Comparative Government

D0434188

Comparative Government
An Introduction

Jean Blondel

EUROPEAN UNIVERSITY INSTITUTE, FLORENCE

Philip Allan
New York   London   Toronto   Sydney   Tokyo   Singapore

First published 1990 by
Philip Allan
66 Wood Lane End, Hemel Hempstead
Hertfordshire HP2 4RG
A division of
Simon & Schuster International Group

Disk conversion in 10/12 Plantin
by Columns Typesetters of Reading

Printed and bound in Great Britain

British Library Cataloguing in Publication Data
Blondel, Jean, _1929–_
    Comparative government : an introduction.
    1. Comparative politics
    I. Title
    320.3

    ISBN 0–86003–419–4
    ISBN 0–86003–719–3 pbk

1 2 3 4 5   94 93 92 91 90

Contents

V

Preface

In the course of the last few decades, the study of comparative government has had a tempestuous journey. First, it moved in the 1960s from a constitutional and legalistic approach to one in which grand taxonomies were elaborated. The idea began to prevail that government formed a 'system' and that the various institutions which were part of this system were related to each other in terms of the 'functions' which they fulfilled. Comparative government had also to be concerned with the newly created developing countries, in which the traditional social base of tribes and ethnic groups was associated with 'modernising' single parties and 'charismatic' leaders. Grand taxonomies seemed necessary: these alone appeared able to take new countries into account, alongside liberal democracies and dictatorships.

Yet these hopes proved illusory: taxonomies were static and descriptive, while what seemed to be needed were dynamic and explanatory theories. In the late 1960s and early 1970s, it appeared necessary, therefore, to use different approaches, which would link political life to underlying social and economic forces at both national and international levels: models based on analyses of developmental factors and on international dependency seemed to provide the answer, at a time when Western liberal democracies were increasingly challenged for perpetuating their control over the countries of the 'South' instead of offering help to solve the problems at hand.

'Developmental' approaches came to be criticised in turn, however, for the explanations which they offered seemed too general and indeed simplistic. Thus, in the 1980s, comparative government has partly returned to its original focus on political institutions and on the state, though in a more sophisticated and more realistic manner. The turbulent period during which constitutionalism, systems analysis, and grand developmental theories had been successively adopted and strongly criticised helped to deepen the analysis; meanwhile, there is a calmer and more mature recognition that studies need to remain close to the structures of government. This new maturity is also the result of the accumulation of data on all countries which has taken place over the last decades, as these have helped to build a more complex picture of political life than had been the case earlier.

This volume is thus written at a time when comparative government aims at being a genuinely cross-national study of the institutions of government and of the interconnections between these institutions. What the models of the 1960s and 1970s made abundantly clear was that comparative government had to be general, but that it had also to be grounded in a concrete picture of individual cases. Thus, as I wrote twenty years ago in an earlier version of a work which had the same aim as this volume, comparative government must consider both 'the general conditions which lead to the development of political systems and the more detailed factors which account for the characteristics of political structures, whether groups, parties, governments, assemblies, or bureaucracies' (*Introduction to Comparative Government* (1969), p. x). This was indeed the purpose of comparative government at its origin, at the time when Aristotle wrote his *Politics*. This is what it is recognised to be once more, in a period in which changes in many countries, and indeed the collapse of apparently strong regimes in the Communist world, show in a striking manner the part which institutions can play in shaping the character of political systems.

It has been particularly pleasant for me to return to a general reflection on comparative government at this point: I am therefore especially grateful to Philip Cross, of Philip Allan, for having given me the opportunity to undertake this task as well as for having helped and encouraged me while this work was being prepared. I wish also to thank my students at the European University Institute in Florence, who gave me numerous occasions to discuss many sections of this text. I am most grateful to Professor J. Schwarze, also of the European University Institute, for his comments on two of the chapters which relate to constitutions. I owe a special debt to Maureen Lechleitner, who typed draft chapters, tables, and bibliography. Finally, I wish to thank Tess for the unfailing support she gave me while this book was being written. I know that, with their help, I have prepared a markedly better volume than would otherwise have been the case: I only hope that this work will be of use in leading to further developments in the systematic study of comparative government.

J.B.
Florence, Italy
1990

Part I

General framework and concepts

1 | The importance and scope of comparative government

Politics, we all know, is a universal activity. Whether in the United Nations or in a parish council, in a trade union or in a papal conclave, in a board room or in a tribe, the decisions which have to be taken involve political action. Many, sometimes for political reasons, deny the universality of politics; but, in everyday language, even if the word is used in a pejorative sense, we talk of the politics of all the groups to which we belong, and rightly so, in the same way as we talk of the politics of governments.[1]

Politics and government

Yet the politics of governments have always occupied a special place in our preoccupations. There is no need to examine here at great length the reasons for this. Governments do more than any other body: they have great financial resources, their decisions have the authority of the law, and the coercion of physical punishment is at their disposal. Whether we belong to a small or a large country, the actions of our government and the actions of the governments of the great powers will shape our destiny. Some may prefer not to think of such things, but the freedom to turn one's eye away from government will have no effect on the power which governments have to direct one's life, except perhaps that governments may be more able to move in an unfavourable direction as a result of one's withdrawal. We cannot contract out of being an object of governmental action, even if we decide that we shall refuse to be a party to the preparation of this action.

It is therefore natural that the study of politics should include, as one of its most important aspects, the study of governments; but the task of studying, explaining, and trying to rationalise government is made particularly difficult because each country has only one government. In the main, we have learnt about our environment because we have been able to observe series of identical or at least similar phenomena. This is how man began to grasp the main characteristics of the 3 physical world and some aspects of social life. Indeed, it took a very long time, even with continued repetition, to distinguish spurious relationships from genuine interconnections; for instance, it was only after much reflection that man discovered the phenomenon of gravitation among physical bodies, both on earth and in the universe in general. A further long period had to elapse before a second type of regularity, statistical regularity, began to be discovered in the biological and the social sciences: this was possible only because of the existence of large numbers of events of the same class; for instance, the progress made in the study of voting behaviour has been in large part a function of the repeated number of instances in which large numbers of electors did cast their ballot.[2]

We do not have the same advantage when we study governments. At a given point in time, each country has only one government; at the top of this government is a supreme authority – whether individual or collective – a single leader or a cabinet. There is sometimes only one party in the country, but, even where there are more than one, the number of these parties is always comparatively small. There is sometimes no national parliament at all, but when such a parliament exists, there is only one. Although it is sometimes possible to analyse larger numbers and to find repetitive phenomena in the fabric of government, some of the most important aspects of this fabric are based on single instances or on instances of which there are very few cases.

The importance of government makes it imperative to study its characteristics and its behaviour: this means that one is inclined to look for 'causes' and, more generally, for regularities: of course, one could argue that all is 'accident' and that the role of individuals and of 'big structures' such as parties or national executives is so large that it is not possible to discover any trend. But this standpoint is both theoretically absurd and practically untenable: theoretically absurd, as events tend to be described as 'accidents' when we do not know the reasons why they occur; practically untenable, as we always want to improve on what we regard as unsatisfactory (and to maintain what we tend to like).[3]

Yet it is not sufficient to believe that regularities exist; we must also be able to discover what these regularities are. This is difficult to do on the basis of 'unique' situations as we have no assurance that any conclusions which we might draw are justifiable: what can we legitimately say about regularities in the context of a single government, of a single parliament, or of a few parties? This is why the search for comparisons naturally becomes central to the study of government and this is why the analysis of comparative government is necessarily the cornerstone of a rigorous and scientific study of government. If we are to be truly serious about discussing government, we cannot do it outside the comparative framework.

The importance of comparative government

If we are to understand better the way governments work, comparison is not only valuable : it is inevitable. Any judgement on the workings of a government or of an institution of that government is based in reality on some underlying notion of how similar governments or similar institutions of government work in other circumstances. It is, admittedly, possible to imagine how a government could work in the abstract; indeed, we do this when we discuss 'ideal' types of government. But, as a matter of fact, such an abstract vision is the result of impressions and ideas which have come to us gradually by learning about similar situations elsewhere. In particular, judgements which suggest amendments to existing sets of arrangements and even judgements which propose a complete overhaul of the system of government are based on implicit comparisons. At the root of comments on electoral systems, for instance, are impressions or conclusions drawn from the workings of electoral systems elsewhere; at the root of judgements about the effectiveness of a parliament are also judgements about the way parliaments operate in other countries. It is immaterial whether we recognise that we do in fact use other examples: what is important is that we use these examples to build our 'theories'.

Thus comparative analysis, in reality, underpins the study of government. It is better therefore to admit explicitly that this is the case and, clearly and systematically, to lay the foundations of the study of government on a comparative approach. The study of particular governments and of particular institutions within each government will be enhanced as a result, for the specific assessments will be guided by a knowledge of the character, shape, and range of similar situations in other governments or in other institutions; our understanding of the mechanics and of the dynamics of governmental life in individual cases will be both enriched and made more accurate.

If comparative government is valuable and indeed inevitable, why is the subject so little advanced and why does it raise so many difficulties and controversies?[4] Is it only that so many aspects are still insufficiently explored? Or is it also that there are inherent theoretical difficulties – some even claim that the goal of a truly comparative analysis of government is impossible?

That the comparative aspects of the analysis of government are insufficiently explored is manifestly the case. Although the idea and even the practice of comparative analysis is old – it goes back to Aristotle who compared the Greek constitutions in a systematic manner – work on the subject has been spasmodic throughout the subsequent period and only in the twentieth century has the endeavour been undertaken by a substantial number of scholars wishing to increase cumulatively our knowledge of government.[5] Yet, despite this improvement, information remains limited, either because access is refused, as in the case of totalitarian and even authoritarian governments, or because, as in more open polities, many aspects of the analysis of governmental life are subjected to various restrictions. Above all, the numbers of scholars involved remains limited; their numbers are markedly smaller, for example, than the numbers of scholars in the natural and biological sciences: only time will gradually improve this knowledge and there is no short-cut in this respect.

Yet some consider that the real problem is more fundamental. It is argued that comparisons cannot ultimately be successful because the 'cultural idiosyncrasies' of each country condemn comparative analyses to superficiality, if not to serious misunderstandings. It is claimed that the government of a country at a given point in time is the result of historical traditions which are so specific that they both shape this government and make it intrinsically different to any other government. The same argument applies to particular institutions of the government, whether the national cabinet, the legislature, or the political parties. To proceed from the assumption that one can compare these institutions leads, so the argument goes, to making links which should not be made and to drawing general conclusions which are unwarranted as they necessarily ignore the specificities of each political 'culture'.[6]

The argument does have force: historical traditions do fashion in a particular way the governmental life of each country. Yet the argument has limitations too, since, in practice, as we saw, comparisons are always made, implicitly or explicitly. The need for comparative analysis ultimately rests on the proposition that we can only apprehend reality by using categories and constructs which are by definition general. The various elements which together form a government – the leadership, the cabinet, the assemblies, the parties, etc., are all 'constructs' which enable us to understand the 'reality' of governmental life. We have to elaborate these constructs even when we are concerned with only one government in its fundamental specificity. Thus the cabinet of Country X may be discussed specifically: it none the less refers to a concept of 'cabinet' which exists beyond the characteristics of Country X. It may be difficult to 'understand' the cabinet of Country X in all its details; and, consequently, it may be true that any comparison between the cabinets of countries X and Y will be deficient to the extent that the detailed description of these two cabinets will be limited. This means, however, that we need to improve our knowledge and the instruments by which we can operationalise these descriptions; it does not mean that comparisons are impossible.

In fact the implication is, on the contrary, that the study of government has to be viewed in universal terms – that is to say that comparative government does not relate merely to comparisons among a relatively small number of countries or among a small number of institutions. Comparison relates potentially to all governments – subject to the proviso that we are able to discover operational mechanisms enabling us to apprehend differences and to give detailed descriptions.

It would seem to follow that comparative government needs to be general: this is the approach which we shall adopt in this book. Indeed, this approach not only stems logically from the fact that the concepts which we use are general; it is also a more valuable approach in practice, because we are then able to develop a better vision of the 'landscape' of government and thus discover more easily the extent to which the characteristics of certain governments are unusual or, on the contrary, rather common. Comments about the effect of electoral systems, for instance, have become appreciably more sophisticated as politial scientists have looked at them in a general manner; comments about the duration of tenure of ministers or of leaders have become less impressionistic as they have been made on the basis of world-wide comparisons.[7] Thus, far from being antithetical to the study of individual governments or institutions, general comparative studies constitute a major help – indeed an irreplaceable help – as they can show the direction which studies of individual governments or institutions should most profitably take.

The scope of the study of comparative government

Assuming that one is to study government in a general manner, what then is the scope of the inquiry and, specifically, what part of political life can be said to be encompassed by the study of comparative government? In the nineteenth century, the answer would have been simple: the (proper) study of government seemed to be co-extensive with the study of constitutional arrangements.[8] The events of the eighteenth century, the American and French Revolutions, themselves in large part resulting from the example of the English Revolution of the previous century, led to two conclusions: first, absolutism was viewed as a thing of the past; second, societies would henceforth be governed on the basis of the rule of law and of constitutional principles. This meant that it was no longer necessary to study absolutist governments, which came to be regarded as out-of-date in the same way as the barter economy was out-of-date for economists of the time; this meant also that the study of government should concentrate on the analysis of constitutions.

This standpoint proved to be both narrow and unduly optimistic: narrow, because it was simply not the case that the operations of governments could be confined to the provisions of constitutions; extra-constitutional bodies, such as political parties, had begun to play a large part even in the nineteenth century; unduly optimistic, because constitutionalism, far from spreading over the whole globe, seemed for a time to be restricted to a limited 'Atlantic area'. While there has been once more an expansion of constitutionalism in the last decades, the large majority of states are still ruled in a non-constitutional manner, even though constitutions may be theoretically in force almost everywhere.[9]

Thus the scope of comparative government had to be broader; indeed, it could not be defined in such a rigid manner. It had to be defined, not in terms of sets of provisions and arrangements, but in terms of the overall *raison d'être* of governmental arrangements. Governments exist, in all their complexity, in order to achieve (or because it is hoped that they will achieve) certain results. The scope of the study of government (and therefore of comparative government) can be discovered only if we discover what governments are for.

The search for a 'realistic' determination of the scope of government has been one of the aims of the analysis of contemporary political theorists. Having moved away from the notion of constitutionalism as being the primary characteristic of modern government, these theorists came to develop the concept of the 'political system' (perhaps wrongly labelled, in that what was being referred to by this expression was more specifically the *national* political system or, in effect, the *governmental* system);[10] yet the idea of a political or governmental system has been fruitful in that it has enabled political scientists to see the governmental machine as being engaged in an activity which brought together the various elements of government. This activity, which we shall have occasion to examine more closely in the next chapter, is concerned with the determination and implementation of policies, both material (the distribution or indeed redistribution of goods and services, such as education, pensions, etc.) and 'moral' or 'spiritual' (decisions about what is allowed or not). As the governmental machine 'pronounces' its decisions in a general manner on the premiss that it can speak for the whole nation, it has been stated that, in the most general fashion, the *raison d'être* of the political (i.e. governmental) system is the 'authoritative allocation of values', to use D. Easton's definition.[11]

The study of government is thus the study of the 'elements' in society which jointly (in conjunction but also more than occasionally in opposition) produce this 'authoritative allocation of values'. These 'elements' are naturally broader and more numerous than the arrangements described in constitutions, even where constitutions are applied: they include the national executive and the parliament; they also include parties, groups, to the extent that these participate in the process of the 'authoritative allocation of values', as well as bureaucracies and indeed courts. What the concept of the political system does is to provide a link between these elements as well as to show how certain elements can be substituted for others when they are missing, for instance when there is no parliament or there are no parties.

It is important to note that these elements constitute the cornerstone of government, as governmental activities are first and foremost the result of the activities of groups, or, to be precise, the result of the activities of individuals within and between groups. There have been many controversies as to whether 'institutional analysis' should or not be given prominence, in part because institutional analysis was often associated with the formal examination of constitutions. It has therefore sometimes been suggested that the emphasis should be placed on behaviour rather than on institutions, particularly when, as in the 1960s, political science moved generally in the direction of behaviourism.[12]

This emphasis is valid to the extent that the analysis of government must not be concerned exclusively, or even primarily, with formal bodies and rules, but must on the contrary be concerned with what actually takes place; this does not mean, however, that formal bodies and rules should be disregarded altogether: their real place in the life of governments must be closely examined. But the point against institutional analysis is invalid and indeed fundamentally mistaken if it is has the effect of de-emphasising the central position of institutions, of 'structures' (formal as well as informal) – as if these institutions were of little importance. Behaviour occurs within the context of institutions: these are the means by which governmental processes occur and which shape behaviour.

It has also sometimes been suggested that institutional analysis should give way to a study of norms and values, as these, in reality, are at the origin of institutional development.[13] Thus parliaments are set up in order to achieve at least some degree of representation; parties are founded in order to enable some groups to have a greater voice or some viewpoints to be better expressed. This, too, is a valid point:

indeed, we shall see that it is not possible to 'explain' institutions purely on the basis of structures, as some have tried to do; what accounts for the structures and for the relationship between these structures are the values or norms which prevail in the society at a given point. But to say that norms account for structures (albeit in a complex manner) does not mean that structures are unimportant: it is through structures that the values or norms are implemented (though often only in part). The study of government must focus on structures, even if the analysis of norms and values is an essential element of the understanding of the way in which structures come to exist and to develop.

Yet structures or institutions are not 'givens' which are maintained indefinitely. On the contrary, institutions emerge, expand, and decay. The study of government must obviously take into account these changes in the characteristics of structures: indeed, the study of such changes is a crucial aspect of the study of government. One type of change which has been given prominence in the last decades has been 'development', often presented as the political parallel to social and economic development.[14] Whether there is, or not, 'development' (or, as it was called in the past, 'progress'), change is an essential part of the study of the elements which constitute comparative government. That study would be wholly inadequate if it were 'static': it is indeed in large part because the traditional constitutional analysis was static that it came to be viewed as unsatisfactory.

Yet the study of change (in the form of development or in other forms) cannot be undertaken without a study of the instruments by which this change occurs. Governmental institutions, as well as the behaviour of individuals within these institutions, can have an effect only if there exists some rapport, so to speak, between institutions and individual behaviour, on the one hand, and what takes place in the society, on the other: when such a rapport ceases to exist, changes will occur in the characteristics of the governmental system. The 'credibility' of leaders and of institutions is thus an essential aspect of governmental life. It has thus naturally been an object of inquiry: it is with concepts which describe this rapport, such as legitimacy, authority, institutionalisation, integration, that one can better grasp, compare, and perhaps ultimately measure the nature and strength of the ties which exist between governments and citizens and the changes in the character of these ties.

Conclusion

Thus, before undertaking a detailed review of the governmental structures and institutions, we need to explore a number of general questions which relate to the overall characteristics of these governmental systems. We shall start from an analysis of what is meant by the governmental or political system; we will move on to the role played by norms and values in shaping the configuration of institutions and thus in giving rise to different types of political system; we will then examine the context within which change (and in particular development) occurs in governmental systems and the processes by which this change takes place; we shall look at the part played by legitimacy, integration, and other factors in giving support to the governmental system or in withholding support from it. Only then will we be sufficiently equipped to investigate successively the role of groups, of parties, of parliaments, of national executives, as well as of bureaucracies and courts, in the functioning of the many types of governmental system which exist in the world today.

Notes

1. On the universality of politics and on the difference between politics and government, see R.A. Dahl, *Modern Political Analysis* (1963), pp. 4–13. See also A. Leftwich (ed.), *What is Politics* (1984), pp. 1–18 and M. Laver, *Invitation to Politics* (1983), pp. 1–16. For an idiosyncratic view of what politics is, see B. Crick, *In Defence of Politics* (1964).
2. The question of the difference between the 'hard' sciences and the social sciences has attracted a vast literature. Indeed, the 'scientific' character of social science investigation is frequently denied. For a broad presentation of the subject see P. Winch, *The Idea of a Social Science* (1958); a more recent presentation is that of R. Trigg, *Understanding Social Science* (1985), in particular pp. 3–40. On the general question of explanation in social science, see E.J. Meehan, *Explanation in Social Science* (1968).
3. The role of 'accident' in politics is, on one level at least, considerable: many governments are elected by very small majorities, for instance, and some leaders, such as J.F. Kennedy, were also elected by very narrow margins. See my *Discipline of Politics* (1981), pp. 1–14.
4. The difficulties and indeed basic inadequacy of comparative analysis have been repeatedly mentioned, especially in the 1950s and 1960s. One frequently quoted article is that of R.C. Macridis, *The Study of Comparative Government* (1955), in which the parochial and truly 'non-comparative' character of comparative politics was denounced. A more fundamental critique was made in the early 1970s by R.T. Holt and J.E. Turner in an article on 'The methodology of comparative research' which appeared in the volume of the same title edited by these authors (1970). See Chapter 2 for a more detailed analysis of developments in the field.
5. Aristotle compiled a study of all the Greek constitutions of his time, but the work has been lost, except for the study of the Constitution of Athens. However, the comparative approach of Aristotle can be discovered in his *Politics*. The study of comparative government only started to develop again on a systematic basis with the Frenchman Montesquieu (1689–1755) who wrote the *Spirit of Laws* in 1748.
6. The debate between supporters of general and individual analyses has been recurrent in comparative analysis. See for instance L.C. Mayer, *Comparative Political Inquiry* (1972), pp. 273–81 and C. Ragin, *The Comparative Method* (1987), pp. 34–68.
7. See Chapters 12, 18 and 19.
8. See Chapter 15 for a discussion of the role of 'constitutionalism' in comparative government analysis. By and large, comparative government studies were based on legal analysis before World War I, though there are outstanding exceptions, such as those represented by the works of Lord Bryce (*Modern Democracies*, 1891) and A.L. Lowell (*Governments and Parties in Continental Europe*, two vols, 1896). For an examination of the evolution of comparative analysis in political science see my *Discipline of Politics* (1981), Chapters 4 and 7.
9. See Chapter 15 and subsequent chapters.

10. This approach was particularly developed by D. Easton in the 1950s and 1960s. See Chapter 2.
11. D. Easton, *The Political System* (1953), pp. 129–48. Many definitions of politics have been given: Easton's definition has the merit of avoiding introducing power into the definition, the concept of power having proved particularly difficult to handle. See R.A. Dahl, *Modern Political Analysis* (1963), pp. 39–54. See also S. Lukes, *Power* (1974), *passim*.
12. The conflict between behaviourists and anti-behaviourists has marked the decades since the 1950s. At first, behaviourism led to the rejection of the importance of institutions. More recently, in part because of the criticisms made against behaviourism, institutions in general and the state in particular have been given prominence. See in particular J. March and J.S. Olsen, 'The new institutionalism', *Am. Pol. Sci. Rev.* (78), Sept. 84, pp. 734–49. On the role of the state, see P. Evans, D. Rueschemeyer, T. Skocpol (eds), *Bringing the State Back In* (1985), *passim*.
13. The role of norms in political analysis has also become important once more after the decline of behaviourism and of functionalism in particular. See L.C. Mayer, *op.cit.*, (1972), pp. 67–81 and M. Landau, *Political Theory and Political Science*, (1979), pp. 43–71. See also Chapter 3.
14. For a discussion of the role of development, see Chapter 4.

2 | The political system and the role of structures in governmental life

For the analysis of government to be applicable to all types of government across the world and therefore to be truly comparative, a general framework has to be found within which the specific characteristics of each government can be described. Chapter 1 alluded to the existence of such a framework: it is based on the idea of the political or governmental *system*. We need now to examine this framework to see whether it is indeed universal and can thus be applied to all countries as well as being sufficiently precise to provide a basis for the detailed description of individual governments.

A general framework must be both universal and precise if it is to meet the needs of comparative analysis. It goes without saying that the conceptual framework is not satisfactory if it is not applicable to all countries. Constitutionalism provided a framework for comparative analyses in the past, as we saw, and indeed for precise comparative analyses: the well-known distinction between presidential and par-liamentary systems continues to be used as it helps to contrast sharply and in detail the relationships between executive and legislature in some types of polities. However, constitutionalism had to be rejected as a general framework for the analysis of governments as it could not help in the description of regimes which were not based on constitutional principles.

The concept which replaced constitutionalism was that of the political system. This seems to be truly universal, as it is based on the idea that all governments are concerned with the elaboration and implementation of decisions applicable to the whole society. From this recognition it follows that the political or governmental system is composed of the set of arrangements which, together, lead to the elaboration and implementation of those decisions which are applicable to the whole community. The notion of the political system thus appears to provide a basis for developing comparative analyses of governments.

Yet a framework of analysis is only truly useful if it is precise as well as universal: it needs to be precise if it is to provide us with the tools with which to distinguish among the many objects of analysis – in this case the many governments

– which are in existence. This is where the notion of the political system has been less successful, and indeed less successful than was the idea of constitutionalism in the past. Efforts have been made to refine and develop various aspects of the framework; but these efforts have been criticised and, so far, while the *elements* which compose the political system give rise to relatively few problems, the precise nature of the *links* between these elements has not been discovered. In the course of this chapter, therefore, after examining the central concept of the political system, we shall successively study the characteristics of the elements which compose this system and analyse the problems posed by the description of the links between these elements.

The political system

The idea of the political system (as it is called, although it would be more accurate to refer to it as the governmental system) stems from the recognition that the *raison d'être* of government is to elaborate and implement decisions for the society; as these decisions can be material or 'spiritual', this process of elaboration and implementation of decisions has been labelled a process of *allocation of values* – of matters which have physical or spiritual value. It has also been labelled an 'authoritative' process, perhaps a little more controversially: what is being referred to in this way is the fact that the governmental machine can claim obedience or acceptance – a point which relates to the 'credibility' of that governmental machine; this question has already been raised in Chapter 1 and it will be considered in greater detail in Chapter 5.[1]

If we leave aside for the moment the question of whether the governmental machine has, indeed, the authority necessary for its value allocation to be 'accepted' by the society and if we concentrate on the fact that what is at stake is the allocation of these values, two general points need to be made. First, the object of governmental activity is not specified: what characterises the political system is that it allocates values, not the fact that it allocates some values rather than others. The political system exists because values have to be allocated (goods and services distributed, spiritual or moral standpoints adopted), not because *some* values rather than others have to be allocated. This is what makes the framework truly general and applicable to any government in any society (unlike constitutionalism, for instance). This does not mean that in specific societies some values are not being allocated rather than others; on the contrary, this is precisely how some systems can be distinguished from others, as we shall see in greater detail in Chapter 3: however, because the concept of the political system enables us to discuss and describe governments which promote and develop values of all types, the concept does provide a truly general framework.

Second, the definition which has been given relates to a political (or governmental) *system*: we are defining a set of interconnected activities undertaken by large numbers of agents. This system, as has already been noted in Chapter 1, is composed of elements which may or may not be in accord but are at least interdependent, as they would not otherwise be part of a system. These elements are the structures of the system: they are the institutions or groups which are considered more closely in the next section.

Before doing so, however, we need to ask: why is there a political or governmental 'system' at all? Why do we need a mechanism to allocate values in the society? The answer lies in the fact that the number of values which might be allocated is larger than the number of values which can be allocated – that is to say that there is scarcity. The scarcity may be of a physical kind, just as, in the economic field, the scarcity of goods creates the necessity for the mechanism called the price system. In a sense, the political system operates an economic system of its own, a parallel economic system, so to speak, by which some goods and services are distributed in the community. As a matter of fact, the situation is the converse one: the economic system is dependent on the governmental system in that it is the governmental system which allows certain goods and services to be distributed by means of the price mechanism. There are, in this respect, variations over time and space: some governmental systems allow more free enterprise than others; some goods and services (in particular health, education, pensions) may be distributed 'free' (i.e. by governmental decisions) or by the operation of the price mechanism.[2]

The scarcity which is regulated by the governmental system is not only physical, however; it is also spiritual and moral. In such cases, we are typically confronted with alternatives among which we have to choose, though there is sometimes scope for compromise. For instance, divorce may or may not be allowed; it may also be allowed more or less liberally. In such matters (and indeed also with respect to many goods and services, particularly those which the government provides directly, such as roads), the scarcity to which one refers is based on the fact that one cannot decide both to do and not to do. With respect to these goods, which are typically labelled 'collective', a decision has to be taken to provide or not to provide them 'on behalf' of the society as a whole.

Thus society needs a governmental system since both goods and services, as well as spiritual and moral values, have to be allocated and it is physically or logically impossible to allocate all of them: 'anarchy' – in the etymological sense of absence of government – is an impossibility because of the constraints which limited resources and life in common impose on society.[3] But the question still remains as to why there are so many values to allocate: values do not 'emerge' spontaneously: they have to be 'presented', so to speak, to the political system. It is clear, for instance, that, however prevalent values may be in a given society, all the possible values will not be on the agenda. Thus the question of the 'value allocation process' raises the question of the reason why values emerge and, specifically, of the mechanisms by which some values, rather than others, are decided on.

The question of the emergence of values has usually been dealt with, following Easton, by viewing the process as one in which 'demands' are made on the political system. Easton thus conceived of the political system as analogous to a computer which processes and thereby transforms 'inputs' into 'outputs', while adjusting mechanisms allow for a feedback from the outputs on the input mechanism (see

Environments

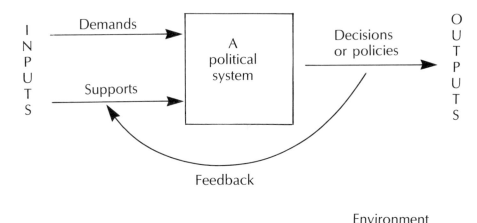

Figure 2.1 The political system

Figure 2.1). The inputs are the pressures of all kinds exercised on the system, which is thus activated by way of the demands and which then elaborates decisions which will become outputs to be presented to the society.[4]

The idea is appealing; it bears a fairly close relationship to reality in many respects and in particular where 'demands' are made by groups and are then taken up by parties, parliaments and indeed cabinets. But it should be viewed more as a limiting case than as a correct representation of the situation in all types of polities, for the political system is not necessarily activated by demands in this clear-cut manner. The situation may be – and often is – appreciably more confused, in that demands may simply not be expressed and ideas may come from within the most central part of the machine, the cabinet or the national leadership, for instance (a point which Easton does recognise, but which is appreciably more common, especially in closed political systems, than he allows for).[5] Moreover, the political system can modify the conditions under which society operates and thus 'manipulate' the demands which may be made – for instance by allowing some groups to exist and not others, or by encouraging propaganda in favour of some policies and against others.

The analogy with the computer is therefore oversimplified and needs to be treated with great care. Yet it remains true that the idea of the political system can constitute the general basis on which, or the framework within which, governments can be compared and the process of government analysed. As this process involves a system, however, we need to turn to the examination of the elements of this system and, to begin with, of the part played by structures or institutions in the overall configuration.

The elements of the political system: structures, institutions and groups

Government has always been conceived in terms of institutions within which actors – leaders in particular – operate. From Aristotle onwards, theorists have discussed government in terms of such bodies as executives, parliaments, 'factions' (in many ways the ancestors of parties), courts and local assemblies; but the analysis of government in terms of a political system led to a reappraisal of the role and nature of the institutions which constitute the elements of the system. First, the role of institutions in the system had to be clarified. Since the idea of the political system entails that politics should be viewed as an *activity*, it seemed that it should no longer be described in terms of a number of institutions. Second, even if institutions were still to be regarded as the key elements, the nature and character of the institutions or structures which are involved in the political system had to be reassessed.

Prima facie, the definition of the political (or governmental) system in terms of decisions aiming at 'allocating values' seems to suggest that the central aspect of government is no longer a set of institutions but a set of activities which result in the elaboration and implementation of decisions. Yet in practice the activity of politics cannot take place without the existence of sets of structures: these are the means – and the necessary means – by which and through which decisions can be made.[6]

To understand the part played by institutions or groups in the political process, let us consider what the definition of politics as an authoritative allocation of values implies. Decisions have to be taken and implemented. If there were no structures, be they institutions or groups, all decisions would have to be taken face-to-face and would involve all the members of the community continuously; the implementation of decisions could be put in question at every point. On the one hand this state of affairs can be regarded as a perfect situation, corresponding to full democracy; but it can also be regarded as a wholly anarchic predicament corresponding to the state of nature as Hobbes envisaged it. It is clear that, in practice, even in a small community, some ordering, some 'structuring' of the decision process has to occur if the allocation of values is to take place at all and if people are to abide by it. This is what institutional arrangements achieve; this is why these arrangements structure the political process.

What are then the fundamental characteristics of the structures of the political process? Whatever differences may exist between them, they have one element in common: it is that they pattern the relationships among the individuals belonging to them. Specifically, an institution or group is characterised by the fact that those who belong to it are more closely related to each other than they would be if they did not belong. An institution or group is a set, to use a mathematical expression: those within the set have links with each other which they would not have if the set did not exist.[7]

The fact that an institution or group is a set of relationships has two consequences for the political process. First, the relationship extends to those who are connected to the group and not to others: decisions made in the name of the group, for instance, will not (normally) apply to those who are outside the group; privileges which those who are connected to the group may receive will not (normally) extend beyond the group. Second, the relationships are also patterned in the sense that decisions within the institution or group take certain forms rather than others: these forms of decision-making are characteristic of the group, although of course they may change and indeed are likely to change over time: thus the way decisions are taken in a group will differ at least in part from the way in which decisions are taken in another group. For instance, decisions will be taken within the group in a certain manner and this manner will be different at least in part from that of other groups.

When structures, institutions, or groups are seen in this fashion, it becomes clear that these necessarily exist in the human context: men and women always have patterned sets of relationships with other men and women in that they are more closely associated with some fellow human beings than with others; the family is the most obvious set of patterned relationships, but there are many others, such as the local community, the workplace, etc.[8]

Thus the national political system has to be viewed as composed of a number, probably very large, of institutions or groups to which individuals belong. These institutions or groups can therefore legitimately be viewed as elements which in turn are linked to each other in many complex ways in the national political system. Institutions and groups have ill-defined borders; often they overlap somewhat in their aims: this stems from the fact that individuals may and often do belong to many groups and thus have relationships with individuals who in turn may belong to many groups. The national political system is based on this large variety of complex patterns while also creating a series of patterns of its own.

The examination of the part played by structures indicates that the structures which form part of the political system cannot be limited to governmental institutions in the commonly accepted sense of the word. Large numbers of groups of all kinds are involved to the extent that they contribute to the authoritative allocation of values. Trade unions, employers' associations, welfare organisations, but also ethnic groups or tribal bodies are or may be part of the political system alongside parties, assemblies, local authorities or national executives.[9]

Admittedly, not all the groups which exist in a polity take part in the national political system. There is of course political activity *within* these groups, but this activity may bear no relationship to national decision-making. For a structure to belong to the national political system, there must be an involvement of that structure in the process of national allocation of values, since this is the definition of the national governmental system. Some structures may therefore be part of this governmental system only occasionally, intermittently, or almost not at all; others, on the contrary, are continuously involved, often because they have been set up in order to help fashion the national decision-making process: parties and parliaments are two obvious examples.[10]

Thus one reason why institutions or groups form the elements of the national governmental system is the fact that, like society as a whole, the national political system is composed of individuals who are necessarily related to others according to various sets of patterned relationships. It could be argued that this situation is merely the reflection, on the plane of government, of the universal social fact that men and women are not ubiquitous but are closer to some fellow human beings than to others for reasons ranging from geographical contiguity to ideological affinity.

There is a further and equally important reason why structures, institutions, or groups constitute the elements of the political system, however: this is the more pragmatic point that these structures allow a considerable amount of time to be saved in the decision-making process. It is often noted that decision-making is extremely slow in large and tumultuous mass meetings in which there is (sometimes deliberately) no organisation at all. The absence of structures in the national governmental system would have the same effect, but on an immense scale. Institutions and groups establish or maintain in existence procedures of decision-making, some of which are set up in a fully conscious manner and some of which are simply the product of habits which go unchallenged: for instance, in traditional societies, where tribes are perhaps the most important structures, the elders may have rights of decision-making which other members of the tribes do not have. As a result of such procedures, decisions are taken more speedily, since they will not involve the consultation, let alone the agreement, of all the members of the tribe.[11]

In this practical sense, institutions and groups can be viewed as established arrangements in which decisions are taken in a certain way, with only relatively few members participating in the decision-making process and even these active participants being subjected to large numbers of restrictions. Whether in a party, in parliament, or even in the national cabinet, the institution or group may be primarily characterised by the way in which decisions are taken within it.

The fact that institutions or groups are, so to speak, machines to speed up the decision process is particularly important to the political system, since the political system is a mechanism by which values are allocated in the society. In the social context as a whole, it may not be so important that institutions or groups should be able to take decisions speedily; indeed some social clubs may be concerned only incidentally with the taking of decisions (though there are always at least some decisions to be taken); but the national political system could not operate without institutions or groups drastically speeding up the process by which values are allocated.

Thus it is doubly wrong to underestimate, let alone set aside structures, institutions, or groups in the context of the political system. Such an understimate amounts to a fundamental misunderstanding of the part which these bodies play. Admittedly, as was pointed out in Chapter 1, this standpoint resulted from a reaction to what had been an overemphasis on purely legal arrangements when constitutionalism was prevalent. It was a mistake to restrict comparative government analysis to legally organised groups and even more to be concerned only with the formal arrangements of these groups. It was necessary to broaden the perspective and to see that the structures which fashion the national political system extend well beyond constitutional bodies and the legal rules under which they are deemed to operate. This, indeed, is what has now come about: the national political system is viewed as being composed of sets of structures, some of which are constitutional, many of which are not; indeed the structures which compose the national political system vary in time since, as we saw, some groups may be involved in the political system only occasionally. In this way, and in this way only, it is possible to understand how the national political system can constitute a mechanism able to allocate values for the society.[12]

Links between the structures in the political system: 'functions' of structures

If structures are the elements of the analysis, the nature of the links between these structures must be discovered in order to make it possible to describe the detailed nature of specific political systems; different configurations of structures will emerge in this way. For instance, we will find that in one country there are tribes, assemblies of chiefs, and a royal council; in another country, there will be interest groups, such as trade unions and business organisations, a number of parties, a parliament, and a council of ministers; in yet another there may only be one party, while the military may be influential, etc. Clearly it will be possible to undertake comparisons on this basis, as different political systems will be characterised by the structures which play a part in the national decision process.

Comparisons between political systems are indeed commonly done in this way. Unfortunately, however, it is still not possible to specify with precision the character of each political system by specifying the exact nature of each configuration. Ideally, one might imagine that one would determine, at each point in time, the 'composition' of a political system in the way one determines the composition of a chemical body: chemical bodies are also composed in varying degrees of elements such as oxygen, carbon, etc. But chemists can measure with precision the proportions of the various elements which form the molecules; so far at least, political scientists have not been able to do anything similar and, like natural scientists of an earlier period, they can only state that, in a given political system, interest groups such as trade unions are 'more' influential than in another or that the parliament or congress is 'more' involved in the process of national decision-making than in another country. The comparisons which are undertaken in the field of government are still rather vague and are likely to remain so for many years.

Some efforts have been made to come closer to a precise description, if not to a quantitative measurement: these efforts have been primarily associated with the idea of functionalism, but after a period of some success, they have been shown to be unsatisfactory. The principle behind functionalism was simple and, at first, appealing: it seemed that the best way to compare different configurations of structures was to look at the activities of these structures in each of the configurations and therefore to discover the link between structures by means of a description of the activities which these structures performed. The activities of parliaments vary from country to country, as some are more involved in legislation, others in the scrutiny of the government. The activities of parties also vary: some are more involved in the preparation of programmes, others in the 'mobilisation' of the population. The activities of the groups which compose the political system also display marked differences. If one were able to assess precisely the activities of every structure, one might then be able to describe in some detail the characteristics of each political system.

If this were done, one might then also be able to compare in a rigorous manner the various political systems which exist in the world. Let us suppose that it were possible to discover a number of 'phases' in the cycle of activities of the political system and that it were also possible to discover that a given structure is concerned specifically with a particular 'phase' of the political system's activities: one could then ascribe structures to 'moments' of the life of this political system and thereby solve the problem posed by the links between structures. The method will be truly satisfactory, however, only if we are not constrained to ascribe to each structure, party or parliament, for instance, an unchangeable position in the political system: there has to be flexibility. One has to be able to assign a particular structure to a given phase of the political system in the case of Country X, but to a different phase in that of Country Y. Otherwise the analysis would be unrealistic, since, as was pointed out earlier, the activities of parties or parliaments are not identical everywhere. Moreover, as some structures may not exist in some countries, other structures must be able to take their place; it is not permissible to suggest that there are phases in the life of a political system and then to leave one or more of these phases without the attendant structures. The idea of linking structures to activities in this manner was given the name 'functionalism' since these activities were regarded – somewhat arbitrarily and a little dangerously from a scientific point of view – as the functions performed by the structures in each particular case.[13]

Functionalism did not provide a satisfactory solution to these questions and, as a result, the problems posed by the relationship between structures and the political system remain unsolved. Admittedly, a number of phases of the activity of the political system were listed, but these phases were too broad and not sufficiently distinct: they could not give more than a broad impression. It was suggested, for instance, rather uncontroversially, that the process of national decision-making begins with a phase of 'articulation', followed, analytically at least, by a phase of 'aggregation' and that these two phases constituted the way in which 'inputs' into the political system were made. Then policies were elaborated, first generally, then in more detail, corresponding to a 'rule-making' and a 'rule-implementation' phase, to which should be added a phase of 'rule-adjudication' when specific problems of implementation arose. This categorisation, which was elaborated by G.A. Almond in the 1960s, was both ingenious and, as a first approximation, valuable. But the problem of the link between structures and the various phases of the political system was not solved by this categorisation: there had to be a further step.[14]

That step was never taken or, more accurately, it was attempted in such a way that comparative government theorists then engaged in rather sterile controversies and lost sight of the original aim. What was needed at that point was to find a means of characterising structures with respect to the phases of the political system; it would also have been necessary to discover more phases than the few listed above. Neither development occurred, for two main reasons. First, the phases which were suggested were constructs of the imagination of individual scholars, and their boundaries were uncertain. When does rule-making become rule-implementation? When does articulation become aggregation? Controversies could be indefinite. Second, it was not possible to locate a particular structure within a given phase of the political system without major empirical analyses for each country. When comparative government was based on constitutionalism, one could look at constitutions to determine whether parliament, the executive, or the courts were engaged in certain types of activities. What was now proposed was to look realistically at the activities of structures, whether constitutional or not, and this could not be done without a detailed examination of every structure in order to be able to state what the activity of that structure was. This was manifestly a major – indeed perhaps a monumental – task, and it was not clear what the pay-off would be, given that so few phases of the political system had been identified and given also the fact that, as was noted above, the boundaries between these phases were imprecise.[15]

These difficulties made it impossible to solve satisfactorily the problem of the link between the political system and the structures which constitute its elements. Despite the high hopes which had been raised, a genuinely satisfactory theory could not be developed from the combination of 'systems' analysis and 'structural-functionalism'. Other types of structural-functionalism then emerged, largely as a result of the failure of this first, wholly descriptive approach: these will be discussed in the next chapter, since they relate in reality to norms rather than to a 'neutral' endeavour to link the structures of the political system to one another.

Conclusion

The failure to operationalise precisely the link between structures and the political system has had many consequences for comparative government; one of them has been that scholars began to move away from attempts at developing a truly 'grand' or general theory and came to recognise that there was a manifest need to build a stronger empirical base for comparative government. Yet the idea of the political system remains important, as indeed is the point that, in general, structures are linked to the political system by means of their activities, even though we may not know yet precisely what is the nature of the link. The notion of the political (or governmental) system suggests that the governmental machine has an overall activity – that of allocating values – and certain broad characteristics; in particular, it is composed of a number of elements (structures) which are linked together by means of the (still rather ill-described) activities which these structures undertake. As a result, while the specific effect of each structure may not be known, we do at least know in broad terms how these structures relate to each other, what the overall character of the configuration is, and that some types of structures can be replaced by others in different political systems or at different points in time in a given political system.

Notes

1. The idea of the political system was particularly developed by D. Easton in the 1950s and 1960s, in his *Political System* (1953), and *Systems Analysis of Political Life* (1965). A similar framework was explored by many other political scientists during the same period and in particular by K. Deutsch who attempted explicitly to apply a cybernetic model to the description of political life in *The Nerves of Government* (1963). For an examination of the importance and value of systems analysis in political science, see in particular L.C. Mayer, *Comparative Political Inquiry* (1972), pp. 48–66, and R. Chilcote, *Theories of Comparative Politics* (1981), pp. 145–62.
2. On the fact that politics has to exist, see M. Laver, *Invitation to Politics* (1983), Chapter 2, pp. 17–46.
3. One can reduce the needs for large collective decisions by means of decentralisation – this will be discussed in Chapter 16 – but the problem cannot be eliminated altogether.
4. See D. Easton, *The Political System* (1953), pp. 96–100, and *A Systems Analysis of Political Science* (1965), pp. 29–33. See also G.A. Almond and J.S. Coleman, *The Politics of the Developing Areas* (1960), pp. 5–9.
5. D. Easton (1965), pp. 54–6: he calls these inputs 'withinputs'.
6. In the 1960s, there was a tendency to dismiss the role of institutions under the impact of 'behaviourism'; this was in part because institutional analysis was regarded as related to and connected to constitutional analysis: while it was right to view a constitutional approach as too narrow, an institutional approach goes far beyond an examination of purely constitutional structures. There is now a more realistic view of these matters; see the article by J. March and J.S. Olsen (1985) quoted in Chapter 1. See also Chapter 14.
7. It is essential to view structures and institutions as sets of relationships among a number, often a very large number, of individuals. The words 'structure' and 'institution' will tend to be used as synonymous in the course of this volume, though institutions have a somewhat more 'organised' connotation: we shall thus refer more specifically to 'institutions' in contrast to more traditional 'communal' groups in Chapter 6. See the distinction made by G.A. Almond and J.S. Coleman (1960), *op. cit*, pp. 33–4.
8. The universal role of groups has been particularly recognised in political science with A.F. Bentley, *The Process of Government*, (1908), though their importance, especially in the American context, had already been stressed by Tocqueville, *Democracy in America* (1835). See Chapter 6 for a discussion of 'group theory' and of the different characteristics of groups.
9. This is precisely why one cannot distinguish sharply between a 'political' and a 'non-political' area in society. The same bodies may be more or less involved in politics at different points in time.
10. On the other hand, bodies such as bridge clubs or sports clubs tend rarely to be involved in national political life. Note, however, that politics exist within these groups to the extent that decisions have to be taken which affect the whole group. We are considering here only the extent to which groups are involved in national (and local) decision-making processes.
11. The fact that institutions are a means of speeding up the process of decision-making is clear. The matter is sometimes presented in terms of institutions being instruments of social 'control': but social control is only one aspect of what institutions achieve for political decision-making. See S.P. Huntington, *Political Order in Changing Societies* (1968), pp. 8-11.

12. See Chapter 6.
13. This is the main idea behind the development of 'structural-functionalism' which was developed for comparative politics principally by G.A. Almond, following the work of D. Easton and T. Parsons. The first volume in which this approach was systematically presented was *The Politics of the Developing Areas*, edited by G.A. Almond and J.S. Coleman (1960); see especially the Introduction, pp. 3–64. The literature on the use of structural-functionalism in comparative government is vast. For a balanced judgement, see L.S. Mayer (1972), *op. cit.*, pp. 143–161 and R.H. Chilcote, *op. cit*, pp. 162–82.
14. See G.A. Almond and J.S. Coleman (1960), *op. cit.*, pp. 15–17. G.A. Almond made a somewhat modified presentation in G.A. Almond and G.B. Powell (1966), *Comparative Politics*, pp. 27–33.
15. An attempt had been made by G.A. Almond and J.S. Coleman in 1960 to present what they called a 'probabilistic theory of the polity' (1960), *op. cit.*, pp. 58–64, but the model was difficult, if not impossible, to apply. In practice, no-one has attempted to describe *systematically* the functions performed by different structures in different political systems, though an effort has been made, in a number of country volumes published under the general editorship of G.A. Almond, to look at the life of these countries through the angle of the functions of various structures (Little, Brown series).

3 | The norms of political systems: patterns of government in the contemporary world

The previous chapter was devoted to the anatomy of the political system. Structures constitute the elements which, in combination, form different configurations. As yet it is uncertain how the relative weight of different structures in different political systems may be described precisely, but it is known that these structures exist and that they perform different activities, and therefore have different effects, in the various political systems. It is now necessary to turn to the overall character of political systems, to their overall 'colour', so to speak. Political systems are concerned with the allocation of values: what are these values and how far do they differ from one political system to another? In order to answer this question, it is necessary to look at the norms of political systems.

The comparison of political systems by reference to their norms is a very old idea and one in common usage. Everyone talks about democracies and oligarchies, about liberal and authoritarian regimes, about 'progressive' and conservative countries. In doing so, people are indeed referring to the norms of these systems, that is to say to the kinds of proposals they make and to the kinds of aims which regimes achieve (or appear to achieve). Making these judgements involves the type of activity in which political scientists have engaged for centuries – at least since Aristotle, who divided societies into such categories as democracies, oligarchies, and monarchies, and who was later followed by many of the great political theorists, such as Hobbes, Locke, Rousseau, and others.[1]

The aim of this chapter is to examine more closely the nature of the norms which characterise political systems and, on this basis, to place the various political systems which exist in the world to-day into a number of categories. The next step will be to investigate how far certain structures can be related more specifically to certain types of norms, on the understanding that, as was discussed in the previous chapter, it is still not possible to describe with precision the various configurations of institutions; nevertheless it is possible to give an impression of the type of activities which characterise these structures.

The three dimensions of norms of political systems

The classification of political systems has always been based on the assessment of the norms which these systems were held to embody or to achieve; examples of these norms include, for instance, liberalism and democracy. Yet, while the existence of norms appears to be universally recognised (although there may be controversies in practice as to whether, for example, a given political system is liberal or not), one problem which arises is the number or range of norms which should be taken into account to characterise political systems. Are liberalism and democracy – and their polar opposites, authoritarianism and 'monocracy' – the only two types of norms which need to be taken into account? Many theorists seem to have thought so and, indeed, Western regimes are commonly described as 'liberal democracies' (or 'polyarchies', to use the expression of R.A. Dahl) in order to stress that these are the two types of norms which these regimes embody.[2] However, a classification of this type does not take into account the substantive policies which a given political system might achieve or want to achieve: two political systems may be authoritarian, but may vary according to their actions with respect to property, the social structure or education. A classification of political systems has surely to take these variations into account, since they appear as relevant to the norms of these systems as democracy or liberalism. This is indeed recognised in 'ordinary' language: governments, as well as other bodies within the political system, such as parties or the military, tend to be characterised by the extent to which they are conservative or 'progressive' as well as liberal or democratic.[3]

So far the examples given include only the norms which have been or may be taken into account in order to classify political systems. It is possible to be systematic, however, and, by referring to the definition of the political system, to determine what areas or domains these norms can be expected to cover. The political system is concerned with the authoritative allocation of values: such an allocation can only take place if the following three questions about norms are answered.

The first question refers to the persons involved in the political process. Who makes the allocation? One answer may be that all the members of the polity take the decisions and that, therefore, in the strict sense of the word, the system is a democracy: no polity of course approximates this situation.[4] The second question refers to the way in which the decisions are taken: are there many restrictions on the examination of alternatives? This question raises the problem of liberalism or authoritarianism. The third question relates to the substantive content of the policies: what does the allocation aim at achieving? Is the goal of the polity to spread goods and services, indeed values in general, evenly and equally, or is it, on the contrary, to create and maintain inequalities in the distribution of these goods, services, and values?

Thus the definition of the political system shows that there are just three types of norms to be examined if one is to characterise a political system. It is immediately apparent, however, that these norms should be viewed as divided, not in a dichotomous manner, but along continuous dimensions. Political systems are not only democratic or non-democratic: they may be located at many points between a democratic pole (participation of all in an equal manner) and a 'monocratic' pole (one person takes all the decisions), although it is clear that no real-world society is located at either extreme.[5] Similarly, political systems are located between a fully liberal pole and a wholly authoritarian pole.

It may seem difficult to define precisely the third dimension, which relates to substantive policies. Yet experience shows that this dimension is concerned with a variety of models of the 'good society' which can be said to range between fully egalitarian and inegalitarian arrangements.[6] At one extreme is what might be described as the 'communist utopia'; at the other pole is the wholly hierarchical society in which one or very few draw the very large majority of the benefits. The grounds for inequality may be diverse: they may be based for instance on inheritance, race, creed, occupation or class; they may be based on some combination of these characteristics. There will of course be many degrees of equality and inequality; but the overall effect is to place societies on a third dimension, which is distinct from the dimensions of liberalism versus authoritarianism and of democracy versus 'monocracy'.

Four point can be made about this three-dimensional distribution of the norms of political systems. The first is that reference is made here to the norms 'of' the political system as a short-cut to suggest the norms which tend to be expressed by the behaviour of the authorities of that political system and especially by the government and the members of the political elite. Clearly, in any polity, there are dissenters from the prevailing norms of the regime, but the views of the dissenters are either repressed or do not have sufficient force (for instance because they constitute the views of a very small minority); as a result, at any rate at the point at which the observation is made, these views do not translate themselves into norms of the polity. Over time, however, these views may contribute to a change in the behaviour of the authorities and thus in the norms of the regime; the existence of these opposing norms is also likely to contribute significantly to the determination of the position of the political system on the liberal–authoritarian dimension as well as, though perhaps to a lesser extent, to the position of the political system on the other two dimensions.

Second, the current ability of political scientists to operationalise these norms remains relatively limited. Yet it is possible to operationalise them in part – and to a greater extent for some countries than for others. For example, degrees of equality or inequality can be assessed by means of income per head and the distribution of capital across the population, although other indicators should also be used, for example the extent to which minorities have equal access to various positions. Degrees of liberalism are typically assessed by the extent to which various freedoms are achieved in the political system, though the indicators are likely often to be of a qualitative rather than a quantitative nature. The extent of democracy can of course be measured in part by reference to the opportunity given to citizens to participate in the electoral process, but other indicators also need to be taken into account, such as the extent of participation in political parties and in groups which are involved in national decision-making. Clearly, the measurement is often based on data which are not wholly reliable and the allocation of weighting to various indicators can give rise to argument. However, it is at least possible – and efforts have already been made in this direction – to arrive at some degree of operationalisation.[7]

Third, the measurements which are made refer to a particular point in time: thus the assessment given to a political system concerns only that point in time. If a regime changes and is replaced by one which has different goals (more or less liberal, more or less democratic, or more or less egalitarian), the location of the system in the three-dimensional distribution of norms also changes. Thus the assessment of the location of a given political system does not by itself give a dynamic picture, but a number of observations can provide the dynamics. This also makes it possible to see whether there are trends which apply to many regimes and thus characterise the evolution of political systems in general.

Fourth, the examination of the evolution of norms over a period of time can provide a means of assessing the extent to which moves according to one dimension of norms have an effect on moves on another. The three dimensions are analytically distinct: liberalism is conceptually different from democracy and egalitarianism; but there are apparent empirical links between positions on the three 'axes'. Thus it could be claimed that a move towards liberalism will be followed by moves towards democracy: this has been the evolution of Western European countries in the nineteenth century and it can be argued that, as a state becomes more liberal, more citizens will be able to participate because they will be able to express demands, in the first instance, for greater participation. It is also often assumed that changes towards egalitarianism will have the effect of reducing, at least to a degree, the opportunities for liberalism, as liberty and equality are at times regarded as antithetical; in practice, rapid changes towards greater equality – or indeed greater inequality – often lead to protests and tension; this might result in more authoritarianism on the part of the regime and in a curtailment of participation as well.[8]

Overall, therefore, the determination of the position of countries at various points in time with respect to the three dimensions of norms is both a way of characterising the nature of political systems and a means of understanding the dynamics of these systems on a comparative basis. So far, knowledge of these positions and of the evolution of these positions is still relatively vague: this is despite the fact that it is common to assess many regimes according to two and often all three of these dimensions, as the description of Western European countries as liberal democracies and of Communist states as authoritarian regimes indicates. It should therefore at least be possible to see in broad terms how contemporary polities can be characterised, examine how far they tend to be grouped into a number of categories which can be clearly distinguished from each other, and discover whether some configurations of structures are particularly important in reflecting or even in part determining the characteristics of these regimes.

The five main types of political system in the contemporary world

The three types of norms described above suggest that political systems may be located at an infinity of points in the three-dimensional space determined by these norms. Indeed, no two political systems are likely to be placed at exactly the same point, and even the most stable political system is likely to vary also somewhat in terms of the norms which it embodies. Yet there are also considerable similarities: as was noted earlier, Western European countries are generally regarded as being close to each other in terms of their norms; they are all deemed to be liberal democracies.[9] Communist states are characterised by a high degree of authoritarianism; indeed, some ceased to be Communist when they became less authoritarian, though there have also been moves among the remaining Communist states, and in particular in the Soviet Union, to become more liberal. The situation is so fluid in this respect that it is difficult to know whether states can remain Communist and not be relatively authoritarian.

Indeed, imitation is one of the reasons why the norms of political systems are similar. Western European regimes evolved in the nineteenth and twentieth centuries on the basis of an adaptation of many of the arrangements of British practices; in the case of European Communist states, norms were openly imposed and maintained by the Soviet Union, to the extent that, for a long period at least, it was relatively difficult to find appreciable differences among the norms of these countries. But the adoption of the norms of one country by another goes beyond Western Europe and the Communist world: the influence of colonial countries over the newly independent states of the Third World, as well as that of the Soviet Union and China, has had the effect of spreading the norms and the institutions of these countries to many parts of the globe.

It is therefore not surprising that there should be clusters in the positions of countries in the three-dimensional distribution of norms. These clusters allow for some differences in the exact position of each country (it is not possible to determine the exact position of each country with respect to the three dimensions and thus to measure the precise difference among the countries in each cluster). Whether because their political systems have originally been set up with norms adapted from other political systems or not, the countries in each cluster display characteristics which are close to those of others, though these positions can be expected to change occasionally, either slowly or in some cases, for instance after a coup or a revolution, rather abruptly.

A survey of the contemporary world suggests that there are five such clusters of positions in the three-dimensional distribution of norms. These clusters can be labelled 'liberal–democratic', 'egalitarian–authoritarian', 'traditional–egalitarian', 'populist', and 'authoritarian–inegalitarian'.

Liberal–democratic regimes

These include the countries of Western Europe and North America, as well as Japan, Israel, some members of the Commonwealth, and in particular India, and some Latin American states, in particular Costa Rica. The list does of course vary over time, indeed vary appreciably: over the post-1945 period, Spain, Portugal, and Greece have entered or re-entered the group, while several Latin American countries (Chile being a good example) ceased to be liberal democratic, at least for a period, in the 1970s and 1980s; on the other hand, a number of Latin American countries adopted liberal–democratic norms in the 1980s. A number of European ex-Communist states have also moved in the direction of these norms in the late 1980s.

These countries also constitute a cluster from the point of view of their substantive policies, which tend to be neither truly egalitarian nor truly inegalitarian. Of course, there are major differences among them from the point of view of the distribution of incomes and of the social services; but the substantive norms which are being embodied and to an extent implemented in these countries tend to correspond to a half-way position between the two extremes. This is probably the consequence of the liberal–democratic formula which these countries adopt: various groups can express themselves at least with a moderate degree of openness and they then compete to obtain support from the population, in particular through elections. The result is a set of policy norms which are in the middle of the dimension, although there are of course movements on either side of this half-way position.

Egalitarian–authoritarian regimes

Communist regimes can be described as egalitarian and authoritarian, though they should also be labelled democratic. The countries of this group have traditionally included, beyond the Soviet Union and the Eastern European countries, China, North Korea, Mongolia and Vietnam, as well as a number of other states such as Cuba, Angola, Mozambique, and Ethiopia. In the late 1980s, Eastern European states have moved out of the group or have taken steps towards doing so. A further set of countries, to be found in particular in Africa, has occasionally adopted norms which are close to those of Communist states, but these norms have not been pursued sufficiently systematically to justify their inclusion in the group.

The fact that the regimes of these countries are authoritarian is well-known and does not need to be argued at length, although the evolution of these states in the course of the 1980s suggests that there is a broad tendency to move away from more extreme forms of authoritarianism. This has resulted in a number of states no longer remaining Communist, but there have also been moves away from authoritarianism among those which did, and in the first place in the Soviet Union. The state of flux is such that it is difficult to be sure that these moves can continue without leading to the end of Communism in these countries as well. Meanwhile, authoritianian norms remain markedly in evidence in a number of Communist states which have refused to be associated with the changes which were initiated in the 1980s in the Soviet Union.

Communist regimes have also traditionally been relatively egalitarian, even if doubts are often expressed about the nature and extent of the egalitarianism of these countries. The fact that there are no substantial concentrations of wealth in the hands of individuals has a considerable egalitarian effect, although the power of managers and politicians does compensate in part, in practical terms, for the limitations upon the economic power of 'capitalists'. Moreover, Communist states are characterised by an extensively developed social security system which provides the whole population with a basic equality of provision with respect to education, health, and pensions.

Finally, Communist states should be regarded as relatively democratic, even when they are or were authoritarian. As was pointed out earlier, liberalism and democracy are two analytically distinct concepts, which tend to be associated in the West because of the evolution of Western Europe in the nineteenth century; however, a political system may be democratic without being liberal if it gives an opportunity for participation without allowing for appreciable competition. Moreover, the democratic character of Communist societies has to be viewed by comparison with the situation which prevails in other countries: in Communist states, the party and the other 'mass' organisations give large numbers of citizens an opportunity to participate.

Traditional–inegalitarian regimes

In the contemporary world, the political systems which are neither liberal–democratic nor Communist are grouped into three clusters. One of these is composed of the systems which have continued to adopt the traditional norms which once prevailed in most of the world and in Western Europe in particular. These countries are absolutist and their head of state, usually a monarch, rules the nation by counting on the loyal support of the large majority of the population; some oligarchical republics have had or still have a similar character. This type of regime is becoming rare in the contemporary world, partly because most Western European monarchs felt the need to abandon their power in order to remain on the throne while others were toppled. Thus only in relatively remote and closed parts of the world (the Arabian peninsula, the Himalayas) have traditional–inegalitarian regimes continued to exist.

The norms of these systems are 'traditional': they preserve inequalities and highly oligarchical structures, like those which characterised pre-revolutionary Europe. Power and wealth are concentrated in few hands and there are few moves towards a political opening up of the society, although in many cases efforts are made by the monarchs to ensure that their popular support is maintained by providing some elements of a constitutional regime and by developing the economy;

regimes such as those of the Arabian peninsula, which have been fortunate enough to be able to disperse substantial resources among the population, have been best able to maintain themselves.

By and large, these regimes are not truly authoritarian, at any rate in the most overt sense. They remain in being on the basis of traditional popular support.[10] Authoritarianism becomes necessary only when a crisis occurs, that is to say when opposition begins to emerge. The regimes may then be toppled or they have to transform themselves into either populist or authoritarian–inegalitarian systems.

Populist regimes

Most of the newly independent states of the 1950s and 1960s , especially in Africa, began as populist regimes,[11] as did some of the South American republics in the early post-independence period. The establishment of a new state requires at least some involvement of the population in opposition to a colonial power, and 'traditional' loyalties are usually insufficient. There has to be some participation by at least a large part of the population; there has also to be a degree of pluralism. Populist regimes are thus typically born in reaction to traditionalism and, consequently, they tend to be half-way between democracy and 'monocracy', between egalitarianism and inegalitarianism and between liberalism and authoritarianism.

These characteristics account in part for the high expectations raised by such regimes at the outset, both within the country and outside; but they account also for their relative instability. Relative pluralism leads to strong divisions among groups and factions: this could result in a liberal–democratic form of government, but only if strong political institutions exist and tensions are not too high, in particular among the minorities which often have a religious, ethnic, or even tribal character: not surprisingly, this is relatively rare in a new country. Not surprisingly, too, a strong leader is not merely a help, but a necessity; if no such 'charismatic' leader exists, the regime is likely to move rapidly to a different form and in particular may become authoritarian–inegalitarian.

Authoritarian–inegalitarian regimes

By and large, authoritarian–inegalitarian regimes occur as a reaction to a liberal–democratic system, as was the case in much of Southern, Central, and Eastern Europe before World War II, with Fascism and Nazism in particular, or as has periodically occurred in Latin America since World War II; they occur also as a reaction to populist regimes, as in Africa and to an extent in Asia since the 1960s: military governments tend then to be the basis on which these regimes are organised. Authoritarian–inegalitarian regimes can also result from the transformation of a traditional system in which the basis of support for the monarch is decreasing: this has occurred occasionally in Europe in the past; examples can also be found since World War II, for example in the Middle East.

These regimes are first and foremost authoritarian: 'normal' political life is reduced to a minimum and there is even the widespread belief among the authorities that politics can be abolished altogether and be replaced by management and administration. Some authoritarian–inegalitarian regimes have had to accept a degree of 'politicisation' and set up organisations designed to enrol the population in a 'mass' party whose primary purpose is to express support for the leader and the regime; but these regimes are typically hierarchically structured: there is emphasis on the 'chief' and on the need to recognise his superior status while the concept of democracy is rejected outright. Society itself is viewed as hierarchical, with everyone having his or her place in an almost biologically ordered set of positions. The aim is to construct – or reconstruct – a society in which there is a loyal following, an aim which often remains unfulfilled.

These regimes are also socially inegalitarian because they have been set up in order to defend a social elite which feels threatened by the growing influence of the 'popular classes' and/or because they are associated with ideas of social as well as political hierarchy. In many cases, there is longing for a return to what is viewed as the well-organised structure of the past in which everyone had his or her place and positions were not questioned. These attempts often end in failure: the effort to remodel the society cannot be pursued for long. The regime is likely to be toppled and be replaced by a populist or a liberal–democratic system, although this new government may in turn be rather weak and have to give way to another authoritarian–inegalitarian system (or, exceptionally, to a Communist system).

The norms of the political systems of the contemporary world thus fall into quite distinct groups, though the sharpness of the differences sometimes becomes blunted as one country moves from one regime to another or when there is oscillation, as often in Latin America, from one type of norms to another. Whether political systems embody the same norms for long periods or not, however, the patterns which emerge are sufficiently clear to provide a satisfactory picture of the variations among types of government.

Types of norm and types of configuration of institutions

The norms which political systems embody provide an image of the broad direction in which these systems move as well as of the manner in which decisions are taken. But, as we know, decisions are taken with the help of institutions which form different configurations in different political systems. There are, as might be expected, close relationships between the norms of political systems and the structures which prevail in these systems. In part, this is because institutions are set up deliberately in order to embody certain norms: this is the case, for example, with parliaments and parties which are set up to provide a means for democratic participation. However, structures may also have an effect on norms: when they are well-established, as for instance in the case of tribes or ethnic groups, they affect the role of these institutions in national decision-making. It is therefore useful to describe the relationship between norms and institutions and see how far some regimes are characterised by specific configurations of institutions. It is not realistic to expect to do so here in detail: structures are too complex to be easily circumscribed; but at least a general impression of the relationship can be given.[12]

Configurations of institutions in liberal–democratic regimes

In liberal–democratic regimes, the configuration of institutions is based in large part – though only in part – on constitutional arrangements deliberately designed to implement the norms of the political system. This is particularly the case with parliaments or congresses, but courts, the executive, and the bureaucracy are also shaped to a varying degree by the constitution.

Yet, ever since the nineteenth century when earlier constitutions were drafted, liberal and liberal–democratic systems have included many institutions not even mentioned in constitutions; the most important of these have been the political parties, but other groups have also played a large part in national decision-making. Consequently, even in liberal–democratic polities, constitutional structures have often become less influential or have remained influential only in conjunction with non-constitutional bodies, such as parties: parliaments and executives tend to be dominated by political parties, both because elections occur on party lines and because day-to-day behaviour takes place on topics and in a manner which corresponds to the decisions of the parties (together with the most influential groups). However, of all types of political systems, liberal–democratic regimes are those where constitutional bodies play the largest part.

The structural configuration of liberal–democratic regimes can therefore be said to be based on a number of well-defined arenas (parliaments, executives, but also local and regional parliaments and executives constituting these arenas) in which there are two main levels of actor, parties and groups, while the bureaucracy is influential in the-wings. The positions of these two types of actor are different: parties play the main parts and occupy the front of the stage, typically executing the main movements or reciting the main lines; groups are normally less visible, except when they suddenly irrupt by means of major strikes or demonstrations. Groups tend to be organised for definite purposes (though their aims may be relatively broad, as in the case of trade unions or business organisations); they normally exercise pressure on the parties, though they also endeavour to have direct links with the civil service.

The level of participation in groups and parties is ostensibly high but it is in practice often small: the mass of the population tends to take a spectator's position, groups and parties being supported from time to time by vigorous clapping or attacked by strong booing. Ties between population and structures are not necessarily much stronger at the local or regional levels. By and large the 'grass-roots' activities of the national parties and groups directly concern only a minority, although there may be variations from area to area and from time to time. Overall, the system is relatively well-ordered, largely as a result of the acceptance of the 'rules of the game' – that is to say the characteristics of the constitutional arrangements – by practically all the actors. Where this acceptance is less widespread the probability of the liberal democratic regime being overthrown is high, as apart from this acceptance there are relatively few means whereby the various arenas and actors may be strongly defended.

Configurations of institutions in Communist regimes

In egalitarian–authoritarian regimes such as Communist states, the determination of the arenas is much less clear , as these regimes have traditionally tended to operate on the basis of a deliberate ambiguity. There is in effect a political superstructure and a political infrastructure, with two different configurations of institutions linked primarily by means of personal ties. The political superstructure is constituted by the state level, in which constitutional bodies are outwardly similar to those of liberal–democratic countries, except that a greater emphasis is given to the bureaucratic side of the machinery than in liberal–democratic countries. The civil service is not 'in the wings', but is part of the configuration itself; indeed, at the level of the state structure, there is little, if any, differentiation between the administrative and the non-administrative elements – a distinction which has become sharp in liberal–democratic countries because political parties wish to control the executive but, by general agreement, do not enter to more than a limited extent in the lower echelons of the administrative hierarchy. In Communist states, the structural configuration at the level of state organisation is essentially based on a large number of administrative bodies whose personnel is both political and technical.

The level of the state organisation is effective only because, at the level of political infrastructure, the Communist party and a host of ancillary bodies both suggest directions for action and supervise the implementation. Thus the Communist party does not have clear and circumscribed areas of activity as parties tend to have in liberal–democratic states; it is at least as active as parties are in Western countries in directing the executive, but it also controls many aspects of the administrative machine and supervises the many 'mass' organisations which it has helped to set up, such as trade unions.

There are thus two levels of structural configuration; the linkage between the two is naturally a source of difficulty, and it can be achieved only by means of key individuals at both levels. A further source of difficulty comes from the fact that, below the political infrastructure of party and groups, there also exists a further, wholly unofficial, level consisting of more traditional bodies (ethnic or religious in particular) as well as of more modern (protest) organisations. The party has woven a closely knit web of groups below itself in order to prevent both traditional bodies and more modern organisations from coming to the surface: it is far from successful in this task and changes which have taken place during the 1980s in particular show that efforts at suppression have been in vain. 'Holes' in the structures have always been large in some countries (such as in Poland, where the Catholic Church has proved particularly resilient), but the problem has erupted in a major way in all Eastern European states except Albania in the late 1980s, to the extent that, as is well known, Communism has ceased to prevail in these countries. Moreover, the grave disorders which erupted in parts of the Soviet Union have raised doubts about the future viability of the Communist system in that country as well.[13]

Configurations of institutions in traditional–inegalitarian regimes

Structural configurations in traditional–inegalitarian regimes are in sharp contrast with those of liberal–democratic and egalitarian–authoritarian regimes as they are in no way the product of deliberate decisions, let alone of imposition on a pre-existing structure. Traditional regimes have the configuration of institutions which corresponds most closely to the social structure: indeed, these are the regimes in which the osmosis between politics and society is the most complete because the only elements which count are the traditional groupings and the hierarchical positions which exist within and between these groupings. Thus there is no political arena as such, whether well- or ill-defined. In particular there are no political parties and there is often no parliament; the bureaucracy itself is relatively limited, at least in the most traditional of these countries. What characterises these regimes are sets of loyalties of a personal or a group character, which start at the level of small units (in villages or among bands, for instance) and move to that of the tribe and of the chiefs.

This situation has two consequences. First, when the system functions well, groupings are very strong and difficult to shake; their domain is by and large geographically circumscribed and they are likely to resist any encroachments. While liberal democratic polities are based on a permanent competition among groups which have specific activities, traditional–inegalitarian systems are based on the principle that there is only one grouping within a particular area, for instance a single tribe.

The second consequence is at the national level. The various groupings may or may not recognise fully the supremacy of the monarch and of the top political personnel. Admittedly, traditional–inegalitarian regimes will be maintained for substantial periods only if some *modus vivendi* is achieved between the geographical groupings composing the nation; otherwise, the polity will break up. This is indeed why ex-colonial countries have rarely given rise to traditional–inegalitarian regimes: oppositions between geographical groups are typically such that, soon after independence, a different regime has to be introduced.

Indeed, it is becoming increasingly difficult to maintain a stable equilibrium between monarch and tribal or ethnic groups, in part because every society is subjected to outside influences which undermine traditional groupings and in part because of the geographical and social mobility of the population. Thus traditional–inegalitarian regimes begin to change: institutions such as the bureaucracy and the military become stronger; new groups with specific purposes, such as business organisations and even trade unions, start to play a part. As long as these developments occur on a small scale, the regime can still be described as traditional; when the supremacy of tribal groupings becomes seriously challenged, however, the regime typically becomes populist or authoritarian–inegalitarian.

Configurations of institutions in populist regimes

The structural configuration of populist regimes is hybrid. It is often characterised by a profound opposition between declining traditional groupings and new groups, such as business or trade union organisations, between which uneasy compromises have to be ironed out. This means that, in populist regimes, the ties between society and the political system are much less close than in traditional–inegalitarian systems and, specifically, that political structures, and in particular parties, are normally set up with the conscious purpose of fostering change in the society. However, these parties have naturally to confront the problems posed by the opposition which exists between the weight of traditional groupings and the pressure towards 'modernisation' which some of the newer groups, as well as in many cases the bureaucracy and even the army, wish to promote. This suggests that parties are likely to be divided between those which represent primarily traditional groupings and those which at least claim to foster and mobilise the demands of the newer groups (though many parties in these countries are characterised by both elements).

Hence there is a degree of tension, which often resolves itself by the (more or less voluntary) merger of political parties and the move towards a single-party system. Yet the dominance which this type of single-party system (or of a dominant near single-party system) exercises over society is different from that which is exercised by Communist parties in egalitarian–authoritarian regimes: single parties in populist regimes usually cannot hold in check the traditional groupings. In Africa, in parts of the Middle East, and to a lesser extent elsewhere, populist single parties have typically tried to balance the interests of the 'modernising' groups, including the bureaucracy, with those of tribal or ethnic forces. In some cases, the regime has been successful, typically thanks to the presence of a popular (or 'charismatic') leader, who has been able to strengthen the political structures and the party in particular through an appeal to the population as a whole. When there are no (or no longer) such leaders, major difficulties occur which are presented, by and large rightly, as indications of the inadequacy of the structural configuration to solve the problems faced by the country. The result is, often at least, the emergence of an authoritarian–inegalitarian regime.

Configurations of institutions in authoritarian–inegalitarian regimes

Authoritarian–inegalitarian regimes tend to develop when internal divisions at the level of the institutions cannot be overcome by compromises. This takes place, as was noted above, when a populist regime is confronted with traditional groupings, such as strong tribes, which have been alienated by the regime; it also takes place when, in a liberal–democratic polity, oppositions between parties and between groups are so strong that the government becomes ineffective. The emergence of an authoritarian–inegalitarian regime is then often presented as an alternative to an authoritarian–egalitarian system of the Communist variety, though there are in fact very few cases in which Communist takeovers have taken place in this way.[14]

While populist regimes attempt, often unsuccessfully, to build new institutions to counterbalance the influence of traditional groupings, authoritarian–inegalitarian regimes typically try to revive these traditional bodies and to base their strength on the loyalties which they generated in the past. This is of course easier to achieve when the authoritarian–inegalitarian regime replaces a traditional system, and in particular when the monarch himself is the originator of the move. Yet there are difficulties even then, as more modern institutions also emerge, within the bureaucracy as well. This is why authoritarian–inegalitarian systems rely mainly on the military, as this not only provides physical power to control and undermine the opposition, at least for a while, but can also help to foster the principles of hierarchy which the regime wishes to maintain. Where a 'mass' organisation (a party) is set up, and especially in cases when the move is from a liberal–democratic to an authoritarian–inegalitarian regime, this is often done on military lines and indeed based on the army. However, such parties are created only after the military has been in power for some time, and this helps to extend the support for the military beyond the army itself.

Thus, while the configuration of institutions in populist regimes is hybrid and leads to serious internal conflicts, the configuration of institutions in authoritarian–inegalitarian regimes is somewhat artificial. Traditional groupings are expected to be the mainstay of the regime; but they are typically too weak to perform this function and an attempt is made to fill the gap by using the army, while the bureaucracy is expected to be concerned with a very large part of the decision-making process. As a result, the configuration of institutions tends to be divorced from the characteristics of the society: compulsion has to be strong, unless the leader can maintain the regime by his own 'charisma'; but this is rarer than in populist regimes, as there is typically no groundswell of popular feeling supporting the rulers. Not surprisingly, authoritarian–inegalitarian regimes face high levels of internal tension and often collapse as a result.[15]

Conclusion

There is a considerable variety of types of political system in the contemporary world, more variety perhaps than in previous periods of human history. Yet one can find broad patterns among these systems; these patterns can be discovered by reference to both the norms and the institutional arrangements. There are liberal–democratic, egalitarian–authoritarian, traditional–inegalitarian, populist, and authoritarian–inegalitarian systems: each of these types corresponds to particular situations characterising contemporary politics. Some of these systems experience greater tensions than others: the configuration of institutions reflects these tensions more than it overcomes them. As these tensions are in large part the result of the oppositions which exist in the contemporary world between loyalties based on tradition and pressures for social change, the question of the development of political systems is central to the current character and evolution of political systems: this is therefore the question which will be dealt with in Chapter 4.

Notes

1. Aristotle, *The Politics*, Book 3, Chapter 7 Classifications of political systems were common practice among political theorists afterwards. Both Locke and Montesquieu developed a constitutional classification (out of which emerged the current distinction between parliamentary and presidential systems); Rousseau's classification, in the *Social Contract*, was based, as was that of Hobbes in the *Leviathan*, on a behavioural distinction among regimes. For a discussion of these classifications, see D.V. Verney, *The Analysis of Political Systems* (1958), pp. 17–93.
2. R.A. Dahl, *Polyarchy* (1971), in particular Chapters 1 and 2.
3. There has been a tendency in political science to classify political systems according to the extent of participation and the extent of freedom only. As a matter of fact, the substantive goals of regimes are important, both for the leaders and the citizens; indeed, the definition of politics – the authoritative allocation of values – suggests that the values themselves are an important part of political life. A comprehensive classification has therefore to take these goals into account. This is what will be done in this and the subsequent chapters of this book.
4. Democracy is taken here in its most extreme and literal sense – government *by* the whole people – a conception which Rousseau, of course, thought impossible for men (*Social Contract*, Book 3, Chapter 4). The point is simply to define a dimension and the poles of this dimension must naturally be the most extreme cases.
5. The term most commonly used to refer to dominance by one person is that of 'autocracy': this was the term used in connection with Tsarist Russia, for instance. Strictly speaking, however, a government by one person is a 'monocracy'.
6. We shall discuss the matter in the next chapter in connection with political development. To discover the wide range of uses of the term by political and social theorists, see A. Arblaster and S. Lukes (eds), *The Good Society* (1971).
7. R.A. Dahl attempts a rigorous operationalisation in *Polyarchy* (1971). Chapter 4 will examine the efforts made to measure political development and to relate it to socio-economic development.

8. The question of the moves along the dimensions of goals is one which has not as yet been given systematic treatment, though it is frequently referred to in general terms in both political science and ordinary political literature: it is typically believed, for instance, that greater freedom of expression will make it difficult at least to maintain legal barriers against participation: the history of nineteenth-century Europe seems to suggest that this view is correct, but it would need to be explored fully, as would need to be explored the relationship between liberalism, participation, and moves on the dimension of substantive goals.

9. There are of course differences in the degree of stability of these systems and indeed in the extent to which liberalism and participation are allowed. One example is voting: it was long restricted to men; only in the 1960s and 1970s has the voting age been lowered to 18; and it is still denied to immigrants, except in some countries and for local elections.

10. This traditional support relates to the type of legitimacy of these regimes. The matter will be discussed in Chapter 5.

11. The expression 'populism' was used in late nineteenth-century America to refer to movements which wished to help the bulk of the people against political and social bosses: it spread particularly in the Midwest. Since World War II, the expression 'populist' has been used primarily in the context of those regimes and leaders who, in the newly independent countries of the Third World, were attempting to 'modernise' their societies, for instance to reduce tribal influence, while avoiding the adoption of a Marxist or communist stance. See for instance S.M. Lipset, *Political Man* (1983), pp. 52–4.

12. Works describing the characteristics of regimes in the various regions of the globe are of course extremely numerous. A selected list of studies on different types of political systems can be found in the bibliography at the end of this volume.

13. Communist states have been in a state of flux since the second half of the 1980s. After the events of late 1989 it could be argued that not just Hungary and Poland, but also East Germany, Czechoslovakia, and perhaps Bulgaria and Romania had moved close to being liberal democracies, while the Soviet Union was on the verge of becoming a 'populist' regime and had ceased to be a Communist system in the strict sense, despite the pronouncements of its leaders. There had been appreciably fewer changes of goals in the other Communist states, except perhaps in some of the peripheral ones, such as Laos, Angola, and Mozambique.

14. Mussolini, Hitler and Franco did claim that their authoritarian systems were the best 'bulwarks' against Communist takeovers. The same argument has been used since World War II in many parts of the Third World.

15. This matter will be examined in Chapter 5 in the context of legitimacy.

4 Political development

The question of change in norms and of the dynamics of political systems, which was alluded to in Chapter 3, leads directly to a further problem: that of the direction which these changes take. Ultimately, what is at stake is the matter of political 'improvement' (or decline), of political 'progress' (or regress): if there is to be change, it is obviously important to know whether such a change will lead to a 'better' society. Political theory has indeed always been concerned with such questions: the main aim of writers such as Hobbes, Locke, Rousseau, and Marx was to contrast what they deemed to be the unsatisfactory conditions of politics around them with the 'improvements' which would result from the implementation of the blueprints which they proposed.

The period following World War II in particular has been characterised by a concern for 'political progress' – typically under the expression of 'political development'. There were three main reasons for this renewed concern. The first was the aftermath of the events of the inter-war period. The period of relative optimism characterising the nineteenth and early twentieth centuries was followed by intense pessimism when dictatorships prevailed in Europe: the victory of the democracies in 1945 seemed to open a new era for political 'progress', with the United Nations as the symbol of this optimism. Second, there was the emergence of 'new' countries, especially in the 1950s and 1960s, most of which were born from the rejection of colonialism and from the concomitant desire to make a fresh start, as had been the case in the United States in the late eighteenth century.[1] Third, and at the same time, improvements in what came to be known as the Third World seemed to imply profound economic and social changes in agriculture, industry, education, health and welfare. Such changes came to be regarded as economic and social 'development'; a parallel improvement or 'development' seemed necessary in the political sphere. Indeed, development was viewed as a comprehensive process which should not be divided into compartments: improvements in one aspect of the society – political, social, or economic – depended on improvements in all the others.

40   Large numbers of social scientists and among them political scientists came

therefore to study development.[2] However, it soon became clear that *political development* at least was difficult to circumscribe and to define: thus L.W. Pye[3] found no less than ten different bases for political development in the literature, ranging from mass mobilisation to the operation of the state and from the politics of industrial societies to stable and orderly change. Although he then proceeded to look for a comprehensive 'syndrome' in order to bring these approaches under a common umbrella, it seemed rather worrying for the intellectual solidity of the concept that there should be so many views about what it entailed. There appeared to be a major contradiction between practical requirements and the logic of the analysis: while everyone wished to improve society, including its political aspects, it seemed difficult to agree as to what 'improving politics' might entail. There was a conceptual impasse on a topic which was a top priority both for practitioners and for the public at large. Before concluding that there is, indeed, no hope of reaching an acceptable single definition, it is necessary to examine this impasse somewhat more closely and, firstly, to discover which points cause controversy or lead to differences in approach: norms and structures are key components in the determination of political development. In the second and third sections of this chapter, the role of structures and norms in the elaboration of the concept will be analysed further.

Problems in defining the concept of political development

Why does the concept of political development raise difficulties? A useful starting point is what the concept aims to cover: it is concerned with progress, which means change in a 'positive' direction. Change can be described, although there may be problems about its measurement; what causes difficulty is the assessment of what is 'positive' or 'negative' change, as such an assessment depends on having previously determined what makes 'good politics': one cannot speak of political development without having a conception of the 'good society'.[4] The real difficulty arises at this point: it is not so much that it is difficult to define what the good society is, but that it seems impossible to find a definition with which all will agree. The decision about whether a society is good or not and whether a change is an improvement or not is a value judgement: what is the good society for one individual may not be the good society for another. Witness the controversies which have raged between 'democrats' and supporters of a 'hierarchical society', or between 'levellers' and those who believe that inequalities are not merely inevitable but indeed just. This explains why political theorists have searched relentlessly for the good society: every political theorist is entitled to renew the search without being bound by the conclusions of others.

If this is the case, should one simply refuse to give a general definition of political development? This is impractical, however, since society exists and political activity takes place in society. Whether we define political development or not, society will have to do it; there will be goals and there will be images of what constitutes a good society. There is thus an 'existential' need for an operational definition of political progress and development, which is valid at least for the immediate future and for a given society. Political theorists are not just entitled to continue to search for a solution: they have to do so, because society needs to have some practical notion of what political 'progress' entails.

It is possible to consider, following Pye, what kinds of definitions of political development have been given and whether there are at least some relatively firm elements. These definitions fall into three distinct categories. The first relates political development to social and economic development by suggesting that political development is concerned with the politics of industrial societies or with a 'multi-dimensional process of social change'. A second group is concerned with what might be called the organisation of the political system by referring to nation-building and to administrative structures. The third links development to political values, such as mass mobilisation, the relationship between mobilisation and power, and the movement towards democracy.[5]

Definitions of the first group, which relate political development to social and economic development, are simple, but seem rather unrewarding. They are simple in that they assume a knowledge of what social and economic development is: in the 1960s and the early 1970s at least, social scientists believed that they did have this knowledge, and even thought that few measurement problems existed, as economic development could be assessed by such means as levels and distributions of incomes and levels of industrialisation, while social development could be traced through levels of educational and social services, all of which seemed eminently measurable and were indeed measured by many UN agencies engaged in collecting and publishing the relevant data. On the other hand, political development was obviously more difficult to grasp *per se*: it was not clear what data would have to be collected; but, as political activity consists in taking decisions, its effect could be understood in terms of policy outputs, that is to say by economic and social outputs. One might then conclude that there was political development where one could trace the existence of economic and social development.[6]

This approach is unrewarding, however: quite apart from making it difficult to perceive the autonomy of politics, it makes it impossible to assess the part played by what may be called political 'bottlenecks', such as corruption, inefficient or wasteful bureaucratic procedures, or the inability of politicians to take decisions speedily. Conversely, it is impossible to discover the political conditions which could favour economic and social progress. A place has therefore to be made for political development as such, alongside and independently of development in the other spheres.

The second group of definitions relates to what might be regarded as a 'minimalist' view of politics. These are the approaches which relate political development to the activity of the state and to the efficiency of administrative processes. Even if it is difficult to describe with precision, let alone quantify, bureaucratic efficiency, it seems at least possible to point to specific examples suggesting that 'progress' in society depends on 'progress' in the administrative sphere. Yet it is hard to see why one should single out the state structure and the bureaucracy as the only elements on which political development should depend. Political decision-making results from the activities taking place within all political structures, including groups, parties, parliaments and executives as well as bureaucracies; inefficiency in any one of them should therefore result in lack of development. Thus political development would seem to relate generally to the way decisions are taken, from the moment they are conceived to the moment in which they are fully implemented, in and by all these structures.[7]

Yet, while the concept of political development acquires a sounder intellectual base as a result, there are practical and theoretical problems. The practical problems of measurement are immense: for instance, it would be necessary to assess whether a party was 'efficient' or not in promoting a given policy at a given point in time; this would entail passing judgements on such matters as the extent to which the population is 'ripe' for the policy, whether it would 'cost' too much in terms of money and energy to undertake such a move, and so on.[8] Comparisons across countries may help to an extent, but the magnitude of the practical problem is obvious. Moreover, theoretical difficulties begin to arise as the investigation moves from what was basically an examination of the appropriateness and effectiveness of means to an assessment of goals. Since it is necessary to consider the role of parties, groups, parliaments, or executives, it is important to look at the grounds on which the decisions were taken. Therefore what is required is to pass judgements on the validity of choosing these grounds rather than others: thus there is a movement from the realm of means to that of norms.

This is probably the reason why some students of political development have opted for a definition of the third type, which takes into account values such as mobilisation and democracy. The difficulty, however, is that, as was stated at the outset, such definitions are based on subjective standpoints. While one observer may regard development as based on democracy, another may claim that a hierarchical society would be more 'developed'. It seems therefore that the argument has run full circle: relatively simple and low-level approaches alone are objective, but at the cost of covering only one aspect of the problem; more comprehensive approaches seem to depend entirely on the personal position of the observer. Nor does a 'syndrome' truly help; the problem of value assessment is not resolved since values are one element of the analysis.

A different solution has therefore to be found. If values play a major part in the determination of the good society, what must be explored is whether there may not be some common ground below the norms and values which appear to be subjective. Meanwhile, it is also necessary to explore the part which all structures (and not merely bureaucracies) play in making the processes of decision-making and implementation more efficient. The previous two chapters showed that political life is concerned with norms and with the way structures shorten and indeed shape its process: it should not be surprising that political development, if it is to be fully assessed, should be based on particular characteristics of both structures and norms.

Political development and the role of structures

Political development unquestionably depends, in part at least, on the efficiency of the structures of the political system; what needs to be determined is what precisely constitutes structural efficiency. The question has two aspects, absolute and relative: first, whether it is possible to discover principles which govern a decision about what makes a structure efficient; second, to what extent other differences within the society may affect the characteristics which make the whole system more or less efficient.

There are no easy answers to either of these questions; nor has it been possible so far to provide precise guidelines. As far as the characteristics of structural efficiency at the level of each institution or group are concerned, attempts have been made to circumscribe the problem by way of an analysis of the concept of institutionalisation. Structures are likely to be more efficient if they operate smoothly, if there are few difficulties about the procedures on the basis of which they are run, and if these procedures are clear. The concept of institutionalisation attempts to summarise these points: it has been defined by Huntington as 'the process by which organisations and procedures acquire value and stability'.[9] In the detailed analysis which he then conducts, Huntington outlines four dimensions along which institutions can be located and which can help to determine their degree of institutionalisation. Institutions have to be assessed, he states, by the extent to which they are 'adaptable' rather than 'rigid', 'complex' rather than 'simple', 'autonomous' rather than 'subordinated', and 'coherent' rather than 'disunited'.[10]

It is arguable as to whether one should conclude, following Huntington, that the highest possible degree of institutionalisation is always to be found at the polar extremes of these four dimensions. There may be a trade-off between the four variables: 'adaptability' may affect the degree of 'coherence'; it is probably better to have some 'disunity' if this means a lower level of 'rigidity'. However, to the extent that the analysis applies to each institution, it provides guidelines which are both theoretically rewarding and practically useful. One can at least gain, at the level of each structure, an impression of what constitutes 'progress' or 'development'; one can for instance compare parties, groups, or legislatures, and see to what extent, by being better institutionalised, they appear to be more developed.[11]

Difficulties are greater when the second and larger problem of structural political development across the polity as a whole is considered. At first, it might seem permissible to assess the overall structural efficiency of a political system by 'summing', so to speak, the results obtained for the different structures which compose the system; such an operation would of course be extremely long and could in practice only be partial, but it would at least give an impression of the level of the overall efficiency of the system, were it not for the fact that a high level of institutionalisation of each structure may not result in a truly efficient political system. For instance, groups which are highly developed may produce a situation in which demands are so numerous that the system cannot cope – a situation typically described as one of political overload.[12] Admittedly, this means that the parliament, the executive, or the bureaucracy are not then truly adapted to the characteristics of other structures and of groups in particular; one must go beyond the institutionalisation of each structure and consider the interconnections between structures, but it is difficult to see precisely how these interconnections can be assessed.

As the first element of a solution, two criteria have been suggested in the literature: they are the level of structural differentiation and the extent of structural autonomy.[13] The first criterion bears some similarity to the idea of the division of labour which, since Durkheim, has been regarded as a characteristic of 'advanced' societies;[14] empirical evidence does indeed suggest that there is greater differentiation of institutions and groups in societies which are less traditional. The second criterion is related to one of the dimensions mentioned by Huntington since, as was stated above, he views 'autonomy' as evidence of institutionalisation;[15] it seems permissible to claim that, where there is a large number of autonomous structures, there is at least the potential for greater political development.

Difficulties subsist, however, beyond the fact that the concepts cannot be easily operationalised. It is not axiomatic that there is a linear relationship between structural political development and the two variables which appear to account for it: for it does not seem *prima facie* evident that the existence of an infinite number of highly differentiated and autonomous structures makes the system *ipso facto* more efficient than it would be with a smaller number of structures aggregating within themselves a variety of standpoints and approaches.[16] While differentiation and overall autonomy may play a part, the nature and extent of the linkages between structures have to be closely examined. The question resembles that of centralisation, which will be examined in Chapter 14. It is typically suggested that there are optimum levels of decentralisation for each situation and that these optimum levels are at some distance from full autonomy. The same could and probably should be said with respect to the efficiency of the structural configuration as a whole.

This approach to political development raises more fundamental problems, however, which ultimately lead away from the realm of structures and into the realm of norms. One is on safe ground if one describes political development in terms of the efficiency of the structures of the political system; one is still on safe ground if one then looks at the way in which all the structures combine to enable society to allocate values in an efficient manner – if one looks, so to speak, at the capability of the whole system to take decisions.[17] One is on less safe ground if one postulates that this efficiency can be assessed by means of structural differentiation and structural autonomy. For, although it seems true that a form of 'division of labour' and some degree of decentralisation may lead to greater development, the relationship between these two characteristics and efficiency has to be empirically tested. One can only state with certainty that the development of the structures depends on the differentiation and efficiency of these structures if this is shown to be the case in all societies.[18]

This strong empirical connection has not yet been proved, however – a state of affairs which might not be truly serious, were it not for the fact that both differentiation and autonomy are characteristics which appear to be value-loaded and lead to the conclusion that the countries which are most developed politically are liberal democracies. Both these characteristics or properties of structures can be found in countries in which groups are numerous and emerge freely in the society – that is to say, primarily in Western liberal democracies.

So long as it is unproven that the capacity of the political system entails the existence of differentiated and autonomous structures, the emphasis on these characteristics constitutes a value standpoint: the discussion no longer concerns structural, but normative elements. This is indeed an accusation which has commonly been levelled at this approach to political development. That is why this approach has been regarded as biased towards the West, as well as somewhat underhand: if we are to suggest that Western liberal democracies are the most politically developed polities, it is more honest to state this openly – on the basis of a value judgement – than to claim that political development is based on apparently 'objective' characteristics of structures.[19]

It is therefore better at this point to turn to the examination of the role of norms in political development. This does not mean that structures should be regarded as irrelevant to political development, but it is necessary to stop short at the point where the normative properties of these structures must be taken into account. It is permissible to state that political development is related to the efficiency of structures and, overall, to the capacity of these structures to cope with the decisions which the system has to take and, when asking whether structures should be differentiated and autonomous for the system to be developed, to test whether these characteristics have the effect of increasing capacity. Any conclusion which goes beyond this point must be seen in the light of the part played by norms in political development.

Political development and the role of norms

The assessment of political development cannot be complete without a consideration of the part which values play in defining the goals of the polity. This seems to point to the conclusion that there cannot be a single concept of political development to which all agree: there will be many views as to what these goals may be. Thus it does not seem permissible to state that political development *is* 'mass mobilisation and participation' or 'the building of democracy', or even 'stability and orderly change', as some have suggested according to Pye's analysis;[20] nor is it permissible to state categorically that the political development 'syndrome' includes a striving towards 'equality', as Pye suggests.[21] It does not seem possible – indeed it is logically unwarranted – to claim that these values *are* the values which all have to recognise as characterising a 'good' society.[22]

The question remains whether there is any way at all out of this impasse, and whether it is therefore necessary to say that each society, each individual even, can have a different concept of the 'good' society and that the concept of political development (at least in so far as it refers to norms) cannot be other than subjective. This conclusion seems at first sight difficult to avoid. It was reached by many in the 1970s, who noticed, as was just pointed out, that writers of the 1960s had somewhat too easily 'demonstrated' the superiority of liberal democracies. New development theories emerged which suggested on the contrary that the alleged value of liberal democracies was the product of the exploitation of the Third World by the West; thus the 'development' of liberal democracies was achieved by maintaining other parts of the world in a form of economic dependency; to this was to be added an ideological dependency by which non-Western states were subjected to the repeated claim that the Western model of government was politically superior.[23]

This approach united political development closely with economic power; meanwhile, supporters of Western liberal democracies tended to make the same connection, since they typically claimed – and indeed to an extent showed empirically – that liberal democracy flourished primarily where living standards were high.[24] Economic and social development seemed to be the key element; political development was merely a 'superstructure', an inevitable consequence. In practice, however, the 'developmentalists' were the ones who had to establish the primacy of political development if they were to break the vicious circle in which they considered Third World societies imprisoned. This led to the emphasis on alternative approaches to development and the strong statement that, at bottom, political development had to be assessed on a normative basis.

Such an approach reinforced the view that there could be no agreement on the bases of political development and that any assessment of what it constituted depended entirely on the individual's ideological preferences. Yet it is questionable whether this conclusion is truly warranted. In this respect, it is worth examining what seems to be an apparent contrast between the characteristics of social and economic development and those of political development, for, on the surface, while the latter concept appears to be based on normative standpoints, the definition of social and economic development, on the contrary, does not seem to raise quite the same fundamental difficulties and indeed appears relatively uncontentious.

It is not true that economic and social development is universally acceptable because the concepts involved are not normative concepts. Economic and social development may be more easily measurable, in some of its aspects, than political development; but, as with political development, it is based on ideas which are normative. For instance, it is neither axiomatic nor logically demonstrable that higher incomes per head are a 'good' thing, let alone that industrialisation or the use of sophisticated machinery are 'good' things; nor is it even axiomatic or logically demonstrable that more education or more social services are 'good' things. These questions are not only debatable, they are indeed to an extent debated; they were often hotly debated in the past and some of them have come to be discussed, in a renewed manner, in the 1970s and 1980s, as a result both of the increased strength of 'environmentalist ideas' and of the spread of conservative views about the state and the individual.[25] These points are debated because they are, like participation or equality in the context of political development, based on value judgements.

If the concepts of economic and social development depend on value judgements about the 'good' society, why do these concepts not encounter the same difficulties as political development? There are two reasons for the difference. The first is somewhat peripheral but it does none the less play some part: economic and social development is more easily measurable in many of its aspects; this means that in practice there is less scope for argument as to what, from a concrete point of view, might constitute development.[26] The fact that countries can be ranked in terms of incomes per head or of educational attainment, while it is not possible to do so with respect to the level of institutionalisation of parties or parliaments, makes economic and social development appear more objective. Second, and more fundamentally, the norms of economic and social development, though theoretically debatable, are debated in fact only to a limited extent: there is a higher degree of agreement on socio-economic norms than on political norms. There are few who believe, let alone state (at any rate at present) that society should not educate its members or take care of the health of its citizens; there are few who believe or state that levels of incomes among the mass of the population should be low. Meanwhile, many believe and indeed state that levels of participation should not be high or that freedoms should be restricted.

It is so manifest that there is a debate on social and economic issues that it has been argued that political systems should be differentiated along a dimension of substantive goals, of outputs, as well as along dimensions of liberalism–authoritarianism and of democracy–monocracy. Yet the debate which occurs along the dimension of substantive goals also leaves considerable scope for broad agreement as to what might be said to constitute 'basic' social and economic values. There is for instance substantial disagreement on levels of equality with respect to property distribution and indeed income distribution, while aspects of social life, such as those relating to health and to an extent education, as well as to a lesser extent some aspects of economic life, for example the increased use of mechanical power instead of human physical force, are broadly accepted.

The point here is not to assess the precise extent to which economic and social development is being debated; it is to point out that a lesser amount of disagreement with respect to the goals of economic and social development does not stem from a fundamental difference *vis-à-vis* political development, but merely from a difference of degree. It is not that economic and social development can be defined in an objective manner while political development depends on subjective assessment: all aspects of development are based on subjective assessments. What makes economic and social development apparently easier to handle is that the level of *intersubjective* agreement is appreciably higher – at least this is ostensibly the case.[27]

Given that the characteristics of development – of progress – depend on a high level of consensus – of intersubjective agreement – if they are to be acceptable, there is a case for examining whether, as for economic and social development, it might not be possible to find a broad intersubjective base for political development as well. The aim is not to discover a 'syndrome' in which the structural elements of political development would, so to speak, reduce the part played by normative elements; it is to see whether some values are sufficiently broadly held in the political sphere to form a basis for an intersubjective approach to the concept.

It is manifestly impossible to discover such values at the level of ideological standpoints which are widely adopted in specific regimes, such as equality, democracy, or 'orderly change'.[28] These concepts are the object of too many public and private debates. The question is, however, whether there are some deeper characteristics of politics which might appear to the large majority – if not to all – as 'positive'. Hobbes noted one characteristic which appears to be of this type, the right to defend one's life. Could one not go somewhat further and, building on Hobbes' premiss in a positive rather than a negative way, consider as 'inalienable' and universally 'valuable' the right to strive, the right to achieve, a view which is perhaps not too far from the idea of the right to 'happiness'?[29]

To return to the definition of politics as the authoritative allocation of values, the question is: whose values? The answer may then be: all the values which exist at a given point in the polity. However, the political system cannot take all these values into account, as was pointed out in Chapter 2; there have to be mechanisms limiting the number of values (goods, services, but also attitudes) which the society can process at a given moment. Does it not therefore follow that *improvement, progress, development* would consist of increases in the number and characteristics of the values accepted by the society? If human beings have a right to achieve and at least to strive, this surely means that a better society is one in which all human beings are in a better position to achieve and at least to strive; this means that a better society is one in which the 'number' of values allocated is larger.

This conception of development is the one which D.E. Apter proposes in *Choice and the Politics of Allocation* (1973), when he states that development is the 'expansion of choice opportunities', a notion which pertains particularly to politics.[30] Such an approach, though normative, is almost certainly intersubjective, as it is likely to carry broad agreement. This does not mean that there cannot be conflicts about the concrete manifestations of these 'choice opportunities'; nor is universal acceptance claimed for the view that political development is related to the expansion of choice opportunities, especially if the matter is considered historically. However, this approach is likely to produce a sounder basis for intersubjective agreement and thus reduce the oppositions which at one point appeared to make it impossible to even discuss political development.

Conclusion

The question of political development raises major theoretical problems; these are unavoidable, given the intrinsically contentious nature of political values. Yet, as the analysis of the concept proceeds, some scope seems to emerge for a clarification and perhaps a narrowing of disagreement. It is true that political development must be viewed in the context of development as a whole, as is also the case for economic and social development: there is no primacy of one aspect over the others. As the analysis proceeds, one discovers that all aspects have objective and subjective components, which are linked and even intertwined. Political development can to some extent be assessed objectively through an examination of the capacity of political structures and, in the first instance, through the determination of the degree of institutionalisation of these structures. This is a difficult task; operationalisation is still a relatively distant goal, but it is not impossible to achieve. The problems posed by values in political development are more severe, but they do not seem insurmountable; if they are directly confronted, the danger of a wholly subjective assessment recedes. By proceeding in this manner, the analysis can lead to a markedly more precise view of the concept of political development and thus contribute significantly to the understanding of the direction of change in modern societies.

Notes

1. The comparison between the newly independent states of the Third World and the *First New Nation* which the United States once was has been made most interestingly by S.M. Lipset in a book of that title (1963).
2. Studies on development are legion. So are those on political development. For a general presentation of the evolution of the studies see J. Blondel, *The Discipline of Politics* (1981), pp. 90–102. For a detailed examination of theories of development, see R.H. Chilcote, *Theories of Comparative Politics* (1981), pp. 271–346.
3. L.W. Pye, *Aspects of Political Development* (1966), Chapter 2, pp. 31–48. Two other earlier presentations of the problem can be found in J.L. Finkle and R.W. Gable (eds), *Political Development and Social Change* (1966) and in R.J. Jackson and M.B. Stein (eds), *Issues in Comparative Politics* (1971), Chapter 1, pp. 19–111.
4. See in particular A. Arblaster and S. Lukes (eds), *The Good Society* (1971), which was mentioned in the previous chapter.
5. L.W. Pye, *op. cit.*, pp. 45–8.
6. This is one of the cases in which political analysis is at a major disadvantage compared to social and economic analysis: despite the difficulties of collection and the problems of measurement, indicators of political development could be used if the raw data were collected, as for social and economic development, by international agencies: this is not done, in large part because governments are unwilling to see the data collected and published by these agencies.
7. In the late 1970s and in the 1980s, it became fashionable to 'bring the state back in' to political analysis and this has sometimes been done almost to the extent of underestimating the role of other groups. See for instance T. Skocpol, *States and Social Revolutions* (1979) and P.B. Evans, D. Rueschmeyer and T. Skocpol (eds), *Bringing the State Back In* (1985), in particular the Introduction by T. Skocpol, pp. 3–43.
8. The measurement of 'outputs' of governments (and of parties) has attracted the attention of increasing numbers of political scientists, especially during the 1980s. The question will be examined in Chapters 14, 18, and 19.
9. S.P. Huntington, *Political Order in Changing Societies* (1968), p. 12. S.P. Huntington is one of the authors who attempted to give first a precise content to the concept of institutionalisation, although an earlier effort at measuring the extent of institutionalisation of the American Congress was made by N.W. Polsby in 'The institutionalisation of the US House of Representatives', *Am. Pol. Sc. Rev.*, 62 (1968), pp. 144–68.

10. S.P. Huntington, *op. cit.*, pp. 13–24.
11. For instance along the lines suggested by N.W. Polsby, *op. cit.*, e.g. by looking at the professionalisation of members, their career, etc.
12. The concept of overload was developed in the context of attempts at measuring the outputs of governments. See in particular R. Rose, *Understanding Big Government* (1984). This question will be further discussed in Chapter 18.
13. These criteria were developed by G.A. Almond and G.B. Powell in *Comparative Politics* (1966), in particular pp. 306–14.
14. E. Durkheim, *The Division of Labour in Society* (English translation, 1933), especially pp. 39–49.
15. S.P. Huntington, *op. cit.*, p. 12.
16. For instance, in some countries, parties and interest groups are quite independent of each other: this is the case in particular in the United States; in other countries, Socialist and Christian parties are related to a series of groups, such as trade unions, co-operatives, etc. It is not clear that the first type of arrangement is by any criterion more 'successful' than the second.
17. The concept of the capabilities of political systems was developed particularly by G.A. Almond and G.B. Powell in *Comparative Politics* (1966), pp. 190–212. While this concept is in theory most valuable, it has so far not proved measurable, any more than the efficiency of the political system.
18. G.A. Almond and G.B. Powell postulate such a relationship between differentiation and efficiency: this is at best not proven; indeed the relationship is probably not linear.
19. The criticism of being Western biassed was addressed to structural-functionalism in general and to the approach of G.A. Almond in particular. For a detailed presentation of the criticisms, see R.H. Chilcote, *op. cit.*, pp. 178–82.
20. L.W. Pye, *op. cit.*. pp. 39–42.
21. *ibid.*, pp. 45–6.
22. R.J. Jackson and M.B. Stein, *op. cit.*, pp. 32–4.
23. See R.H. Chilcote, *op. cit.*, pp. 296–312, for a presentation of the different varieties of 'dependency' theories which aimed at moving out of the apparent Western bias of functional theories in particular. Many of these theories were based on the Latin American experience and were developed in the 1970s; they have in turn been subjected to criticism.
24. This type of analysis was first pioneered by S.M. Lipset in *Political Man* (1983) and by P. Cutright in 'National political development' in N.W. Polsby *et al.*, *Politics and Social Life* (1963), pp. 569–82. The question will be examined in Chapter 5.
25. The development of 'green' movements and parties, especially in Western liberal democracies, since the 1970s, has led to a strong questioning of the worth of economic and even conventional social development. The idea of 'rolling back the state' which characterised also the policies of a number of Western liberal democracies, such as Britain and the United States, had too the effect of leading to a questioning of the worth of conventional economic and social development.
26. The question of the measurement of economic and social development has also tended to be raised increasingly; the comparison of the *per capita* GNP of highly diverse countries, for instance, is very controversial.
27. The idea that normative standpoints could achieve some degree of generality by being shared by many, if not all, members of the society is not new. The notion of intersubjectivity has developed in particular from critical theory. See for instance J.H. Turner, *The Structure of Sociological Theory* (1986), pp. 188ff. and pp. 328ff.
28. To take the expressions used by L.W. Pye, *op. cit.*, Chapter 2, pp. 29–48.
29. T. Hobbes, *Leviathan*, Part I, Chapter 14.
30. D.E. Apter, *Choice and the Politics of Allocation* (1973), p. 10.

5 | Legitimacy, integration, coercion and the question of dictatorship

It is widely believed that governments and political systems need support to remain in existence, yet many governments remain in office for many years without being ostensibly accepted by the population. The phenomenon of coercion is widespread and the concept of dictatorship is not one which has little or no practical application. This apparent contradiction between a recognised 'need' for support and the reality of coercive governments has to be explored.

Support relates to legitimacy, a concept which should be sharply distinguished from legality, though there are connections between the two ideas. Cases abound of legal regimes which are not, or have ceased to be legitimate because they no longer enjoy support (Tsarist Russia at the time of World War I is an example); there are also governments or regimes which enjoy support without being legal, or at any rate without yet being legalised (for instance if a coup has toppled a regime). In most situations, however, the legality of the government helps to increase legitimacy, because many will support the government because it is legal.

The type of support referred to above is based on the sentiments of individuals; but there is another type, which stems from the relationship between groups and the regime or government: parties, interest organisations, but also tribal, ethnic, or religious bodies ostensibly play a large part, as was already indicated in Chapter 3 and as will be discussed at greater length in the coming chapters. The support given by groups determines the extent of political integration in a country: while legitimacy refers to the overall level of acceptance of the regime or government throughout the polity, political integration is concerned with that part of legitimacy which is based on the ties between groups and the political system. The two concepts are manifestly related: we need therefore to look both at legitimacy among individuals and at political integration in order to assess the extent of the support which a regime or government enjoys.

A regime or government which does not have (sufficient) support has to rely on coercion or imposition: such a regime is referred to as a dictatorship. The history of the world, including the contemporary world, suggests that dictatorships are a common feature and therefore that coercion can be a substitute for the absence of support in many circumstances, despite the claim (or hope) that dictatorships might not be viable. Putting it differently, although many regimes give rise to apparent discontent among the population, the incidence of rebellion is relatively limited; moreover, successful rebellions (and revolutions) are relatively rare, at least in comparison with the extent of discontent. It took a world war to force the end of some of the European dictatorships, while others have sprung up in various parts of the globe since 1945. Although rebellions took place in Eastern Europe and toppled several regimes in late 1989, one must also remember how long these regimes had lasted; and one must remember that such rebellions would probably not have taken place, let alone been successful, had not the Soviet government directly or indirectly encouraged major changes in these countries. Dictatorial government is thus a persistent feature of political life, alongside regimes which have support and rely on consent.

One of the keys to the understanding of the apparent contradiction between the need for support and the existence of dictatorships lies in the recognition that these situations, like most of those which we have already encountered, refer to continuous dimensions and not to dichotomies. The extent of individual support for a regime does vary; the integration of groups in the political system can be more or less pronounced; similarly, there are manifest differences in the extent to which governments rely on coercion, from that used in mildly repressive regimes to that of fully blown totalitarian states. Consequently, one should not simply state that all these regimes are dictatorships, but instead one should view them as being characterised by various degrees of harshness, while all regimes enjoy different levels of individual support and of integration. It can also be assumed that there are almost certainly no regimes at either extreme of these dimensions. If the problem is viewed in this manner, it becomes unnecessary to attempt to explain the existence of support and of coercion *per se*; more realistically, one has to attempt to account for variations in support and coercion on the assumption that in all cases there is always a minimum amount of both support and coercion.

Legitimacy and the characteristics of individual support

The concept of legitimacy is used widely both in the specialist political science literature and in common political parlance, yet it remains relatively ill-studied from a formal point of view. Neither its origins, nor its growth and decline (just as support varies in extent, so does legitimacy), nor its effect have so far been systematically analysed.[1] This is indeed probably one of the reasons why exaggerated claims are made about its effect or, more precisely, why, since degrees are not measured or even assessed with any accuracy, particular effects of given amounts of legitimacy cannot be related to particular outcomes. As a matter of fact, there has so far been little effort to operationalise the concept and compare regimes in order to examine possible effects of different levels of legitimacy on outcomes.[2]

The analysis conducted here will therefore lack the solid empirical base which it should have and which will no doubt eventually be developed.

Legitimacy stems from individual support. The most elementary forms of this support will be considered first. There is support when members of the polity are favourably disposed towards the political system, the regime, the government (clearly support may or may not extend to all three, and this has important consequences). No attempt will be made to examine here the reasons why someone supports the national political authorities; such an examination would lead into the realm of individual and group psychology, which is beyond the scope of this work. It is enough to note that support may come from the socialisation process and thus from outside pressures as well as from the characteristics of the 'personality' – the whole personality, including its affective and cognitive elements. Whatever the origins of the positive view which citizens may have of the regime, its object may vary widely; the support may relate in a diffuse manner to the system as a whole (though this does not mean that it is weak), or it may be directed specifically to a number of measures which the government has taken or has promised to take; indeed, in practice, especially with reference to the national political system and to the government, whose range of activities is very large, the support of individuals for the regime is likely to be composed of a combination of the two elements – general and specific, vague and precise – but to a varying degree: there will be both some overall system support and some support for individual policies.[3]

The existence of a combination of types and objects of support suggests that this support varies in strength over time, if only gradually and in many cases only to a limited degree. The rate of change is also likely to differ: where support is specific, variations can be expected to be more rapid. Regimes depending primarily on specific policy support therefore appear vulnerable, as they may be subjected to sudden variations in support; such a situation, however, is unusual in national political life, perhaps even purely hypothetical.[4] In general, support for the regime is based more on habits and/or a general ideological stance than on detailed calculations about specific issues; however, ideological standpoints and traditionally held views also change, if rather slowly, for instance as a result of the influence of the environment or of variations in personal life conditions.

Although it is clear on an impressionistic level that changes in support levels occur, the extent and rate of these changes has not so far been measured.[5] Theoretically, such a measurement is not impossible; in practice, it has not been attempted: we cannot therefore assess at this point how much time it takes for a regime to become more or less popular as a result of variations in the characteristics of the society or as a result of specific policies. So long as this is the case, the study of legitimacy will remain rather vague and, as a corollary, conclusions about the amount of legitimacy needed by a regime to remain in power will remain imprecise.

As changes in the level of support manifestly take place, however, it is at least possible to conclude that the intensity of support does also vary and that support can range from being very active to being wholly passive. The citizens may be inclined to behave positively in favour of the regime; they may, on the contrary, be willing only to refrain from acting against the authorities and merely tolerate these as long as they are not personally affected. Passive support is widespread: large segments of the population have typically little to do with national authorities, except when there is an emergency or a war. This is particularly true in traditional societies in which concrete manifestations of the activity of the state are rare and in which the dependents of the state are not numerous: in overwhelmingly rural societies, the impact of the regime on citizens is low: the degree of state 'penetration' in the society is said to be low.[6] Only in industrial societies does the majority of the population become affected by social services, public works, and regular taxation: yet, even in these polities, the involvement of the state in the daily life of millions of citizens remains relatively small.

Support is therefore characterised in many cases by a passive and vague sentiment *vis-à-vis* the regime and/or the government. Of course, the support which has been discussed so far with respect to each citizen has to be 'aggregated', so to speak, to provide an impression of the overall level of legitimacy of the regime or government. Naturally, each member of the polity does not display the same amount of support: some are intensely positively inclined towards the authorities, others are strongly opposed, while many are neutral or at most passively in favour. The overall level of legitimacy enjoyed by the regime or government is based on the 'sum' of these reactions, a sum which, however, has not so far been adequately measured or calculated. Where positive and passive support exceeds negative reactions, the regime can be said to be relatively legitimate; the greater the difference in favour of positive support, the higher the amount of legitimacy.

In the absence of a measurement of these positive and negative reactions to the regime, it is impossible to go further, except to state that, in view of the characteristics just outlined (relatively slow change where habits are the basis of support, and an extensive level of passive support), most regimes probably enjoy a substantial, but not a very high amount of legitimacy. This enables the public authorities to continue in office, especially if they do not make large new demands (which could alter the supportive habits of many), unless changes in the society provoke changes in attitudes among the population. In such cases, the authorities have on the contrary to introduce policies designed to satisfy these demands, as otherwise support is likely to shrink and the possibility of outright manifestations of discontent, leading perhaps to rebellion, might increase. Such a strategy poses problems, however, as there will also be opposition to these changes. Tension is therefore likely to increase whatever is proposed and the government may have to resort to coercion.

Yet, even in such a situation, the erosion of legitimacy may not lead (or at least may not lead quickly) to the collapse of the regime, since there may not be a credible alternative. In the last resort, public authorities really need support only when they are directly challenged. Of course, when support declines, such a challenge may emerge, but this is unlikely to occur spontaneously and in particular without a group providing a focus. This is indeed why rebellion, let alone revolution, rarely develops from a 'spontaneous' uprising of the people, but more often from an organised body which was not integrated in the system. What support achieves, when it is strong, is to render the emergence of a strong challenge unlikely, even within the context of a group; indeed, if some elements are to voice their opposition, they will find little echo. Even when discontent is large and support very passive, moreover, there will always be at least some delay before consequences are felt: the regime is likely to benefit from the fact that it takes time for discontent to be turned into an effective challenge.[7]

The role of political integration

To say that the regime or government has, so to speak, the benefit of the doubt and can survive on passive support as long as there is no focal point around which a challenge might emerge means that a crucial element of the equation is constituted by the group configuration. In practice, the only elements which are in a position to mount a challenge are groups, as only they are sufficiently strong and durable to gather around them the potential opposition. Thus conversely, to be safe, a regime or government needs a high level of political integration to exist in the society.

Political integration has been defined as a 'pool of commonly accepted norms regarding political behaviour and a commitment to the political behaviour patterns legitimised by these norms'.[8] The parts of the political system have to be related to each other in such a way as to make a coherent whole. There must be an absence of groups which continuously, strongly, and over a wide range of issues oppose the actions of the regime and government.

Political integration relates principally to groups which are closely involved in political life, but, as was pointed out in Chapter 2, many others are also engaged intermittently in politics and occasionally play a major part. The only bodies which are wholly excluded from consideration are purely 'social' clubs, while even cultural organisations which are outwardly non-political may be important in supporting or oppposing a government or regime. However, the bodies which are characteristically involved in political life and are critical for the assessment of political integration are, in the first instance, the constitutional bodies, including local authorities, parties and large interest groups, such as trade unions and employers' associations, as well as bodies promoting or defending a cause, environmental and regional organisations, for instance. In many polities, moreover, the most relevant groups are those which form part of the traditional fabric of society, such as tribes, ethnic groups and religious bodies.

Political integration relates to the extent to which these groups are tied to the regime and to the government. For these ties to be strong, as Ake states, 'norms regarding political behaviour' have to be shared by the groups and by the government. There are manifest variations in the degree to which these norms are shared, admittedly. Nowhere are all the groups involved in political activity in full agreement with the norms of the regime or government. One should therefore refer to political integration as ranging from very high – though never complete – to very low, though probably always above a minimum level, for below such a minimum the polity would disintegrate. So far, as is the case with levels of legitimacy, levels of political integration have not been measured or even assessed with precision, but there can be no doubt that these levels do exist.[9]

The extent of political integration is also affected by the importance of the group: an occasional conflict between a very large group and the regime can be more serious for that regime than the permanent opposition of a very small group, even that of a group which is frequently involved in political activity. Thus political integration needs also to be assessed by reference to the weight of groups in the polity and indeed by reference to variations in this weight over time. This importance has not so far been measured, but one can give an impression of its contours and this will be attempted in some detail in Chapters 6 and 7. At this point, however, it is sufficient to note that the importance of groups depends on two elements, the size of their following and the breadth of the problems which they cover. The breadth of problems covered by the group is obviously critical: groups which are concerned with all aspects of the life of an individual, such as tribes in traditional societies, can be expected to play a truly large part in the determination of the overall level of integration, while the more specialised interest groups which one finds in industrial societies are likely to have a less determinant role.

The nature of the following is also fundamental in determining potential effects on integration: groups have an impact only if they can count on reliable support from their members. Thus while legitimacy relates to the support which the political system has directly in the population, political integration relates to the support which each group has in that population. Political integration can be viewed as 'indirect' legitimacy: it is legitimacy channelled and mediated by the groups. Governments and regimes are therefore naturally anxious to reduce the part played by groups in this equation: they obviously prefer to depend primarily on 'direct' legitimacy.

This desire may not be achieved, and indeed can almost never be achieved because groups exist and it is not within the power of the government to abolish groups altogether; to be more precise, the stronger the group following in the population, the less it is possible for the government to abolish them: where some groups have a truly massive support, the government is, so to speak, at their mercy. So long as these groups accept the political status quo, the regime and the government are relatively safe; but if one or more among them challenge the public authorities, these are in serious danger.

This places leaders of important groups in a strong position: they appear able to undermine or even break the political system at will. Yet this is only true provided they can carry their following with them. The leadership of the group needs the support of followers to be legitimate in the same way that the national government needs the support of the population. Support within the group naturally has the same characteristics as support within the political system. It can be more or less diffuse or more or less specific, it can vary over time, and it can be more or less strong: many members of these groups are likely to be passive supporters, for instance. This means that the 'government' of the group is no freer to move in any direction it wishes while keeping its support intact than are the national political authorities with respect to the whole population. The freedom of group leaders is particularly restricted when, as Ake states, there is a 'pool of commonly accepted norms' among the population: political integration is then maintained because the group leaders cannot act beyond certain limits without endangering their own status within the group or even the very existence of the group.[10]

Thus political integration is about the extent to which groups both act in broad harmony with the political authorities and are in a position to confront these authorities. Not all groups can do so, but some can do so in an effective manner. By and large, the groups in which support is based on habits are more likely to do so than groups whose support depends on instrumental calculations; there is therefore a greater likelihood that groups will be strong and independent if they are long-established and indeed belong to the fabric of society, as is the case for example with tribal, ethnic, or religious groups. Admittedly, new organisations can acquire strength and be in a position to challenge the authorities, but this is more difficult to achieve, especially in the early period of the group's development. Moreover, even at later stages, the regime or government is more likely to be successful in imposing restrictions on new groups, while these may be also opposed by older bodies which fear they will be undermined.

As was stated with respect to legitimacy, the extent of political integration – or the extent to which groups are effectively in a position to challenge the regime or government – is affected by variations in general social and economic conditions. If the society is static and relatively insulated from the influence of other polities, the relative strength of groups *vis-à-vis* the regime or government will tend not to change: thus, where integration was high, it will remain high. Where groups and political system were not in harmony, conflict will remain high, as occurs in plural societies, that is to say in those polities where some groups (usually tribal, ethnic, or religious) are strongly entrenched and are in permanent confrontation with the national political system and with other groups. These are indeed the situations when rebellions tend to occur; examples abound, from Northern Ireland to Uganda and from Cyprus to Sri Lanka.[11]

The overall conditions within which the relationships between groups and the political system operate are rarely stable in the contemporary world. The social structure is likely to change under the impact of industrialisation or of geographical mobility; the social, economic, and indeed political influence of neighbouring countries can be large, as for instance when these support some groups against others. As a result, the rules of the game being played by groups and government will be altered. The level of political integration will change, sometimes to the benefit of the groups, sometimes to the benefit of the political system. Support for traditional groups may become eroded and 'national sentiments' may increase; new groups may also emerge and these may conflict with the government. Thus the problems which political integration poses for many regimes are extensive and permanent, especially if groups with a substantial following appear to be entrenched. In extreme cases the very existence of the state may appear to be in danger. Not surprisingly, governments are often tempted to solve this problem by using force. The question is whether this can provide a genuine solution, and whether there are limits to the extent of coercion which a regime can impose without endangering its own future.

The spread of coercion and the conditions for dictatorships

Coercive regimes are widespread: in the contemporary world, a majority of regimes probably deserve to be described in this manner, and a substantial minority apply very harsh coercion: the repeated incidence of coups – military and otherwise – is evidence of the magnitude of the problem, though coups (and revolutions) occur with the aim of installing dictatorial regimes as well as toppling them. The means by which coercive regimes are able to maintain themselves in power are well-known: not only are the more sophisticated freedoms, such as the freedom of the press or the right to demonstrate, curtailed or abolished while elections are rigged, postponed, or not called at all; the 'basic' rights of individuals are set aside and opponents of the government are rounded up, imprisoned, or shot. Meanwhile, government propaganda dominates the media, thus ensuring that information is restricted to the news which the regime wishes to broadcast in the hope that, gradually at least, the minds of the population will be influenced in the direction which the regime favours. There seems to be almost no limit to the coercive measures which a 'totalitarian' state can adopt, modern technical discoveries having substantially added to the instruments of control and 'education' which were traditionally at the disposal of governments.[12]

Yet the fact that such regimes are often successful only for a limited period suggests that it is probably not possible for a harsh dictatorship to be truly viable or at least that there are conditions under which these dictatorships are more or less likely to prosper. The main practical problems which are encountered result from the financial costs of the coercive apparatus and from the fact that at least a minimum of support is required among those who operate this apparatus. Little needs to be said about costs: these obviously pose major problems for countries which are very poor. The setting up of a variety of controls implies that the police and the army are sufficiently large to be able to exercise surveillance over all parts of the country; this is rarely achieved in Third World dictatorships, so that, in practice, the extent of coercion which takes place at grass-roots level is often less widespread than might be expected in a dictatorship.[13]

An even more serious problem is posed by the need to deploy reliable forces to exercise coercion. If the population is truly antagonistic, the regime will have to select carefully those who will be charged with the operation of repression. In some situations, this can be achieved with relative ease, for instance when the opposition is concentrated in a particular tribe, ethnic element, or religious body: members of other groups can be used to force compliance and this method is often adopted.[14]

But the fact that the regime can count on one element of the population to oppress the others also means that the regime enjoys some support in the population: if there is no support at all, or if there is a tiny amount of support, there is a very high probability that the regime will not find – or will not find for very long – a sufficiently large number of persons on whom it can rely.

Of course, the regime can then attempt to create such a reliable group artificially by a combination of personal favours and 'political education'. This is the rationale behind the creation of 'mass movements', and of political parties, in many coercive regimes. This development has been particularly common in contemporary dictatorships, in part because of the technical facilities which are now available. Yet it is also costly to build such organisations and, even more important, it takes time – indeed a long time – to ensure that active members are truly reliable. This is why many such organisations exist more on paper than in reality, as is often the case in the single-party systems of Black Africa; this is also why those which are really alive tend to be found where special conditions have enabled them to develop, for instance during a protracted war of independence or if the occupation by a foreign nation adds external resources to the coercive effort, as has been the case in Eastern European Communist states.[15]

Coercive machines are difficult to build because they need to be extensive precisely in those countries in which the mass of the population is antagonistic. A government will wish to build a mass organisation such as a party in order to modify the views of the population in its favour and in particular in order to lure that population away from the traditional groups and from the norms which these groups support. But these norms tend to be embodied in groups which have a strong hold on their members; this is the case with tribes, ethnic groups or religious bodies. Alternatively the government may primarily want to 'build the nation' by attempting to unite a polity divided into a number of opposed groups and where, therefore, integration is low. In both types of situation, the opposition of the traditional groups is difficult to break. In post-independence Black Africa, for instance, governments had in many cases to abandon their opposition to tribes and to ally with the strongest of them. Sometimes, after a coup, a new regime tries to impose a tougher policy, but this is usually to no avail. Even in Communist states, determined efforts to abolish traditional groups have only been partly successful; latent oppositions remain and sometimes emerge on the surface, the most obvious case being that of Poland. Even when there are special circumstances, therefore – for example after a long war of independence and where there is a strong leadership – dictatorships experience major difficulties in attempting to reduce long-standing group ties and they never seem to be fully successful.[16]

The coercion of groups is thus not easily achieved. Conversely, however, some societal conditions may make it likely, if not altogether inevitable, that dictatorships will emerge. By and large, as was suggested earlier, a dictatorial government is likely when conflicts among groups are such that no accommodation can be found because political integration is low. In such circumstances, the dictatorship can be described as 'structural'; in contrast a dictatorship is 'technical' if it emerges as a result of personality clashes. In practice, the distinction is more analytical than empirical, as many dictatorships include both personal and 'societal' elements.[17]

Structural dictatorships tend to occur when societal divisions are deep since, as a result, the different segments of the polity are unwilling to agree to compromises. Such a situation can be found primarily where there are profound socio-economic changes: the traditional structures lose support and new groups emerge whose members want to accelerate the pace of change. The climate is often made worse because of the direct or indirect influence of neighbouring countries; the realisation that other societies are economically and socially more 'advanced' acts as an incentive for those who want progress. Major divisions occur which correspond to different models of society. Even where the political system previously enjoyed high levels of legitimacy and integration, a peaceful solution of the new conflicts is difficult to achieve: this is why structural dictatorships tend to occur during the 'take-off' stage of the economy. The dictatorship may be 'progressive', if the forces which wish to accelerate the pace of change are able to coerce the traditional groups; it may be 'conservative' if the converse obtains.[18] Indeed, there will often be oscillations between one form of dictatorship and the other, as, in view of what was pointed out earlier, the costs of organising an effective dictatorship are often so high that the opposition may find the means to topple it within a few years.

Dictatorships thus occur frequently during the take-off stage, while they are less likely to emerge in stable traditional societies where large groups predominate, and are very rare in highly developed societies in which the more specialised interest and promotional bodies are less able individually to exercise direct control over the government. Moreover, during the take-off stage, countries may not be ruled by a dictatorship if tension in the society remains relatively low: this will occur if the society was originally well integrated, if the pace of change is relatively slow, and if some political structures bridge the gap between the traditional and the modern society, for instance if political parties are able to represent elements of both. This peculiar combination of factors leading to gradual change will therefore be found primarily in homogeneous societies which have had a relatively long history and whose geographical boundaries have remained unchanged for generations.[19] It is not surprising, however, that most societies, and in particular most newly established polities should find it difficult to avoid periods of dictatorial rule.

Conclusion

The numerous dictatorships of the contemporary world are largely a consequence of the major changes which have taken place in recent decades; their number has been boosted by the unprecedented creation of new countries in the post-1945 period as well as by the high expectations in the rise of living standards which remained largely unfulfilled. In these countries, support was originally low because traditional groups had had little time to become integrated in the national polity. Yet the existence of these dictatorships does not suggest that support is of no importance in human societies: not only does it play a part in other regimes, but some element of support must exist around the government in all political systems. Dictatorships cannot be sustained in a completely hostile environment. Support and coercion are two components of political life which, although and indeed because they are diametrically opposed, have to be seen in combination; only in this way can one understand the characteristics and the dynamics of political systems. Whatever distaste one may have for dictatorships, they are often the result of forces and of changes which societies experience in their move towards development. Only an analysis of the conditions under which dictatorships emerge and are maintained can provide the means of discovering how their impact can be minimised and legitimacy become more widespread.

Notes

1. The concept of legitimacy has attracted considerable interest for generations, yet it has so far led to little true systematic analysis. One of the most interesting earlier presentations was that of the historian G. Ferrero, *Principles of Power* (New York edition, 1945). D. Easton examines the effect of legitimacy in *A Systems Analysis of Political Life* (1965), pp. 278–310 in the context of a much longer discussion of support. See also W. Connolly (ed.), *Legitimacy and the State* (1984). The question of the conditions under which rebellions and revolutions occur has naturally been explored extensively. See for instance R.J. Jackson and M.B. Stein, (eds), *Issues in Comparative Politics* (1971), pp. 265–408. See also T.R. Gurr, *Why Men Rebel* (1970), *passim* and T.R. Gurr (ed.), *Handbook of Political Conflict* (1980), *passim*.
2. The most systematic attempt at measuring some aspects of legitimacy in the context of divided societies is that of R. Rogowski, *Rational Legitimacy* (1974).
3. See in particular D. Easton, *op. cit.* (1965), pp. 311–19. See also P.L. Berger and T. Luckman, *The Social Construction of Reality* (1966), pp. 110–46.
4. Here the case of the support for *regimes* in general is being considered; governments, in the narrower sense of the government of the day, receive specific support for their policies. Opinion polls tend to measure government support rather than regime support in general.
5. Support for governments can be and is measured (and fluctuates markedly); but support for regimes is appreciably more difficult to assess precisely, much of it being, as was pointed out, vague and diffuse. The converse of support is of course protest, rebellion, and revolution. The conditions under which rebellions occur have been analysed in particular by T.R. Gurr, *op. cit.*, (1970). See also R.J. Jackson and M.B. Stein, (eds), *Issues in Comparative Politics* (1971), pp. 265–84 and 347–59.
6. In traditional societies and indeed in many developing societies, the ability of the state authorities to 'penetrate' in the provinces is very limited, in part because the state does not have the resources to post officials widely throughout the country and in part because of the resistance of traditional groups which are well-implanted. Indeed, by the same token, active opposition is likely to be rare, because it requires action (and often dangerous action): hence the relatively limited number of rebellions.
7. It is difficult to organise opposition from scratch, especially in a society in which communications are difficult, even if levels of coercion are relatively mild. This is why many regimes in which there is a limited amount of coercion are often not subjected to widespread active opposition, let alone rebellion. An interesting example of the problems posed by such the organisation of opposition in an authoritarian regime is found in mid-

nineteenth-century France; see T. Zeldin, *The Political System of Napoleon III* (1958), in which the 1852 election is examined. See Chapter 10.

8. C. Ake, *A Theory of Political Integration* (1967), p. 3. The concept of integration is discussed systematically by H. Teune in G. Sartori (ed.), *Social Science Concepts* (1984), pp. 239–63. For a systematic examination of the problems of 'plural' societies, see A. Rabushka and K.A. Shepsle, *Politics in Plural Societies* (1972), C. Young, *The Politics of Cultural Pluralism* (1976), and A. Lijphart, *Democracy in Plural Societies* (1977). See also Chapters 6 and 7.

9. See R. Rogowski, *op. cit.*, for an effort at measuring the extent of integration, especially at pp. 143–97 in relation to what is described as 'segmented society'.

10. For an analysis of support within groups, see P.M. Blau, *Exchange and Power in Social Life* (1964), especially Chapters 7 and 8.

11. See A. Rabushka and K.A. Shepsle, *op. cit.*, and A. Liphart, *op. cit.* On rebellions and revolutions, see T.R. Gurr, *op. cit.*, (1970).

12. Works on totalitarianism are numerous. Among the most influential are those of C.J. Friedrich and Z. Brzezinski, *Totalitarian Dictatorship and Autocracy* (1956) and C.J. Friedrich (ed.), *Totalitarianism* (1954). After a period in which Communist states, in particular, were viewed almost universally as totalitarian, analyses have become more complex and the distinction between totalitarian government and other forms of authoritarianism, including within Communist states, has come to be made more widely. See in particular L. Holmes, *Politics in the Communist World* (1986), especially Chapters 3 and 15.

13. It is in particular in this context that the extent of penetration by the state becomes important: there cannot be totalitarian government unless there is a high level of state penetration.

14. The technique of sending administrators, policemen, and indeed the army to different parts of the country is widely used in centralised states in order to ensure greater levels of compliance. This method continues to be adopted in several Western European countries: in the Italian south, for instance, members of the police forces almost never come from the local area. The technique is not always successful, however; it can even lie at the origin of discontent and rebellions, as it increases feelings of ethnic, tribal, or religious opposition.

15. See Chapter 11 on single-party systems.

16. This has been noticeable even in countries such as Algeria, Angola, Mozambique, Vietnam, or Zimbabwe, where protracted wars of independence might have been expected to create an overwhelming sense of national identity.

17. See in particular M. Duverger, *De la Dictature* (1961), where the distinction between 'structural' and 'technical' dictatorships is discussed.

18. Examples of 'progressive' dictatorships are numerous, especially as a result or by imitation of Communist regimes: in Africa, post-1975 Ethiopia can be regarded as a prime example. Examples of 'conservative' dictatorships are also numerous, both in Africa and in Latin America: Pinochet's Chile is one of the best-known cases, but there have been many others in the 1970s and 1980s, often (but not always) based on the military, such as that of Stroessner in Paraguay.

19. The cases of Great Britain and Sweden can thus be contrasted with those of France, Germany, Italy, or Spain.

Part II

Society and government

6 The social bases of political systems

It is commonly recognised that the political life of a country is related to the socio-economic sub-structure. Marxists and non-Marxists seem to agree that some association exists; few students of politics, if any, would doubt that the structure of society, as defined in Chapter 1, is the origin of the conflicts which come to be reflected on the political plane. If a nation has profound social cleavages based for instance on class, race, or religion, the political system can be expected to be concerned with these cleavages; the complexity of the political problems will be in some measure the consequence of the complexity of the social problem.

The difficulty arises in attempting to give some precise content to the relationship. It arises .partly on the socio-economic side: some socio-economic characteristics are less 'objective' than others and even the 'objective' characteristics do not have the same meaning everywhere: the definition of a per capita income, for instance, is far from clear in the case of societies in which cash is not the main basis for the exchange of goods and services among large sections of the population. Yet the 'subjective' elements of social life, such as belief systems and attitudinal characteristics, are considerably more difficult to measure: in some countries, mainly Western, the concept of 'subjective social class' has been defined, examined and carefully operationalised, but the same cannot be said about other subjective elements, in particular for non-Western countries.

By and large, however, the relationship between the socio-economic base and political systems has become better known, especially with respect to liberal democracies. Yet two other aspects are potentially of great significance. One of these was encountered in the previous chapter when considering the question of integration: impressionistic evidence suggests that there are strong differences between the political life of plural societies, which are sharply divided by ethnic, linguistic, or religious cleavages, and the political life of homogeneous polities, but so far the evidence is insufficiently precise to be conclusive. In the second place, political life appears to vary according to the 'culture' of the country, that is to say the general social 'norms' which have come to be accepted throughout the nation's history. For instance, it has been thought for a long time that countries characterised by a 'protestant ethic' behave politically in a different manner from other nations. Yet culture, whether social or political, is difficult to ascertain and to measure as there is no universally accepted view as to what its components are. Efforts have none the less been made to circumscribe the concept more closely and, whatever the objective social conditions, to see how far the political characteristics of a country are likely to differ as a result of differing cultural conditions. The main findings in this field will therefore be examined after the relationship between socio-economic characteristics and political life has been considered, together with the impact which ethnic, linguistic or religious divisions may have on political life.[1]

Political systems and the socio-economic structure: the social 'prerequisites' of liberal democracy

In the contemporary world, about 50 countries – or a third of the total of about 160 nations – can be loosely classified as liberal democracies, although of course the number varies slighly from year to year and although, as was pointed out in Chapter 3, the appropriate concept is not a single point, but clusters allowing for substantial variations. Even a quick examination shows that these countries are not distributed at random (see Table 6.1): all Western European countries fall within this category, while the proportion of liberal democracies is small in Africa south of the Sahara and in the Middle East, and Communist states long formed a block of authoritarian–egalitarian polities. Latin America and South-East Asia are the two geographical areas where the proportion of liberal democracies is largest after Western Europe and North America, but, especially in the Latin American case, there are substantial variations over time.

Table 6.1 Liberal democracies around the world (among 147 countries in the mid-1980s)

	Atlantic	Communist	Middle East and North Africa	South and East Asia	Africa (South of Sahara)	Latin America	Total
Liberal democracies	23	0	3	8	3	11	48
Non-democracies	0	15	19	9	41	15	99
Total	23	15	22	17	44	26	147

Source: Calculated from Vanhanen (1987), pp. 39–42.

The study of the prerequisites of liberal democracy

On the basis of this preliminary impression, economic conditions seem closely related to political life. Per capita income is highest in Western Europe and North

America: these are the areas where liberal democracies are concentrated. Indeed, liberal democracy came first to Northern Europe, which was richer earlier than Southern Europe. Moreover, a scatter of other rich countries, such as Australia, New Zealand and Japan, are also liberal democracies. Yet wealth alone cannot constitute the whole explanation: India has a low per capita GNP and is a liberal democracy; some Latin American countries, such as Argentina, whose GNP per capita is relatively high, have known a number of authoritarian or populist regimes.

One solution to the problem could be to develop a ranking: an early study by P. Cutright suggested that the fit between liberal democracy and the socio-economic infrastructure was better if one took into account degrees of stability (while the pioneer in this line of analysis, S.M. Lipset, had only distinguished between 'stable' and 'unstable' liberal democracies in *Political Man*).[2] Yet even a ranking based on the number of years during which a country has been liberal–democratic is not sufficient: exceptions such as India, Malaysia, Jamaica and Mauritius remain.

For a while, therefore, political scientists looked for explanations other than the strictly economic. On the one hand, it became fashionable to argue that the presence or absence of liberal democracy was markedly affected by the 'dependency' of the nations concerned: this view was expressed in particular in relation to Latin America, as this was the area where one found the most authoritarian–inegalitarian countries which should, on economic grounds alone, be liberal democracies. Such an approach suggested that authoritarian government was directly or indirectly the result of the policies of 'core' countries (i.e. of the United States and Western Europe). This view has come to be less widely held since the 1980s, as Latin America entered a period (admittedly perhaps temporary) of resurgence of liberal democracy.[3]

It has also been suggested that one should not forget the part played by 'culture' and by purely political elements. Bearing in mind the fact that, in pre-World War II Europe, some countries remained liberal–democratic while others did not, it seemed permissible to claim, as has been suggested by Linz, that political factors could 'increase or decrease the probability of the persistence and stability of a [liberal–democratic] regime'.[4] Yet, although these factors are likely to play a part, the socio-economic substructure is an important variable: the weight of this variable has therefore to be measured precisely.

Vanhanen's multivariate approach

The most sophisticated development in this field has been the result of the work of Vanhanen. In a series of studies which appeared between 1979 and 1987 and which ultimately extended to 147 countries, this author took into account, not merely per capita GNP, but five further variables, namely the percentage of urban population, the percentage of non-agricultural population, the number of university students per 10 000 inhabitants, the percentage of the literate population and the percentage share of family farms in the total area of holdings.[5] A sixth variable was also considered, but its operationalisation was held to be too soft to allow for a truly precise measurement: this attempted to assess the extent to which non-agricultural resources were decentralised and were in effect controlled by relatively independent groups.[6]

The five main variables are aggregated in what is described as an Index of Power Resources which is then correlated to an 'Index of (Liberal) Democracy'. This in turn is based on two variables, which measure liberalism and democracy through the extent of competition and the level of participation by considering the share of the votes of different parties and election turnout. Though these can be regarded as reflecting only partially the richness of the two political variables, they do at least provide a realistic start for an empirical analysis.

Vanhanen finds that per capita GNP does correlate with the combined Index of (Liberal) Democracy (0.555), but he also finds that the correlation is appreciably higher when all the variables are taken into account (0.762). About 70 per cent of the variation in liberal democracy in 147 contemporary states is explained in this way; on the other hand, about 30 per cent of the variation in democratisation can be said to be due, among other things, to 'unique historical circumstances', to 'cultural and national peculiarities':[7] overall, therefore, 'one explanatory variable, the Index of Power Resources, seems to explain the major part of variation in political systems from the aspect of democratisation'.[8]

The apparent 'exceptions' to the influence of socio-economic factors

Yet about 30 per cent of the variation *cannot* be explained by the factors which Vanhanen uses in his analysis. It is interesting to discover whether some 'exceptions' at least can be accounted for by special circumstances. Vanhanen thus examines the case of 18 countries (out of 147) which do not 'fit' the expected relationship (though there are a further eight countries, including India, which also constitute 'exceptions' but which are not specifically considered).[9] Four of these 18 countries are liberal democratic while they 'should' not be and the reverse is true in the other fourteen cases.

The few polities found to be liberal–democratic in the early 1980s and yet scoring very low on the index of power resources are Gambia, Papua New Guinea, the Solomon Islands and Uganda. While the first three are very small and may be regarded as having an idiosyncratic political behaviour, Uganda was indeed liberal–democratic for only a few years in the early 1980s: the socio-economic index seemed to predict this political change.

The fourteen countries at the other end of the scale are even more interesting. As Vanhanen points out, 'pressure for democratisation has been strong in nearly all of [them]'.[10] Four had become liberal democracies by 1987 – Argentina, Uruguay, the Philippines, and Turkey; there were moves towards liberal democracy in South Korea, Singapore, and Panama, while Jamaica rated low on the index of liberal democracy because the 1983 parliamentary elections were uncontested by the opposition as an act of protest. This leaves six countries on the threshold, Lebanon,

Jordan, Mexico, Poland, Yugoslavia, and Chile. Poland and Yugoslavia are with Hungary the Communist countries which were the first to come closer to becoming liberal democracies; Mexico has had a dominant, but not a strict single-party system and has indeed moved since the late 1980s towards a less dominant party system; the civil war in Lebanon made it no longer possible for the country to function as a liberal democracy; pressures against military rule have been strong enough in Chile to force the end of the regime. Finally, in Jordan, elections took place in 1989 for the first time in decades and some moves towards democratisation also occurred.

The method suggested by Vanhanen thus helps to predict which countries are likely to be liberal democracies (and vice versa); it also identifies and accounts for a high proportion of the 'exceptions'. The tendency for the social basis of political systems to have a strong influence on the norms of the political system is therefore marked, at any rate with respect to the distinction between systems which are and systems which are not liberal–democratic. Since a substantial proportion of the variation remains to be explained, however, we need to turn to the examination of the exceptional part played by some groupings in plural societies and to the role of the 'national culture'.

The case of plural societies

A first impression of the contemporary world suggests that the stability of political systems can be markedly impaired by the existence of sharp conflicts of a societal character and in particular by ethnic, linguistic, or religious conflicts (or by a combination of these). In Western Europe, the cases of Northern Ireland and of the Basque country are prominent as well as the deep division in Belgium; elsewhere, civil wars and/or partition have affected countries in which such cleavages are prominent, for instance Cyprus, Lebanon, Sri Lanka, Uganda or Nigeria. Yet this first impression is also compensated by examples of much greater political calm: without even considering the case of Switzerland,[11] nations such as India or the United States are based on strong ethnic differences, as are Malaysia or Trinidad: yet these polities seem to have absorbed or broadly overcome these differences. While ethnic divisions in the Soviet Union erupted in the late 1980s, the unity of the country was maintained for many decades. To be sure, this was done on the basis of a large amount of coercion, but none the less unity was maintained. Thus ethnic or linguistic diversity may not immediately or automatically result in instability; to put it in terms of the analysis of the previous chapter, levels of integration may be sometimes sufficiently high to contain the conflicts resulting from ethnic or linguistic diversity.

The extent of ethnic and linguistic diversity

An examination of the extent of ethnic and linguistic diversity across the world shows that it is widespread but does not correspond to the expected divisions. The Index of Ethnic and Linguistic Diversity calculated by Vanhanen on the basis of Kurian shows that, while slightly over a third of the countries can be said to be homogeneous (52 out of 147), a comparable number (53) are intermediate and over a quarter (42) are truly heterogeneous.[12] These countries are spread unevenly across the world, as Table 6.2 shows.

Table 6.2 Ethnic and linguistic homogeneity (1984)

	Atlantic	Communist	Middle East and North Africa	South and East Asia	Africa (South of Sahara)	Latin America	Total
80–100%	14	7	11	4	4	12	52
60–79%	4	4	6	2	5	7	28
40–59%	5	2	1	7	6	4	25
Under 40%	–	2	2	5	30	3	42
Total	23	15	20	18	45	26	147

Source: Calculated from Vanhanen (1987), pp. 35–9.

The Atlantic, Communist, Middle Eastern and Latin American areas can be said to be relatively homogeneous; they are also the regions in which the proportion of old and established countries is the highest and where we can therefore expect the mix of linguistic and ethnic groups to be greater. South and South-East Asia is at an intermediate level, while the proportion of truly ethnically and linguistically divided countries is large in Black Africa. Two-thirds of the highly heterogeneous countries belong to that region, which comprises less than a third of the nations of the world.

Yet, even in the Atlantic area, the proportion of somewhat divided countries is not insignificant. In five countries – the United States, Canada, Switzerland, Belgium, and Spain – linguistic or ethnic cleavages affect about half the population. The mere listing of these countries shows, however, that the type of division and the political consequences of these divisions are sharply different: while Switzerland and even the United States have been affected to a limited extent only, the foundations of the state have been shaken from time to time in Canada and Belgium; in Spain, the separatist problem has clearly strongly contributed to the weaker democratic traditions of the country.

Conclusions of this type could be drawn for the rest of the world. The countries which have been most affected, ostensibly at least, by sharp cleavages, are not those where divisions are objectively the largest: for instance Cyprus, Lebanon and Sri Lanka are in the middle of the range, as are Switzerland and the United States. Thus, not surprisingly, Vanhanen finds the level of correlation between the ethnic and linguistic cleavage and liberal democracy not to be high. He notes that 'usually requisites of democratisation are slightly better in ethnically homogenous countries than in ethnically less homogeneous countries', but he further points out that there may also be divisions of power resources which are favourable for democracy (as in Switzerland).[13]

Ethnic and linguistic diversity and level of conflict

The most relevant factor seems therefore to be, not the extent of ethnic or linguistic diversity, but the extent to which this diversity is *perceived* by members of the polity as a conflict, and indeed as a conflict without apparent solution. For this to be the case, the society must be plural without being pluralist. As Rabushka and Shepsle point out:

> . . . cultural diversity [is] a necessary condition for a plural society: if a society is plural, then it is culturally diverse. However, nearly every modern society is culturally diverse. Thus, although the existence of well-defined ethnic groups with generally incompatible values constitutes a necessary condition of the plural society, it is not sufficient.[14]

For a plural society to exist, that is to say for basic ethnic and linguistic divisions to become the source of major conflict, there has to be a sense that the conflict is preponderant: 'Permanent ethnic communities acting cohesively on nearly all political issues determine a plural society and distinguish it from a culturally heterogenous, non plural society'.[15] It is therefore not the percentage of ethnically or linguistically diverse groups which *per se* creates the conflict and leads to low integration, but the fact that the 'cultural sections are organised into cohesive political sections'.[16]

The central part played by the perception of the conflict naturally leads to an examination of the conditions under which such a perception is likely to occur. A crucial factor is the distribution of the cleavages among the population: ethnic or linguistic cleavages will have a direct effect on the level of the perception of conflicts if they are reinforcing rather than cross-cutting. Indeed, ethnic, linguistic, or religious cleavages are not the only ones which can and do give rise to conflict: class, for instance, is likely to play a strong part; even political opinions can be an important source of division. Yet, in the large majority of cases, these divisions do not produce mutually exclusive groupings. Indeed, as Rae and Taylor state: 'linguistic cleavages, for example, seldom produce mutually exclusive groups, for many individuals may be multi-lingual . . .'[17] Nor do ethnic groups always do so. In general, if these or any other cleavages cut across other divisions, the probability is high that no group will be mutually exclusive. Too many people will belong to more than one.

One can see at this point why Vanhanen found the correlation between linguistic or ethnic diversity and democracy to be relatively low. A cleavage is unlikely to lead to major political conflicts where its impact is reduced by the presence of other cleavages: in practice, societies in which there is substantial wealth and where geographical and social mobility is high are unlikely to be characterised by the preponderance of only one overwhelming conflict. As Rabushka and Shepsle state: 'In the United States, Italian and Irish highway contractors view themselves as businessmen, not ethnic representatives, in competition.'[18] By and large, the greater the wealth, the greater the level of education, and the greater the decentralisation of resources, the more other cleavages will develop and the more these will cross-cut the linguistic, ethnic, or religious division.

Yet one can also see that the 'perception' of the cleavage will vary and depend on incidents which may at a given point lead to the predominance of a cleavage; there may be reinforcement of one cleavage by another. This occurred to a substantial extent in the 1970s in Belgium, when the Flemish majority *felt* deprived linguistically although it had come to acquire economic superiority; in Northern Ireland, the sense of economic deprivation of the Catholic minority was combined with the sense of religious difference; a similar consciousness has been visible in America on the part of the Blacks since the 1960s. Thus, while it is true that in general economic prosperity will lead to the emergence of more cross-cutting cleavages, there may also be periods during which a group, hitherto deprived but unable to voice this deprivation, perceives its deprivation in the context of some uplifting of its economic situation. What does remain then, however, is that *potentially* plural societies are markedly more numerous than effectively plural societies and that the impact of cleavages of a linguistic, tribal, ethnic, or religious type (and indeed of others) has to be viewed in the context of the specific configuration (reinforcing or cross-cutting) of these cleavages in the society.

The existence of major divisions of a linguistic, ethnic, or religious character is thus likely to affect appreciably the character of the political system, but these divisions are mediated by the general framework of the socio-economic basis of the society. Where the nature of the division is, so to speak, sustained by the socio-economic base, the effect will be sharp. Thus the less mobility there is in the society, and the less economic wealth and the social services are spread within that society, the more a linguistic, ethnic or religious cleavage can predominate. To these conditions has to be added another, which stems from the general character of political and administrative life: a cleavage which is clearly geographically marked is more likely to be predominant than one which is not, as representation and policy implementation both tend to take primarily territorial forms. When all these conditions are favourable, the 'sectional' effect of a basic division can be expected to be maximised and indeed to bring the polity to such a low level of integration that even the strongest authoritarian regime may be unable to prevent civil war and ultimately the break-up of the nation.[19]

The impact of cultural characteristics

The wealth of problems posed by the analysis of individual social variables on political life is only matched by the richness of the findings which emerge out of the study of culture – both at the political and at the general level. As a matter of fact an immense, though highly impressionistic literature (including works of fiction) has over the decades and indeed centuries stressed the fact that political and social behaviour, both national and regional, has been markedly affected by the specific conditions in which countries developed. Differences between North and South in Europe for instance fascinated writers in the eighteenth century – Montesquieu and Madame de Stael were just two of the most prominent. As was suggested earlier, a frequently held view is that the 'protestant ethic' lay at the root of major differences – ranging from the 'rise of capitalism' (Weber) to the development of liberalism and democracy.[20]

Yet, while these general conclusions have been repeatedly drawn and indeed seemed highly plausible, the effect of 'culture' on politics has long escaped precise measurement. Thus it has been difficult to disentangle the part played by 'harder' and more easily recognisable variables such as those just examined from the less tangible factors which 'culture' encompasses – all the more so since it seemed both intuitively correct and empirically valid to state that economic and social 'indicators' also had an effect on culture. Thus what occurred for psychological variables in general occurred also for national (and regional) cultural factors: as the identification and the measurement of economic and social indicators was simpler, these were given priority and the tendency to consider as merely residual cultural elements, as well as psychological characteristics, spread.[21]

This state of affairs began to change in the 1960s as a number of authors, such as G.A. Almond, S. Verba, and G.W. Pye, gave prominence to the analysis of political culture, while a major study by Hofstede, *Culture's Consequences* (1980), constituted the first systematic attempt at measuring, on a truly world-wide basis, the characteristics of culture.[22] Though it is still not possible to state with assurance the extent to which 'cultural factors' affect, and affect independently, political behaviour, one can at least begin to describe the proportions in which the components of culture are distributed among nations and groups of nations. Work to ascertain more precisely what are the effects of various components has also been progressing fast, for instance in particular countries and over time, especially in relation to the development of a 'post-industrial' type of political culture which appears to stress values of a less 'materialistic' character.[23]

The first problem which has to be faced in such an analysis is that of definition: culture is an elusive concept, precisely because it is all-embracing. Hofstede suggests that 'culture is to a human collectivity what personality is to an individual'.[24] This may not be an altogether helpful remark since the concept of personality is itself rather elusive: the main problem relates to the time dimension. It may be true that personality is, according to Hofstede (quoting Guilford's work on *Personality*): 'the interactive aggregate of personal characteristics that influence the individual's response to the environment.'[25] However, even if we think we know what this definition covers at a given moment, we are in greater difficulty when we consider the life of an individual. No one would deny that personalities 'grow' or decay, and at any rate change, if only to some extent and relatively slowly. As this is the case, the 'response to the environment' will not be identical at different points in time and the reality of personality escapes us. Although psychologists recognise the need for a concept such as personality since underlying characteristics of individuals seem to exist, change only gradually, and in some manner 'synthesise' the various 'traits' of these individuals, the concept is clearly difficult to handle: this undoubtedly played a part in slowing down analyses.[26]

A similar conclusion can be drawn about culture. Culture, too, embraces a large number of 'traits' which have only been identified gradually and whose interrelationships are still somewhat obscure. Culture, like personality, varies gradually over time. But a further complication arises with respect to culture: while one can at least observe an individual and subject him or her to various tests which can help to reveal the underlying personality, no such facilities are available with respect to culture. Morevoer, comparisons are necessary in order to determine what is specific about the culture of each country: there are difficulties with these comparisons, however, as there is a risk that one might attribute to individuals characteristics which truly belong to a group.[27]

Yet, despite these problems, the study of culture has progressed, as efforts have been made to discover specific components, the underlying dimensions characterising these components and the relationships among these components. The pioneering study of Almond and Verba, *The Civic Culture* (1963), first came to a three-fold distinction suggesting the existence of a parochial, a subject, and a participant political culture taking into account the three elements of the personality of citizens, namely cognition, affectivity and evaluation.[28] It was also suggested that there could be mixed situations; thus states such as the Ottoman Empire had a 'parochial–subject' culture, while France, Germany, or Italy had a 'subject–participant' culture.[29] The study covered five countries, studied on the basis of interviews – the United States, Britain, Germany, Italy, and Mexico; it succeeded in showing great variations among these countries, despite problems posed by the fact that interviews, especially at the time, could reveal only part of the reality.

This analysis led to the elaboration of dimensions in a subsequent study by Pye and Verba, *Political Culture and Political Development* (1965), which covered ten countries on the basis, not of interviews, but of a general survey of political (and especially elite political) behaviour in these countries. The four dimensions which were elicited by these country cases were those of 'national identity', 'identification with one's fellow citizens', 'governmental output', and 'the process of making decisions'.[30] An effort was made to bring political beliefs together, especially in the context of change. It was pointed out that there may be various developments, for example:

> The belief that (the citizens) can participate meaningfully in the governmental decision-making process can replace the belief that he is essentially the subject . . . or the participant orientation to government can develop on top of, without replacing, the subject orientation to government.[31]

These distinctions led to studies of change, and in particular to the examination of the reasons why countries (those of Europe in the inter-war period and of Latin America since 1945) experienced a breakdown in democracy;[32] they also led to the examination of changes in value patterns and to the stress on a move from 'materialist' to 'post-materialist' values among Western societies from the 1970s onwards.[33] Overall, it was clear that cultural 'development' was not merely a characteristic of 'modernising' societies but of societies at all levels of socio-economic development and that these values could cut across the divide between highly industrial and 'developing' societies: one of the clearest examples is the fact that Commonwealth countries have many political characteristics in common which contrast with those of non-Commonwealth countries.[34]

The contribution made by these studies to the analysis of political culture has therefore been considerable; it helped to circumscribe the concept and to show the directions in which a systematic analysis should go. Meanwhile, the assessment of national culture in general and indeed its measurement began to be undertaken in earnest, in particular as a result of Hofstede's study. On the basis of the examination of the values of large numbers of respondents in forty countries, the author was able to discover the existence of four components of culture, 'power distance', 'uncertainty avoidance', 'individualism', and 'masculinity'. The first of these dimensions relates to inequality and to its acceptance; the second refers to the fact that 'the tolerance for uncertainty varies considerably among people . . . in different countries';[35] the third is based on the recognition that 'in some cultures, individualism is seen as a blessing and a source of well-being [while] in others it is seen as alienating';[36] and the fourth stems from the fact 'that the sex role distribution common in a particular society is transferred by socialisation in families, schools, and peer groups, and through the media.'[37] But these four dimensions were not 'imagined', so to speak, by Hofstede. They form 'a generalised framework that underlies the more apparent and striking facts of cultural relativity'.[38] As the author notes, they come close to the 'standard analytic issues' which have been identified in the literature on the 'national character'.[39]

On this basis, Hofstede was able to discover a number of clusters which were defined as 'culture areas' on a more subtle and systematic basis than had previously been the case.[40] A variety of clusters were identified, described as Latin (divided into more and less developed), Asian (also divided into more or less developed), Near Eastern, Germanic, Anglo, and Nordic. Apart from many specific differences (and in particular the fact that Nordic countries were found to have, together with the Netherlands, an essentially 'feminine' culture), two major findings emerged which are essential for the analysis of the social bases of political life. The first is the unexpected discovery that cultural divisions were strong in Switzerland and almost non-existent in Belgium: the accommodation between the linguistic groups in Switzerland is thus the result of major cultural differences, while the difficulties experienced by Belgium correspond to a more 'superficial' opposition between linguistic groups. This helps to understand a large part of the history of centralised Belgium (as well as the continued differentiation between the Netherlands and

Flanders). The finding also has more general implications in that it suggests that there is not yet one type of plural society: there are likely to be many different models.

The second main finding relates to the relationship between culture and the socio-economic variables which were examined earlier in this chapter. The fact that both Latin and East Asian countries have to be divided into 'more' and 'less' developed suggests that there is a relationship among and a distinction between the two types of factors. In the case of Latin countries, while both groups score high on power distance and on uncertainty avoidance (in contrast, for instance with Anglo and Nordic countries) the more developed Latin nations are highly individualistic and have a medium score on masculinity; the less developed Latin countries have a low individualism score and are either very masculine or relatively feminine (but less so than Nordic countries).[41] It is not possible at this point to state categorically that these differences can be linked to socio-economic development, but they at least appear to be related to socio-economic development, while socio-economic development does not appear to have a marked influence on views about power distance or uncertainty avoidance. Generally speaking, Hofstede finds – and in this respect his findings come close to those of Inglehart on 'post-materialism' – that economic development has an effect on changes over time: the 'need' for 'dependence', for example, tends to diminish, though this may result in higher conflicts.[42]

It is thus possible to understand better both the characteristics and the 'consequences' of culture. We are no longer confronted with a vague concept which can be used only to explain 'accidents' for which socio-economic indicators do not seem able to account. Achieving a definition based on precise components which in turn are measured by popular attitudes means that culture can become an integral part of the systematic analysis of the social bases of politics. It may still be impossible to quantify the impact of culture on political behaviour, but it is at least possible to assess the ways in which its components help to form the bases of political life.

Conclusion

It has always been felt that the political characteristics of nations were related to the social conditions within which states developed. For a long period, however, and indeed until very recent times, the shape and even more the extent of this influence remained mysterious. This is no longer the case: variables have been identified and have begun to be measured; the interrelationships between socio-economic and political variables are described and assessed. The relationship between society and politics is obviously not simple, nor does it take place in one direction only: the correlations which exist leave room for two-way influence. But it is at least possible to be definite about the strength of some of the connections. On this basis the discussion can now turn to the part played by structures (both social and political) in political life and seek to establish the relationships between these structures and the government.

Notes

1. The question of the relationship between socio-economic cleavages and political life has been one of the main areas of research in political sociology in the course of the last decades and major advances have been made, despite the fact that many aspects, and political culture in particular, have remained difficult to circumscribe and analyse. In a sense, this analysis originated from the founders of political science, whether Aristotle, Montesquieu, or Rousseau, each of whom saw in different ways how such elements as class, religion, or ethnic divisions could affect political life. Marx and, to a lesser extent, Weber have profoundly shaped the nature of the interpretations and indeed the type of investigations which have been conducted. More recently, the studies undertaken by S.M. Lipset and by S. Rokkan contributed markedly to the development of these analyses, in large part by showing the need to take into account all the major cleavages (class-based, but also religious, ethnic, linguistic, and geographical, as well as broadly cultural) which play a part in the framing of political identities. See in particular S.M. Lipset and S. Rokkan (ed.), *Party Systems and Voter Alignments* (1967), especially the Introduction, pp. 1–64. Since this volume appeared, new cleavages have begun to emerge, especially in Western industrial nations, as has been shown by the emergence of 'green' movements and parties: these cleavages appear linked to the development of 'post-materialist' values which were first systematically analysed by R. Inglehart in *The Silent Revolution* (1977).
2. S.M. Lipset, *Political Man* (1983), pp. 31–45; P. Cutright, 'National political development', in N.W. Polsby *et al.*, *Politics and Social Life* (1963), pp. 569–82. See also D. Neubauer, 'Some conditions of democracy', *Am. Pol. Sc. Rev.*, 67 (1967) pp. 1002–9.
3. For a survey of the critical approaches to the liberal–democratic approach, see R.H. Chilcote, *Theories of Comparative Politics* (1981), in particular pp. 271–346. These criticisms have been to an extent superseded at the end of the 1980s, with respect to Latin America at least, as a result of the development of the 'consolidation of democracy' thesis.
4. J.J. Linz, *Crisis, Breakdown, and Reequilibration* (1978), p. 4.
5. T. Vanhanen,'The level of democratisation related to socio-economic variables in 147 states, 1980–85' in *Scand. Pol. Studies*, vol. 12, no. 2 (1989), p. 104.
6. *ibid.*, p. 106.
7. *ibid.*, p. 110.
8. *ibid.*, p. 110.
9. *ibid.*, p. 115.
10. *ibid.*, p. 116.
11. There have occasionally been problems in Switzerland: linguistic conflict thus led to the setting up, after some struggle, of the new canton of the Jura.
12. See T. Vanhanen, 'The level of democratisation related to socio-economic variables in 147 states in 1980–85' (1987), paper for *Eur. Consortium for Polit. Research*, p. 13. See G.T. Kurian, *The New Book of World Rankings* (1984).
13. *ibid.*, p. 14.
14. A.A. Rabushka and K.A. Shepsle, *Politics in Plural Societies* (1971), p. 20.
15. *ibid.*, pp. 20–1.
16. *ibid.*, p. 21.
17. D.W. Rae and M. Taylor, *The Analysis of Political Cleavages* (1970), p. 14.
18. *ibid.*, p. 21.

19. On the question of the causes of rebellion, see R.J. Jackson and M.B. Stein, *Issues in Comparative Politics* (1971), pp. 265–332. See also T.R. Gurr (ed.), *Handbook of Political Conflict* (1980), *passim*. The case of the eruption of linguistic, ethnic and generally cultural nationalism in the peripheral areas of the Soviet Union since the late 1980s is evidence both of what coercion can achieve for a substantial period and of what it does not resolve in the long run.

20. See for instance Montesquieu, *The Spirit of Laws*, Books 14–19; M. Weber, *The Protestant Ethic and the Spirit of Capitalism* (English edn, 1976).

21. See for instance F.I. Greenstein, *Personality and Politics* (1969), Chapter 2, pp. 33–62.

22. See in particular G.A. Almond and S. Verba, *The Civic Culture* (1963) and L.W. Pye and S. Verba (eds), *Political Culture and Political Development* (1965). See also G.A. Almond and S. Verba, *The Civic Culture Revisited* (1979).

23. R. Inglehart, *The Silent Revolution* (1977). See also H. Gerstenberger *et al.*, 'Politische Kultur', *Österreichische Zeitschrift für Politischewissenschaft*, vol. 13, (1984), pp. 1–121.

24. G. Hofstede, *op. cit.* (1980), p. 25.

25. F.I. Greenstein, *op. cit.*, pp. 2–5. G. Hofstede, *op. cit.*, (1980), quoting R.R. Guilford (1959), p. 25.

26. On the nature and role of traits in personality, see J. Blondel, *Political Leadership* (1987), pp. 115 and 124–36.

27. This extrapolation from the characteristics of findings in a particular region to the individuals within it has been shown to be unwarranted: such an error is known as the 'ecological fallacy'. See W.S. Robinson, 'Ecological correlates and the behavior of individuals', *Am. Soc. Rev.*, 15 (3), (1950), pp. 351–7

28. G.A. Almond and S. Verba, *op. cit.* (1963), pp. 17–20.

29. *ibid.*, pp. 23 and 25.

30. L.W. Pye and S. Verba (eds), *op. cit.* (1965), pp. 529–43.

31. *ibid.*, pp. 543–4.

32. See J.J. Linz and A. Stepan (eds), *The Breakdown of Democratic Regimes* (1978).

33. R. Inglehart, *op. cit.* (1977).

34. See for instance J. Blondel, 'Political leadership in the Commonwealth: the British legacy' in H.D. Clarke and M.M. Czudnowski, *Political Elites in Anglo–American Democracies* (1986), pp. 311–37.

35. G. Hofstede, *op. cit.* (1980), p. 153.

36. *ibid.*, p. 213.

37. *ibid.*, p. 261.

38. *ibid.*, p. 313.

39. A. Inkeles and D.J. Levinson, 'National character' in *Handbook of Social Psychology*, vol. 4 (1969).

40. G. Hofstede, *op. cit.* (1980), pp. 333ff.

41. *ibid.*, p. 336.

42. *ibid.*, p. 368.

7 | Groups, demands and political systems

Groups are naturally the first type of structure which is encountered in the analysis of political systems. The machine of the political system may or may not be activated as a result of the groups which exist, but it is unquestionably through groups that many demands are made or pressures exerted in most political systems, whether these demands are made gently and peacefully or take the form of protests, including violent protests. Indeed, even beyond the fact that the machine is set in motion by the activities of the groups, these bodies, at any rate the most important among them, play an even greater part in the political system: they can be said to sustain it, to be so to speak its foundation. The political characteristics of a traditional society are shaped by the fact that tribes exist and define the relationships among leaders and between leaders and the people; plural societies are largely organised around the cleavages of ethnic or religious groups; parties often draw their strength, even in Western liberal democracies, from the groups, ethnic, religious, or class-based, from which they originated; authoritarian societies which attempt to ignore the major cleavages are likely to encounter problems, as is the case in the Soviet Union with respect to its many 'nationalities'.

Thus groups are both pillars of political system and instruments by which demands are channelled into these systems. However, the study of groups raises serious practical and theoretical problems. This is because groups as such are not part of the study of politics: they need to be studied to the extent that they enter the political process. Some may be involved so often in politics that they cannot easily be separated from political life, but even these are not 'wholly' in politics. Conversely, however, any group, or almost any group, is involved from time to time in the political process. Practically all the groups which exist in society must be studied – a huge number of bodies, of all types and character, from large to small, from episodic to permanent, from well-organised to loosely structured. This renders the study of groups so complex that it has to be drastically streamlined. In this chapter, the analysis will be limited to the examination of the general part played by groups in different types of political systems.[1]

81

Modern political science was profoundly affected by the 'rediscovery' of the role of groups. In the classical theory of politics, groups were disregarded as they were considered to be harmful. According to Rousseau, and to the authors of the *Federalist Papers*, groups divided the polity into factions; they were felt to represent the semi-feudal past and to prevent the will of the people from being expressed clearly. Interestingly, many leaders of developing countries in the second half of the twentieth century have had the same motivations as eighteenth-century theorists.[2]

This normative theory affected behaviour, particularly when constitutions were drafted; it also affected empirical analysis. Groups were disregarded or played down. Only heterodox writers at both extremes – either defenders of the 'old order' or radicals – pointed to the role of groups in the new 'bourgeois' political order, in particular business groups. For most political scientists of the nineteenth century and even later, the study of politics remained the study of constitutional bodies.

The change came about in two ways. Firstly, mainly in Europe, a form of limited 'pluralism' came to be recognised through parliaments and parties, as well as economic groups. Second, a new general theory developed in America. The legislatures of the federal and state governments were sought for favours of various kinds and the behaviour of legislators (and indeed of members of the executive branch as well) could not realistically be described unless lobbyists and those representing interests were taken into account. Thus the situation could not be understood, let alone explained, within the framework of a classical 'constitutional' theory: groups had to be reintegrated. This was to be done by means of a wholly new approach which changed the previous way of thinking about groups. Instead of accounting for political developments in terms of the actions of individuals within institutional structures, 'group theory', as the new approach was to be called, did not merely state that groups were 'important' or even 'essential': it claimed that groups were the centre of social activity. Individuals were characterised by the group interactions in which they were involved, instead of groups being characterised by their members; overlapping or cross-cutting membership became a key characteristic accounting for the fact that groups followed different or opposite courses.[3]

The new theory also reassessed the old institutions of government, including constitutional bodies, on the basis of the same principles. Institutions came to be seen as groups of a special kind, divided into sub-groups and expressing different points of view and different policies. In this way, the whole political system could be explained in terms of a gigantic network of interlocking groups and political action could be conceived as resulting from shocks between group structures.

Though such an analysis was ostensibly empirical and 'neutral', it had normative undertones and policy implications. The classical theory was opposed to groups, since they were viewed as splitting the 'general will'; the new theory not only accepted groups as facts: it tended to suggest that it was best not to interfere with group activity, as society had built-in equilibrium mechanisms by which the defects of the system could be automatically redressed. If, in one field of activity, a group or groups became too vociferous, an anti-group or anti-groups would emerge which would combat the aims of the original organisation. Just as the classical theory of the price mechanism suggested that the combined effect of fall in demand and rise in production of goods in short supply would check price increases without any deliberate intervention, the automatic development of groups opposed to policies hitherto successfully put forward by other groups would, without intervention – and indeed better if there was no intervention – prevent decisions from getting out of hand and being contrary to the views of the majority. Though 'group theorists' did not necessarily reach these extreme conclusions, one can see how by starting from an opposite standpoint from that of the classical theorists, their views were 'optimistic'; they could posit that the polity would gain from competition between groups. The new 'will of the people' would emerge only from and through group activities and group oppositions.

This normative aspect of group theory came in turn to be questioned, in the same way and indeed for the same reasons as the classical theory of groups.[4] It was obvious that groups were interfered with everywhere. Some societies were dominated by large groupings which did not allow competing bodies to manifest themselves. Authoritarian polities controlled groups drastically, but even liberal polities were not characterised by complete openness: in particular, the collusion among some of the larger groups such as employers' organisations and trade unions seemed occasionally to lead to what might be regarded as 'cartel' arrangements, a state of affairs which was described as 'neo-corporatism'.[5] In this way, demands could be restricted and even the creation of new groups was made difficult. While it might still be the case that, were groups to be truly established and not interfered with, a situation corresponding to that described by group theory might prevail, the reality of both liberal and authoritarian states as well as of relatively egalitarian and of inegalitarian polities seemed to be far distant from the model. Thus, while groups had to be allocated a major part in the analysis of government, that part was manifestly extremely complex and could not be regarded as stemming directly from one and only one interpretation.

Groups and political systems

Given this complexity, the first step in the analysis must be to discover the ways in which groups become part of the political system. There are large and small groups; there are powerful and insignificant groups. The most important distinction, however, is different: it is based on the contrast between groups which embody long-standing and even permanent relationships and those which exist to promote specific goals, a division which should not be viewed as a dichotomy but as corresponding to two poles of a continuum. At one extreme are bodies such as families, tribes, ethnic, religious or even class-based groups to which members are associated by the fact that they happen to have a common characteristic: an accident of birth can thus have life-long implications. These groups exist because they express deep and almost indissoluble 'traits', so to speak, among those who belong to them. At the other extreme are the groups which exist in order to achieve some purpose, whether it is to defend a section, promote an idea, make money or enjoy a game. Those who join such organisations may not always only do so because they wish to achieve the stated purpose of the organisation, but, by and large, the membership is brought and kept together because of the group's aims. In a sense, groups which express patterns of relationships are based on the past, while those which exist to promote an aim are oriented towards the future.

The distinction between communal and associational groups

Groups which embody patterns of social relationships may be called *communal* and those which are constituted in order to pursue a goal, *associational*. However, in practice, 'pure' communal and 'pure' associational groups are polar positions on a continuum.[6] To the extent that men recognise themselves and/or others as members of a communal group, they recognise themselves and/or others as being 'expressed' – represented would be too precise a term – by the communal group. The bond between member and group is the 'image' which the member has of what he or she is, at least with respect to the human relationships which the communal group embodies. Thus a member of a tribe or a family is linked to the group by the image of the relationship to other members of the tribe or family, by characteristics shared in common, by a common 'heritage'. On the contrary, members of an associational group (again in the most extreme form which this type of grouping can have) are tied to the association and the other members by the aim which is common to all and by the fact that they are achieving or want to achieve something in common. This has major consequences for the authority of the leaders of the organisation. Leaders of communal groups are related to members as a result of the broad pattern of relationships, while leaders of associations have authority only in relation to and within the frame of reference of the goal of the group. Consequently, the limits of action within communal and associational groups will be different: the sphere of legitimate activity of associational bodies is narrow because it is related to the aim of that group; the legitimacy of communal groups is broad as it is co-extensive with the 'organic' relationship which exists among the members.

Because of these characteristics, communal groups tend to be old and indeed to develop around relationships whose origins cannot easily be traced. New communal cleavages may none the less emerge in a polity, but often as a result of changes in the social composition, for instance through waves of immigration or because industrialisation results in the arrival of large numbers of workers to the cities. Communal relationships may also develop on the basis of the institutionalisation of a political or administrative body, such as the army or the bureaucracy.[7] In such organisations, one can expect an *esprit de corps* to emerge gradually; as a result, feelings of belonging will develop within the institution which will give it the characteristics of a communal group. Such bodies can be referred to as *institutional*, in contrast with the *customary* communal groups which arise from traditional patterns of social relationships.[8]

New groups and especially new associational groups may be strengthened through the transfer of the legitimacy of a strong grouping, in particular of a traditional communal grouping. This will tend to happen when, in a society, existing patterns of relationships begin to be eroded and therefore need to be reinforced by the creation of new links. If, in a highly religious community, the church begins to notice that the young are losing some of their faith, the parish priest may be induced to create a special organisation in order to maintain his hold on adolescents; but this organisation comes alive, at least at the beginning, only because it is sustained by means of the 'parent' body, the church, which thus transfers to it some of its capital of legitimacy.

The concept of transfer of legitimacy or of support is of crucial importance in understanding the development of groups. Communal groups are able to control new trends in society and stop or retard their independent development. Tribal, ethnic, or religious leaders may thus succeed in keeping within their 'wing' segments of the population which might otherwise have come under the allegiance of counter-bodies. But support transfer can also take place in other ways: 'modernising' rulers may use the legitimacy which they draw from the tribal or ethnic group from which they originate to foster allegiance for new groups which they attempt to develop.

One can indeed go further, as the effect of transfers of legitimacy extends to the political system as a whole. In a traditional society, the state tends to be dominated by customary bodies such as tribes or ethnic groups; indeed, it can be argued that the authority of the state has emerged almost everywhere as a result of a transfer of legitimacy from these customary groups. Gradually, however, almost in the same way as any other large group, the state comes to be regarded, at any rate by many, as the embodiment of patterns of relationships and it therefore attracts feelings of loyalty, which translate themselves in terms of nationalism. Some bodies within the state, and in particular institutional groups such as the army and the bureaucracy, but also other communal groupings and indeed parties, can thus exploit these feelings of allegiance to their profit and in turn obtain allegiance because they appear to represent the state. Thus the transfer of legitimacy may extend downwards to more specialised organisations which are set up to control the population: this is particularly the case in authoritarian polities, and especially in Communist or populist states; thus trade unions, youth organisations, cultural centres and a variety of other 'voluntary' associations come into existence and help to promote the goals which state leaders wish to pursue. These feel able in this way to push forward their views better and educate the population, though they are likely to find themselves in opposition with the leaders of traditional customary groups whose way of life and traditions are opposed to these 'modernising' leaders. This is why, in many societies, bodies which are ostensibly associations are in fact instruments used by a variety of communal groups in order to defend or establish their influence. Such associations are not independent, but are truly dependent bodies of communal groups.

Political systems and types of group

It is possible then in a broad sense to relate types of group to types of political system. The simplest way is to start with the two extreme cases. One pole is that of the society which has only customary communal groups; indeed, at the very extreme is the tribal society in which there is only one broad customary group and where demands are articulated exclusively through the tribe. At the other extreme, one finds the wholly associational society, in which communal groups have disappeared or almost disappeared and in which demands are formulated and articulated by as many associational groups as there are goals, with perfect freedom for any new demand or goal to be translated into the political system through new associations.

The intermediate positions which correspond more adequately to the real world need to be considered. It was noted that these new groups could develop in one of two ways. The society itself, by developing new patterns of relationships and by making demands for new goals, could 'press' for the creation of new groups or the taking over of these new patterns or goals by old groups. Alternatively the leaders of the political system could aim at modifying the conditions under which the system operated by introducing new patterns of relationships and new goals. In the first case, the development of patterns of relationships and goals and of the groups which embody them can be said to be *natural*; in the second case the development can be said to be *imposed*. It must be remembered that the distinction between these two types of developments is conceptual and that real-world situations are a combination of both types: one should therefore assess the relative extent to which one or the other of the two forces, 'natural' and 'imposed', plays a part in any given system.

If, first, developments arising from 'natural' forces are examined, three successive stages can be identified (they are chronologically and logically in sequence, though the time lag may not necessarily be the same in all systems). First, new communal groups are created under the impact of the development of new patterns of relationships: some of these groups are of a 'customary' type, such as those which are based on class, religion, or race; some are of an 'institutional' kind, such as the army or the bureaucracy. Second, specific demands begin to be made through communal groups and through the development of 'subsidiary' associations to the parent communal group. Third, associational groups come into existence gradually, partly because these subsidiary groups start to acquire some independence, partly because other associations are created to combat some of these subsidiary groupings; these owe their legitimacy to this goal. At the end of the third stage, the older communal groups have lost much of their original legitimacy: their 'reserves' have shrunk so much that they might disappear, modify the basis of their support, or come to be supported by the very subsidiary groups which they had created. Churches may for instance regain influence in view of the part played by religious associational groups in articulating some demands. At the end of this process the situation is no longer far from the associational pole which was referred to earlier.

The characteristic stages which stem from the imposition of norms on a society by the political system are different. Systems which attempt to impose patterns and goals have to try to maintain their support in the community. Such political systems will therefore create both new institutional groups and new associational groups in opposition to pre-existing communal groups and use their capital of legitimacy to maintain these new groups. This will raise conflict levels, however, and the reserves of legitimacy may prove insufficiently large; coercion will have to be used, the amount of coercion being inversely correlated to the legitimacy possessed by the system. The imposition of new norms will have 'authoritarian' consequences; the same would of course be true if, conversely, a system tried to maintain traditional norms while 'natural' developments were leading to the emergence of new types of organisations.

It is now possible to assess the extent to which, even in imposed systems, groups reflect demands in the society. To begin with, there will be narrow 'selection' rather than 'articulation', as the demands which the system will accept will tend only to be those which are in line with the ideology of the leaders and as dependent associations are set up primarily in order to educate the population. Tension is likely to be strong and, over time, even despite coercion, some demands are likely to make their way into the system. This could be avoided only if existing dependent associations were continuously reshaped and even reconstructed, to prevent them from acquiring any autonomy. This is what both Trotsky and Mao Tse-tung had in mind when the former favoured a 'permanent revolution' and the latter launched the 'cultural revolution', but neither succeeded in this goal. Of course, coercive regimes often do not last long enough for such a slow change to occur within the dependent associations; but, if they do, their characteristics are likely to be altered gradually and demands are likely to filter through the network of dependent associations.[9]

Three further characteristics need to be mentioned. The first concerns the ambiguous character of associational groups. A 'pure' association constitutes an extreme case: in practice, in almost all societies, there are many groups which have a near-associational rather than a pure associational character. This is true of the 'dependent' associations of communal groups and of the state which were described earlier; this is true even of more independent associations as these often, if not always, acquire – and indeed strive to acquire – the loyalty of their members irrespective of, or at any rate beyond, specific goals. Precisely because leaders of groups are severely constrained by the goals of the groups in a 'pure' associational context, they are typically anxious to build and develop patterns of interpersonal relationships among members in order to be able to enlarge their sphere of activity. This is noticeable in some of the promotional groups and social movements which will be discussed in the next section (women's groups, ecological groups or regionalist groups, for instance) and which characterise societies which are otherwise 'associational' rather than 'communal', such as Western liberal democracies.

Second, institutional groups often constitute a key to the understanding of the process of demand articulation and selection. They may develop 'naturally' or be 'imposed' by the leaders of the political system. But in both cases the presence of institutional groups indicates that the society has moved from early socio-economic development to a 'transitional' stage. Moreover, institutional groups constitute, in these transitional societies, means by which demands can be formulated more explicitly than through customary communal groups. This is what occurs in many developing societies where institutional groups such as the army or the bureaucracy are important channels for demands.

Third, customary groups, whether wholly traditional (as ethnic or religious groups) or newer (as class-based groups) continue to play a substantial part in all societies. Neither liberal democracies in general nor Western countries in particular are wholly associational, even in the less 'pure' sense which was just considered. Communal groupings are often very strong, if not throughout whole nations, at least in some regions and among some segments of the population.[10] Their reserves of legitimacy not only helped associational groups to become accepted and, indeed, as will be seen in Chapter 9, political parties to become legitimate; they continue to constitute important elements of the group configuration both in terms of the articulation of demands and in more general aspects of the decision-making process. Thus societies are composed of a mix of relatively communal and relatively associational groups, of dependent and less dependent associations. The measurement of the specific mix is still far from possible; but it is at least possible to have an impression of the nature of the mix.

Communal and associational groups in the contemporary world

Communal patterns of relationship

Communal groups, directly or through the dependent associations which they help to create, play a major part in most societies. There are substantial differences among communal groups, however; these stem in large part from the fact that some patterns of relationship are more recent or less all-embracing – less fully communal, in reality – than others. The consequences in terms of internal organisation and of the extent of the autonomy of dependent associations are important. Overall, four broad types of social relationship patterns have played and continue to play a major part in binding men and women together and thus have a considerable influence on the overall characteristics of political systems. These relationships are tribal or clientelistic, ethnic, religious and class-based. Tribal or clientelistic organisations can be defined as either those which link people together by an assumed bond of blood (large families in which fictitious cousinhoods may well be more numerous than real family trees) or those which link natural leaders of a clan or elders to 'clients'.[11] Ethnic relationships associate members by reference to alleged physical characteristics of colour or features. Religious relationships are organised around beliefs, usually involving belief in an after-life. Class relationships are associated with the status of men and women in society and have spread widely in industrial societies, though they have occasionally existed in the past.

Tribal or clientelistic relationships have given rise to the most traditional customary groups, while ethnic, religious or class-based groups have typically emerged later. But some tribal or clientelistic groupings have developed by means of immigration, as was noted earlier; moreover, ethnic, religious or even class-based groups can emerge from existing tribal or clientelistic bodies. These can subsume all the demands in an early stage of socio-economic development; indeed, very undifferentiated social systems will be characterised by the symbiosis of at least ethnic and religious patterns within a tribal organisation. Conversely, tribal or clientelistic groups are least likely, and class-based groups are most likely, to set up associations with a semi-dependent status. It is, therefore, through ethnic, religious or class-based patterns of relationships that new communal groups and dependent associations come to exist.

Ethnic groups are likely to emerge as a result of immigration or when the constraints which were previously imposed on them begin to loosen. The first type of development seems characteristic of the evolution of many Western countries, and in particular of the United States where waves of immigrants changed the character of the basic group structures. The second type has recently characterised a number of Latin American countries, notably those which have a large Indian population.

Religious groups have even more commonly set up dependent associations, particularly the churches which are hierarchically organised, as is the Catholic church.[12] This has occurred especially when the religious body feels threatened by anticlerical bodies or by competing churches. In such situations, a number of dependent organisations have commonly been set up, many of which have succeeded in achieving considerable success and indeed in extending beyond the group of those who can be said to be truly faithful.

Class-based patterns of relationships developed later, at a point at which many industrial societies had already become somewhat associational, the strength of clientelistic and even of religious bodies having by then substantially declined. Thus class-based relationships took a more markedly associational form from the start, but communal feelings were also strong, in particular at the origin. The confraternal and almost religious aspects of early trade unions have often been noted; reverence and loyalty to the organisation has been a widespread feature of these bodies. Trade unions are created in order to exercise pressure for concrete demands; but these demands are aimed at promoting the status of the membership at large. As a result, trade unions are genuinely ambiguous: in a sense they are associations, but associations located at some considerable distance from the associational end of the continuum. They are also communal bodies, but they are further away from the communal end of the continuum than religious bodies.[13]

Where the political system itself attempts to organise the group structure in an imposed manner, communal and associational feelings are also mixed. Institutional bodies such as the bureaucracy or the army often buttress the state and the customary groups on which the state may in part be based. But, in order to impose goals on the society, specialised associations have to be created or the existing ones controlled. If the goals of the political system are essentially inegalitarian and non-democratic, the system can operate by simply abolishing or dominating existing associations. If the goals of the political system are egalitarian and/or democratic, new associations have to be set up to propagate the goals of the system of persons. This happens for instance in Communist countries where trade unions or youth organisations have traditionally been large and powerful dependent associations. The same development has occurred in many 'progressive' Third World countries.[14]

Tribes, ethnic groups, religious bodies and class-based organisations thus both correspond to different levels of socio-economic development and are characterised by correspondingly different sets of group structures along a continuum. Tribal or clientelist groups scarcely give rise to semi-autonomous groupings. Ethnic groups develop primarily as new customary groups and do not typically create subsidiary associational groups. Religious and class-based organisations, on the other hand, typically create semi-independent associations though class-based organisations do so more commonly than religious bodies, and the latter tend to do so because the institutional structures of some churches have maintained very effective patterns of relationships among the believers.

As a matter of fact, the bodies which have emerged out of religious or class-based groupings vary markedly in degrees of associationalism both over time and, as a result, from nation to nation. The Catholic workers' or youth organisations which were created in many European countries in the later part of the nineteenth century were more dependent on the Church organisation at the time than they came to be in the second half of the twentieth century; their dependence remained greater in parts of some countries than in others. Similarly trade unions became more quickly 'associational' in character in some countries than in others and indeed in relation to some social groups than in others: American trade unions have always been viewed as more 'associational' than European trade unions; miners' unions have typically been characterised by greater 'class loyalties' than trade unions of shopworkers; and the extent of class loyalty characterising European trade unions has seemingly markedly declined as 'associationalism' appeared to prevail in the minds of many members.[15]

Somewhat similar developments occur in imposed political systems. The networks of dependent organisations acquire some autonomy as the regime lasts, and cannot wholly impede the emergence of demands among the members: this is why this movement is more noticeable in imposed regimes which last for a long period and which constitute only a minority. However, populist regimes, in Black Africa for instance, have been characterised by outbursts of strong autonomous activities on the part of trade unions which were originally truly controlled. In Communist states, too, both in Eastern Europe (including the Soviet Union) and in China, manifestations of trade union independence have occurred, quite apart from the vast development of the independent trade union Solidarity in Poland in the late 1970s. The dependence of class-based groups, and indeed of religious or ethnic groups, on 'parent' customary or institutional bodies thus gradually diminishes, even though some communal feelings remain in existence.

Associational developments

Communal feelings do not disappear because, conversely, associations are rarely 'pure' in that their members are rarely linked to the group exclusively through its goal. One can in reality rank associations from the point of view of their 'associationalism'. The most associational groups are those which are organised around a specific activity such as the defence or promotion of an opinion or a problem, while the least associational are those which protect persons.[16] Indeed, one can further subdivide the groups which belong to these categories. Bodies which defend points of view or opinions which are wholly acceptable to the national culture are likely to be highly associational. This is because, in such cases, the group will not have to make substantial efforts to gain and retain members: membership will come naturally. Less associational are the groups whose goals are at any rate somewhat opposed to generally accepted points of view: efforts will have to be made to maintain membership, and it will therefore be valuable to build patterns of social relationships extending beyond the expressed goals. This is often the case with the social movements, such as women's movements, environmental movements and regionalist movements, which have come to be regarded, since the 1970s, as a special feature of liberal democratic societies, though the novelty of the development is not as great as is often claimed.[17] Less associational still are groups which defend people's status and working conditions, especially when those represented constitute a minority: often, in such cases, the group will be – or at any rate was at the outset – a dependent association of a communal group (such as an ethnic, religious, or class-based organisation).

It follows that, particularly in countries which have large numbers of relatively independent associations (developed liberal democratic polities, for instance), the distinction between associations protecting persons or classes of persons and associations putting forward opinions is important. The first category, that of protective groups, includes a wide variety of bodies, ranging from trade unions and professional associations to trade associations. The second category, that of promotional groups, is composed of an equally large variety of bodies ranging from the most 'politicised', such as the social movements, to the most 'social' and hence politically 'innocuous', such as bridge clubs or angling associations.

In Western countries, protective associations are typically better established than promotional bodies; they are also more tightly organised, and richer. But protective groups also tend to have more general aims than promotional bodies; trade unions, professional or trade associations take up the contentious issues of the moment. Trade unions are the most general; but trade associations and business organisations feel competent to discuss matters of general economic policy, social matters which are related to economic policy, and even in some cases international affairs. On the contrary, promotional bodies are usually concerned with matters pertaining to their own sphere; they typically find it difficult or hazardous to tread outside their original goals. If they enlarge their sphere of activity, as social movements often try to do, they quickly find that their following dwindles. The most political of these bodies endeavour to expand their activities, however, and become political parties: Chapter 9 will consider to what extent these efforts can be successful without the support of a broader communal feeling.

Differences among associational bodies are therefore sharp, and the sharpness of the differences becomes truly noticeable where associations are numerous and relatively stronger than communal groups. The sharpness of these differences stems from the fact that the legitimacy of associations is limited in scope: if they are true associations, these bodies cannot call on the support of their membership beyond the goal for which they are created. This means that their leaders will be constrained and that their membership is likely to fluctuate. In societies in which communal feelings are strong, associations are unlikely to develop, whether the system is highly authoritarian or not: there is simply little scope for 'pure associations' to emerge, just as there is little scope for a very tender plant to grow in the shadow of luxuriant bushes.

Communal feelings have thus to be eroded through competition among communal groups and through the emergence of dependent associations for 'pure' associations to have a higher probability of developing. Yet, even in such cases, associations remain fragile if they are solely concerned with a particular issue. Thus it is common for leaders of associations to attempt to move away from the associational end of the continuum by emphasising the existence of a pattern of relationships, of a way of life, behind the associational goals. It is the discovery of this development which has given rise to the suggestions that 'social movements', rather than interest groups, characterised many of the 'developed' Western societies towards the end of the twentieth century.[18] Thus it is remarked that women's movements, ecological movements and regionalist movements are not solely in existence in order to achieve specific, 'instrumental' goals, but in order to present a new blueprint for society within which relationships among members would be different from those which characterise advanced industrial societies. Members are thus brought and kept together as a result of feelings of comradeship which the ideal of a different type of society fosters: new forms of communal groups would appear to be developing as a result, rather than new associations.

In practice, however, these groups do not appear to have a sufficiently widespread development to justify the conclusion that a new form of communal feeling has emerged. The organisations stemming from or embodying these movements are also typically constrained to be more instrumental and to adopt specific policy goals which they press upon the political system. Although the ideal of the social 'movement' is nurtured and may from time to time, under special circumstances, emerge with great force, it is more common for the organisations to have a real impact with respect to particular objectives which are relatively narrow and which do not result in a fundamental questioning of the society.[19]

Many societies have increasingly large numbers of protective and promotional groups of an associational character while, by and large, communal bodies and even dependent associations are being eroded. In the nineteenth and early twentieth centuries, America and the other Anglo-Saxon countries were the only nations in which associationalism could be said to have taken roots: it spread widely across Western liberal democracies in the second half of the twentieth century; a similar movement is occuring in other parts of the world, although it is less carefully monitored and indeed often difficult to measure.[20]

Conclusion

These developments suggest a general trend, though the speed with which changes are taking place is not known and the final stage of evolution is as yet difficult to predict. There is certainly diversification and specialisation; very broad patterns of relationships are being undermined. To this extent societies are all moving some way towards associationalism. But the fact that pure associations have a narrow area of legitimacy acts as a brake on the emergence of the type of fully associational society which 'group theory' appeared to predict. While 'indelible' patterns of relationships may be eroded, feelings of belonging still constitute an important element in the development of groups; loyalty to the organisation plays a part alongside interest in a goal. Thus it is probable that societies will move towards some middle point where groups are relatively numerous but limited in scope, and not to a wholly associational model. Meanwhile, if interest groups of all kinds play an important part in many polities, and in particular in the liberal democracies of the West, communal groups continue to be – in the West, let alone elsewhere – an essential base for political life as well as a means by which demands are pressed on the political system.

Notes

1. For an assessment of the internal life of groups, see P.M. Blau, *Exchange and Power in Social Life* (1964). The political involvement of groups has been studied extensively at the level of individual countries or of individual groups (such as trade unions), but a systematic mapping has only been undertaken in part. A general overview, though old, can be found in F.G. Castles, *Pressure Groups and Political Culture* (1967).
2. Classical democratic theory is traditionally represented by the *Social Contract* (1762) of J.J. Rousseau and by Letter Ten of the *Federalist Papers* (see Hamilton *et al.*, 1981): in this letter the evils of faction are mentioned and advice is given as to how to meet the problems of groups in a society. This approach was widely accepted for a long time in Western Europe, although it appeared increasingly unrealistic. Group theory emerged as a realistic answer to the problem.
3. Group theory was first articulated by A.F. Bentley in *The Process of Government* (1908). It was further developed by D. Truman in *The Governmental Process* (1950), in particular in Chapter 2. See also C.B. Hagan, 'The group in political science' in R. Young, *Approaches to the Study of Politics* (1958), pp. 38–51.
4. The normative implications and indeed a general critique of group theory can be found in L. Weinstein, 'The group approach' in H. Storing (ed.), *Essays on the Scientific Study of Politics* (1962), pp. 153–224.
5. The theory of 'neo-corporatism' was fashionable in the late 1970s and early 1980s as it

appeared to account for the way in which, in some Continental liberal democracies in particular, such as Austria or the Netherlands, employers' and employees' organisations, as well as representatives of the state, came together to formulate policies, instead of being in competition with each other. See G. Lehmbruch and P.C. Schmitter (eds), *Patterns of Corporatist Policy-making* (1982).

6. The distinction originates from F. Toennies, *Community and Association* (London edn, 1955).
7. Religious groups are somewhat ambiguous. They might equally be classified as institutional or customary, as some religious are highly institutionalised (the Catholic church, for instance), while others have a very 'fluid' type of organisation.
8. G.A. Almond and J.S. Coleman (1960), p. 33, make the distinction between 'institutional', 'non-associational', 'anomic', and 'associational' interest groups.
9. This has been particularly the case in Communist states where the network has been markedly developed. See L. Holmes, *Politics in the Communist World* (1986), pp. 216–29.
10. Such communal groupings can be found for instance in Northern Ireland or in the Basque country as well as parts of the Italian South.
11. The notion of 'client' stems from Roman political and social life, but it has remained widespread in many parts of the world and even in Western Europe. The relationship is one of personal dependence, based on favours and protection. Clientelism can arise in both rural and urban areas, though it is more widespread in the former type of context.
12. The highly developed character of subsidiary associations of the Roman Catholic church is well-known: these range from sports clubs to trade unions. Other Christian churches have not developed such a vast network.
13. These confraternal aspects of trade unions were particularly marked in the nineteenth century; they are still more marked in Western Europe than in America, but they are decreasing everywhere.
14. During the 1980s, the dependent organisations of Communist parties have begun to acquire some independence, in part because, as in Poland, independent organisations have developed in parallel. In the Third World, dependent organisations of political parties have not been normally as extensive as in Communist countries – in the same way and for the same reasons as those which have led to parties being also less extensive, as will be seen in Chapter 11.
15. On the characteristics of trade unions on a comparative basis, see A.J. Taylor, *Trade Unions and Politics* (1989).
16. The distinction between 'protective' and 'promotional' organisations was made in the context of Britain by S.E. Finer in *Anonymous Empire* (1966), pp. 3–5. It is universally valid.
17. Feminist movements were strong in Britain, America, and other countries in the early part of the twentieth century. There were also environmental movements at various points in the nineteenth and twentieth centuries.
18. On social movements, see for instance B. Klandemans, H. Kriesi, and S. Tarrow (eds), *From Structure to Action: Comparing social movement research* (1981).
19. The increase in the strength of 'green' parties does not suggest necessarily that the links between electors and these parties are communal.
20. Tocqueville, in his *Democracy in America* (1835), was among the very first to note the importance of associations in the United States. The relative strength of associations was first assessed systematically in five countries by G.A. Almond and S. Verba in *The Civic Culture* (1963). Large differences were found: they are probably smaller at present.

8 Popular information and the role of the media

In the course of the last few decades, the importance of communication in political life has become universally recognised. It is interesting that this recognition has been associated with the analysis of group behaviour: thus group theory can be said to have been at the origin of the study of communication. 'It became clear to Bentley [the originator of group theory] that society and politics were indeed processes and that the central phenomenon of social process was communication.'[1] Thus we have become fully aware of the fact that no operation of the political system can take place unless each part of the system communicates with the others; more specifically, there are operations in the political system only to the extent that there is communication among the various parts. This is true both within groups – which act as mechanisms for communication among members – and among groups. Indeed, communication also links the present with the past and the future, so that demands are followed by policies.

Of course, the recognition of the over-riding importance of political communication and of communication in general has been triggered by the development of the mass media and by the belief that these media made it possible for those who controlled them to manipulate opinion and thereby behaviour. 'Assumptions about the political impact of the mass media have played a formative part in guiding the direction of mass communication research ever since its inception.'[2] It had been originally felt that these media could so increase the opportunities for leaders to influence citizens that the bases of the political system would be wholly transformed. It was therefore only natural that the main thrust of research be devoted to the study of the media; only when it became clear that the amount of influence exercised by these new forms of communication was manifestly less substantial than had been originally thought did the study of political communication become truly general, directed towards the universal phenomenon of information.[3]

If communication is viewed as the dynamic movement of demands and decisions from one part of the political system to another, it follows that the study of the operation of communications extends far beyond the study of the media of communication. The distinction is important, because communication gives its dynamics to the political system. The study of political communication should 95 therefore be approached in the same way as the study of the political system as a whole, namely in terms of the interpenetration and reciprocal influences which exist between structures and behaviour. Scattered throughout the political system are complex networks of communication 'processes' as well as communication institutions and structures. Depending upon the levels of development and the norms of the system, these structures will be more or less specialised, and the growth of engineering techniques of communication has a substantial effect on the development of these specialised structures.

The study of political communication therefore raises three main questions. First, what consequences follow from the general principle that the study of communication is truly the study of the dynamics of the political system? Second, what is the nature of the processes and of the specific structures of communication in various types of societies, and what is the relationship between these processes and structures? Third, what are the effects of these structures and processes on the communication levels of a given polity? If, on the basis of a general analysis of communication, we can identify the characteristics of 'perfect communication' and the ways in which 'real world' communication departs from the ideal model, it should be possible to see to what extent the communication patterns which take place through specific structures and processes succeed in establishing communication 'levels' in a given polity at a particular point.

Towards a general theory of communication

A general theory of communication should test all the variables which interact at any point in the system. In practice, the best method is to start by considering a 'perfect' system, and to examine the ways in which the real world is 'imperfect' and thus reduces communication levels.

Perfect communication

Communication takes place between two points, A and B, if there is a link between these two points and a coding–decoding device at each end. Communication is perfect if the link functions clearly and continuously and if the two coding–decoding machines understand each other fully and are entirely able to perceive what is to be emitted. Similarly, a perfect system of communication between any number of points requires that all the points be related to each other, two by two, by perfect coding–decoding devices so that anything that happens at any of the points is transmitted fully to all the other points.

Real-world communication

In a perfect system, there is complete and immediate transmission of all the signals. In the real world, however, the communication process can be 'imperfect' in a number of important ways. First, the machine at each end may only register a proportion of the signals which are in A, or it may only register these signals to a certain extent, and may transform what are continuous variations of intensity into a series of discrete levels. This is likely to occur because machines are usually adapted to 'perceive' happenings only within a given range or at a given depth.

Second, the machines at each end must be able to 'understand' all that is emitted by the emitting machine: yet the 'translation' which takes place through 'decoding' increases the number of ambiguities in the communication process. In order for this not to happen, the machines at both ends would have to be identical (or perfectly matched). This is difficult to obtain even with mass-produced machines; it will not happen with human communication machines, since the 'understanding' of individuals varies in relation to their social background, education, psychology, etc. Thus a signal emitted by A with a certain meaning will often be decoded by B with a different meaning. If A and B are strangers, the danger of misunderstanding and even incomprehension is large. Communication will of course be low if A and B know each other's language imperfectly; but some aspects of the message will always be lost.

Third, reductions in communication will also result from imperfections in the link. For communication to be perfect, the link between A and B must be in continuous two-way operation. This is practically impossible: no communication process allows for full simultaneous two-way communication. When A emits to B, B cannot emit to A; B has to interrupt A to communicate his or her information or B in effect ceases to listen to A. In most cases, the situation is worse, as A or B may simply not be able to emit at all and is temporarily or permanently on the receiving side.

Finally, the communication process must be in continuous operation, or there must at least be a system (such as a telephone bell) through which A and B may constantly communicate with each other. Real cases, even of two-person relationships, rarely approximate this ideal: A and B will simply not be able to reach each other in many circumstances.

Thus real-world communication is imperfect in four ways: because the zone or area of information is limited, either in range or depth; because there is some incompatibility between emission and reception, and misunderstandings or errors in translation occur; because it is not two-way and fully reciprocal; and because it is not continuous. As these types of imperfections can be combined in different ways, it might even be possible to measure the extent to which communication between A and B is imperfect, although such a measurement has not so far taken place.

Real-world communication processes are of course rendered even more imperfect because of the numbers of persons involved; yet a further type of 'imperfection' arises when the number of persons involved is greater than two, resulting from the existence of clusters of communication patterns, since groups privilege communication among some members of the society. The measurement of some aspects of these clusters has indeed begun, for instance by examining amounts of correspondence or the physical movement of persons. This suggests that, not surprisingly, real world communication is only a minute fraction of what perfect communication could be, despite the recent development of the mass media.[4]

Autonomy, influence and feedback

The imperfect character of communication leads to influence because the information which is imparted is selective and not fully two-way. Where information is not complete, it can be manipulated; where two-way communication does not take place, it is possible to ignore reactions, to prevent information from developing laterally and thus to maintain one-sided information in the polity.

On the other hand, however, the presence of social clusters or of individual psychological barriers tends to reduce influence. While leaders may sometimes be able to take decisions more easily as a result, since opposition will not manifest itself sharply, they may also be less able to ensure acceptance afterwards, as information on the decision may not have been given. Influence may be increased by imperfections in two-way relationships, lateral two-way relationships and the selective sending of messages, but it is decreased by bad 'reception' due to psychological or social characteristics. If it were possible to maximise reception without at the same time increasing two-way relationships or lateral relationships, it would be possible to increase influence indefinitely.

Such an indefinite increase is impossible. A point in a system can be said to be autonomous if it is not subjected to influence; yet for a point to be able to communicate, it must have information about the state of the receiving system of those to whom messages are sent. This cannot be done without prior information about the state of other points in the system and information will only have maximum effect if it is adjusted to the receiving mechanisms. Consequently, those who emit the messages lose at least some of their autonomy.

Moreover, limitations in autonomy are increased by self-adjusting or feedback mechanisms. These will tailor the messages to be sent to what can be understood. The autonomy of the emitting body will therefore become constrained to a point at which it does not even realise the real nature and extent of the constraints under which it operates. The process by which information is gathered, processed, and sent thus eventually ceases to be within the control of the body which emits the messages and can, ultimately, be operated automatically.

As yet too little is known about the ways in which feedback and other mechanisms operate in political systems to be able to state precisely where the equilibrium point lies nor whether this point varies from society to society, although this would seem to be the case. But it is clear that influence cannot be indefinitely increased in the polity. Assuming that the general socio-economic conditions of the system remain constant, the choice is between more interaction and less interaction, and this will affect both autonomy and influence.

Communication processes and the communication media

An exhaustive analysis of communication processes in a polity would require the measurement of the 'imperfections' relating to transmission, reception, clustering, two-way traffic, and continuity of communication among members of the polity: even the description, let alone the measurement, of these phenomena is markedly beyond what empirical analysis can currently achieve. On the other hand, the mass media can be described adequately, their relative extension and even their content can be measured and therefore compared, and some aspects of their impact can be fairly precisely assessed. Yet, restricted to the mass media, the study of communication is partial. The mass media constitute only the most sophisticated technical development of public communication, just one of the two forms which political communication takes in political systems. Alongside public communication, there is private communication, which has also been affected by the impact of various technological developments. Indeed, private and public communication constitute the two poles of a single dimension; they are often intermingled in political life.

Private communication

Private communication processes are those which are characterised by the exchange of information on the basis of an adequate or at least an elementary knowledge of the person or persons to whom information is being given. Private communication tends therefore to take place within very small groups and, in particular, by means of two-person discussions, though it does not need to be face-to-face. Indeed, not only correspondence, but also telephone conversations have markedly diminished the need for physical proximity in private communication. Though private communication is more intense, it is, of course, not perfect. As we noted, full continuous two-way traffic is theoretically impossible: this is obviously the case when the exchange of information takes place by correspondence. Although those who exchange information know each other, there are often difficulties in interpretation and in assessing the messages which are being exchanged.

Private communication tends to develop within and along the lines of the group structure of the polity, as the group structure gives rise to the private relationships which are at the origin of the communication. Thus patterns of private communication can be described by considering the network of groups. Where these tend to be communal, private communication will take place both almost exclusively within these communal groups and according to the socio-psychological characteristics which have developed within the groups. Where, on the contrary, group patterns tend to be associational, private communication will be less exclusive and more varied, though it may also be more superficial, as members of the associations are likely to know each other less well.

Public communication

Public communication has always been characterised, on the contrary, by a lack of personal knowledge of the members of the 'audience' to which the communication is being addressed. The mass media have extended dramatically the size of this audience, but the principle by which a signal is emitted without adequate knowledge of the receivers is not new. In political life in particular, this type of communication has always constituted a large part of the activities of leaders. Thus it may be that it is more in other fields (except perhaps in those of literature and the arts) that the mass media have dramatically modified the conditions of communication, by opening up a wide range of hitherto impossible forms of public communication.

Public communication is clearly less adequate or more 'imperfect' than private communication. First, it maximises lack of understanding, as it is not known whether the 'language' used will be understood by those who receive the message; thus no prediction can be made about whether the expected effect will occur. Second, public communication minimises two-way traffic since, except for somewhat anomic outbursts and perhaps a limited number of 'questions', those who receive the message cannot participate actively in the communication process. Third, such a communication process is scarcely continuous, while private communication relationships can usually be started at the will of each of the communicators. Fourth, it is highly selective in that the zone or area chosen by the communicator is generally rigidly predetermined.

The 'dysfunctional' aspects of public communication are therefore large. They are, of course, balanced by an immediate practical advantage: an individual can address himself or herself to large groups at one moment in time. Since politicians came to deal with large groups as soon as political life started to have an element of popular appeal, public communication developed long before the mass media. But public communication is also likely to be less imperfect than private communication in that it can extend beyond specific groups; it can therefore help to break sectionalism. It may of course take place within sections and thus promote sectionalism. Yet it *may* be used against sectionalism or as a means of appealing from a narrower to a broader form of sectionalism, to the tribe from the family, the party from the occupational or social group, the nation from the party.

Structures

Private and public communication have hitherto been discussed in terms of different processes, but reference has also been made to the structures through which these processes take place. In the case of private communication, the underlying structures are the very structures of the political system, groups, parties, bureaucracies, governments: private communication rarely cuts across these. In the case of public communication, the mass media added a new range of structures; but these act also as constraints on politicians. Newly created mass media can start developing independent tendencies which politicians may not easily control, unless these impose control on the media. This does of course often happen, but some aspect of legitimacy has then to be used in order to maintain this control.

Seen in this light, the constraints placed on public communication by the mass media do not appear to be different in kind to the constraints which earlier forms of public communication and all forms of private communication have also imposed on communication. They chiefly have an impact on selectivity. Public communication is more imperfect than private communication in all aspects except one (it may help to break sectionalism); but politicians and public leaders generally have to concentrate on public communication because of the size of the audience which can be reached in this way. The mass media are thus the form of public communication in which the characteristics of public communication are stretched to extremes, and the choice made in favour of large audiences is seen as the counterbalancing factor in the equation.

Techniques, media and processes of communication

Two broad points therefore emerge from the analysis of private and public communication. They are both structured, and the structures within which they operate vary with different types of societies. The impact of techniques is considerable: this is usually acknowleged in the case of public communication, but the impact of new techniques in the field of private communication is probably equally large, although it may still not be possible to describe this impact with the same degree of precision. Since techniques play a large part in both aspects of communication, it is tempting to relate levels of communication to levels of socio-economic development. Cutright used an index of communication, relating political development to communication development (both in the private and public senses of the word), and found the association to be high, although only easily identifiable indicators of communication, such as newsprint, letters, etc., were used.[5]

The examination of political communication should be conducted at three different levels, only one of which is usually considered. One level is that of techniques. It assesses the extent to which various polities use various communication media. The data are generally available, and, as can be seen in Table 8.1, the residents of countries which are socio-economically advanced have greater access to the media, though there are interesting differences between parts of the developing world.

Table 8.1 Spread of the mass media across the world

	Newspapers: daily circulation per 1 000 (1973–5)		Radios per 1 000 (1973–5)		Televisions per 1 000 (1972–5)	
	No. of countries	Average	No. of countries	Average	No. of countries	Average
Atlantic	18	306	23	451	23	267
Eastern Europe and Northern Asia	10	222	13	197	14	115
Middle East and North Africa	11	65	16	183	20	48
South and South-East Asia	9	97	16	133	20	31
Africa south of Sahara	31	15	40	56	44	3
Latin America	17	73	26	216	27	58

Source: C.L. Taylor and D.A. Jodice, *World Handbook of Political and Social Indicators* (3rd edn, 1983), vol. 1, pp. 175–84.

The second level is that of the media themselves, and of the structures within which the processes of private and public communication tend to take place. In this respect too, socio-economic development appears to affect both private and public communication. In private communication, there will be more barriers but also perhaps greater depth in societies characterised by communal groups: patterns of private communication which exist are less imperfect, but both within each group and from group to group private communication is more narrowly circumscribed. The opening up of the society and the development of different types of groups (including political parties) coincides with a decrease in the 'quality' of private communication.

The structures of public communication are also obviously closely related to socio-economic development. The structures of the mass media become more sophisticated with socio-economic development, though an 'imposed' transformation can lead to greater concentration, rigidity, or 'dependence' of the mass public communication system than would occur naturally. However, the situation is patterned on the development of other structures. Where the development is 'natural', the press, radio and television tend to be created as 'semi-legitimate' dependent associations of the broad (or some of the broad) legitimate groups. As radio and television are technically more advanced and more expensive to run than a newspaper, only some groups will be in a position to start their own channels. Where the development is 'imposed', the various media are used in the same way as other dependent associations, though, because they provide the means by which leaders can (apparently) influence the people most easily, much more is sometimes made of the control of the press, radio and television than is made of the control of other organisations. However, as with other associations, the public communication structures may gradually become somewhat autonomous and disengage from the organisation on which they originally depended.

Third, processes of communication take place within the context of these structures and it is in relation to processes that difficulties mostly tend to arise, both conceptually, because structures, processes and techniques are not sufficiently distinguished, and in practice, because efforts to 'organise' the mass media have not always been made in the light of this distinction. Three types of arrangement are possible and are indeed in existence. These are as follows:

1. The mass media can be wholly independent associations; relationships between the mass media and the political parties are then random; and processes are 'free'.
2. The mass media are controlled by each major political party, and are thus 'dependent' associations of these parties; processes would then be half-imposed.
3. There is only one national organisation, which is controlled in a pluralistic manner; processes vary in imposition according to the degree of 'balance' among the controlling groups.

As technical problems increase from the press through radio to television, a solution has sometimes been for the press to be organised on the basis of independent associations, and for radio and television to be organised on the 'single national institution' pattern. The United States and the USSR correspond to the two extreme situations, while most Western European countries adopted an intermediate model (see Table 8.2).

If the ordering of the three major media is kept in mind, patterns outside the developed world can also be accounted for. First, costs will play a major part in countries of low socio-economic development: not only television and radio, but also the press will tend to come to be under a 'single national plan' in countries where income per head is very low, unless, as was for instance the case in many colonial countries, capital costs for newspapers and even radio and television were met by organisations from the colonising country. Second, an imposed political system will only allow the creation of one dependent national organisation and will attempt to impose this organisation on all the mass media. The combination of both these factors will make an imposed plan of public communication more easily successful (i.e. will require the use of fewer political resources) where socio-economic development is low: it will be more successful for radio and television than for the press. Where the level of socio-economic development is low, even the press is likely to be controlled with relative ease: few printing presses will be created. Where socio-economic development is relatively high, for instance in richer authoritarian countries, more difficulties will occur in relation to the press than in relation to radio and television.[6]

Table 8.2 Examples of legal arrangements relating to press, radio and television

		Press	Radio	Television
1.	Pluralistic and wholly based on commercial arrangements	USA Japan Brazil Britain France West Germany Italy Sweden	USA Japan Brazil	USA Japan Brazil
2.	Intermediate: partly state, partly private		Britain France West Germany Italy	Britain France Italy
3.	Monopoly	USSR	Sweden	Sweden West Germany (but changing)

The analysis of the control of public communication media suggests a close relationship between technique, structure and process; yet the conceptual distinction must be kept, because control is partly independent from structures and because influence also depends on processes of private communication which are always less easily and less satisfactorily controlled. Processes vary within the single national institution organised for the media; so do the processes in what are ostensibly sets of independent public communication agencies. When mass media structures are imposed on the polity in order to buttress the political system, the processes of private communication may lag behind. Zones of silence or misunderstandings may render the public communication processes ineffective; more traditional means of public communication (meetings, for instance) may therefore have to be used to buttress the mass media.[7]

The effect of public communication

Conceptual difficulties surround the analysis of public communication. Since both private and public communication exist, rates at which and ways in which both develop are different, and technological advance, structural arrangements and processes have to be kept distinct despite obvious inter-relationships, the analysis of the effects of communication raises complex problems, most of which have not as yet been solved.

What can be measured: the disturbance

The absolute effects of all communication processes cannot be measured: they are too embedded in society to be disentangled from it. What can be measured are the changes in the effects of one communication medium over time, and indeed over a short time period; this can be referred to as the *disturbance* in the communication patterns as a result of the introduction of a new communication medium. Moreover, it is difficult, if not impossible, to measure very small disturbances occurring over a long period. This means that the effect of communication media which do not grow rapidly or which grow scarcely at all, and which are therefore likely to lead to a small disturbance over time, will rarely be observed. This also means that, when comparing the effects of communication media, one has to concentrate on those which grow roughly at the same rate. This situation poses problems for the comparative analysis of media as, in recent decades, the rates of growth of the various forms of public communication – public meetings, the press, radio, television – have been widely different and only the last two, and indeed in many countries only television, have had marked rates of growth. Thus it is inappropriate to compare the apparent effects of television to those of the press or public meetings at present; it might be valuable to draw comparisons over time, for instance by examining the disturbance caused by television during the present period and the disturbance caused by the press at the time during which it grew rapidly. Cross-national studies are hampered by the same problem; in order to assess the effect of a particular medium, such as television, it is necessary to concentrate on those countries in which the medium developed at roughly the same rate throughout the period of investigation, thereby obviously restricting the field of investigation.[8]

Effects of communication structures and processes

A number of conclusions can none the less be drawn about the role of the media, and of television in particular. They all suggest that the impact is less striking than had originally been thought. 'The scope of early media studies was primarily concerned with a search for direct, immediate, and deterministic "effects".'[9] It is now clear that these effects are more indirect and less determinant.

First, there is more influence on information than on values and norms. In particular, television increases knowledge but does not significantly modify norms, at least in the short run. Indeed, even if the medium is very biassed, the effect is likely to remain limited because the psychological barriers of the pre-existing forms of communication, and in particular of private communication, will buttress existing norms. Evidence for this conclusion has tended to be drawn from developed societies, and especially from election campaigns; but the effect of television and radio seems to be of the same type in developing countries. In all cases, the only significant changes which can be observed relate to information.[10]

Second, where the norms expressed by the new media go in the same direction as those of the polity, the media do reinforce these norms. Studies of the disturbance resulting from television at election time show that party supporters are reinforced in their views by the campaign conducted on television: this reinforcement also results from other media of public (and presumably private) communication. Where the disturbance is large, as a result of the appearance of a new medium coinciding for instance with an election, the reinforcement is substantial. This is not surprising: the media of political communication are typically not divorced from the cultural characteristics of the polity. Private communication is structured around and within the groups which exist in the polity; the newer mass media are not different in this respect. They are related to the norms of the polity; they are appendages (sometimes, as we saw, legal appendages) of the groups, political or otherwise, which exist in the polity. Their main effect is therefore reinforcement.[11]

Third, if any new medium is used in order to change norms, other aspects of the communication process have also to be altered; specifically, private communication patterns have to be modified. The impact of media of public communication is greater on 'opinion leaders' than on the population as a whole. This has been shown to be the case in relation to television, but it would seem that the point is general: meetings, the press, and radio as well as television are all primarily used by opinion leaders, as these attend or listen to them more frequently. Moreover, opinion leaders are better able to understand the messages which are emitted by political leaders.[12] As a result, only by a combination of the action of public communication and private communication media can changes in norms permeate down through the whole population. If norms are to be altered, the structure of private communication has also to be altered, but this is not usually possible, at least in the short run. All that can be done is to alter somewhat the content of the messages exchanged by opinion leaders. The change in the political norms which the mass media can achieve is therefore small in the short run; it may be greater in the long run, but any change which then occurs has to be related to other variations in the society as a whole. There is a 'systemic' relationship between communication structures and processes and the political and social system.

There are two aspects in which the new communication media have a substantial effect, since they have a characteristic advantage which was mentioned earlier, namely that they can 'nationalise' political norms and political views. First, they increase information. This has been shown vividly to be the case in developed societies – largely of course because more research has been done in these countries. This is particularly the case in connexion with television, mostly, it is suggested, because television is the medium which has caused most 'disturbance' recently; were it possible to analyse the effect of the press in the nineteenth century, the same finding might emerge. It is at any rate manifest that television helps citizens to acquire information of a general character which private communication networks cannot impart because these function in a narrower framework. There is no consequential change in norms, however, at any rate so long as there is no trend in the society for norms to be modified.[13]

Second, the public communication media appear able to close the gap between norms and policies where this gap becomes apparent. Where the norms of members of the polity (or of an important fraction of its members) are not implemented or cannot be implemented by existing policies or existing political leaders – when, therefore, there is a gap between norms and policies – a medium of public communication (and *a fortiori* a new medium which can create a large disturbance) seems able to fill this gap, for instance by building the reputation of someone who appears to correspond to the norms of members of the polity. But, in doing so, the communication media do not change the norms; an attempt is simply made to implement them.

If this point is combined with the fact that the media help to increase knowledge and if one concentrates on the situation in developing countries in which means of private communication are essentially clustered around tribal or other closed communities, the consequences may be or at least may appear dramatic. This is why it is often stated – and in this sense rightly – that media of public communication, and in particular television and radio, have contributed markedly to the development of the 'rising expectations' of the citizens of Third World countries. It is not that demands have been engineered, but there was a gap between norms and policies.[14] The 'disturbance' may appear large, and so it may well be in some countries, in relation to the fact that traditional private communication operated only within the clusters of tribes or other communal groups. But the norms have not been engineered in this way; the new media of public communication fill a gap between norms and policies which emerged in many countries of the Third World from a combination of imitation of practices of developed countries and from limited, and indeed patchy, socio-economic development.

Conclusion

The analysis of the effects of communication is one in which vast zones of obscurity are separated by small areas of detailed findings. Political scientists have naturally concentrated on those aspects which were most topical (such as television) and where the impact seemed to be the greatest. Meanwhile little effort has been made to measure the impact of private communication or of the more traditional forms of public communication.[15] A truly comprehensive empirical theory of political communication will emerge only when it becomes possible to relate private and public media in countries where both types are relatively 'primitive', in those where public media are 'in advance' of the private media and in those where both are relatively 'developed'. One can only hypothesise that rates of growth of knowledge are greatest in countries of the third type, and smallest in the first, and that the gap between the three types increases – although it may be found empirically that countries of the first type are becoming increasingly less numerous. When such an empirical theory is developed, the study of political communication will come to occupy the place which it truly deserves in the analysis of comparative government.

Notes

1. J.E. Combs, 'A process approach' in D.D. Nimmo and K.R. Sanders (eds), *Handbook of Political Communication* (1981), p. 49. The idea of applying a communication model to political life was originated primarily by K. Deutsch, whose *Nerves of Government* (1963) truly opened up a new whole dimension of analysis.
2. M. Gurevitch and J.G. Blumler, 'Linkages between the media and politics' in J. Curran *et al.* (eds), *Mass Communication and Society* (1977), p. 270.
3. The role of the mass media was originally thought to be capable of truly shaping the views of whole populations. This view was particularly widespread before World War II. It was also fairly common in the 1950s: see for instance R. Williams, *Communications* (1962). There has been a considerable toning down of this role as a result of empirical research. See D. McQuail, 'The influence and effects of the mass media' in J. Curran *et al., op. cit.* (1977), pp. 72–4.
4. See in particular K. Deutsch, *Nationalism and Social Communication* (1953), *passim* and in particular Chapter 4, pp. 60–80. For an examination of these indicators, see C.L. Taylor and D.A. Jodice, *World Handbook of Political and Social Indicators*, (3rd edn, 1983).
5. P. Cutright, 'National political development' in N.W. Polsby *et al.* (1963), pp. 569–82.
6. The experience of Communist states in particular showed that the press, in the form of underground newspapers, began to develop in an independent fashion considerably before radio and television started to open up.
7. The fact that people do not really 'listen' to official propaganda has been shown repeatedly by the fact that, in East Germany, for instance, West German television has been a greater source of news for the population than the official media. The same could be said about the fact that Western radio stations have provided citizens of Eastern countries with information in which they were more interested.
8. The detailed studies of the impact of television in a number of Western countries have shown the extent to which the impact of this medium in terms of influence had previously been exaggerated. See D. McQuail, *op. cit.* (1977), pp. 73–6. See also M.L. De Fleur and S. Ball-Rokeach, *Theories of Mass Communication* (4th edn, 1981), Chapter 12, pp. 232–50.
9. C. Zukin, 'Mass communication and public policy' in D.D. Nimmo and K.R. Sanders (eds), *op. cit.* (1981), p. 362.
10. On the influence of television, see in particular J.D. Halloran (ed.), *The Effects of Television* (1970). See also M.L. De Fleur and S. Ball-Rokeach, *op. cit.* (1981), pp. 232–55, for the effects of the media in general.
11. On the reinforcement effect of television, see M.L. De Fleur and S. Ball-Rokeach, *op. cit.* (1981), pp. 240–50.
12. On the role of opinion leaders in filtering the effect of television and other means of public communication, see E. Katz and P.F. Lazarsfeld, *Personal Influence* (1956), in particular pp. 31–42.
13. 'Only under rare conditions would we expect mass media information to be able singlehandedly to alter . . . basic beliefs', note M.L. De Fleur and S. Ball-Rokeach, *op. cit.* (1981), p. 247. See also D. McQuail, *op. cit.* (1977), pp. 80–2.
14. An early examination of the role of communication media in developing societies can be found in D. Lerner, *The Passing of Traditional Society* (1958), pp. 19–107, on the Middle East. For a more recent presentation of their role, see F.W. Frey, 'Communication and development' in I. de Sola Pool *et al.*, (eds), *Handbook of Communication* (1973), pp. 337–418.
15. At the limit, the effect of private communication forms part of the socialisation process, and in particular of the process of child socialisation. It is therefore difficult to disentangle the specific effect of private communication from the general characteristics of socialisation. See S.H. Chaffee, L.S. Ward and L.P. Tipton, 'Mass communication and political socialisation' in J. Dennis (ed.), *Socialisation to Politics* (1973), pp. 391–409.

Part III

Political parties

9 Origins, nature and goals of political parties

Political parties are one of the major developments of the nineteenth and twentieth centuries. They are an invention of modern political systems, an invention which, curiously at first sight, has served and even truly made effective both liberal–democratic political systems and many types of coercive regimes. Some contemporary dictatorships also attempt to operate without political parties; they usually do so, however, for short periods only and with difficulty. Political parties are fundamental to modern society because they are the main institution by which conflicts are dealt with. As a result, they have a two-sided aspect: they help legitimise conflict and give it, so to speak, a voice in the public debate, but they are also instrumental in reducing and indeed in extreme cases repressing conflict. This very ambiguity is what makes them crucially important, indeed truly unique, though this ambiguity also lies at the root of their limitations.

Before examining the anatomy of parties (their structure) and their physiology (how they combine and fight each other in the form of political systems), it is necessary to consider why parties are particularly associated with modern polities; it is also necessary to examine the nature of parties and specifically how these organisations resemble and differ from other groups in society and thus how they come to be the political groupings *par excellence*, the bodies through which and by which both representation and at times imposition occurs. It is important to examine the social bases of their strength as well as their goals, social bases and goals being in part related to each other and in part independent from each other.

Political parties in the contemporary world

The widespread presence of parties

Political parties are one of the main features of contemporary political life, as we said. Although various types of factions existed earlier and were sometimes well organised and durable, as in ancient Rome or in the Italian cities of the Renaissance, only since the later part of the nineteenth century have parties come to be recognised as the normal means by which to fight political battles. It was noted in Chapter 7 that the dislike for factions which characterised late eighteenth-century political theory was gradually undermined as parties developed and became strong, first in Europe and North America, and gradually throughout most of the world. In this process, parties emerged not just in liberal polities but in authoritarian or totalitarian societies, as a means of holding the country together. Firstly by accident, and later consciously, the single-party system came to be used as a means of imposing regimes, apparently more effectively than seemed possible by other political or administrative structures, such as the military or the bureaucracy. In this way, parties have come to play a part in countries hitherto characterised by non-party arrangements. It has been suggested that such parties are different in kind to the parties which emerge in pluralistic political systems:[1] in reality, as will be seen in the course of this and the following chapters, the distinction between these two types of parties is not clear-cut, and there are gradations from one to the other. As a matter of fact, the role of parties in single-party and pluralistic systems is often not markedly dissimilar.

Parties have thus become a common feature of contemporary political systems. They are not present everywhere, however; throughout the second half of the twentieth century, between a fifth and a quarter of the countries of the world (admittedly mostly not the same ones) have indeed lived under regimes which excluded parties. However, to refer to this global statistic means exaggerating markedly the number of systems without parties, for these are of two types, traditional and military, and only the first of these is truly a 'no-party' system. The traditional system survives in countries where political life is dominated by absolute or near-absolute monarchies, of which there were about a dozen, mostly in the Arabian Peninsula and the Himalayas, by the 1980s; their number is regularly declining. Military regimes, on the other hand, are not true 'no-party' systems: they are set up *against* parties. They formally abolish parties, but these typically simmer under the surface; furthermore, these regimes often end up by creating an 'official' party in order to control the polity. Military regimes, which will be examined more closely in Chapter 21, are a significant feature of contemporary societies, but they are an indication of the pathology of parties (and of governmental systems), not a real alternative to party politics.

While parties are a common feature in modern societies, they do not have the same importance everywhere. It is not sufficient to distinguish between systems which have and systems which do not have parties; a further distinction needs to be made, both among single-party and pluralistic systems, between regimes in which parties are strong and well-established and those in which the 'weight' of parties is limited, for instance because they have been set up artificially by a ruler. The weight of parties also can vary over time: this is indeed what happened in the course of the nineteenth century in Europe; as will be seen in Chapter 14, it can be argued with some justification that the strength of parties may now be diminishing in many countries.

Reasons why parties are widespread

Before examining why parties exist at all and, if they exist, how strong they are, it is necessary to answer a preliminary question. Why are parties so widespread in the contemporary world, when they were rare in the past? This cannot result solely from the spread of liberal democracy, since many authoritarian governments are also based on parties. The reasons are to be found in three characteristics of the modern world, namely the perception of the existence of conflicts in society, the need for the government to be linked to the population, and the belief that 'unity means strength'.

First, parties emerge when members of the polity begin to recognise the existence of problems which they wish to promote or defend. These problems may relate to the overall structure of the society, to aspects of its organisation, or to policies. The problems may be openly discussed or suppressed (as in many single-party systems). But the existence of problems and therefore of conflicts, open or concealed, is a *sine qua non*. It is because, in traditional societies, such conflicts are not perceived that these polities can be true 'no-party' states.[2]

Second, parties exist where government and political system have to be linked to the population and cannot rely on external sources of legitimacy such as the divine right to rule. When the government needs, even if only in a broad manner, to justify its existence by relating to the people, it has to develop links with the population. The need for parties then arises, as parties can, more than other groups, and in particular more than the military, develop regional and local branches, and thus create ties between the top and the bottom of the pyramid. Such a need for the government to be linked to the people is a characteristic of the modern world.

Third, for parties to exist, the belief has to be widespread that unity means strength. This belief is indeed commonly held in the contemporary world, as it is usually thought that better results can be achieved if a large organisation is built. However, not everyone adheres to this belief. Some political activists feel, on the contrary, that small bodies, tiny cells, can achieve more than big parties as far as changing society is concerned. Moreover, the question of the relationship between 'unity' and 'strength' has consequences for party life, as it suggests that a divided party will not be effective; yet such a view clashes with the suggestion that parties should allow 'internal democracy'. Parties therefore often experience tension between an underlying belief in the strength provided by unity and the divisions which generally accompany the growth of organisations.

Parties tend therefore to be characteristic organisations of modern political life. Yet it is not surprising that they should not exist everywhere or that they should not have the same strength in every polity. It is also not surprising that imitation should play a large part in the life of parties: new organisations are likely to imitate successful ones elsewhere to which they feel ideologically close, as happens with other political institutions, such as legislatures or executives. Thus Socialist parties and, but less so, Christian parties spread throughout Europe in the late nineteenth and early part of the twentieth century; thus one-party systems, which first emerged in the Soviet Union, gave rise to a large number of similar developments, not just among Communist states but also in other parts of the world. Yet imitation creates problems, as institutions which are imported may be alien to the basic social structure and to the cultural patterns of the society: the new parties may therefore not have substantial strength.

Definition and functions of political parties

Parties are groupings, but groupings of a particular kind. It is not sufficient to say that they are 'political' while other groups are not: as was noted in Chapter 7, a body is political only to the extent that it participates in the procedure of solving conflicts. It is necessary to look for more precise criteria in order to account for the increased probability of involvement of parties in political life and indeed for the claim that parties are essentially political. One criterion which is sometimes used is that parties aim at taking power, while other groups aim only at influencing decisions which are taken by others.[3] This distinction is valid, though more as a rough-and-ready rule than as a true conceptual contrast. It is based on a distinction between decision-makers and mere influentials which is somewhat oversimplified; moreover, it involves taking aspirations into account even if these are wholly unrealistic, for instance among small parties. It is particularly unsatisfactory when considering change, since it does not help to determine the dynamics by which an 'ordinary' group may gradually become a party. Thus this distinction is more in the nature of an indicator than of a criterion.

It is necessary to return to groups and examine the changes which are likely to take place when a group becomes 'more' political. Firstly, parties are 'associations'; they are not 'communities' like tribes or ethnic groups. They are associational in that they have some aims, whether these involve taking or keeping power or using power to implement some goals. However, parties are associations of a special kind: unlike most promotional associations, parties need to have general aims; unlike protective associations, they tend to be broadly open to all members of the society.[4]

There are some exceptions, however, or at least borderline cases. One of these exceptions is that of the minority party which exists to defend a particular section of the polity and resembles a protective group; another is that of the 'single-issue' party which is set up to put forward a particular cause and resembles a promotional group. These are genuine borderline cases and, in the course of time, changes are likely to occur. Minority parties will attempt to appeal to other sections in order to increase their influence, for instance by making alliances with other minority parties or even with national parties. Similarly, special-issue parties will gradually develop general policies and broad ideologies: 'ecology' or 'green' parties have increasingly done this, for instance. At the end of the process these bodies may acquire all the characteristics of other political parties.

It is because aims are general and membership open that parties want to take power and are highly politicised. They do not confine themselves to a limited number of issues; they are interested in all the national decisions. They cannot therefore be confined to intermittent 'influence', but are concerned with overall influence. They are confronted with all the contentious issues which the polity has to face; they are involved in all the aspects of the political process, while other groups are involved in only parts of it. A political party will therefore be defined as any group whose membership is open and which is concerned potentially with the whole spectrum of matters which the polity faces.

From this definition follow the main characteristics of parties and their role.[5] This role can be described at three levels, those of the society as a whole, of the political system, and of daily political life. At the level of the society as a whole, political parties are general mechanisms by which conflicts are handled: they are one of the main means by which rulers exercise influence and endeavour to induce the population to accept their policies, while, conversely, they are the means by which the population (or at least its most active part) attempts to exercise influence. Conflicts thus both arise through parties and are solved (by compromise or repression) through parties. This role of parties translates itself in terms of the development of ideologies and programmes which may partly come from the bottom but are likely to emerge mostly from the top.

More instrumentally, at the level of the political system, this role is achieved because parties are the institutions *par excellence* by which the people are both represented and mobilised. Parties are thus a two-way means of communication of influence between rulers and population. The success of the mechanism depends on the strength of the parties (on what may be called their weight in the community), which in turn depends on the effectiveness of the party structure, and in particular on the extensiveness of the party throughout the country. This question will be examined in Chapter 10. Moreover, depending on the particular case, either the 'representative' or the 'mobilising' aspects of the party are more prominent: some parties 'aggregate' or, to use Apter's expression, 'reconcile' more than others; they can be used more or less as instruments enabling the rulers to exercise influence and control.[6] This question is closely connected to the social bases of parties and to their goals.

Finally, at the level of daily political life, parties play a major part in recruitment. They bring to the fore men and women willing and able to share in ruling the country: as a matter of fact, they are the main mechanism by which such recruitment takes place continuously and smoothly, though the political 'class' can be recruited from other groups as well, such as the bureaucracy or the army. Party recruitment can be regarded as the most natural in the contemporary world, since parties are an obvious training ground where the skills of politics are learnt. Consequently, the function of recruitment is sometimes viewed as the most important one in political parties, if not the most exalted.

Social bases of parties

The notion of the legitimate party

The importance of the concept of legitimacy was noted in Chapter 5, while recognising the difficulties relating to its measurement. Chapter 7 also showed that legitimacy plays a major part in the development of groups; a similar analysis can be extended to parties. Legitimacy does require the passage of time, however. In the intervening period, parties have to be supported and strengthened: this is where the concept of 'legitimacy transfer', which was identified in relation to groups, is essential. For parties, not being 'communal' groups, have to emerge from and be supported by pre-existing groups, either communal or associational, though one of the groups supporting the parties can be the polity itself, the nation, in the same way as the polity can support institutional groups such as bureaucracies or the army.

Two consequences follow. First, parties are not legitimate, they *become* legitimate. They become legitimate when the transfer of support from the 'parent' group has lasted long enough to lead to a situation in which the supporters of the party no longer refer to that group in order to support the party. The support ceases to be indirect and becomes direct.

Second, this process of legitimisation of parties can be said to be natural if and when the parties emerge from a parent group whose goals are accepted by the polity or large sections of the polity; this has been the case with most Western parties of the right or left. The process of legitimisation can be said to be imposed if the party aims at substituting new goals for those which prevailed in the polity: this has been the situation in Communist countries, for instance. In this case, extra resources are required from the 'parent' group to maintain the party in existence, although the party may later be one of the bodies buttressing the 'parent' group. In practice an imposed development of this kind can take place only when the parent group is, or at least includes, the state itself, as this alone possesses the coercive powers which will maintain the party's dominance. However, the coercive power of the state can also be associated with a communal group, for instance a tribal, ethnic or religious body, if such a group aims at modifying radically the goals of the polity.

The process of legitimisation of parties thus results from movements coming from two directions: on the one hand, by a 'natural process', the legitimate groups in the society gradually produce party organisations, when the need arises. Such a need is likely to arise when the society becomes modern: thus many Socialist parties were supported by trade unions and religious parties by churches. On the other hand, the national leaders may use the state to back parties which they create. Examples of parties of this kind are imposed parties in Communist states and in developing polities; these can be of the right or left. This process is difficult and often unsuccessful, however, as these parties may remain artificial: the fall of many Third World parties and the decline of many Eastern European Communist parties are examples of these difficulties.

Modes of legitimisation of parties by natural development

The process of legitimisation of parties by natural development takes place on the basis of the four types of broad groups (tribal, ethnic, religious, and class-based) which were examined in Chapter 7, though not by all of them in every society.[7] On the other hand, one of these broad groups may give rise to more than one party if there are several tribes or churches in a polity.

Tribal or clientele parties

Tribal or clientele groups have produced many parties in the past, for instance in England in the eighteenth century and, more recently, in some developing areas, such as in Latin America. These parties can be truly tribal or 'clientelistic'; they can even be geographically based, and this is a growing tendency. The association is then not with a clan but with a given region which is to be defended; modern nationalistic parties can therefore be said to have originated in this way.

This type of origin characterises the oldest parties, and in particular the oldest European parties. The English Tories and Whigs, for instance, were based on clientelism, from which they gradually became independent in the course of the nineteenth century; they thus acquired a legitimacy of their own. A similar evolution characterised the oldest conservative and liberal parties of other Western European countries, whatever ideological differences gradually emerged among them.

Parties of this kind are, and indeed were in the past, particularly associated with the hold of individual chiefs and chieftains. There tended to be an almost feudal pyramid of personal allegiance. This has become rare, though in parts of the Third World, including parts of Latin America, this type of party 'vassalage' does remain. Traces of it also remain in Western Europe, especially in more peripheral areas. Expressions borrowed from the army are often used to describe the relationships. Thus one speaks of 'lieutenants' of various kinds (the 'corporals' of the traditional Brazilian party structure) who exercise influence on behalf of the main chief (a 'colonel'). Clientele parties therefore tend to have a personalised rather than a well-developed bureaucratic structure.

Ethnic parties

Ethnic groups also give rise to parties, though in some cases the basis of the party combines bonds of clientele or race. They often give rise to minority parties, but this is not always the case. Indeed, some of the oldest parties of the world, the American parties, combined important ethnic elements with a more traditional local group basis: thus the Democratic Party has long been a 'federation' of various ethnic groups. Ethnic minorities – or a combination of tribal and ethnic minorities – have also contributed to the emergence of many parties in Europe and in the developing world, and indeed continue to do so, to a greater extent than had been expected.[8]

Religious parties

Churches are likely to place parties in 'orbit', but the creation of such parties depends on the church structure and on the size of the religious organisation. The more hierarchical the church, the more a church-based party is likely to emerge: Roman Catholic, Moslem, or indeed Jewish parties, as in Israel, are thus more likely to emerge than parties based on other churches. A church-based party is also more likely to emerge where the church is strong but not overwhelming, for example in Germany or Italy rather than in Ireland.[9] A religious party may also emerge from more than one church if these churches feel, as was the case in Germany after World War II and in the Netherlands in the 1970s, that they need to create a single party to maintain their influence.[10]

Church-based parties tend to develop where other communal groups have not already set up a strong party, for instance if there is no well-established conservative party or if such a party is strongly antagonistic to church interests. Thus Christian parties gained a larger foothold in many Continental countries than in Britain or Scandinavia, partly because the Catholic church is stronger on the Continent, partly because it has been under attack at times, and partly because traditional conservative parties have tended to be weaker.

Class-based parties

Class-based parties are perhaps the best-known of the parties which developed naturally, at least in Western Europe and in various European outposts such as Australia or New Zealand, where the political system is characterised by the presence of large Labour or Socialist parties allied to and often supported by the trade union movement. Class-based parties are less conspicuous elsewhere in the world, although in the United States and some parts of Latin America class has played a part, with other components, in the process by which other parties became legitimate.

There are manifest reasons for the development of class-based parties in Europe: industrialisation led to the expansion of the working class and to the development of strong trade unions. Where this 'objective' base did not exist, class-based parties scarcely developed. Socialist (and Communist) parties are thus closely connected to a particular type of social structure; elsewhere clientele, ethnic divisions, and churches are the groups which generate parties. Moreover, class-based parties are unlikely to become strong where other communal groups form the basis of strongly implanted parties. In Canada and the United States, ethnic allegiances (often combined with religious allegiances) have been strong, thus undermining the potential class cleavage. In Western Europe, too, there are examples of relatively weak Socialist parties, for instance because religious groups were strong, as in Ireland, or because ethnic or clientelistic cleavages were prominent, as in Switzerland.[11]

Parties depend on groups in order to acquire legitimacy naturally. This is why some parties never succeed in becoming legitimate, while others remain small. Some parties are also 'satellites' of larger parties in that they are kept in being by these larger parties for tactical reasons. Their fate varies; some may succeed in acquiring the legitimacy of an existing broad party and dislodge it from the forefront of the political scene, in the way that Socialist class-based parties typically weakened liberal parties in Western Europe in the early part of the twentieth century – however, this occurred only because Socialist parties had a large group following. In general, parties which have a small communal group base tend to remain small; they are not placed in 'orbit'. Only by imposition do they succeed in coming to the forefront. It is perhaps not surprising that some of their leaders should be tempted to resort to such means.

Modes of legitimisation of parties by imposed development

When a government wishes to see society follow different goals from those which are currently followed, imposition becomes the order of the day. The situation may arise from a number of factors, as was seen in Chapter 5; it can aim at preserving as well as at radically changing the status quo. Such parties need to be buttressed by the state, which then acts in a way similar to that of a communal group lending its legitimacy to a party of the type which we just examined. However, the state adds another element which communal groups do not possess to the same extent, namely coercion: it is expected that the party will be placed in 'orbit' more quickly as a result. Not surprisingly, some – perhaps many – of these attempts fail. As a matter of fact, success will occur only if some internal resources, both short- and long-term, can be mobilised, and, in particular, in the short term, the special appeal of individuals and groups as well as, in the long term, the 'education' of the population towards new goals.

Such parties typically use the strength of national leaders (who, indeed, are precisely those who create these parties). Such a leadership is of a 'charismatic' and not of a clan or clientelistic nature, though some support, in some areas, may also have a clientelistic character. The bond is based on trust in the ability of leader to bring the party and the nation to a more exalted destiny, a bond which does not exist in traditional leadership.[12]

These parties cannot be based on leadership alone, however exalted it may be. Indeed this charismatic leadership is often associated with an 'idea', national or ethnic, as in many parts of the Third World. In some cases it is also religious or even class-based: the frame of reference is then placed in the future and the group which is exalted, far from being natural and 'accepted', is opposed to and contrasted with the natural groups; nationhood is then referred to as more valuable than the old clans or tribes.

Yet these means are typically insufficient to build the party on a sound basis: coercion has to be used. In the long term, however, the aim is to educate the population so that it supports positively the goals put forward by the party and its leaders, and to combat, rather than aggregate, traditional demands. If this strategy succeeds the party may in turn help the legitimacy of the whole political system. The goals of the regime may become more accepted and the party may channel some demands and aggregate them within the framework and the context of the party 'ideology'. Coercion may then be reduced.

In practice, however, these expectations are rarely fulfilled. The rate at which the acceptance – or legitimisation – of the party takes place depends on the effectiveness of actions designed to oppose short-term demands and on the extent to which the attitudes of the population can gradually be changed. An equilibrium is difficult to reach: the capital consumed on short-term action may be exhausted before long-term 'education' can produce major results. Some imposed regimes appear to have been relatively effective in broadening their support and, indeed, in surviving, but the fact that they survived does not necessarily mean that they succeeded in bringing the population close to their goals; the Communist systems of the Soviet Union and China are two obvious examples. The problems which the regimes of these countries have continued to face after decades in which an *indigenous* radical system was implanted suggest that the goal may be impossible to achieve. Indeed, it seems that these regimes may be able to survive only if a major 'revision' of goals takes place, as has indeed occurred in Mexico – the only other country in which an imposed party appears to have been put successfully in 'orbit' for a very long period.[13]

The goals of political parties

The five main groupings of parties in ideological space

An essential aspect of party activity concerns the elaboration and implementation of policies. Of course, in some cases, parties exist only for the benefit of leaders and policies are merely used as cover-ups. Moreover, some parties claim to be purely pragmatic and not to be concerned with 'doctrinaire' points of view. In reality, such an attitude is ideological, both negatively and positively – negatively in that it rejects the suggestion that countries can be better run if there are general guidelines in the determination of policy, and positively in that it sees the current situation as broadly satisfactory. Thus truly pragmatic parties basically accept the tenets of the existing system.[14]

In reality, ideology plays a significant part in the life of most parties, both symbolic and practical. The goals of parties are important signposts to this ideology, although it may at times be difficult to determine these with precision. First, the goals of the leaders are not necessarily identical to those of the followers and intermediate leaders; indeed, there is a high probability that there will be disagreements among them.[15] Second, the actual policies of a party in office may be different from the programme put forward before gaining power. However, as an approximation, parties can be characterised by the three types of broad goals which were described in Chapter 3 and which are concerned with participation, means of implementation, and policy content. Indeed, it is possible to locate parties broadly in five ideological clusters within this three-dimensional space – the same clusters as those identified for political systems.

The predominance of liberal–democratic parties in Western Europe and North America

In Western Europe and North America, in terms of the dimensions which were delineated, parties occupy a middle-of-the-road position between egalitarianism and inegalitarianism. They are broadly liberal, and they tend towards democracy rather than monocracy. These parties can therefore be labelled *liberal–democratic*. The variations between parties with respect to each of these three dimensions tend to be relatively small.

There are some exceptions, but these are limited in number and character. The main ones are constituted by Communist parties, as parties of the extreme right have been rare since World War II and have usually had a short life. Communist parties profess a different ideology concerning equality and appear to have very different views on freedom, though they have markedly altered their standpoints (a change which has often been associated with Eurocommunism). Moreover, Communist parties have become markedly weaker in the six countries in which they were traditionally strong – France, Portugal, Italy, Greece, Finland, and Iceland.

Eastern Communist countries ruled by authoritian–egalitarian parties

In the fifteen countries of the Eastern Communist bloc, on the other hand, the ruling parties have traditionally been, at least until the late 1980s, authoritarian–egalitarian. Admittedly, even in the heyday of Communist control of these countries, the Communist parties have not always ruled alone: in Poland, Czechoslovakia and East Germany, other parties were permanently associated with the Communist party and remained to some extent distinct from it, in particular the Catholic party in Poland. But the control of the Communist party over these satellite parties was traditionally so strong that ideological differences were scarcely relevant to government policies. The ideology of Eastern Communist parties must thus be defined as authoritarian–egalitarian. The changes which have taken place since the mid-1980s suggest that the ideology of Communist parties may become different, quite apart from the emergence of genuinely liberal–democratic parties in these countries. The reforms initiated by Mikhail Gorbachev in the second half of the 1980s in the Soviet Union constitute a major shift, however, which might bring the Communist party of the Soviet Union close to the liberal–democratic parties of the West in the future.[16]

The three main types of party in the Third World

In the rest of the world (Latin America, Africa and the southern half of Asia), parties are more varied in character. Some countries have, or have had, parties of a liberal–democratic type: this is true of Israel, of several Latin American countries and of Costa Rica in particular, while India has long been the largest liberal democracy in the world. Morever, parties in Japan, Australia and New Zealand closely resemble North American or Western European parties, as do parties in some other countries of the new Commonwealth such as those in the Caribbean. Some countries also have Communist parties which closely resemble the Eastern model; this is especially true in the case of Cuba, which has been run for three decades on Eastern European Communist lines; it is less true of some other Marxist states, such as Angola or Mozambique.

Yet, by and large, parties in the 'developing world' have different ideologies from those of Western or Eastern parties. To a limited extent, this is because *traditional* parties still exist. These have similar characteristics to those of early nineteenth-century Europe; however, they have markedly diminished in number. Among them can be included the traditional Colombian parties, some parties in some Central American republics, and parties in a few African countries such as Lesotho, in some South-East Asian states such as Malaysia, and in the smaller countries of Central and Western Asia. Such parties may be labelled traditional–conservative, as they have conservative goals and usually have no desire to change an inegalitarian status quo in which the members of an oligarchy (and sometimes a monarchy) control the wealth of the country and are truly above the rest of the citizens in status. Levels of participation in these parties are also low.

As the idea of development caught on in the Third World, traditional–conservative parties began to decline and traditional groups began to lose their influence. The first manifestations of such a change occurred in Mexico and Turkey after World War I; similarly, Nasser set up a new type of party in Egypt in the 1950s. In Asia, new types of parties have not spread widely, partly because of stronger underlying structures. In Africa, on the contrary, the struggle for independence reduced the role of tribal groups who played little part in it. Meanwhile, in Latin America, traditional parties were gradually challenged by new parties. As a result, by the 1970s, the majority of Third World parties could be defined as belonging to this new *populist* type, though with larger variations among them than between the liberal–democratic, authoritarian–egalitarian or traditional parties; this has meant, as was pointed out in Chapter 3, an emphasis on increasing development and popular participation, by and large using the state as the means by which these achievements can be obtained.[17]

The main underlying reason for the growth of these parties has been the desire of new groups such as the bureaucracy, and sometimes businessmen or workers, to raise the country from economic under-development and social backwardness. Populist parties are therefore less conservative and more egalitarian than traditional parties. This goal is sometimes expressed in terms of Socialism (as in Tanzania), but of a brand of Socialism which is indigenous to the country and in most cases less comprehensive than that which was traditionally put forward in the Soviet Union and other Eastern states. Meanwhile, although populist parties are more democratic than traditional parties, participation is less institutionalised than in the West or East: the idea is to provide some 'communion' between people and government rather than government by the people.

The leaders of these parties are also often charismatic; this accounts for some (but only some) measure of liberalism. Many countries – indeed the majority – are based on single-party systems and opportunities for citizens to express, and more particularly to organise, opposition are limited. Yet these single parties occasionally attempt to take into account the viewpoints of a variety of segments of the society, perhaps at the expense of being practically effective. Populist parties are thus half-way between the authoritarianism of Communist parties and the liberalism of Western parties.

Populism is widespread among Third World countries. Indeed some countries in which the military has banned parties also have populist leaders; but, more often, especially until the 1970s, the military came to power to put forward an *inegalitarian and authoritarian* ideology. Sometimes, however, these regimes are based on a party, single or dominant, as was the case in Paraguay under Stroessner until the late 1980s. These parties are the Third World replicas of the inter-war European fascist parties. They wish to maintain rather than reduce inequalities of wealth and status; they are also authoritarian, indeed more so than traditional–conservative or even populist parties; they are oligarchical, indeed almost monocratic, since the people's place in decision-making remains negligible. Typically, such parties emerge after a few years of a military regime, in Black Africa for instance, and are set up by the military ruler to consolidate the regime – often unsuccessfully, however.

This broad characterisation of parties is only an approximation. In particular, the goals of parties can vary over time. Western European Communist parties have become less radical; some Eastern Communist parties may be becoming more liberal and less egalitarian; many African parties started as left-populist and have gradually moved to the right (as in Egypt); the same movement occurred in Mexico. Indeed, some populist parties have become authoritarian–conservative, even when the same leader remains in power, as with Banda in Malawi. Yet parties broadly cluster around the five main ideological types, partly because of imitation. Liberal–democratic ideas spread throughout Europe in the nineteenth century; Communist parties have traditionally been modelled on the Communist Party of the Soviet Union and changes are far from being universal; populism spread from Mexico and Turkey to many parts of the world, and seemed particularly relevant to the needs of Third World countries. The ideologies of political parties therefore correspond to the characteristics of the various countries in which they have emerged in the last decades of the twentieth century.[18]

Socio-economic structure, groups and goals of political parties

As was pointed out in the first section of this chapter, different groups are likely to lie behind the parties which develop naturally. Thus non-industrial countries are likely to be characterised by parties of the clientele, ethnic and possibly religious types, while industrial countries are likely to be characterised by parties of the class-based type as well as by parties based on clientele, ethnic groups or religious organisations, though particular combinations or exclusions vary in ways which were examined earlier in this chapter.

The relationships between groups and parties appear at first sight to be less clear in the case of 'imposed' parties. Yet these need some groups as well if they are to acquire real strength. Thus, not surprisingly, egalitarian parties tend to develop in industrial countries, China and Cuba being the main exceptions; the difficulties in implementing the Communist regime in China led to the development of a new form of 'rural' Communism ostensibly more adapted to the country, although even this system cannot be said to have been very successful. On the other hand, authoritarian–inegalitarian parties are more likely to succeed where traditional tribal groups are still strong: this is why these regimes are more likely to be found in small or isolated countries.

Populist parties, as was shown earlier, are helped by the emergence of new groups, such as the bureaucracy, as well as by the gradual spread of developmental and 'nationalistic' values. This is sometimes associated with a religious frame of reference, particularly in the Middle East, where the Moslem religion is institutionalised and has been associated with nationalism in the course of the pre-independence period. However, while these developments, which are also often linked to the charisma of the leader, help many parties, and in particular populist parties, the weakness of these organisations often becomes manifest in the long run. Populist parties are therefore often handicapped by the fact that they do not have a strong base: this is one of the reasons why many have proved unable to surmount effectively both their internal divisions and also any opposition coming from outside, and in particular from the military, as has often occurred in Latin America.

Conclusion

The spread of parties in the contemporary world has been rapid and diverse. Parties exist almost everywhere, but their characteristic bases and their goals differ widely, both because of the nature of the society and because of the 'will' of rulers – who often benefitted from favourable circumstances, and in particular from independence movements, in putting forward their ideology. The variety of arrangements has therefore to be examined before one can assess whether, behind the facade of substantial strength, they have a strong organisation and can – or indeed want to – represent and/or mobilise the population; closer examination is also needed in order to assess to what extent parties manage, domesticate, or repress conflict, which is, as we saw, one of the main reasons for their existence. This is the object of the coming chapters which will consider both the structure of parties and the way they form 'systems' within which popular views are channelled. It will then be easier to assess the part they have played and continue to play in contemporary political systems.

Notes

1. See G. Sartori, *Parties and Party Systems* (1976), pp. 42–7.
2. S.P. Huntington, *Political Order in Changing Societies* (1968), p. 407.
3. This is the classic view about the role of parties. See for instance S. Neumann, *Modern Political Parties* (1956), pp. 395–400.
4. See Chapter 7 for a discussion of the distinction between protective and promotional associations.
5. For a discussion of the functions of parties, see S. Neumann, *op. cit.* (1956), *loc. cit.*
6. The distinction was first coined by D.E. Apter in *The Politics of Modernisation* (1964), pp. 182–7 and 206–12.
7. See Chapter 7.
8. The development of ethnic or minority parties in Western Europe has been substantial in the course of the 1970s and 1980s. They sometimes have a geographical dimension, as the minority is also often primarily located in a given area. The growth of these parties has sometimes corresponded to an attempts by 'peripheral' areas to obtain a bigger voice in the political system (or alternatively to demand independence). But the growth has been on a larger scale than might have been anticipated, given the expected trend of advanced industrial countries to become more uniform. On these cleavages see M. Lipset and S. Rokkan (eds), *Party Systems and Voter Alignments* (1967), pp. 23–30.
9. Church parties will tend not to emerge in a country where the influence of the church is overwhelming as the church does not need then to defend its position: thus there is no church party in Ireland.
10. Both the German CDU and the Dutch CDA were created as a result of the widespread belief that the appeal of the church parties would increase in the population if divisions between the denominations were not reflected on the political plane.
11. The question of the failure of Socialist parties in North America, and in particular in the United States, has attracted attention. At its peak, in 1912, the Socialist presidential candidate obtained only 6 per cent of the votes; there were then, however, a number of elected Socialists in a number of states. A number of factors, ranging from the 'immigrant' character of America to the federal and presidential character of the political system, have typically been stressed to account for this failure. The debate is no longer markedly alive, however, possibly in part because of the relative failure of Socialist parties in many Western European countries as well. See L.D. Epstein, *Political Parties in Western Democracies* (1967), in particular at pp. 138–45.
12. On charismatic leadership, see Chapter 19.
13. The Mexican *Partido Revolucionario Institucional* (PRI) is the most successful example of a dominant and near-single party outside the Communist world. See Chapter 11. On the PRI, see R.J. Alexander, *Latin American Political Parties* (1973), pp. 263–79.
14. If a party is purely pragmatic, it will, at least in general, accept the status quo. It has therefore an ideology which is 'conservative' in the sense that it does not wish to make more than minor adjustments as they appear 'necessary'.
15. The ideological differences between leaders and followers have been both noted impressionistically and studied systematically. See for instance L.D. Epstein, *op. cit.*, pp. 290ff.
16. The changes which have taken place in some Communist states, in particular since Gorbachev came to power in the Soviet Union, have of course been considerable and unquestionably resulted in the collapse of the Communist regimes in Eastern European states in 1989, although slow and indeed substantial changes had been underway for some time in Poland and Hungary. Yet these changes have not led to the collapse of Communist regimes everywhere; Communist regimes continue in particular in the Soviet Union and China, as well as in the Third World states in which Communism had been adopted.

17. The notion of 'populist' parties has been widely used to refer to many Third World parties: the term is therefore often used somewhat loosely. Yet the idea does correspond to a type of party which is, in its principles at least, markedly different from both traditional parties and 'reactionary' parties. For a discussion of these parties, see S.M. Lipset, *Political Man* (2nd edn, 1983), in particular pp. 52–4.
18. A massive effort at classifying political parties has been undertaken by K. Janda, *Political Parties: A cross-national survey* (1980). See also A.J. Day and H.W. Degenhardt, *Political Parties of the World* (1980).

10 The structure of political parties

The life and characteristics of political parties markedly depend on their organisation and structure. A party will be representative only if there are mechanisms by which the views of the rank-and-file are transmitted to the top; a party cannot be mobilising unless it has structures which ensure that leaders induce party members and supporters to act according to their wishes. A poorly organised party is manifestly unlikely to achieve representation or mobilisation and therefore to fulfil its basic role.

Not surprisingly, therefore, questions of structure were investigated by early students of political parties. The conclusions which were drawn – and which have not been truly challenged to this day – were that, despite many appearances to the contrary, parties tend to be run in an autocratic or oligarchical manner, whether they are ostensibly 'democratic' or not. Michels thus spoke of an iron law of oligarchy under which all parties operated: the top leadership – the executives and the secretaries – could run the party as they wished; they remained in power for very long periods. Socialist parties, being more 'bureaucratic' than others, were perhaps even more likely to be dominated by oligarchies.[1]

These views have remained by and large conventional wisdom, though they seem less appropriate than in the early part of the twentieth century. This is not so much because the organisations themselves have become more 'democratic'; as a matter of fact, organisations have probably become weaker in many countries, especially in Western Europe, despite the fact that the formal bodies, including councils, executives, regional federations and local branches, still exist and are probably more numerous than in the past.[2] The decline in the effective role of internal organisations is due to two developments which have so to speak squeezed or to some extent by-passed these structures. One of these elements is the larger part played by the population in political life, and in particular the part played by a variety of local interest groups, at least in the West, but to an extent also elsewhere.[3] The other element is constituted by the leadership, which is obviously personalised 127 in much of the Third World and is also probably more personalised than in the past in some of the older parties of the West.[4] As a result, the 'bureaucratic' organisation of the party comes to take second place in a game in which leaders often appeal directly to the people or at least to party supporters; as a result, too, it becomes a little more difficult to decide whether parties are, or are not, oligarchical: to an extent at least, the views of the people – if not necessarily of the party rank-and-file – are taken into account, indeed sometimes against those of the party rank-and-file.

This chapter will therefore examine successively three aspects of the structure of parties. First, the internal arrangements need to be considered in order to see how far parties are centralised and how far they are responsive to the views of the 'activists'. Second, the relationship between parties and the broad mass of their supporters, individually or in groups, needs to be assessed. Third, it is important to look at patterns of leadership: personalised and 'charismatic' leaders are obviously critical to the life of some parties, but there are also other types of rulers. Overall, it is necessary to see how far a responsive leadership emerges in political parties and thus how mobilisation and representativeness can be associated at the top.[5]

Internal structure of parties

The internal structure of parties raises two connected problems. One is technical and relates to the 'extent' of organisation, while the other is 'ideological' and is concerned with the degree to which the party is more or less democratic and more or less representative. Both questions are connected at the level of a third problem, which is that of centralisation: the implantation of a party will have a more or less centralised character depending on the views of founders and leaders about the extent to which the party has to be responsive to the rank-and-file.

Extensiveness

The first question which arises is that of the extent of implantation of political parties at the regional and local levels. An inextensive party is one which does not aim at or does not succeed in being present at the periphery. This can be simply because the party is very small: a party with little electoral support, for instance, is unlikely to be extensive; but parties can also be inextensive because they do not need to cover the country as a result of the clientelistic structure on which they are based. In traditional societies the very idea of 'branches' or 'sections' is simply meaningless: the landlord and his subordinates *are* the articulation of the party at the local level. Parties can also be inextensive if they rely heavily on the support of a parent group, for instance an ethnic or religious group, but even, at least in the early years, on a trade union.

There are substantial differences even among extensive parties. Communist parties have always tended to be more extensive than other parties; Christian and

Socialist parties are usually more extensive than conservative parties, though in northern and central Europe all parties have tended to be very extensive; on the contrary, in France and in North America parties are relatively less extensive.[6] By and large, authoritarian conservative parties are less likely to extend antennae than populist and other left-wing parties, as the former type of party constitutes a rather weaker challenge to existing norms than the latter types. Generally speaking, the more the goals of the society are challenged, the more the party will tend to be extensive. Extensiveness also varies from area to area: a party may have support from a particular group in some areas while trying to implant itself elsewhere.

Centralisation and decentralisation

Centralisation refers to the amount of decision-making which takes place at different levels, but these levels have to be defined. Parties which are above a minimum of extensiveness have at least two levels of activity, central and local; generally, parties can be said to have a maximum of four levels of activity, national, regional (provincial or 'state' in a federation), local (town, constituency or district) and precinct, branch, section or cell. For an assessment of the extent of centralisation, it is reasonable to discard the lowest level as no sizeable party is likely to be run from its branches. The relative position of the second (regional) and third (local) levels can perhaps be examined. Although systematic empirical evidence is still lacking, it seems that parties endowed with a strong second level are more decentralised than parties not so endowed; American and German parties are more decentralised than British or French parties. Where the provincial element is weak and the local element is the stronger of the two, the party is likely to be centralised.[7]

Moreover, centralisation does not need to be (and usually is not) merely territorial; functional decentralisation commonly takes the form of special organisations for women, young people, trade unionists, students, etc. In practice, however, functionally decentralised organs are weaker than territorial organs of decentralisation, possibly for the same reasons as those which account for the strength of territorial sectionalism – the strength of the party organs appears related to the fact that political and administrative organisations are territorial.[8] Functional organs remain ancillary and peripheral and often exist only on paper: this appears to be the case even when the party makes a special effort to implant its functional organs, as is true in Communist parties. Although factory cells have been developed alongside territorial cells, territorial units seem to have remained the strongest elements.

Parties can be ranked in broad terms along a continuum of centralisation–decentralisation. First, authoritarian parties are more likely to be centralised than liberal–democratic parties, whatever formal structure each of them adopts: thus Western European parties, for instance, are decentralised in relation to parties in populist or Communist countries. Second, centralisation increases with the programmatic character of the party within each of the categories. Third, centralisation is affected by the type of broad communal group on which the party is based: parties based on clientele or ethnic groups are likely to be less centralised than parties based on churches or class.[9] Indeed, the extent of decentralisation of the party is likely to depend on the extent of decentralisation of the group. By and large, parties which started from ethnic organisations, such as American parties, are more decentralised than parties which were based, originally at least, on trade unions, while parties based on churches (such as Christian Democratic parties) constitute intermediate cases.

Ideological aspects of structure: 'democracy' and representation

The basic organisation of parties raises a further problem, that of the extent of democracy. Indeed, the problem of centralisation and of decentralisation is related to the question of democracy, as decentralisation might be regarded as a means of enabling the rank-and-file to exercise some influence, though a traditional conservative party may be decentralised and yet be undemocratic, as decisions taken at the intermediate echelons are likely to be taken by small oligarchies.

Moreover, overall, democratic aims may militate against democracy in the party organisation, as a high level of internal democracy will result in more demands coming from the rank-and-file and, therefore, in more *representativeness*: a party with programmatic aims – one which wishes to *mobilise* the population – will therefore be continuously tempted to reduce the extent of democracy within the organisation. In order to appear to resolve the contradiction, authoritarian parties with a 'democratic' ideology (populist and Communist), and to a lesser extent liberal–democratic parties which occupy borderline positions, have developed a theory of representation known in the Communist world as 'democratic centralism' whereby policies are presented to the lower echelons for discussion before the decision is taken – but decisions arrived at (presumably on a majority basis) must not only be obeyed, they must be actively and positively accepted by all. As will be seen in the next section, this tends to affect the type and characteristics of the membership of the party; but the principle of democracy in the context of a 'mobilising' ideology appears formally preserved.[10]

The overall problem of structure and the dynamics of development of structure

The concept of democratic centralism plays a part in determining the extent of centralisation, as well as of democracy and representation, within a political party. It is by considering the impact of such a concept that one can measure and compare, for instance, the role of organs which characterise all large political parties claiming to be democratic, such as party congresses, central committees, inner executives and secretariats. However, the situation is fluid, and although the time span during which parties have been in existence is relatively short, the dynamics of party development have already become complex. The extensiveness of parties is in part related to the type of social environment in which the party developed; the extent of centralisation is also related to the type of social structure. As the polity and the political system change over time, parties which are maintained over a fairly long period tend therefore to be modified. Among liberal–democratic parties, the more conservative and the more progressive have become more alike, in that the former have spread their tentacles and become more centralised, while the latter have become less characterised by 'democratic centralism'. The very inextensive parties of traditional countries have, more often than not, been replaced by more extensive populist parties, but, in some cases, they have themselves become more extensive as many Western conservative parties did in the early part of the twentieth century. Meanwhile, some Communist parties, in Yugoslavia in particular, but also in the Soviet Union, have become more decentralised while also becoming more representative.

External aspects of party structure: members, supporters and associated groups

Members and supporters: the concept of the mass party

Parties wish to affect the environment: they need therefore to be related to the rest of the country. This takes place through various circles of supporters. The large majority now have 'members' in the strict sense of the word, that is to say persons who are legally within the party, while supporters are only psychologically tied to the organisation. But this distinction is often more apparent than real. It was previously given considerable prominence: for instance, Duverger defined as 'mass parties' those which were based on members, while 'cadre parties' were based on clientelism. It seemed to him that the distinction was critical in that it explained the difference between modern and non-modern parties, in both modern and non-modern societies.[11]

There are difficulties with this, however. The distinction is too rigid: an index of 'massness' based on the percentage of card-carrying members among the electors of a party would be of little significance, as some parties which do not define members in this way, such as American parties, would not qualify as mass parties.[12] However, it is not just because of this problem that the distinction needs to be questioned. More fundamentally, Duverger clearly exaggerates the importance given to membership. Studies of party members have repeatedly shown the small, if not even almost wholly insignificant, part played by most members. Membership is not a sign of participation; it merely means association, often of a tenuous kind. It reflects attitudes more than behaviour, and at the same time is an indication of the ability of the organisation to attract sums of money by putting canvassers and other helpers in the field.[13]

However, if membership is viewed as an association, not as a promise of participation, it can be understood in terms of the broader linkage between parties and their supporters. Party membership is a legal manifestation, prompted by party organisation, of a wider notion of party identification, a concept which is more helpful, as it suggests that there is a natural and perhaps permanent allegiance to the political party, similar to the adhesion to a church, an adhesion which is part of the socialisation process.[14]

Such a support will be 'natural' and long-lasting if the party is legitimate. As was noted in Chapter 9, a legitimate party is one which no longer needs to be supported by a group; it therefore has large numbers of direct supporters, who may or may not be members. Rather than define the party by its membership, it is more critical to find the extent to which the party has *identifiers* among its supporters and to see how large is the group of direct and long-lasting supporters who are associated with the party by a bond of allegiance which remains wholly, or almost wholly, unquestioned.[15]

The distinction made by Duverger between 'cadre' and 'mass' parties can be restated in terms of identification, moreover. When a party draws support from the population indirectly, through the allegiance members have to the groups which have helped to constitute the party, there is no element of 'massness' at the basis of party support. This does not mean that such parties are inherently unstable, because the groups (tribal, ethnic, religious, or even class-based) on which the parties are founded may well be legitimate; but the party as such does not have legitimacy or, more precisely, 'mass legitimacy'. What is therefore crucial in the distinction is whether the party has direct mass support or whether groups are a link in the chain: it is on this, and not on the existence or non-existence of legal membership, that the distinction between mass parties and other parties rests.

Parties of a legitimate mass type emerge when they do not need to rely on one or more communal groups for support. Their legitimate mass character develops gradually, as more and more of their supporters identify with them directly and cease to use the 'parent' communal group as their reference point. As a result, the development of legitimate mass parties is a sign that political life is increasingly autonomous and probably often increasingly national.

Legitimate mass parties emerge in a context of natural party development. Yet, in the case of imposed parties as well, attempts are often made to develop party identification in order to strengthen the party and the regime. This is obviously a slow process: the basic lack of legitimacy of the political system as a whole makes for a limited insertion of the party members into the community. Thus such parties are rarely of a real 'mass' type, although membership figures may be high.[16] Indeed, membership is high precisely in order to help the party to proselytise among the population. As a result, in these parties, one can sharply distinguish members from supporters; basic party organisations (cells in Communist parties) are also more closed than the branches or sections of legitimate mass parties. Gradually, the party may become a legitimate mass party but, for this to occur, the distance between members and supporters needs to be reduced and, in reality, the concept of membership needs to lose its clear and sharp character.

Associated groups

Socialist parties are sometimes singled out as being closely linked to groups and associations. Duverger does indeed feel the distinction to be of sufficient importance to warrant the dichotomy between 'direct' and 'indirect' parties being applied to parties on the basis of whether their membership comes from individual members only or from groups such as trade unions and co-operatives.[17] In reality, the association with groups is general and it is a two-way process, from groups to parties and from parties to groups.

First, we know that parties become legitimate through being supported by a broad communal body such as a tribal or clientelistic, ethnic, religious or class-based group. The association gradually becomes less close, however, and, in extreme cases, wholly legitimate parties cease to have any 'special' relationship with any group or, alternatively, have relations with all associations on the basis of the intrinsic importance of their demands. Before this happens, however, the link between party and communal group remains strong and has a special character.

Second, and conversely, imposed political systems often create parties and groups in order to spread their goals and increase the support which they enjoy.[18] The function of general propaganda is mainly exercised by the party, while the (dependent) groups have more specific purposes: they deal for instance with special sections of the population, such as women, the young, etc. If the party (and the political system) become more open, either because the new goals become accepted or because the party compromises its original goals in order to maintain itself in existence, groups also become more independent of the party. The end of this process coincides with the end of the process in the case of natural development; broad communal groups cease to play a part, while parties and associations become independent of each other.

Thus associations are linked to parties when new goals are promoted as with Socialist or Communist parties, or old goals defended against attacks as with authoritarian–inegalitarian parties. But dependent associations may also be created by the party in an effort to free it from being too closely linked to the broad communal group from which it emerged: this occurred in Western Socialist and Christian parties, for instance. The objective is then to achieve the independence of the political party from the broad communal group by building new dependent associations which strengthen that party. The result is a complex criss-crossing of associations and of patterns of allegiance which can be summarised in the following way.

When there is no, or little conflict of goals in the political system, the dependence of groups on political parties is small (as in the United States) and vice versa, the level of dependence at any given moment being measured by the extent to which the party is legitimate in the community – in terms of party identification, for instance.[19]

Where the conflict of goals is sharper, parties are likely to be based at least to an extent on broad communal groups, while they will also create dependent associations, especially if they want to proselytise and mobilise the population.

There will be a criss-crossing of lines of dependence, leading to reciprocal relationships and sometimes competition. As parties become more legitimate, they become more independent from the broad communal groups, but the associations dependent on the parties also tend to acquire more autonomy. Such an evolution may also take place in the context of an imposed system: the evolution of the relationship between the Communist party and the trade unions has taken this form in the Soviet Union in the late 1980s.

On this basis, it is possible to describe the relationship between groups and parties in different types of societies and, more specifically, in the five categories of parties which were identified in the course of the previous chapter.

Traditional conservative parties

Traditional conservative parties are dependent upon broad communal groups, mainly of the clientele or ethnic types (though perhaps in some cases on religious groups as well). Only if a conflict of goals emerges will they produce dependent associations; by then the parties may well have become legitimate. In practice they are more likely to have been superseded by populist or authoritarian–inegalitarian parties: this has been the fate of many traditional conservative parties in Latin America, for instance in Brazil in the early post-war period.

Liberal–democratic parties

Liberal–democratic parties grow through a process of legitimisation which places them near the legitimate mass end of the continuum. They may have developed in a context in which conflicts of goals are relatively low; in this case, dependent organisations are not set up. They may alternatively have developed in a context in which conflicts are higher; in such a case dependent organisations are likely to be created. The first situation corresponds to that of the American parties and of those Conservative and Liberal parties which became legitimate before class-based groups succeeded in becoming important (in Britain in particular). The second corresponds to that of most Western European parties. One can see why not only Socialist parties, but also Christian parties depend on the broad communal groups which helped to make them legitimate. Moreover, the higher the conflict, the more there will be a criss-crossing of group–party special relationships; when conflicts of goals diminish (as is at present the case in Western Europe) these special relationships also tend to diminish. Unless conflicts of goals are once more on the increase, the relationships between Socialist parties or Christian parties and, on the one hand, the broad communal groups from which they started or, on the other hand, the dependent associations which they created will become increasingly looser.

Authoritarian parties

The three groups of authoritarian parties vary depending on the extent to which they propose to introduce new goals and on the extent to which they are legitimate: a populist party such as the Mexican PRI is more legitimate than, for instance, most African parties, and the various associations which are linked to it are also relatively less dependent on it. In general, the more 'progressive' the party goals, the higher the dependence of associations, as the need to proselytise and to mobilise is strongly felt, provided levels of legitimacy are about the same.

The links between parties and individual citizens as well as between parties and groups are thus essential elements in the life of these organisations: their importance dwarfs the question of the relationship between the higher echelons of the party and the activist rank-and-file. This is all the more so since, in many contemporary parties, the mass of the citizens and even the groups to which they are associated often relate directly to what îs perhaps the most crucial element in the life of parties, the leadership.

Leadership patterns

Party leaders are, or may become, national leaders; less frequently, they have already been national leaders. Thus, not surprisingly, there exist relationships and often mutual reinforcement between party leadership and national leadership. But there are also relationships between party leadership and party structure. Indeed they influence each other in a number of complex ways.

Classifications of leadership have been based, for many decades, on Weber's distinction among three types of authority – traditional, bureaucratic–legalistic, and charismatic, the last being more properly referred to, in the reality of political life, as personalised leadership.[20] These are of course ideal types and, in political situations and in particular in modern political and party situations, mixed types are most frequent.

The gradual decline of traditional leadership in contemporary political parties

Given the decline of traditional party structures in the contemporary world, traditional leadership has also declined; it has not disappeared altogether, however. Many leaders, including those of political parties, owe part of their political power to the traditional influence they hold, for instance to the status of their family in their district. Even at present, the influence of aristocratic leaders may be substantial in some Third World countries and indeed in some Western (although not, apparently, Eastern) parties as well. More widespread, however, is the occurence of a relatively limited local following embedded in the social structure: thus doctors, lawyers, middle-sized farmers or industrialists enjoy an advantage in standing for political office in the West, especially in the less industrialised and socially mobile areas, such as parts of Italy, rural France, or the periphery of Europe and North America. The same is true, and indeed to an even greater extent, in many countries of the Third World, and not only in those which are conservative.[21] What is also true, however, is that only in about a dozen countries, located mostly in Central America and in

Western and South-Eastern Asia, does the *top* leadership rely primarily on the authority given by traditional social relationships; this number is slowly declining.

The spread of bureaucratic leadership in Western, Eastern and some Third World parties

Alongside traditional leadership, bureaucratic leadership is relatively more common: bureaucratic leaders are professional politicians who have moved gradually within the party hierarchy on the basis of their talent. This form of leadership is most prevalent in the better established Western parties and in the Communist countries, while it has developed only to a limited extent in the Third World.

In Western European countries, in North America, and in the few other countries of the world where socio-economic developments have followed Western lines (Japan, Australasia and Israel) most parties have been established for long periods – usually for at least half a century and sometimes longer. In these parties, whether of the right or left, the person holding the position of leader, chairman, president, or secretary general has some real authority to lead, not merely the party but indeed the whole nation, as he or she is the recipient of the legitimacy of the party while he or she is leader.

Bureaucratic leadership has traditionally also been common in Eastern Communist countries: it is indeed consistent with the ideology of these regimes that party leadership should be bureaucratic. This seems also a natural consequence of the vastness of the party organisation in all Communist states: those in charge at the various echelons of the party hierarchy are endowed with an aura of authority stemming from the patronage attached to their positions and, traditionally at least, from fear. As time passes, parties become so strong that the power of the leaders and sub-leaders seems to be almost entirely natural.

In the Third World, bureaucratic leadership exists where parties are relatively strong and durable. Many Latin American parties are of recent creation or have had major ups and downs in their fortunes; some, however, have been in existence for long periods. This is the case in particular of the Mexican *Partido Revolucionario Institucional* (PRI), whose leaders owe their influence to the party and to the party alone. Bureaucratic leadership is also strong in the better established parties of the Commonwealth, particularly in the West Indies, East Africa and South Asia.

The relative importance of charismatic leadership around the world

It is charismatic leadership which is typically associated with developing countries, although it exists also in Communist states and indeed even in the West. Pure charismatic leadership is, admittedly, relatively rare in the West. It occurs when the political, social or economic structure faces a major challenge. The depression of the 1930s created situations of this kind, as did decolonisation in the 1940s and 1950s in

France: forms of personalised leadership have thus emerged in Italy, Germany and France. To a lesser extent, a similar development took place in Britain during World War II, when Churchill came to power more as a personalised leader than as a loyal member of the Conservative party. However, partly because the problems faced by Western countries are usually less fundamental and partly because parties are better able to cope with the nation's political problems, *purely* personalised leadership usually plays a minor part in the politics of the West. Yet an element of charisma is also often injected into the professional leadership of parties; it is sometimes claimed that this element is increasing, though this is unsubstantiated by firm evidence.[22] Reagan and Thatcher had a personal following, but then so did F.D. Roosevelt, Lloyd George, Disraeli and Gladstone. Whatever the trend, it is clear that some contemporary Western leaders have a personal following while in power; but these leaders are not necessarily more powerful than those without it. J.F. Kennedy, a relatively charismatic American President, was less successful in policy-making than was Lyndon Johnson, who had little popular support of this kind.

Personalised leadership is common in the East, although this may not appear consistent with Communist ideology. Despite repeated efforts to install 'collective leadership', not merely after Stalin's death in the Soviet Union, but at other times and in other Communist countries, a type of leadership continued to prevail which went beyond the confines of party committees and left a large gap between the top leader and his colleagues.[23] This is partly because several Communist regimes were installed after successful resistance against an occupying country, the original resistance leaders remaining in office for long periods. Not only Mao in China and Tito in Yugoslavia, but Kim Il Sung in North Korea and Castro in Cuba, Ulbricht in East Germany and Stalin himself in the Soviet Union, as well as others, owed their strength to the personal prestige gained during wars of independence or in guerilla action. It was through resistance against the Soviet Union itself, in the 1950s and 1960s, that Tito in Yugoslavia, Gomulka in Poland for a period, and Ceauçescu in Romania also acquired a personal following.

In the Third World, personalised leadership is widespread: a substantial number of parties (and of states) have been built around the strength of individual leaders.[24] However, it is not present everywhere: in Latin America, for instance, despite the personalisation of power which the presidential system tends to achieve, many party leaders can be said to be 'bureaucratic–legalistic' rather than 'charismatic'.[25] Moreover, even in Black Africa where personalised leaders have been strong in the political parties, they have often been unable to build extensive organisations and to ensure that they are not toppled by military coups. This has been particularly the case outside the Commonwealth.

The achievements of leaders in strengthening political parties

Throughout the Third World, though to a greater extent in Africa and Asia than in Latin America, strong leaders have created political parties. These parties seem to dominate the political life of the country, at least for a time, usually as a result of severe restrictions brought to bear on opponents. In perhaps a third of the countries of the world, political life in general, and the party system in particular, would be different if parties had not been created by a powerful leader.[26]

It is more difficult to disentangle the reality of party strength from that of the leader, however.[27] In many countries which are characterised by a party system centred around the founder of the sole or major party, the extent and effectiveness of that party are not well-known; moreover, as the political party – and indeed the state itself – are often recent creations, neither the long-term effect of the party nor its chances of survival can be predicted with even moderate assurance. A measure of the success of the party can be gauged by examining the respective fates of parties created in the post-war period, however. In sixty-four countries, a party was created by the deliberate action of a leader, in most cases in the late 1950s or early 1960s. In eighteen of these countries the leader was still in power in 1990; in twenty-one of them, the leader and his party had been toppled by a coup; in twenty-five, the disappearance of the leader (by death or succession) was followed by the maintenance of the party at least as an important force in the community. Assuming that leaders who remained in office were somewhat stronger than those who were deposed, we may conclude that the contribution of leaders to the creation of effective political parties has been significant in a substantial number of countries of the Third World.[28]

The 1950s and 1960s were exceptional, however, as a large number of new states became independent – a development not likely to recur in the coming decades. A better guide to the 'normal' rate at which new parties are founded and maintained by charismatic leaders is provided by Western Europe, where two parties were created or recreated by a leader (the French Gaullist party and the German CDU), and by Latin America where four parties – the Peronist party in Argentina, the Venezuelan *Accion Democratica*, APRA in Peru, and MNR in Bolivia – have survived their leader despite military coups. This much smaller rate of emergence of successful parties corresponds more closely to that pertaining before World War II: in every generation, perhaps a handful of leaders maintained and developed a really strong party in their countries (Mexico and Turkey being the main examples in the 1920s).

Thus leaders can occasionally build a party successfully. They can also help to strengthen an existing party, but this is rather difficult to measure. In the West and in the Third World a number of them had a strong effect on the fate of the parties which they led – among the best known examples are Brandt in the case of the German Socialist party, Mrs Thatcher in the case of the British Conservative party, Mitterrand in the case of the French Socialist party, Craxi in the case of the Italian Socialist party and Mrs Ghandi in the case of the Indian Congress party (despite its splits). Conversely, it is also possible to find numerous examples of leaders who inherited a rather strong party and only succeeded in weakening its strength. Thus while party leaders may not have as much power as is sometimes claimed, in particular in the Third World, they appear to have a definite influence on the fate of the organisations which they lead and, occasionally, may place in orbit a party which will survive their disappearance.

Conclusion

Parties have such varied structures that a brief analysis can show only broad lines and elicit trends, while leaving most concrete developments to more detailed (and hopefully comparative) studies. But trends and broad lines exist. Parties do not resemble each other by accident, nor do they differ for fortuitous reasons. It may be fortuitous that a particular Socialist party should include among its members about 10 per cent of its electors while another includes only 5 per cent; it may be fortuitous that a particular country should have gained a particular leader, for instance at independence, rather than another. But if one looks at patterns of party development, structural characteristics tend to emerge clearly. Traditional parties have common characteristics, though 'pure cases' become increasingly rare through the combined development of legitimate and imposed parties. Parties of the 'legitimate mass' type have many common traits. This is sometimes seen as a sign of decrease in the weight of parties, and deprecated on grounds of 'convergence' between right and left, but this convergence appears inevitable. The dilemma between charisma and bureaucracy in imposed political parties has to be faced everywhere, and affects party extensiveness and centralisation, the nature of the bond of allegiance between leaders or supporters and the relationship with other organisations. Thus the dynamics of party structures are real even if not wholly apparent, and even if many studies need to be undertaken before a truly general model is fully developed.

Notes

1. The three 'classics' on political parties are M. Ostrogorski, *Democracy and the Organisation of Political Parties* (1902), R. Michels, *Political Parties* (1914), and M. Duverger, *Political Parties*, first published in French in 1951 and in English in 1955. Duverger's is the only truly cross-national work, though within the context of Atlantic and Communist countries only (with occasional references to Latin America, Turkey, and Israel). Weber's work was not primarily directed to the study of parties, but his presentation of three types of leadership remains of great importance for subsequent studies on parties. See in particular *The Theory of Social and Economic Organisation* (1947) and *Basic Concepts in Sociology* (1962).
2. There is still no comprehensive study of party members and of the liveliness of party organisations across Western Europe. Some evidence about trends can be found from national monographies. A systematic examination of membership of socialist parties was undertaken by S. Bartolini, 'The membership of mass parties: the social democractic experience, 1889–1978' in H. Daalder and P. Mair (eds), *Western European Party Systems* (1983).
3. The development of referenda is one of the ways in which the population is becoming more involved. See Chapter 23.

4. See Chapter 19, on leadership.
5. See H. Daalder and P. Mair (eds), (1983) *op. cit.*, *passim* and L. Epstein, *Political Parties in Western Democracies* (1967).
6. French parties are notoriously weak and little organised, even since the advent of the Fifth Republic. See for instance J.R. Frears, *Political Parties and Elections in the French Fifth Republic* (1977).
7. The decentralised character of American parties is well-known: it is typically argued that there are as many parties as there are states. Western European parties are typically markedly more centralised, except Swiss and perhaps German parties. See for instance, L.D. Epstein, *op. cit.*, Chapter 5, *passim* and in particular pp. 98–103.
8. The structure of the state is important in this context: in general parties are more decentralised in federal countries, though there are exceptions, both outside Europe and in Europe (for instance in Austria). See also Chapter 6, on sectionalism.
9. Parties based on clientele or on ethnic groups are often territorially based and therefore naturally decentralised. This also happens in some church-based parties, as in the Italian *Democrazia Cristiana*, though this is in part for reasons of clientelism. See R.E.M. Irving, *The Christian Democratic Parties of Western Europe* (1979).
10. The reality may be very different and, in practice, there may be little democracy.
11. See M. Duverger, *op. cit.*, pp. 62–90. See also J. Blondel, 'Mass parties in industrialised societies' in J. Blondel, *A Reader in Comparative Government* (1969), pp. 117–26.
12. See L. Epstein, *op. cit.*, pp. 98–129.
13. See S. Bartolini, *op. cit.*, pp. 182–91.
14. One can understand why strong supporters of parties would have wished members to be truly closely linked to their parties. Yet it is also quite understandable that, in practice, loyalty should be more limited and closer to a vague sense of belonging than to a genuine feeling of communion.
15. For an examination of party identification, see A. Campbell *et al.*, *The American Voter* (1960), pp. 120–67. The concept has been used since in connection with European countries. See in particular, I. Budge *et al.* (eds), *Party Identification and Beyond* (1976).
16. Party membership figures were high in countries under the Communist regime, though it is sometimes argued that they were low, in the sense that the whole population could theoretically have belonged to the sole party; in reality, one of the constraints is that it has been typically difficult to join the Communist party in Eastern countries, as the leaders have wanted to be sure of the reliability of members. Overall, these parties do not seem to be really of a 'mass' type, precisely because membership is only achieved after some efforts on the part of the potential candidates.
17. M. Duverger, *op. cit.*, pp. 5–17. The most common example of an indirect party is the British Labour party, but the Mexican PRI also has this character, as it is constituted on a 'corporate' basis and includes large numbers of bodies which form its constituent parts: see R.J. Alexander, *Latin American Political Parties* (1973), pp. 263–79.
18. It was noted that many associations were in fact the dependent organisations of parties. See Chapter 7.
19. In the United States, groups and parties are almost completely independent of each other, though some trade unions have tended to be often associated with the Democratic party.
20. On personalised leadership, see Chapter 19, and also M. Weber, *Economy and Society* (1968), vol. 1, pp. 215–6.
21. The advantage which professional groups enjoy can be seen in particular from the memberships of legislatures. See Chapter 17.
22. Among the reasons which are given for the increase in personalised leadership in the West is the growth of the mass media and of television in particular. See Chapter 19.
23. The growth of personalised leadership in Eastern Communist countries is both paradoxical and very real. It is paradoxical, since Marxism is based on the primacy of the 'underlying forces' in society and denies the strength of personalities as real engines of

history; yet it is very real, as the part played by such leaders as Stalin, Kruschev, Gorbachev, Tito, Mao Tse-tung, and many others indicates. See also Chapter 19.

24. See Chapter 19. For a typology of leadership in the Third World, see T.H. Jackson and C.G. Rosberg, *Personal Rule in Black Africa* (1982).

25. Examples of 'bureaucratic–legalistic' rule can be found for instance among Venezuelan, Colombian, Costa Rican, or pre-1970 Chilean presidents.

26. The number of parties created by leaders is vast. It is relatively small in Western Europe, although a well-known example is that of the Gaullist party in France. A large number of African parties have been created by individual leaders, for instance in Egypt, Zaire, Malawi, or so developed by their early leaders that this was tantamount to creation, as in Tanzania, Zambia, Kenya, Ivory Coast. Similar examples can be found in Asia and Latin America, though on a more limited scale.

27. See Chapter 14, for a discussion of the 'weight' of parties in different societies.

28. See the Appendix for a list of countries in which party development was stable or unstable in the post-independence period.

11 | Single-party systems

Types and broad characteristics of party systems

Parties do not exist in isolation: they are parts, as Sartori suggests.[1] The character and strength of each part cannot be fully understood without taking into account the character and strength of the other parts. This is obvious in the case, which would seem to be the most natural, of systems consisting of more than one party; but it is also true when only one party officially or apparently exists – that is to say in single-party systems. Alongside this single party which is in the limelight, there will exist, in the wings, other organisations. Sometimes these are forgotten because they are small and insignificant; sometimes they are potentially large and are repressed by a variety of means since they constitute a threat to those who are in power. However, in all cases, the setting up of a single-party system indicates that the rulers wish to organise the population towards a goal which not everyone shares or shares with the same intensity, and which therefore is (or could be) undermined by opposition parties.[2]

The total absence of opposition thus manifests itself, not in the single-party system, but in the system where no parties exist at all, provided, as was pointed out in Chapter 9, that this 'no-party' system is truly natural and is not the result of the repression of pre-existing parties by rulers (typically military) who wish to establish a new order. Real 'no-party' systems, widespread in the past, have become rare in the contemporary world, as was also pointed out in Chapter 9. From the late 1960s to the 1980s, the number of true no-party polities has been reduced to about a dozen, five of which are oil-rich dynastic states which often employ large numbers of immigrants who cannot and may not wish to participate in the political life of the host country. Meanwhile, the states where parties have been forcibly abolished have been relatively more numerous, though they decreased markedly in number in the 1980s. Moreover, the group does not include the same countries at different points in time: no military non-party regime of 1970 was still in existence twenty years later

(see Table 11.1)

Table 11.1 Party systems around the world in 1989

	No party		One party	More than one party	Total
	Traditional	Military			
Atlantic	0	0	0	23	23
Eastern Europe and North Asia	0	0	15	0	15
Middle East and North Africa	8	0	8	6	22
South and South-East Asia	5	2	4	13	24
Africa south of Sahara	1	8	32	5	46
Latin America	0	2	5	26	33
Total	14	12	64	73	163
Percentage	9	7	39	45	100

The contemporary world is thus divided essentially into single-party systems and systems of more than one party, with very few countries permanently outside one or the other group and rather more being temporarily, so to speak, on the sidelines. The conditions under which the military is likely to intervene and replace a civilian regime and (temporarily) abolish parties will be examined later; such an intervention is clearly indicative of the inability of parties in that country to command sufficient authority and is thus evidence of party weakness.[3] The main distinction which has to be accounted for is therefore that between single party systems and systems of more than one party, which has become the *summa divisio* of contemporary political systems.

While this distinction is manifestly crucial, it is not altogether clear-cut, nor is it exclusively a question of the number of parties. It is not clear-cut because single-party systems can be viewed more as an extreme case than as a self-contained category. There are countries which have only one party: this is indeed more likely to be the result of official imposition than of a natural development. But, in many other cases, the system is *de facto* one party because that party is so dominant that the other organisations are, for practical purposes, irrelevant; yet these other organisations nonetheless exist. This being the case, there is no longer a precise boundary between single-party systems and systems of more than one party: there is in reality a borderline area between single-party systems and systems of more than one party. This borderline area is or has been occupied by a substantial number of countries, from Mexico to Egypt, from Nicaragua to Taiwan, and from Madagascar to Singapore. Indeed this borderline area could be said to include systems in which a number of parties are permanently linked in a 'forced' coalition dominated by one partner: this has been the case for decades in East Germany, Poland and Czechoslovakia.[4]

It seems reasonable to state that a system is, in effect, single-party if one or both of two conditions obtain. One would be where one party is truly dominant; this can be measured in terms of votes or seats in the legislature. Thus a single-party system could be defined as one in which the dominant party obtains at least 80 per cent of votes or seats in at least two elections (in order to exclude what could be viewed as freak situations). The other would be where one party forces other parties into an electoral and governmental pact such that electors have no other choice but to vote for the candidates of the coalition or to abstain.

Party systems are obviously defined, in the first instance, by the number of parties which compose them; indeed, as will be seen in Chapter 12, the relative strength of these parties is also important in systems of more than one party. But party systems are also defined by other characteristics: it is obvious that a Communist single-party system is different from a traditional conservative single-party system. Overall, taking into account the elements which were analysed in the previous two chapters, three further characteristics of party systems, whether of one party or of more than one, need to be taken into account.

The first of these characteristics is constituted by the nature of support for the party or parties. Are the parties of a legitimate mass kind or do they depend heavily on a group, which may indeed be the state? Second, the analysis of party systems has to take ideologies into account: a two-party system in which both parties agree on most issues differs from a two-party system in which the parties are widely separated; a single-party system in which the prevailing ideology is of a traditional conservative kind differs from a Communist single-party system. Third, the analysis needs to take into account the structural characteristics of the party or parties: extensiveness, centralisation, nature of leadership all give parties a different outlook.

The result may well be that some single-party systems are more similar to systems of more than one party than to other single-party systems, as the difference among single-party systems and among systems of more than one party can be very large. This chapter, which is devoted to single-party systems, will examine the spread of these systems across the world and the variations over time of this spread as well as the duration or longevity of these systems, and will consider the bases of support, the goals and ideologies, and the structure of single-party systems. It will then be possible to assess whether one can genuinely refer to single-party systems as a type or merely as a broad category.

Overview of single-party systems

In the late 1980s, two-fifths of the world polities could be classified as single-party systems. The proportion has increased a little over the post World War II period, but not appreciably since the 1950s; it has decreased somewhat in the late 1980s. Geographically, as Table 11.1 shows, single-party systems can be found primarily in three areas of the world – the Communist Eastern European and North Asian area, where all the countries were single-party systems until the late 1980s and in many of which major changes took place suddenly in 1989, Black Africa, where two-thirds of the States are single-party systems, and the Middle East and North Africa, where the proportion of single-party systems is about average. There are no single-party systems in the Atlantic area (since Portugal and Spain became liberal democracies in the mid-seventies); in South and South-East Asia and in Latin America this type of rule exists in almost one-sixth of the polities. Thus Communist regimes have long constituted, since well before the 1990s, a minority of the single-party systems, even if one includes among them countries such as Ethiopia and the ex-Portuguese colonies, such as Angola and Mozambique: consequently, one can expect the structure of the state, the goals, the bases of support and the organisations of the party to vary markedly among single-party systems.

Although single-party systems are now appreciably more numerous outside the Communist world than inside it, a situation which is reinforced by the fact that single-party systems are on the decline in the Communist area, single-party systems are often regarded as being typically a Communist phenomenon. There is some justification in this impression, as Communist systems are those which have both elaborated the theory and implemented the practice of single-party rule to the highest level. The nature of the Communist ideology, combined with the concept of the 'vanguard of the proletariat', placed the (single) party at the centre of the political system, while the organs of the state (government, legislature, local bodies) were reduced to a dependent position. It is therefore true to state that such a 'total' conception of the single-party system gives Communist regimes a very special position.

Yet Communist systems were not alone in 'inventing' the model of the single-party system in the early part of the twentieth century. The conservative and inegalitarian version was developed and indeed implemented by Italian Fascism and German Nazism in the inter-war period; these were imitated in turn by a number of European rulers, in particular in Portugal and Spain where a Fascist-type single-party system remained in existence until the 1970s. Meanwhile, Turkey had a 'populist' single-party system after World War I and this example was followed by Mexico, which was to have the most successful single-party system of the non-Communist world. Thus, although the Communist ideology was a crucial element in the development of the theory and practice of single-party systems, it was not alone; with the multiplication of both populist and inegalitarian–authoritarian single-party systems, the Communist model had come to constitute only a minority.[5]

The formal status of single-party systems

It was noted earlier that the borderline between single-party systems and systems of more than one party is rather difficult to locate; indeed, the distinction between single-party systems and 'no-party' systems is somewhat unclear. The extent to which a system can be defined as 'one-party' depends on the role which that party plays in political and social life. If the party is very weak and rather formal the decisions taken by the government are only nominally those of the party. In a number of cases, in particular in Black Africa, it is difficult to say whether the party – which may have been set up by the national leader, often a few years after a coup has taken place – is more than a formal organisation designed to give more credibility to the regime.

Single-party systems arise in three types of situation. The first, which is the most common and also the most rigid and formal, is that which results from a constitutional or legal position. This has traditionally been the case in the Soviet Union and in the large majority of Communist states, from Yugoslavia to North Korea and from Cuba to Vietnam: the party has the legal monopoly of representation and mobilisation in the nation, and there may not be any other political organisations designed to unite parts of the population. Technically, this situation contrasts with the enforced coalition arrangements which have existed traditionally in Poland, East Germany and Czechoslovakia: a number of other parties have been allowed in these countries but their representation has been ensured, until the late 1980s, through a combined list presented to the electors. There is therefore little difference in practice between such systems and those of the other Communist countries, although the situation has been described as 'hegemonic' rather than 'monocentrist'.[6]

Legally enforced single-party systems do not exist only in Communist states, however, even if one includes among these the African countries which, like the ex-Portuguese colonies, have fully adopted a Marxist system of government. The single-party system is also a legal requirement in such diverse political systems as Benin, Zaire and Malawi. In such polities the single-party system can be as rigidly enforced as in Communist countries, although conceptions about the character of the party may be vastly different, in particular because it is assumed that every citizen should be a member of the party.

The second form of development of single-party systems arises from what might be termed extra-constitutional repression of opposition: this occurs by means of preventive action against opponents. The extent of this repression is difficult to measure, but it appears common. This type of development is often the prelude to the legal establishment of a one-party state: in Kenya, Zambia, or Zimbabwe, for instance, a number of years elapsed between independence and the official installation of the single-party system. During that period, the opposition was harrassed in a number of ways; in the case of Zimbabwe (as indeed in some other countries) the single-party system was achieved by means of a forced merger of a previously harrassed opposition party. Perhaps the best example of such a single-party system is that of Mexico where, for over fifty years, the *Partido Revolucionario Institucional* (PRI) managed to remain the overwhelmingly dominant force without the country ever being technically single-party: the other parties were simply given little chance at the polls.[7]

The third type of one-party system is of a 'natural' kind: it emerges when a party is, without overt repression, the dominant force in the country; any pressure which might be exercised would be of a cultural rather than of a political or legal kind. This type of natural single-party system has become less common in the last decades of the twentieth century, although prior to this it prevailed more frequently; it tends to exist more at the level of regions than at the national level, and to remain in existence more frequently in small states, such as the Gambia in West Africa or some of the smaller countries of the Caribbean. At the regional level, the predominance of one party can sometimes be found in Western countries: the large dominance of the Democratic party in some of the southern States of the United States had this character, as did the dominance of conservative or Socialist parties respectively in some remote areas and in some traditional industrial areas. In practice this type of situation tends gradually to give way to a more competitive system – or else the dominant party has to use a variety of repressive measures in order to maintain its hold.[8]

The goals of single-party systems

The distinction between legally entrenched, *de facto* repressive, and natural single-party systems suggests that there are major differences in the goals of these parties. Moreover, it can be recalled that Nazi Germany, Fascist Italy or Franco's Spain were single-party systems: these regimes had strongly different aims from those of Communist systems. If one refers to the three dimensions of goals which were described in Chapter 3 (participation, means of intervention, and socio-economic aims), one can find single-party systems corresponding to almost every goal, except true fully fledged liberalism, although, even in the dimension of means, the extent of repression put forward by single-party systems can vary appreciably.

The best-known single-party systems of the contemporary world are of course the Communist systems, whose goals are authoritarian, relatively participationist, and egalitarian. Even among the more orthodox regimes, however, there are increasing moves towards liberalisation (as well as a decreasing emphasis on socio-economic equality). One of the ways in which some liberalisation within the party has taken place has been by allowing a degree of choice at elections, especially at the local level: all candidates are sponsored by the party, but electors (or party members) can choose among a larger number of candidates than there are posts. This process is leading gradually to greater competition and to a loosening of the stringent rules which characterise selection mechanisms in Communist states. Both this change and the move in the direction of 'free enterprise' suggest that even Communist single-party systems are no longer so distant from liberal–democratic parties.[9]

Yet Communist single-party systems constitute a minority of single-party systems, even if one adds the six to ten Black African polities which describe themselves as Marxist. The majority of single-party systems propounds a variety of other goals, specifically traditional conservative, authoritarian–inegalitarian, and populist, this last category being the largest of the three.

Traditional conservative single-party systems have become relatively rare: this is to be expected, as a result of the widespread emphasis towards development in the contemporary world as well as because such single-party systems are likely to be unable, over time, to prevent the emergence of opposition parties unless they increase repression and thus in part change their goals. The best examples are thus dominant single-party systems in small and isolated countries, although, even there, the threat posed by opposition leads frequently to greater imposition. The traditional conservative parties of Lesotho or Brunei have thus reinforced their hold over the population by means of repressing the opposition.[10]

Thus traditional single-party systems of the dominant variety either lead to systems of more than one party or change their goals and become authoritarian–inegalitarian. This last category is appreciably smaller than in the inter-war period, when Fascist and Nazi ideologies were on the ascendant, or in the 1940s and 1950s; a number of Central American Republics (El Salvador, Honduras, Nicaragua) were then ruled by authoritarian–inegalitarian single-party systems for long periods. By the 1980s, this group included primarily countries which appeared to be remnants of the past, such as the fully fledged single-party system of Malawi or the dominant authoritarian–inegalitarian single-party systems of Paraguay and Taiwan, although, in these last two cases, some changes occurred, perhaps temporarily, in the second half of the 1980s.

In the late 1980s, populist single-party systems were the largest group of the forty to forty-five single-party systems outside the Communist world, at least thirty of which could be described as populist; the large majority were in Black Africa (which accounted for almost exactly half the single-party systems in existence). Their socio-economic goals vary appreciably, although there is an overall emphasis on development. Some populist single-party systems can thus be described as 'right-wing' since they espouse a 'free enterprise' philosophy: the prototypes are the Ivory Coast and Kenya, while the PRI in Mexico probably has the same aims, and Zaire may also be associated with this group. There are also single-party systems with middle-of-the-road goals where some part is played by private business alongside state enterprises: Tunisia and Cameroon fall into this category. In the case of Iran, which has been a dominant single-party system since the fall of the Shah, the economic goals are relatively egalitarian, but the basic objective is to apply Muslim principles, though these have been somewhat toned down since the death of Khomeini. Third, there is a substantial group of populist countries with overtly Socialist aims, though the kind of Socialism which they practice is different from that of Communist countries: this is or was the case in Algeria, Zambia, and Tanzania. Changes have occurred in the goals of some of these polities, in part as a result of the economic difficulties which they encountered since the 1970s; some of them, Algeria in particular, have been moving towards more middle-of-the-road socio-economic policies (and indeed, in theory at least, towards a system of more than one party). Finally, a number of regimes are – or claim to be – Marxist, though they have eventually come to adopt populist goals: Benin, the Congo, or Ethiopia are examples. Madagascar was also Marxist for a short period, after having had first adopted a somewhat conservative form of populism.

These single-party systems are populist because of the stress placed on development; they are also populist because some importance is given to participation, though also to a varying degree. Some countries, such as Tanzania, allow for a multiplicity of candidates from which electors can choose, though all are within the party; others do not. The level of repression also varies: it is appreciably milder in some countries, such as Mexico or Tunisia, than in others, such as Zaire.[11] There is in all cases, however, a limit to the extent to which opposition is tolerated: even in the mildest of populist single-party systems, indeed in the mildest of single-party systems *tout court*, some degree of repression takes place. While single-party systems can come relatively close to liberalism, they do not and probably cannot practise fully-fledged liberalism.

Bases of support

Single-party systems are characterised by a high percentage of organisations lacking natural bases of support. They often emerged after a long and difficult process of decolonisation, with the help of a foreign power, or on the basis of a military regime: this gives an artificial character to their development and accounts for many of the difficulties which they encounter. These problems are compounded by the fact that this artificial development takes place in societies in which traditional communal groups are often strong. In Black Africa, for instance, traditional tribal groups constitute the main way in which the population is organised: a problem of nation-building thus usually arises, as was seen in Chapter 6, since the geographical boundaries of these traditional groups rarely coincide with the boundaries of the state which emerged after the decolonisation process. The development of single-party systems thus takes the form of a battle between a newly established organisation attempting to broaden its base and communal groups which are likely to maintain their hold over large segments of the population.

Admittedly, this is not always the case; the traditional single-party systems are based, on the contrary, on the strength of traditional groups, tribal, ethnic, and occasionally religious, but rarely do such groups coincide with the boundaries of the state. This is why traditional single-party systems are likely to be found in small countries in which there is limited potential for the geographical coexistence of more than one tribe. Elsewhere, the groups are likely to lead to the development of more than one party, as will be seen in the next chapter. Consequently, single-party systems tend to exist at the regional rather than at the national level, a situation which has occasionally resulted in secession attempts, as occurred in Zaire or Nigeria in the 1960s. This situation is a further reason, alongside the desire for development, which has militated against the emergence or the maintenance of traditional single-party systems.

Granted therefore that, both in order to achieve their 'modernising' goals and in order to strengthen the nation, single-party systems come in conflict with at least some of the pre-existing structures, most of them are faced with a dilemma. Either they forge ahead in the direction in which they wish to go, attempt to modify the social structure, and hope to undermine the traditional groups after a period; or they try to accommodate these groups, for instance by accepting within the party chiefs and other traditional leaders, at the risk of having to modify their policy goals and of still being unable to unify the nation.[12]

Communist single-party systems are those which pushed furthest in the former direction. They endeavoured to break traditional groups; some of them even claimed that they wished to create a 'new man'. These efforts have had to be buttressed by considerable repression; in the Eastern European states, occupation by the Soviet Union was, to say the least, a considerable help to regimes which might not otherwise have emerged at all (this was the case even in Czechoslovakia where the Communist party was naturally strong) and which almost certainly would not have lasted. Moreover, Communist regimes in Europe and Asia did not have to face the issue of nation-building (except in East Germany); they could even rely to an extent on some support of a nationalistic character. Nor were they confronted with strong tribal or ethnic groups; only in Poland did they face the organised resistance of the church – a resistance which the Polish Workers, (i.e. Communist) party did not succeed in breaking and which indeed formed the basis of the independent trade union Solidarity. Yet, despite these relative advantages, Communist single-party systems did not succeed in achieving the transformations which they hoped for: the 'new man' did not emerge. As liberalisation began to take place and indeed increased, changes in policy goals resulted in a move away from socio-economic egalitarianism in some countries while, in others, the regime collapsed altogether.[13]

The single-party systems which have adopted similar aims in Black Africa (such as the ex-Portuguese colonies or Ethiopia) have been engaged in considerable repression and even in fighting civil wars, a situation which resulted at least in part from the policies which were put forward in a context where the base of support of these regimes was somewhat limited. Populist systems which adopted less egalitarian goals usually avoided such major conflicts, but they typically encountered problems of support, even where, as in Tanzania, tribes were relatively weak and did not constitute a major threat to the regime: in the course of the 1980s the Tanzanian single party has had to tone down many of its goals.[14] The opposition from the tribal groups, or at least from some of them, has been strong in many countries; it has in a number of cases led to the overthrow of the single party – one of the first and best-known cases of such an overthrow being that of Nkrumah's Convention People's Party in Ghana in 1966.[15]

It is thus not surprising that many single-party systems should have attempted to diminish these tensions by 'accommodating' tribal groups. Indeed, most single-party systems accommodate some tribal groups because their leader and his entourage originate from these groups. On this basis, some populist systems appear to be trying to push forward their goals for the whole nation with the support of only a fraction of the population – a support which is given, not because of the policy goals themselves, but for tribal reasons. Such a state of affairs naturally leads to tension. In some cases, as in Burundi, these tensions resulted in major tribal violence; in Uganda violence was also considerable, and even in Zimbabwe and in Zambia tribal oppositions led to major acts of repression. In Iran, repression of opposition to the religious philosophy of the regime has also been fierce.[16]

Regimes which wish to avoid being associated only with some of the groups and which attempt to increase the base of their support will therefore practise a policy of overall 'accommodation'. The country is consequently more peaceful; nation-building may even take place more smoothly. But these strategies cannot be adopted without to some extent abandoning the original populist policy goals. The party may become so dominated by traditional groups that it ceases to be populist and, in effect, becomes traditional. The danger is then of a different character: the modernising elements of the society may become so disaffected that they want to stage a coup. This occurred in Liberia, a country which was ruled for a very long period by a traditional single party, the True Whig party.[17]

The problem of the bases of support in single-party systems appears intractable. Single-party systems have a relatively narrow social base unless exceptionally they emanate from a traditional group. Efforts to extend this base lead to major conflicts or entail a degree of 'accommodation' which results in 'modernising' policies being toned down and the goals of the party severely curtailed. Only in very few cases, as in Kenya, the Ivory Coast or Mexico, have single-party systems appeared able to steer a middle course, though, even there, they had to abandon many of their original goals and thus created discontent among the 'progressive' groups. The problem of support in single-party systems cannot be avoided: sooner or later, all are confronted with it.

Structure of parties in single-party systems

Given the extreme diversity of goals and bases of support of parties in single-party systems, it is not surprising to find that the structure of these parties is also extremely varied. Single-party systems also differ markedly in the extent to which the reality of the structure differs from what is formally claimed by leaders. This is to be expected among parties which attempt rapidly, if not suddenly, to achieve goals of nation-building and of development: the resources required to achieve these goals and to educate the population are simply not available.

Traditional single-party systems have almost no structure at all; they depend entirely on the social groups, tribal or clientelistic, on which they are based to recruit their leaders and run the country. The party is then no more than a loose confederacy of local and regional notables who remain unchallenged because of the strength of their hold on the population.[18] Such traditional single-party systems have become rare, as was seen earlier. They are more commonly found in the contemporary world in association with other types of arrangements and in certain regions; they are important because they help the observer to understand many of the characteristics of single-party systems of the 'accommodating' variety, such as those of the Ivory Coast or Kenya.

What could be labelled the 'modern' single-party system is based on a wholly different model of organisation, which is epitomised by the structure of Communist parties. The aim, here, is to mobilise the population towards new goals by creating a dedicated elite whose main function is to proselytise, not to represent. This means both a considerable presence of the party across the country and a degree of restriction in the size of the membership. Extensiveness is further helped by the setting-up of large and numerous dependent associations covering specific sections of the population and various types of activities. Yet the dominance of the centre is ensured, or at least was traditionally ensured, by the technique of 'democratic centralism', which was referred to in the last chapter.[19] Restrictions on membership are relative rather than absolute. With a membership of over 17 million the membership of the Communist party of the Soviet Union cannot be said to be small by any standards; it constitutes about 10 per cent of the adult population of the country. The Chinese Communist party has 35 million members; although this constitutes 'only' about 6 per cent of the adult population, the figure is clearly impressive. None the less, the conception put forward by Communist organisations is that membership should be obtained with some difficulty, after a time of apprenticeship, during which the proselytising capabilities of the candidates can be tested.

In the Soviet Union and the European and Asian Communist states, the party is or was a truly powerful organisation, though there have always been degrees of effectiveness. The Polish United Workers' party suffered a considerable loss of prestige in the early 1980s at the height of the Solidarity campaign; it never recovered from this setback, as the first free elections which took place in 1989 and their aftermath demonstrated. The events of late 1989 showed that the Polish party was not the only ruling Communist party whose future was in question. While the Communist parties of Hungary, Czechoslovakia, East Germany, and Bulgaria endeavoured to prevent a catastrophic decline by changing their goals, their basic structure, and in some cases even their name, the Romanian party could not stop a strident backlash arising from the sudden collapse of its leader Ceauçescu. This last development occurred in large part because the Romanian party displayed, alongside the North Korean party, another characteristic of many populist or authoritarian–inegalitarian single-party systems, namely a marked dependence on the rulers; they can be regarded as huge praetorian guards working for the benefit of these rulers.[20]

While the Communist single-party model may be in part imitated in the Third World, major variations stem both from the diversity of goals and from the conditions under which the parties are set up. There has indeed been some deterioration of these conditions since the 1960s. Earlier, some relatively well-structured parties were established, for instance in the Ivory Coast, Kenya, Guinea and Zambia, in Tanzania during the pre-independence struggle, in Syria and Iraq (the Baath party) against what was viewed as a reactionary regime, or in Egypt (the Arab Socialist Union) after a military coup. The structure of these parties is less tight than that of Communist parties: this had already been the case with the *Partido Revolucionario Institucional* (PRI) which has dominated Mexican politics for over half a century. That party combines representation and mobilisation by being based on a number of component bodies which 'cover' the various productive forces in the nation (workers, peasants, etc.). Its pyramidal structure coincides with the social structure, but, unlike a traditional dominant party, it is not based purely and simply on the existing social structure; it aims (or aimed) at introducing change by enabling 'new' social classes to rule the country. Admittedly, since the 1970s, the PRI has come increasingly under challenge and its capacity to mobilise has decreased; but, for several decades, it has constituted a successful model – indeed *the* successful model – of the non-Communist single party.[21]

The fate of the single parties created in the 1940s and 1950s has not been as uniformly good. The Baath party has technically been in power in Syria and Iraq for several decades, but this has been more in name than in reality as very strong leaders have given a highly personalised character to the regime. In Ghana and later in Guinea, the leader who created the party used it increasingly as a personal tool – and the party collapsed when the leader was overthrown. The party has remained in existence – and survived changes of leadership – in Egypt and, in a different manner, in Kenya and Tanzania, as well as, under the same leader, in the Ivory Coast and Zambia. In these countries, however, as well as in some others, party organisation appears to have weakened; in the Ivory Coast in particular, the dependence on the traditional structure of chiefs and notables has become an essential element of party life.

Yet these parties are more alive than many of those which were set up in the 1960s and 1970s, usually when a military leader felt it necessary, after a few years in power, to strengthen his hold on the population and combat opponents. Whether these parties claim to be Marxist (as in Congo or Benin), populist or authoritarian–inegalitarian, the aim is to strengthen support for the leader. This is sometimes achieved by stipulating that the whole adult population has to belong to the party (as in Zaire or Rwanda): it is presumably hoped in this way to both control and influence more quickly the bulk of the citizens. It is questionable, however, whether these aims are achieved, since, unlike Communist parties, these single-party systems lack the manpower required to truly mobilise the population. Almost certainly, these parties are primarily organisations designed to control potential opponents.

The difficulties experienced by the single-party systems of more recent creation stem in large part from the fact that, as was noted in the preceding chapters, time is necessary for parties to acquire legitimacy and to enlist the active support of the population. Yet even the single parties which have had more time to develop, for instance during the pre-independence period, have not had much success in mobilising citizens permanently. Indeed, the dramatic changes which took place in Eastern Europe (except Albania) in 1989 suggest that the Communist parties in these countries can no longer rely on mobilisation alone and that they will need to be based on a representative structure if they are to survive at all. The future of Communist parties in Eastern Europe and the nature of the part which they will play elsewhere, including in the Soviet Union, are among the most problematic questions of the end of the twentieth century.

The dynamics of single-party systems

Since two-fifths of the countries of the world are ruled by a single-party system, it must be concluded that this form of government is both 'popular' – in the sense that it satisfies the needs of at least substantial numbers of political elites – and relatively effective. Evidence for this apparent effectiveness and for this relative popularity results also from the fact that both the number and proportion of single-party systems has grown over the post-1945 period, at least until the 1980s, both at the expense of systems without parties and, though to a lesser extent, at the expense of systems of more than one party: of the seventy-seven countries which existed in 1945, twenty-three or just under 30 per cent were single-party systems in the late 1940s (including six Eastern European countries in which the single-party system was introduced between 1945 and 1949); between 1950 and 1989 the net growth of single-party systems was forty-one countries or 10 per cent.

This growth is largely accounted for by a change in the character of single-party systems during the intervening period. Of the twenty-three countries which were single-party systems in the late 1940s, thirteen were Eastern European or North Asian (all Communist states), while a further five were Latin American, two were European (Spain and Portugal), one was East Asian (Taiwan), one was African (Liberia) and one was Middle Eastern (Turkey). Most of the non-Communist single-party systems among them were authoritarian–inegalitarian; except for Paraguay and Taiwan, these systems disappeared.

What developed in their place were mostly populist systems, which emerged, in particular in Black Africa, either immediately at the time of independence or very shortly afterwards. As most Black African countries became independent in the first half of the 1960s, that period was also that of the great surge of single-party systems: by the mid-1960s, twenty single-party systems were set up in Black Africa alone, while single-party systems had also been introduced in a number of Middle Eastern and North African countries (Iraq, Syria, Egypt, Tunisia, Algeria), in Singapore and in Cuba.

The fate of these single-party systems has not been as straightforward as that of those which were instituted earlier. The experience of the 'older' generation of single-party systems suggested that Communist regimes were at least durable, while the others were likely to be replaced by systems of more than one party. On the other hand, the mainly populist single-party systems of the 1960s proved to be neither as durable as Communist regimes nor as endangered as traditional or conservative inegalitarian regimes: a substantial proportion of these populist systems remained in existence throughout the period; indeed, in the course of a few years, the single-party system replaced the system of more than one party in a number of Black African countries, in particular in ex-French colonies, for example Senegal, Cameroon, Burkina Faso and Benin;[22] similar examples can also be found in Commonwealth countries, such as Uganda and, a little later, Sierra Leone. During the subsequent period, however, many of these single-party systems encountered difficulties and were toppled by the military: the Ghana coup of 1966 was followed by others in Uganda, Burkina Faso, Mali, Niger, Mauritania, Rwanda, Equatorial Guinea, Burundi, Guinea. Some countries did eventually return to single-party rule, but the military leaders who re-introduced it did not necessarily have the same goals. There had in any case been a break in the continuity of the regime, which suggested an inherent weakness: single-party systems appeared therefore not to be truly strong, but more to be formulas adopted by regimes in search of legitimacy (see Table 11.2).

Table 11.2 Stable and unstable single-party systems

	Stable	Unstable		
		Moved or returned to single	Moved to no party	Moved to two + party
Middle East and North Africa	3	5	–	2
South and South-East Asia	3	1	1	1
Africa south of Sahara	15	17	8	2
Latin America	4	1	1	4
Total	25	24	10	9

The populist single-party system seems therefore somewhat transitional in character, whether or not it is set up by 'founders' of nations or by military rulers wishing to maintain their regime by other means. Communist single-party systems appeared less shaky for a long time: their numbers had even increased somewhat in the 1970s (with Laos and Kampuchea on the one hand and the ex-Portuguese colonies on the other). Yet, in the late 1980s, the hold of the Communist party in almost all of Eastern Europe was suddenly shaken and it seemed in question almost everywhere else, including China.

Single-party systems seem therefore to correspond to a transitional phase of political life. The authoritarian–inegalitarian regimes experience most difficulties; they are replaced gradually by systems of more than one party, by military regimes, or by another form of single-party system. Populist single-party systems seem more stable but they depend markedly on their leader being willing and able to establish a strong party structure. They also need to become more open and even to move to a position where they are no longer the sole party and become 'merely' dominant. This may result ultimately in the emergence of a system of more than one party, albeit perhaps somewhat unstable, as occurred in Egypt or Senegal and as has taken place in Mexico since the late 1980s. If this evolution does not take place, populist single-party systems are liable to be replaced by military regimes; though these may in turn set up a party, that party is likely to suffer from even more serious drawbacks than the one which it replaced, as the new party is unlikely to be well-implanted. Communist single-party systems have been ostensibly stronger; they have been durable, but they have depended on the support, including armed support, of other Communist states and of the Soviet Union in particular. Their future is increasingly in doubt. This suggests that, in the history of the development of political regimes, single-party systems may be both essential and transitional.

Conclusion

Single-party systems are numerous in the contemporary world; they are also varied and complex. They form a category only in the sense that the rulers of the country succeed each other and maintain themselves in office by means of a single organisation. They are somewhat shaky because the one political structure which ostensibly dominates the polity is, in reality, attempting to control other organisations which simmer under the surface; the strength of state power and the personal influence of leaders are insufficient to achieve this aim. Yet single-party systems are important, as they are a means by which a variety of goals and ideologies can be pressed on the polity, and in particular the ideology of development. Moreover, the single-party system is also a formula by which political structures are set up and some linkages, however tenuous, are organised between population and rulers. This is why it is difficult to assess the speed at which single-party systems will evolve and the extent to which they will remain in existence. The least that can be said is that they will clearly remain a force to be reckoned with in the coming decades.

Notes

1. G. Sartori, *Parties and Party Systems* (1976), p. 4ff.
2. The proof that opposition did exist is shown by the way in which the political scene changed in Eastern Europe when an opening took place in the late 1980s.
3. See Chapter 21 on the role of the military in politics and on the way in which military regimes tend to civilianise themselves.
4. Indeed, in some Communist states, and in particular in Poland and Hungary, the existence of these smaller parties has to an extent helped with some aspects of the transition away from total dominance by the Communist party.
5. G. Sartori, *op. cit.*, pp. 39–51, characterises Communist single-party systems as 'party-state' systems, in view of the extent to which these parties have tended to dominate the society and indeed refused to accept the view that there could be other political forces in society. There is a considerable literature on Fascist and Nazi single-party systems: see for instance M. Duverger, *op. cit.*, Part II, Chapter 1, Section 3. The literature on single-party systems in Third World countries is now also large, both on the Mexican PRI and on African and Asian single-party systems. See, for instance, V. Randall (ed.), *Political Parties in the Third World* (1988).
6. The concept of a 'hegemonic' party system was first developed by J.J. Wiatr in 'One-

party systems: the concept and issue for comparative studies', in E. Allardt and Y. Littunen (eds), *Cleavages, Ideologies, and Party Systems* (1964), pp. 281–90.

7. For the characteristics of the PRI, see V. Randall (ed.), *op. cit.*, pp. 99–112. See also P. Smith, *Labyrinths of Power: Political recruitment in twentieth century Mexico* (1979).

8. As electoral competition develops, areas of one-party dominance tend to diminish. An analysis of the decline in the number of very safe seats has been made by N.W. Polsby, 'The institutionalisaton of the US House of Representatives', *Am. Pol. Sc. Rev.*, 62 (1968), pp. 144–68. See also Chapter 12.

9. Moves in the direction of more open debates within the context of a general control by the Communist party were attempted in Hungary from the second half of the 1980s and in 1989 in Poland and in the Soviet Union. While, in the Soviet case, the result can be described as having been, for a period at least, a success for the regime and for Gorbachev, the Polish semi-free elections of 1989 were such a defeat for the Communist party that they were one of the factors in the sequence of events which resulted in the collapse of the Communist regimes across Eastern Europe in late 1989.

10. Perhaps the most developed single-party system of this type was that which prevailed in Brazil before 1930, where there was one party and only one party per state of the federation. The situation of the first Republic of Nigeria, between 1960 and 1966, was somewhat analogous.

11. The single-party character of Mexico has become questionable in the late 1980s, while, since the fall of the founder of Tunisia, Bourguiba, that country has ceased to be a full single-party system.

12. The distinction between these two types of single-party systems was first made in the 1960s by African specialists and in particular by D.E. Apter. See for instance *Politics of Modernisation* (1965), pp. 199–212.

13. The real exception to these liberalisation trends is to be found in North Korea, while China has oscillated over the period. This oscillation is likely to continue. It is the consequence of the tension between the desire to bring about change and the need to achieve some legitimacy and therefore to accommodate a variety of groups in the population (a need which is made particularly difficult to achieve because major economic transformations have to take place).

14. The Tanzanian party, the Tanzanian African National Union (TANU), long regarded as a model of a single party which was able to maintain itself without excessive authoritarianism, has come to be subjected to increased tension and criticism as a result of the economic difficulties encountered by the country in the 1980s. See for instance L. Cliffe, *One-Party Democracy: Tanzania* (1967).

15. Ghana gained independence in 1957, the first Black African state to do so, under the leadership of Nkrumah and of the Convention People's Party (CPP) which he had helped to build. For a period Nkrumah acquired considerable international prestige, in particular in Africa and in Asia. The tensions created by the authoritarian, strongly anti-tribal, and at least avowedly egalitarian policies of Nkrumah led to the fall of the regime as a result of an army coup in 1966.

16. Burundi and Uganda are examples of countries where tribal oppositions led to major violence and to coups. Inter-tribal opposition appears to be such that integration cannot be achieved. See Chapter 6.

17. The coup which took place in Liberia in 1980 aimed at introducing a left-populist regime in a country where the single party had become very conservative. Yet accommodation has been relatively successful in some countries, in particular in the Ivory Coast under the leadership of Houphouet-Boigny.

18. The Northern Peoples Congress in the First Republic of Nigeria (1960–6) was a good example of such a party.

19. See Chapter 10.
20. Kim Il-sung of North Korea and Ceauşescu of Romania came gradually to dominate their party to such an extent that they instituted a wholly personalised distortion of Communist systems, probably an even greater distortion than that which characterised the Soviet Union under Stalin (though repression was less bloody).
21. The Mexican PRI did lose much of its populist character after the 1960s and it was subjected to considerable opposition on a number of occasions (in particular from students). Its electoral dominance finally came to be questioned in the late 1980s: even according to the official results, whose validity was widely criticised, the PRI candidate only had a small majority at the presidential elections of 1989.
22. A system of more than one party was later re-established in Senegal, though the presidential party remained dominant (to an extent resembling the developments in Egypt or earlier in Mexico).

12 | Systems of more than one party

Systems of more than one party are, unlike single-party systems, based on open competition among political groups in society, a competition which normally takes place through elections. These systems are indeed the only ones where elections are critical to the public decision-making process. To this extent, they would appear to be intrinsically pluralistic and liberal and to develop in a 'natural' rather than in an 'imposed' manner. Yet they are not ostensibly more successful than single-party systems. They are not appreciably more numerous; they are not on average more durable and many of them have been abolished by military coups or replaced by single-party systems. Indeed, some of them do not even allow real competition, as opposition can be heavily restricted or interfered with, while, as was seen in the previous chapter, some single-party systems allow a modicum of dissent within the party or alongside it.[1]

The characteristics of systems of more than one party thus differ widely. While many have liberal–democratic goals, some are populist, others are traditional–inegalitarian and a few are even authoritarian–inegalitarian. These ideological differences correspond in large part to the social bases of the parties and are accompanied by variations in the party structure. Thus some parties are highly dependent on a parent group while others relate directly to their supporters and electors. In parallel, the party organisation may be rudimentary and may rely on the structure of a communal group, or it may be extensive and highly developed, and may include large numbers of active members.

The characteristics of competition in systems of more than one party

These differences have a marked effect on the extent, the nature, and the configuration of competition in systems of more than one party. At one extreme, competition can be so restricted that the regime appears to be imposed. This occurs when a social group – based on class or race for instance – denies the rest of the   159 population the opportunity to participate in political life, as in twentieth-century South Africa; in a somewhat parallel manner, literacy requirements have resulted in substantial proportions of the inhabitants being disfranchised in a number of Latin American countries. Severe restrictions are sometimes introduced by military leaders who wish to maintain an appearance of pluralism. Thus in Brazil a two-party system was imposed for two decades, between 1964 and 1984. More commonly, one or more parties are not allowed to be constituted or reconstituted, as occurred in Argentina with the Peronist party for long periods or in Turkey with the Democratic party.

Thus systems of more than one party can develop in a context of restricted and even contrived competition. More generally, competition in these systems raises three inter-related but analytically distinct questions. There is, first, that of the extent of competition. Are societal conflicts freely reflected in the party system or are there some legal or *de facto* barriers? The cases just mentioned were extreme, but competition can be limited by more subtle means: pressure may be put on electors, there may be outright electoral fraud, or, and indeed very commonly, as will be seen in the next chapter, the electoral system may have the effect of making it difficult or even impossible for some conflicts to be represented. In pratice, there are always some limitations to the 'transparency' of conflicts in all systems of more than one party.[3]

Second, the nature of the competition characterising the system can vary, ranging between two extremes. Competition can be at the level of groups or at the level of individuals or, more commonly, it may result from a combination of both types. Competition is at the level of groups when, was seen in Chapter 7, parties are closely dependent on a 'parent' organisation – tribal, geographical, ethnic, religious, or class-based – it is then a war between well-defined camps, a 'war' which is waged (normally) by electoral means. Elections determine the strength of each group by calling on the loyalty of group members. From time to time, there can be a truce and parties can come to some arrangement: this type of arrangement between the 'pillars' of the society has been labelled 'consociationalism'.[2]

When parties cease to be dependent on a 'parent' body and can call directly on the support of those who identify with them, some change gradually occurs. Parties then begin to look for new 'identifiers' from outside the groups which supported them originally, as in this manner they can increase their share of the electorate, although they may also lose some of their original supporters as other groups become involved in similar forms of 'poaching'. The purpose of elections changes profoundly in the process: from being essentially a means of expressing old loyalties, they become markets at which parties attempt to 'sell' their programmes. Traditional loyalties break as the independence of electors grows. Meanwhile, the competition between the parties becomes close, as each one of them is affected by the actions of the others. There is then a 'party *system*' in the strong sense of the word.[3]

Legitimate mass parties play a key part in this evolution, since they are not directly tied to a social group and are, on the contrary, autonomous organisations.

As parties take time to become legitimate mass, the evolution from group-based to individual competition also takes a long time. Thus, by and large, countries in which the system of more than one party is new are likely to experience a 'group-based' type of competition, while countries in which it has lasted for a long period will experience forms of competition closer to the 'market' end of the continuum.[4]

Yet this development may be prolonged or made more complex as a result of a third element, namely the type of party configuration. Systems of more than one party differ markedly in terms of the number and relative strength of the significant parties, often because, originally, tribal, ethnic, religious, or class-based groups, in varying numbers and with varying strengths, emerge in the different polities. There may therefore be two, three, four, or more significant parties; these may be more or less equal or may differ markedly in the size of their support. This configuration is unlikely to cha..ge to any great extent, or at any rate quickly, even when the party system ceases to be 'group-based' and becomes progressively 'market-based'.

General overview of systems of more than one party

In the late 1980s, 73 countries out of 163 (45 per cent) were ruled by a system of more than one party. These included all the Atlantic countries, three-quarters of the Latin American and half of the South and East Asian states. However, there were only a quarter of the Middle Eastern and one-tenth of the Black African polities in the group. The success of systems of more than one party is thus uneven in the Third World, while it is large in the Atlantic area.[5]

Indeed, old and continuous systems of more than one party are overwhelmingly drawn from the Atlantic area. Of the seventy-three countries which were ruled by a system of more than one party in 1989, only forty-nine – or two-thirds – had been ruled continuously in this way since the end of World War II or since independence. Twenty of these forty-nine countries are in the Atlantic area, twelve in Latin America, ten in South and East Asia and the other seven in the Middle East and Black Africa. While Atlantic countries formed 30 per cent of the countries ruled by a system of more than one party in 1990, they formed two-fifths of the group of the countries which were continuously ruled in that way. They even account for two-thirds of the countries which have had an uninterrupted system of more than one party for four decades or more. Newer systems of more than one party include many countries of the Commonwealth where, as was already noted, liberal traditions have by and large been stronger than in the rest of the Third World. On the other hand, the older Latin American countries have tended to oscillate between military regimes and systems of more than one party during the post-1945 period and very few of them have been ruled by a system of more than one party continuously for more than two decades (see Table 12.1).[6]

Systems of more than one party have thus tended to be durable primarily in the Atlantic area: this corresponds to the view, discussed in Chapter 6, that liberal democracy is significantly associated with economic wealth. Given that, as was

Table 12.1 Stable and unstable systems of more than one party

	Stable	Unstable		
		Returned to two +	Moved to no party	Moved to single party
Atlantic	20	3	–	–
Communist	–	–	–	–
Middle East and North Africa	4	2	–	2
South and South-East Asia	10	3	3	1
Africa south of Sahara	3	2	5	14
Latin America	12	14	1	1
Total	49	24	9	18

pointed out earlier, systems of more than one party tend to change their character over time, it follows that one should first examine Atlantic countries and only afterwards turn to the examination of systems of more than one party in the rest of the world.

Long-standing systems of more than one party and their characteristics: the case of Atlantic countries

The large majority of Atlantic countries have been ruled by a system of more than one party continuously from the 1940s to the 1990s (nineteen out of twenty-three polities). These systems display substantial differences, however, primarily in terms of the configuration of the parties, which ranges from two-party to multi-party systems, but also, though to a lesser extent, in terms of their social base, their organisation, and their goals.

By and large, the parties of the Atlantic area are liberal–democratic, and have an autonomous and relatively well-structured organisation. They are – and indeed often were before 1945 – of a legitimate mass character: the support which they receive from the electorate takes the form of a direct identification with the party. The groups from which they originally emanated are no longer critical to the maintenance of these parties. This suggests that competition among them has been undergoing the type of evolution which was described earlier. Indeed, the second half of the twentieth century has been a period during which most parties of the Atlantic area have moved progressively away from a 'group'-based appeal to an appeal to electors on a 'market' basis. This has had an effect on the solidity of many of the parties and, consequently on the stability of the party configurations in many of the countries.

Admittedly, in certain countries, some parties are closely tied to an ethnic or national minority, as is the case in Britain, Finland, Belgium, Spain, or Switzerland, but these parties are small and only in Belgium do they constitute a basis for potential separatism. There are also, within the larger parties, remnants of communal loyalties of the personal or territorial types, but these are of little electoral significance. Since these pockets of 'communalism' are found mainly in rural areas of difficult access, they have declined in importance with the marked decline of the rural population everywhere. They used to be relatively strong in particular in France before 1958, but the advent of the Gaullist party and its perpetuation since the 1960s reduced communalism to insignificance in that country as well.[7]

Ethnic groups were the basis of party support in America in the past, while religious groups, principally Roman Catholic, and class-based groups provided support for parties in Western Europe in the nineteenth and early twentieth centuries. Gradually, however, as with personal and territorial communalism, only traces of the phenomenon can be found in contemporary Europe and North America. There are some exceptions in scattered areas throughout the various countries, but, in general, direct legitimate identification with parties has superseded indirect allegiance taking place through 'parent' groups.

Personalised leadership is of considerable significance, but within parties, rather than in order to build a party. Only in the case of the French Gaullists did a leader both create and sustain a large party. In Germany and Italy after World War II, Christian democracy was strongly helped, but not truly created, by Adenauer and De Gasperi respectively; a similar phenomenon occurred with the French Socialist party, which was remarkably boosted by Mitterrand in the 1970s and 1980s.[8] Indeed, even the development of the Gaullist party can be said to have corresponded to a deeper move within the society: the build-up and the perpetuation of the party corresponded to the need to replace the old communal 'factions' which had existed in the past and to set up a large conservative organisation.[9] Thus it is truly the case that legitimate mass parties have spread generally throughout the Atlantic area, though, in doing so, they have become increasingly divorced from their social base; the independence of the electors has increased and, as a result, Western European parties have become less stable than in the past.[10]

Differences in structure and ideology are rather more marked in the Atlantic area than differences in the social bases, but these too are rather limited compared to the differences which can be found between systems of more than one party in the Atlantic area and those which can be found elsewhere. It was noted in Chapter 9 that there are substantial differences in the extent of decentralisation, in the relationship between parties and particular groups (even among Socialist parties in Western Europe, for instance), and in the concept of membership itself.[11] However, because the large majority of Atlantic parties are of the legitimate mass type, these differences are dwarfed by the fact that one of the key elements – the direct relationship between electors and party – is common to all or practically all organisations. Thus it does not seem to be of considerable significance, ostensibly at least, whether the proportion of members is larger among social democrats in Sweden or Austria than among Socialists in Germany or France;[12] by and large, policy-making appears to be in all cases markedly constrained by the need to appeal to the electorate while retaining as many as possible of the ideological traditions of the party.

Ideological differences are obviously more marked. However, the truly large variations are at the margin, among 'extremist' parties, but these have a rather small and often only intermittent following. These ideological differences are of two types. There are macro-variations: some parties are not truly liberal–democratic. This is the case of some organisations of the 'radical right', which have typically been small and appear ephemeral. They are apparently often triggered by outbursts of racism, as in France in the 1980s with the National Front, but the spread of their influence remains limited, even at their peak (about 10 per cent of the votes).[13]

The other type of macro-variation is constituted by Communist parties, though it is arguable whether Western Communist parties are still markedly different from other parties. Their importance is diminishing and, after a long period during which they were very significant in four (but only four) of the nineteen countries (France, Finland, Iceland, and Italy), with about 20 per cent of the votes, they came to decline so substantially by the 1980s that only in Italy did the Communist party remain truly a force and, even there, it was a declining one.[14]

No single explanation has satisfactorily accounted for the long period of strength of Communist parties in these four countries. The socio-economic argument is scarcely valid, given the wealth of these countries; the cultural argument, suggesting that 'Latin' countries are more susceptible to Communism than others, has some validity, but Finland and Iceland have to be explained. It seems that these parties remained strong in large part because they had succeeded in building a sub-culture after World War II, having been helped by the conditions of the war and the resistance: once they had reached middle-sized strength, they could remain for long periods at the same level, as they were able to sustain a large network of dependent associations which in turn helped to maintain them.[15]

What is more apparent than macro-variations in ideology are the micro-variations. Differences may loom large at particular times and on particular issues, but they are relatively small by comparison with ideological differences among other parties elsewhere. Differences between Socialists on the left and some of the 'centre' parties, such as the Christian democrats, are not, or no longer very clear;[16] some Conservative parties have become more 'right-wing' in the 1980s, in particular on economic issues, but others have not and, traditionally at least, Conservative parties in Western Europe had come to accept the Welfare State.[17] Liberals are probably to the left of Christian democrats on religious issues and to the right of these parties on economic and social matters.[18] There are also some 'agrarian' parties, principally in Scandinavia, but the shrinking of the rural vote has led these parties to rename themselves and to adopt the label of 'centre', which places them fairly close to Socialists and to Liberals.

The ideological differences between the significant Atlantic parties are thus relatively small; they are probably declining, not only in that neither Conservatives (despite the more 'radical' character of some of them) nor Socialists truly put forward major programmes of change, but also in that all Atlantic parties have tended to pick issues as they have come up, often on the basis of group pressure, some of which have given rise to new parties and in particular to 'green' or ecology parties.[19] As a result, the most important characteristic of Atlantic parties is their configuration, which has tended to reflect some of the group origins of the parties as well as some of the effects of differing electoral systems – this will be discussed further in the next chapter. Yet the gradual move towards a 'market' basis has affected party configurations as well, with the result that party systems, which remained stable throughout the 1950s and 1960s in most of the Atlantic area, have tended to vary appreciably in the 1970s and 1980s.

In the 1960s, Western party systems could be classified neatly into four categories. There were two-party systems, in which the two parties obtained close to 50 per cent of the votes and where any third party which might have existed was very small and politically insignificant: these were the systems of the United States, New Zealand, Australia, Britain, and Austria. There were two-and-a-half party systems in West Germany, Luxemburg, Canada, Belgium, and Ireland, where one party obtained 40–45 per cent of the votes, another around 35 per cent, and the third about 15 per cent: these systems were therefore doubly unbalanced since the second party was structurally smaller than the first and the third was markedly smaller then the other two.[20] There were multi-party systems with a dominant party, where the first party also obtained 40–45 per cent of the votes, but where three or even four other parties shared the rest of the votes more or less equally; this was the case in most of Scandinavia (Denmark, Sweden, Norway and Iceland) as well as in Italy, and the situation in the Netherlands also approximated this model. Finally, there were multi-party systems without a dominant party, as in France before the 1962 election, Finland and Switzerland, where no party obtained more than 25 per cent of the votes and where four or five parties shared fairly evenly the votes of the electors. The large majority of countries thus operated on the basis of at least one party being close to a majority of the votes. True multi-party systems were exceptional. Large countries which had had such a system in the past (such as Germany and Italy) had abandoned it, while, since 1962, France appeared to be moving away from a configuration which seemed to have been at the origin of the very unstable governments it had had until the late 1950s.[21]

Atlantic party systems can no longer be characterised so neatly in the 1990s. The four broad types of party systems do remain as a general framework, but there have been considerable movements in many of the countries and, overall, the percentage of votes obtained by the larger parties has tended to decline. The movement has been particularly pronounced in Britain, Luxemburg, Belgium, and Denmark, this last country having become a multi-party system without a dominant party. In the 1980s, and especially in the second half of the decade, it has taken place also to a more limited extent in New Zealand, Austria, Germany, Iceland, and Norway, as well as in Finland and in Switzerland, which were already multi-party systems. Indeed, in Western Europe, only in Sweden has the party system remained stable, although, even there, some movements have begun to occur. In North

America and in Australia, on the contrary, the traditional party systems seem still to remain broadly unchanged.

It is possible to give two different interpretations of these developments. One consists in concentrating on specific country explanations. In Britain, for instance, the polarisation of the two parties, and in particular the Labour party's move to the left, alienated a segment of the electorate – these voters chose instead to cast their votes for the Liberal party; the creation of the Social Democratic party was also an indication of this alienation. In Belgium, the linguistic problem led to the emergence of Flemish and (temporarily) of Walloon parties as well.

Yet both electoral fluctuations and the emergence of new parties, and in particular of the 'Greens', suggest a deeper trend. The proportion of 'independent' electors has increased in many countries, while party identification has become less strong: evidence for this development has been accumulated in the United States, but there are also indications of the same phenomenon elsewhere in the Atlantic area.[22] Thus party systems in the Atlantic area, especially in Western Europe, appear to be in a state of transformation. Legitimate mass parties are still central to the definition of the party system, but they seem to be increasingly treated by the electorate as instruments to obtain certain policy results, though enough direct allegiance to the parties remains for the change to be taking place slowly and for the configurations in most countries to continue to keep the shape which they had in the past.[23]

Systems of more than one party throughout the world

Atlantic countries are a small proportion of the polities which are or have been ruled by a system of more than one party: at the end of the 1980s, 50 other states had a pluralistic party system, and a further 27 polities had been governed in this manner at some point after World War II. Thus a system of more than one party had been in existence in exactly 100 of the 163 nations of the world.

Yet most of those pluralistic party systems which existed or had existed outside the Atlantic area were not fully developed or were relatively fragile. As was just noted, the pluralistic party system did not survive in twenty-seven of these polities, presumably because it could not withstand pressures. In a further twenty-four, the system of more than one party had not been in continuous existence since World War II or since independence and, in several cases, there had been more than one successful attempt at overthrowing it. Moreover, eighteen of the remaining twenty-nine Third World countries which had been ruled continuously by a system of more than one party were relatively new states, and in a number of cases very new. Thus only in eleven countries, beyond the Atlantic area, had the system of more than one party lasted since the 1940s: even in this category serious difficulties arose in a number of polities. It is therefore worth examining in some detail the characteristics of systems of more than one party in the seventy-seven Third World countries in which this type of rule has existed continuously or for a period and to assess in what ways and in which countries pluralistic party systems have proved more resistant and more durable.[24]

Long-established and continuous systems of more than one party

In eleven countries, a system of more than one party has existed continuously since the 1940s. Yet, in about half of these polities, the system cannot be said to have developed fully; indeed, competition has been severely restricted in some of them. These eleven countries are Israel and Lebanon in the Middle East, India, Indonesia, Japan, South Korea and Sri Lanka in South and East Asia, South Africa in Black Africa, and Brazil, Colombia and Costa Rica in Latin America. Of these, only Israel, India, Japan, Sri Lanka and Costa Rica can be said to have had a truly working and continuous system of more than one party, although Colombia comes very close to qualifying, since, from the end of the 1950s, after the fall of the dictatorship of Odria, its two-party system has been almost fully unimpeded, although – or perhaps because – it was based on a power-sharing arrangement between the two parties for a substantial period.[25]

In the other countries, restrictions have been severe and durable. The war in Lebanon has almost disintegrated the country; while there was still theoretically a system of more than one party (highly based on communal ethnic groups) at the end of the 1980s, its operation was in fact truly hampered by the absence of elections and the *de facto* dependence of the country on its immediate neighbours. Indonesia and South Korea have been technically ruled by systems of more than one party, but they have been so dominated by the government party that they come close to having a single party system, though changes which occurred at the end of the 1980s, especially in Korea, suggest a move towards a more regular operation of the system. A similar conclusion can be drawn in the case of Brazil for the period 1964–84 during which a two-party system was imposed by the military rulers. Finally, South Africa is at best an oligarchical two-party system, and indeed one in which one of the two parties has traditionally been dominant within the white electorate.

Thus only five or at most six countries outside the Atlantic area can be said to have had a truly working pluralistic party system throughout the period from the 1940s to the 1990s. This in itself justifies the conclusion that, so far at least, systems of more than one party are primarily a characteristic of Atlantic countries. As a matter of fact, it is not surprising that Israel and Japan should have had a fully working competitive party system. Israel's party system has been successively of the multi-dominant and of the two-and-a-half party variety; Japan's began as multi-party and moved to a multi-dominant form, and was of the two-and-a-half type between 1958 and 1967. The fact that India, Sri Lanka, and Costa Rica should be in the group is more surprising. Costa Rica's balanced two-party system has functioned effectively throughout the period; Sri Lanka and India experienced greater difficulties: indeed, in India, the emergency period of the mid-1970s seemed to suggest a move towards a one-party system, from which Mrs Gandhi retreated. Sri Lanka has experienced considerable tension arising from communal conflict and its constitution was altered in a semi-presidential – and somewhat authoritarian – direction. Yet, whatever their difficulties, these two South Asian countries remained under pluralistic party rule – this being an undeniable success for this type of regime.

Continuous systems of more than one party among newer countries

Eighteen other Third World countries and one Atlantic country (Malta), which gained independence during or since the 1950s, have been ruled continuously by a system of more than one party. Two of these eighteen are in the Middle East and North Africa (Cyprus and Morocco), two are in Black Africa (Gambia and Mauritius), while five are in Asia and the Pacific and nine in the Caribbean.[26]

These systems have generally operated in a regular manner. Major difficulties have been encountered in only four of them. Cyprus split into two states, Greek and Turkish, but the system remained pluralistic on both sides of the communal divide. In Guyana, considerable pressure and a degree of imposition was introduced by Burnham towards the end of his presidency. In Jamaica, elections were boycotted by the opposition in 1983, but the system remained broadly pluralistic. It is in Morocco that the greatest amount of manipulation and imposition took place, with elections being postponed on more than one occasion by royal action. In the other countries, on the other hand, the pluralistic party system prevailed and was generally fully effective. The majority of these countries (twelve) had a working two-party system throughout their independent period, while there was a two-and-a-half party system in two (Mauritius and St Christopher), a multi-dominant party system in a further two (Papua New Guinea and Cyprus) and a multi-party system without a dominant party in two (Morocco and the Solomon Islands). Only in one country (Malaysia) was there strong dominance of one party but, in this case, the dominance was that of an alliance based on a permanent working relationship between Malay and Chinese organisations.

The fact that these systems have in general operated satisfactorily since independence may be ascribed to the peculiar characteristics of most of the countries of the group. First, seven of these polities are very new, being creations of the late 1970s or early 1980s, while only two (Malaysia and Morocco) date from the 1950s. Second, the large majority of these countries has a very small population – less than a million in a number of cases; in fact, only Malaysia and Morocco have a sizeable population. Third, the large majority of these countries (thirteen out of nineteen) are islands or groups of islands in which there is a high degree of cultural identity. Fourth, a large majority are members of the Commonwealth and were given substantial autonomy before independence (some became independent reluctantly). Not only has a tradition of parliamentarism been established for many years in imitation of Britain, but, again in imitation of Britain, a two-party system was successfully implanted. This has been the case in both the Pacific and Caribbean countries of the group, though in some cases the party system has been based on different ethnic groups, as in Mauritius and Guyana.

These countries are therefore not representative of the countries of the world and their peculiarities appear to account in large part for the permanence of the pluralistic party system. Only Morocco and Malaysia appear to resemble an 'average' polity. It was noted that Morocco was truly a borderline case, with amounts of imposition analogous to those found in Korea or Brazil; thus, in this group, Malaysia alone can be regarded as being an example of a truly successful working pluralistic party system in a sizeable country. It is interesting to note that Malaysia belongs to the same geographical group as India and Sri Lanka and that it is also part of the Commonwealth.

Relatively recent returns to a system of more than one party

In twenty-four countries, a system of more than one party was in existence in 1989, but after periods in which a single party system or a system without parties (traditional or military) had prevailed. The majority of these countries (fourteen) are in Latin America, including eleven in Spanish America proper. Of the other ten, three are in the Atlantic area (Greece, Portugal and Spain) and two each in two of the other three regions of the Third World – Egypt and Turkey in the Middle East, Senegal and Sudan in Black Africa, and the Philippines, Pakistan and Thailand in South-East Asia. While the group of continuous, but recent, systems of more than one party is predominantly drawn from the Commonwealth, slightly over half the countries which developed or returned to a pluralistic party system are from Spanish America.

The influence of Western Europe is manifest in the move of Greece, Portugal, and Spain to a pluralistic party system; the entry of these countries to the European Community appears to guarantee the maintenance of such a regime. Indeed, the party system of these countries has become relatively stable, though, in Spain, the disappearance of the major centre-right party, the UCD, has given the Socialist party a position of dominance which is almost unique in Western Europe. In both Greece and Portugal the party system has shown considerable strength; the Greek system is of the two-and-a-half party variety while Portugal has oscillated between a multi-dominant party and a multi-party system. The Turkish party system (also of the two-and-a-half party form) might also become stable, though the role of the military remains important, despite a return to civilian rule after two periods of army rule.

Outside Spanish America, the system of more than one party does not seem to be truly well-established among the countries of this group. In Egypt and Senegal, the single-party system was replaced, in the mid-1970s, by a pluralistic party system as a result of a presidential decision, but this pluralistic party system remains strongly controlled. The same can be said of Trinidad, though pluralism went further, since, after the death of the founder of the country, an electoral upset brought the opposition to power. In Thailand, the influence of the military is such that civilian coalitions, which emerge from the multi-party system, seem to exist only on sufferance; an analogous situation prevails in Surinam, where the competitive process has been allowed to take place after the military stepped down. Indeed, in these two countries, there was no truly large party: this accounts perhaps for the ease with which the military could maintain and justify its hold on power. In the Philippines, the orderly succession of the two parties in power was interrupted by Marcos in 1970; the political situation which developed after his demise in the second half of the 1980s has been marked by profound instability and by the absence of a strong party system. In Pakistan, a pluralistic system was re-introduced in the late 1980s, after a second period of military rule. Finally, in Grenada, a single-party system introduced by the left was abolished by US military intervention; however, the return to a pluralistic party rule is probably more secure than in other countries of the group, as the characteristics of the country are similar to those of other islands in the Caribbean.[27]

Thus, outside the three Western European countries of the group, and possibly also Turkey and Grenada, the system of more than one party does not appear to have developed in a direction which is either fully competitive or truly stable. These countries constitute examples of pluralistic party systems which might, over time, become established, but which are not as yet 'consolidated'. The same can probably be said of at least the majority of the eleven countries of the Spanish American group which returned to pluralistic rule. There is one clear exception only, that of Venezuela, which has been ruled by an effective competitive two-and-a-half party system since 1958, when the dictatorship of Jimenez was overthrown. This result was obtained largely as a result of the careful manner in which the two major parties, AD and COPEI, endeavoured to maintain the pluralistic system, though difficulties have emerged since the 1970s, in part because oil depletion led to a major reduction in the revenues of the state.[28]

Apart from the Dominican Republic, the other Spanish American countries in the group have returned to a pluralistic party system in the 1980s. In the Dominican Republic, the party system has since the 1960s been subjected to a substantial degree of manipulation in favour of the party of Balaguer, who has repeatedly been president of the country. Thus it is hazardous to claim that the 'return to democracy' which has characterised these countries is likely to be long-lasting. There have already been periods in the past in which at least a number of these countries have experienced a pluralistic, and indeed apparently viable, party system – notably Uruguay and Peru. It is true that in three of the four Central American countries in the group the pluralistic party system appears more viable. These are Guatemala, Honduras, and El Salvador; Guatemala having a multi-dominant party system, Honduras a two-party system, and El Salvador a two-and-a-half party system. The fourth is Panama, where the party system was long severely controlled by the military ruler, Noriega. It is also the case that, in Ecuador and Peru, two elections in succession had taken place in the 1980s and that the competition between Peronists and Radicals in Argentina remained electoral: for the first time since World War II, a president was replaced by another in Argentina by means of a vote rather than by military action. Yet time has to elapse before these party systems become sufficiently 'consolidated' for the pluralistic party system to cease to appear to be fragile and for the parties to become legitimate mass.[29]

The casualties of systems of more than one party

If Spanish America is the region where pluralistic party systems appear revitalised, if not truly strong, Black Africa is the region *par excellence* where these systems have been abolished. Nineteen of the twenty-seven countries belonging to the group come from that area, four of the other eight being in Asia and two each in the Middle East and in Latin America; moreover, six Eastern European States (Bulgaria, Czechoslovakia, East Germany, Hungary, Poland, and Romania) could be included, but the Communist take-over took place so rapidly after World War II in these countries that they are more realistically classified as single-party systems having lasted throughout the period.[30]

The eight countries which belong to this group and which are not in Black Africa are truly diverse. They range from apparently working pluralistic party systems to cases in which there was only a fleeting experience of competitive systems. Among the first category are Chile, which was a truly effective multi-party and multi-dominant party system until the military coup took place in 1973, and Fiji, which had a stable two-party system before the military coup of 1987. At the other extreme are Nepal, Iran, and Cuba, where parties were extremely weak or even non-existent for long periods before a competitive party system was briefly introduced, only to be replaced by a return to the traditional no-party system in the first case, a dominant single-party system in the second and a full single-party system in the third.[31]

Between these two extremes, Bangladesh and Burma experienced periods of pluralistic party rule which were terminated (in both cases on more than one occasion) by coups through which strong rulers emerged. These two countries have had the opposite experience to that of India, Malaysia, and Sri Lanka: in these countries, the pluralistic party system prevailed, albeit with some difficulty. This seems to have been due to the capacity of the dominant party (in Malaysia of the dominant coalition) to expand its roots in the population and thus to achieve relatively effective government within a pluralistic context. This was not the case in Bangladesh or Burma, though the periodic return to a pluralistic system suggests that future experiments in party pluralism will take place, albeit perhaps equally temporarily.

There is less likelihood of a return to a pluralistic party system in Syria (which has had a dominant single-party system since the late 1950s) and in the nineteen African states which, in general, were ruled by a system of more than one party only for short periods immediately after they achieved independence in or around 1960.

In the majority of cases, the system of more than one party was – or was held to be – too inchoate or too closely based on tribal or ethnic cleavages to form a basis for nation-building. The military took over, often in the mid-1960s, but in many cases afterwards – in Sudan this happened in 1989. Parties were abolished, though, after a while, a new single party tends to be set up, as was seen in the previous chapter: this was the case in Benin, Burkina Faso, Congo, Rwanda, Somalia, Togo and Zaire, though, in Burkina Faso, a second (and apparently equally unsuccessful) experience in party pluralism took place somewhat later. The Nigerian case has similar characteristics, though it perhaps resembles more closely that of Pakistan, in that the system of more than one party was established at independence, suspended by the military, then re-established, and once more abolished. In Sudan, the military took over power for the third time in 1989, partly because of the divisions among the parties (as had previously been the case in Sudan as well as in Somalia before 1970) and partly because of the apparently never ending civil war in the south of the country.

In some other cases, as in Cameroon, Chad (before the military eventually took over), Zambia and Zimbabwe, the pluralistic party system, also based on tribal or ethnic divisions, was replaced by a single-party system as a result of the action of the head of state: a merger was obtained in some cases, while in others the opposition was repressed. There are also cases where both experiences were combined, as in Sierra Leone, where the pluralistic party system led to the arrival of the opposition party in power and the subsequent establishment of a single-party system, or in Ghana, where the military first helped to instore a pluralistic party system after the fall of Nkrumah but was subsequently instrumental in the rapid abolition of this system on two successive occasions.

Overall, the system of more than one party clearly has very few roots in Black Africa, most of the Middle East and North Africa. In these regions, it is not even fragile, as it appears to be in Latin America or, with a number of major exceptions, in South and South-East Asia. However, elements of a system of more than one party are beginning to emerge in Africa, primarily as a result of a degree of competition in some of the single parties (as in Zambia or Tanzania) or through very dominant systems such as those of Senegal and Egypt. By and large, especially in Black Africa and in the Middle East, the countries in which the system of more than one party has been abolished have been those in which the party system was part of the colonial legacy and not truly adopted by the political elite, as was the case, on the contrary, in the Caribbean and in many of the small states of the Pacific area.

Conclusion

The experience of the one hundred countries which have adopted a system of more than one party suggests that such a system is truly implanted in limited parts of the contemporary world. It originated in the Atlantic area, and this is still the region where it is truly well-established. It has expanded to small polities with a well-defined cultural identity, as can normally be found in islands, especially if these islands had been under British influence. It has also expanded in a substantial part of South Asia; it appears truly well-implanted in the three large countries of the Third World, India, Sri Lanka, and Malaysia.

Elsewhere, systems of more than one party have had a chequered development. They do not appear to have had the ability to meet the many requirements of most Third World countries, either in terms of nation-building or in terms of their ability to provide a strong and sustained basis for governmental action. As a result, these systems have not had the time required for the parties to establish strong roots in the population and become truly legitimate: they are thus liable to be destroyed or set aside by military rulers or by civilian leaders wishing to exercise full control. Systems of more than one party flourish when full and open competition among social groups is allowed to last for a substantial period, a situation which, so far, has not been characteristic of many countries outside the Atlantic area.

Notes

1. See Table 11.2, p. 155, for a distribution of stable and unstable single-party systems.
2. On consociationalism, see Chapter 6. See also A. Lijphart, *Democracy in Plural Societies* (1977), *passim.*
3. The notion of an electoral market stems in large part from the general model developed by A. Downs, *An Economic Theory of Democracy* (1957), in which the author shows that, under certain conditions, and in particular if there is a two-party system, parties will tend to move towards the centre as this is where they can find the electors who are critical if they are to win a majority.
4. The most extreme case is that of the United States, where large proportions of electors are 'independent' from the parties, even if they 'identify' with these parties. This kind of 'independence' appears also to be growing in Western Europe, including countries in which electors were traditionally associated with a particular 'pillar' of society, as in the Netherlands or Austria. See for America R.E. Wolfinger, 'Dealignment, realignment, and mandates in the 1984 election' in A. Ranney (ed.), *The American Elections of 1984* (1985), pp. 277–96. See also P.A. Beck, 'The dealignment era in America' in R.J. Dalton *et al.* (eds), *Electoral Change in Advanced Industrial Democracies* (1984), pp. 240–66.
5. Systems of more than one party are in the process of development in Eastern Europe. What the configuration will be is unclear, as groups in opposition to the Communist party tend to be loose and often inchoate, although they appear to share the support of the population. As a result, the new systems of more than one party which will emerge are likely to oscillate and may not prove durable.
6. Commonwealth countries of the Third World have tended to have more stable party systems, as has already been noted: in Latin America in particular, the large majority of stable party systems can be found in the Caribbean Commonwealth countries. See J. Blondel, 'Political leadership in the Commonwealth: the British legacy' in H.D. Clarke and M.M. Czudnowski (eds), *Political Elites in Anglo-American Democracies* (1986), pp. 311–37.
7. Yet parties are still not truly solidly established in France, in particular in the centre. The classical image of shifting and higly indisciplined groups is still to an extent valid. On the characteristics of French parties, see J.R. Frears, *Political Parties and Elections in the French Fifth Republic* (1977), pp. 58–83.

8. On personalised leadership, see Chapter 10. By and large, it seems that leaders have been able to build or markedly develop a party, in the Western European context, when there was a break or a major reconstruction of the regime (such as in Germany, Italy, France in 1958 and Spain after the end of the Franco regime in the mid-1970s).

9. Yet, as was pointed out earlier, parties have not been fully established in France, particularly in the centre of the political spectrum.

10. There has been a large degree of instability in electoral patterns in many Western European countries since the 1970s. See M. Pedersen, 'Changing patterns of electoral volatility in European party systems, 1948–1977: explorations in explanation' in H. Daalder and P. Mair (eds) (1983), pp. 29–65; I. Budge and D.J. Farlie, *Explaining and Predicting Elections* (1983), pp. 115–28; R.J. Dalton *et al.* (eds), *op. cit.*, (1984), pp. 240–66; I. Crewe and M. Denver (eds), *Electoral Change in Western Democracies* (1985).

11. See Chapter 10. Some Socialist parties are organically tied to the trade unions (as in Britain and Sweden), while others are not (as in Germany, Italy and France). The effective difference may not necessarily be very large.

12. See Chapter 10. On variations in membership, see S. Bartolini, *op. cit.*, in H. Daalder and P. Mair (1983).

13. Despite the growth of the National Front of Le Pen in France, as well as of the Republicans in West Germany in the late 1980s, the strength of radical right parties remains rather limited. Experience of the post-1945 period suggests that these parties remain marginal to political life.

14. The Communist party has also been relatively strong in Portugal and Greece (where the party system has not been continuous since World War II), but it has also been declining in both countries.

15. The number of dependent associations of the Communist party in Italy is very large, extending into the productive sector (co-operatives, etc.). A network of dependent associations of the French Communist party has also existed in the past, but it has declined in strength with the decline of the French CP.

16. On Western European Christian Democracy, see R.E.M. Irving, *The Christian Democratic Parties of Western Europe* (1979).

17. Under Mrs Thatcher, the British Conservative party moved markedly to the right; but this has not been the case of Conservative parties in general, which exist primarily in Scandinavia: the Danish Conservative party is a case in point.

18. The Austrian Freedom party is an example of a liberal party which is to the right of the Christian Democrats; indeed, it made gains in the late 1980s on a platform which is close to that of the radical right.

19. The ability of the 'green' parties to develop and maintain themselves in the second half of the 1980s has been remarkable. See F. Muller Rommel (ed.), *New Politics in Western Europe* (1989).

20. True 'three-party' systems have never existed; the closest to a situation in which three parties were almost equal was in Peru in the 1960s: but the situation was not stable.

21. The characteristics of the four types of Western party system were analysed in J. Blondel, 'Party systems and patterns of government in Western democracies', *Canadian Journal of Pol. Sci.*, June 1968, pp. 180–200.

22. The growth of 'independence' and the corresponding decline in party identification have been substantial in the United States since the 1960s. See the references listed in note 4.

23. One sign of 'independence' is found in the fact that electors tend to be 'instrumental' in their voting patterns: it has been shown that many take their decisions on the basis, not of ideologies, but of programmes and of past record (so-called 'retrospective' voting). See M.P. Fiorina, *Retrospective Voting in American National Elections* (1981), especially pp. 20–62.

24. There has not so far been any systematic study of party systems in the Third World. A number of studies have considered the 'return to democracy' in Latin America: see for instance G. O'Donnell, P. Schmitter, and L. Whitehead (eds), *Transitions from Authoritarian Rule* (1986). There are also specific studies of African and Asian parties related to particular parties or to particular countries: see for instance V. Randall (ed.), *Political Parties in the Third World* (1988) for an examination of a number of important cases.

25. The arrangement which took place in Colombia between the two main parties followed the dictatorship of Odria in the 1950s; it resulted in the decision that each party would occupy the presidency in succession for a period. This system did appear to help maintain a liberal system in the country, despite many difficulties.

26. The countries in the Pacific are composed of a number of islands or groups of islands most of which became independent in the 1970s and which have very small populations. The most important is Fiji, where however the system of more than one party was abolished by a military coup in 1987. Many of the Caribbean countries also gained independence in the 1970s and are islands with small populations, with the exception of Jamaica and Trinidad, which, together with Barbados and Guyana, gained independence in the early 1960s.

27. Sudan belonged to the group until 1989, when a military coup abolished the system of more than one party for the third time.

28. Social tension is indeed very high in Venezuela, to the extent that riots were repressed in a very bloody manner in 1989. The pluralistic character of the party system has not been affected, however.

29. See G. O'Donnell *et al.* (eds), *op. cit.*, (1986) for a discussion of the extent to which the pluralistic party system can be said to be 'consolidated' in Latin America. It is interesting to note that elections for a regular second or third presidential mandate have taken place in Ecuador, Argentina, and Peru in the late 1980s or early 1990s.

30. These sytems remained one-party until 1989. There are doubts about the robustness of any party system which is likely to emerge in Eastern Europe – see note 5.

31. Elections have taken place in Iran since the fall of the Emperor in the late 1970s: these elections have had a limited pluralistic character and some degree of opposition has indeed been manifested in the parliament.

13 The role of electoral systems

Among the forces which determine the character of party systems, and in particular the configuration of parties, electoral systems are commonly singled out for attention. The literature on the subject is vast.[1] Naturally enough, as soon as elections started to play a part in the political process, discussions on the consequences which would follow from the manipulation of electoral systems began to take place. Yet the precise character of the relationship between electoral systems and party systems is still an object of controversy, partly because the problem has often been approached unsystematically, and partly because large numbers of observations of a homogeneous kind have been difficult to obtain: the numbers in each cell are small and the variations among electoral systems numerous.[2] Yet perhaps the overwhelming reason for the fascination with the study of electoral systems has been the belief that electoral arrangements are powerful instruments of political engineering, able to shape the characteristics of party systems.

The direction of this causal relationship is now somewhat in doubt, though the existence of a relationship is undeniable. Yet controversies about the impact of electoral systems on party systems have tended to obscure the fact that the problems posed by electoral systems are more general. Electoral systems are not merely mechanisms by which votes are translated into seats; they are also broader arrangements about procedures. They are indeed a way of behaving politically. They are rules according to which voters and candidates should act if party competition is to reflect the conflicts which exist in the society. They are therefore not merely means by which party configurations come to emerge; they are also – and perhaps more fundamentally – concerned with the extent and nature of competition. They are so by helping to determine both the conditions to be fulfilled by individuals in order to become electors and the conditions under which individuals and parties are entitled to participate in electoral contests. Thus, while the extent to which electoral mechanisms are related to different configurations of party systems will be examined, it is also necessary to look at the ways in which general electoral provisions help to create a framework within which party competition can truly develop.

Electoral systems and the extent and nature of party competition

Electoral systems and the voter

Electoral systems affect the extent and nature of party competition by determining who is entitled to vote and by providing various types of protection to electors. The question of the extension of the suffrage to all classes and groups has historically been the main issue raised by voter entitlement. By and large, restrictions based on property, literacy, or sex have been abolished but racial restrictions still constituted, by the 1990s, a major issue in the context of the South African government's refusal to grant voting rights to blacks. The main development of the 1970s and 1980s has been to bring the voting age down to 18; nationality is still a requirement almost everywhere, but that restriction is being slowly eroded in favour of a condition of residence only, thus ensuring that immigrants may have a vote, at least in local elections.[3] Overall, one can list nine types of restriction – age, nationality, criminal record, residence, the holding of some office, sex, literacy, property, and race. In general, the first four types can and do occur in a universal suffrage situation, though the manipulation of the residence qualification can seriously limit the franchise and it has sometimes been used to this effect; the next type of restriction constitutes a borderline case; finally, with any of the last four, the suffrage is clearly not universal.

Entitlement to vote does not mean the effective ability to vote: a procedure has to be devised, in particular to avoid fraud, by which electors are registered on a list. In practice this procedure can constitute a barrier to voting if it is administered bureaucratically; in any case there will always be some delay. This is why permanent registers, amended at periodic intervals or at prescribed periods (for instance before elections) are more efficient and ultimately less costly than registers periodically created *de novo*. European countries tend to have permanent registers, but, in the United States, as registration periods are felt to have a mobilising effect, the periodic register has been maintained.

The existence of a register imposes a place of voting, specifically a polling station. This introduces some rigidity, which can be alleviated by means of postal or proxy arrangements, but these entail obvious administrative costs and the opportunities for fraud are increased. A truly comprehensive system of postal voting requires both a highly developed administrative structure and a low level of fraud. In practice, the demand for postal vote facilities increases as the population becomes more mobile, that is to say with socio-economic development: not surprisingly, these arrangements have become more common in the Atlantic area in the second half of the twentieth century.

Overall, whatever the system, a substantial number of potential electors are likely not to be registered – probably at least 5–10 per cent and in many cases more.[4] Absence, illness, or pressing business result in some registered voters being unable to cast their ballot on polling day or being unwilling to take the trouble to do so, especially where a postal or proxy vote is difficult to obtain. Compulsory voting has been introduced in some countries (Australia, Austria, Belgium, Italy and some Latin American states) in order to remedy this problem, but the requirement is somewhat ineffective as the fines incurred are usually small and may not even be collected.

Electoral systems, candidates and parties

Traditionally, electoral systems were concerned almost exclusively with what might be called formal or negative equality, that is to say with the task of ensuring that all candidates were treated equally. The most important advance in this context has been achieved by the secret ballot, a requirement which is sometimes reinforced (as in Britain and Belgium) by the legal requirement that votes should not be counted at the level of the polling station, but at that of a larger unit. The secrecy requirement has been both simple and successful; once rejected by the USSR authorities on the grounds that it was a 'bourgeois' practice, it has probably come to be recognised everywhere as the protection par excellence for electors and candidates.

Other 'negative' requirements relate to the repression of fraud, which can take many forms. Permanent registers aim at stamping out impersonation and double voting, for instance. Other forms, such as bribery, threats, or blackmail, are more difficult to eradicate, partly because some of these practices cannot easily be defined with precision: for instance, the rumour that some threats may be carried out may lead electors to vote in a certain way. In rural areas in particular, citizens who are in a position of dependence and on whom employers can exercise influence may be too frightened to consider voting for an opposition candidate. Fraud can also take place at the count, for instance by spoiling ballots of the opposition or by secretly introducing piles of ballots for favoured candidates. It is therefore typically required that ballot boxes be opened before the vote begins to show that they are empty and that they be opened at the end of the process in the presence of representatives of various parties. Voting machines, which are in use in the United States, are of considerable value, as they are less easily tampered with than ballot papers; European countries have resisted the introduction of these devices, probably on the grounds of tradition.

In Atlantic countries in particular, the focus of attention has moved more recently to positive requirements designed to achieve 'real' equality. In the first phase, mainly immediately following World War II in Western Europe, an attempt was made to limit expenditure by candidates and to provide a number of services in kind, such as the mailing of election addresses and, more importantly, access to radio and television on an equal footing, a requirement which raises problems of apportionment of time among the candidates. In the second phase, which started in the late 1950s, it became suggested that campaigns and political parties should be directly financed out of public funds, in order to offset the increased costs incurred and the consequential inequalities among candidates. Despite criticisms that such developments might lead (and indeed perhaps did lead) to a decline in party mobilising efforts as the need to obtain funds from individual citizens would be reduced, public funding of campaigns and parties has spread widely across the Western world in the 1970s and 1980s.[5]

Electoral systems thus include a vast panoply of devices designed to ensure that campaigning and voting take place in conditions of fairness for candidates and electors. Some of these techniques are well-established though they are far from being universally adopted (in part because many governments are not particularly anxious, to say the least, to abolish fraud); other arrangements are in a process of development. In the West, matters of electoral fairness, except perhaps the question of party finance, are no longer regarded as sufficiently controversial or as raising sufficiently large theoretical issues to deserve detailed study – yet they are manifestly fundamental, as they determine the framework without which matters of seat allocation, to which the discussion now turns, do not even have occasion to arise.

Electoral systems and the principles of seat allocation

Much has been written about the mechanics of allocation of seats and about techniques designed to improve them.[6] Originally, this allocation was conceived as stemming directly from the majority principle: it seemed logical that seats should be given to candidates having the most votes. Later, however, it was felt that this allocation should be made on a proportional basis and 'proportional representation' (PR) thus became an alternative to the majority system – an alternative felt by many to be an improvement.[7] However, this development led to the recognition that another matter was at stake, namely the question of the number of seats to be allocated within each area – a question which is also of major importance, though it is still sometimes not given prominence in assessing the fairness of electoral systems.[8]

Methods of seat allocation

Majority systems

The method of allocation of seats is based in broad terms on the distinction between majority and proportional systems. There are, however, a number of subdivisions of both techniques which lead to appreciably different results. The first method is the simplest: candidates are elected on a simple majority basis; this is the 'first-past-the-post' system, widely used in Anglo-Saxon countries, specifically in Britain, the United States, Canada, New Zealand, and many new Commonwealth countries.

As this system is often felt to be too harsh on minorities, it can be modified in four different ways. One consists in deciding that there shall be *two ballots* and that, at the first, only those candidates who obtained at least 50 per cent of the votes will be elected. There is then a second ballot for those seats not filled at the first, but, at that point, only the top two candidates can stand or else some other arrangements are devised to limit the number of candidates. This system has been in use in France at most General Elections since 1870 (in the Third and Fifth Republics), while it was also widely used on the continent of Europe before 1914; it is also adopted in some 'run-off' American primaries.

Another method, known as the *alternative vote*, which is in use in Australia, avoids the second ballot by asking electors to express an order of preference among the candidates. The bottom candidate or candidates are then eliminated at the count and preferences are re-distributed until an absolute majority is obtained for the top candidates.

In constituencies which have at least two seats, two other methods can be used. One consists of deciding that, though constituencies have more than one seat, electors will have only one vote. Medium-sized minorities are thus represented, though complex strategies have to be devised by the parties in order to decide how many candidates they need to field to maximise their chances. Despite these difficulties, this system, which is known as the *single non-transferable vote*, is far from unworkable: it has operated for decades in Japan.

Finally, one can decide that no party can present more than a *limited* number of candidates (less than there are seats): minorities are therefore necessarily represented. This system was in force in Britain in some constituencies during part of the nineteenth century and is currently in use in some American local elections and at the national level in Mexico.

PR systems

Proportional representation systems can also be divided into a number of categories, which display different degrees of proportionality. A system is perfectly proportional if no vote is wasted, a requirement which is obviously difficult to satisfy, first because there will be 'remainders' when the votes cast for the parties are translated into the much smaller number of seats to be filled and, second, because some candidates will have more votes than are needed for election: if three seats have to be filled in a given district, for instance, a candidate who obtains more than 33.3 of the votes has 'excess' votes. These difficulties can be overcome, however, by adopting a method analogous to the one used in the alternative vote, that is to say by re-distributing to other candidates both the votes which are in excess and those which result from the elimination of candidates who receive very few 'first preferences'. To simplify the process, which could be long if every preference in every ballot was taken into account, a quota, known as the Droop quota from the name of the author who proposed it, has been calculated: it states the minimum necessary to ensure that there are not more candidates elected than there are seats. This is given by the formula $V/(S + 1) + 1$.[9] If there are 120 000 votes and three seats to be filled, it is not necessary to redistribute every vote; one can stop at the point when three candidates obtain 30 001 votes, as no other candidate can obtain more than 29 997. The determination of the elected candidates is thus more rapid, but, in the process, up to nearly a quarter of the votes, in this case, are indeed wasted; contrary to what is sometimes suggested, this system, which is known as the *single transferable vote* (STV) and is in use in Ireland, is thus not fully proportional. But it is 'very' proportional and it has also the advantage of enabling electors to express preferences, even against party wishes.[10]

The other broad method of proportional representation has given rise to the *list systems* which, on the contrary, are in large part based on a pre-ordering of candidates by the parties, though preferential voting may help to introduce some flexibility, as in Belgium or Italy. Such systems are in force in most countries of Western Europe, in Israel, and in Latin America.[11] They are known as 'list' systems because the candidates are presented on party lists. A quotient is calculated (V/S), which a list must reach to be allocated seats. However, as the totals obtained by the lists are not normally exactly multiples of the quotient, there are unfilled seats and there are 'remainders': these seats are then attributed on the basis of the *largest remainders*, a rough-and-ready method which is scarcely proportional.

In order to improve proportionality, an alternative technique of allocation of seats is that of the *highest average* (or D'Hondt system, from the name of the author who proposed this arrangement), whereby lists are compared – and given seats – by dividing the totals of their votes by the series of integers: thus a list will be given seats if the average number of votes, divided by the number of the seats which it is obtaining, is higher than the average obtained in the same manner by the other lists. This system is closer to proportionality than the system of the largest remainder, but it does favour large parties because, as the number of votes of a large party is divided successively by the series of integers, the absolute distance tends mechanically to diminish: thus the number of extra votes needed to obtain a fifth or sixth seat is less than the number needed to obtain a second or third seat.

To remedy this situation, Scandinavian countries have tended to adopt a variation on the D'Hondt system, known as the *Sainte-Lague system*, which consists in using as divisers, not the series of integers, but numbers which come nearer to producing a proportional result; these numbers are not necessarily integers.

As it is often felt that the representation of very small parties – those which obtain 1, 2, or 3 per cent of the votes – should be discouraged, it is sometimes decided to introduce a minimum below which parties will not be allocated seats: the hurdle is thus 2 per cent in Denmark, 4 per cent in Sweden and 5 per cent in West Germany. The introduction of such a clause may reduce by perhaps as much as 10 per cent, overall, the proportionality of the system, as the experience of West Germany has shown.

Finally, there are mixed systems, which include elements of both proportional representation and majority systems. Sometimes, the idea is to give a boost to a large party or an alliance of parties which agree in advance to be related (*apparentés*) to each other: this was devised in France and Italy in the 1950s, with limited success. Sometimes, as in West Germany, some seats are allocated on a majority basis while others are allocated on proportional representation; in this case, however, as seats given to parties on a majority basis are deducted from the totals to which parties are entitled after the allocation of PR seats is made, the result is in effect proportional.

The distinction between PR and majority systems thus covers a complex set of arrangements which lead to different levels of proportionality. In fact, the eleven types which we have just described can be ranked in increasing order of proportionality as follows:

1. First-past-the-post.
2. Two-ballot.
3. Alternative vote.
4. Single non-transferable vote.
5. Limited vote.
6. Mixed *apparentement* systems.
7. Minimum percentage clauses.
8. Largest remainder.
9. D'Hondt system.
10. Sainte-Lague system.
11. STV.[12]

The size of districts and the results

Although the technical method of allocating seats is the most obvious way in which electoral systems affect results, the number of seats in each district also plays a major part, both within each constituency and between constituencies. Within constituencies, the effects of the first-past-the-post system and of STV are the converse of each other: with STV, the larger the number of seats in the constituency, the more proportional the system, as one can easily understand;[13] in the first-past-the-post system, on the contrary, as the largest party obtains all the seats, the larger the constituency, the less proportional the result, since local variations are then submerged in the bigger constituency. Other electoral systems have intermediate effects, because there can be deals among the parties (two-ballot system), because electors can exercise different preferences (alternative vote), or because the largest remainder system tends to favour smaller parties as the number of seats in each constituency increases.

The question of the effect of electoral systems across constituencies raises the matter of the general impact of electoral systems on the national result and on party systems over time, which will be examined in the next section; but it also raises the more technical problem of the consequences which inequalities in population size have on this result. Clearly, electoral systems will have different results if the number of votes per seat varies markedly from one district to another. Naturally enough, parties which benefit from the current arrangements are anxious to maintain the status quo; the matter is further complicated by the question of the 'gerrymander' (where curiously-shaped constituencies have their boundaries drawn to minimise the chances of opponents) and therefore by the need to find impartial authorities empowered to draw the map of the constituencies (such as 'Boundary

Commissions' in the United Kingdom). Yet there are also administrative and political difficulties in approximating equality, as one may have to cut across local or regional boundaries; moreover, frequent redrawing of constituencies creates problems for party organisations, which are therefore often opposed to such changes. The question is particularly serious when the number of seats is small, and it is especially difficult to solve with single-member districts. At the opposite extreme, it is completely by-passed when the nation is one large constituency (as in the Netherlands and in Israel) or when the remainders are allocated on a national basis.

Given the multitude of electoral systems and the almost infinite permutations which can be obtained by playing both on the allocation of seats and on the number of seats in each district, it is not surprising that the technical problems posed by these systems should have fascinated both political theorists and mathematicians.[14] The direct effects of these mechanisms on the result in each district and even on the overall result are manifestly large. As a result, moreover, it is not surprising that there should have been interest in examining whether electoral systems also, indirectly, have broader effects on the overall party system, both at each election and over time. Hence the question of the relationship between electoral systems and party systems to which the discussion will now turn.

Electoral systems and party systems

Electoral systems and the national representation of parties

The effects just described occur mechanically, but they occur at the level of each constituency. The impact of electoral systems at the national level is naturally regarded as more important, but this impact results *only indirectly* from constituency results. We have therefore to discover the nature of the link between constituency and national outcomes. To begin with, for a link to exist at all, parties have to be the same from one constituency to the other. Thus fully valid conclusions can be drawn about the national result only if parties are essentially national in character; this condition can be somewhat relaxed by stating that, the more parties are national, the better one can extrapolate from constituency results to the national result. As socio-economic development tends to 'nationalise' parties, the relationship between the constituency effect and the national impact of electoral systems can be expected to increase with development; specifically, conclusions on the national impact of electoral systems can therefore be drawn more easily for Atlantic countries than for other polities.

In proportional representation systems, the result is increasingly proportional as the number of seats per constituency increases. It follows that the impact will be different if there are appreciable variations in the number of seats per constituency in different parts of the country. This means that parties which are thinly spread throughout the country are at a disadvantage if the average constituency size is small, but that they will gain somewhat if some of the constituencies are large (as sometimes happens with big cities). Generally, if constituencies have three to five seats only, parties which obtain 15 per cent of the votes or less will be ill-represented; thus, in a multi-party system in which five or six parties receive a significant share of the votes, constituencies should have six to eight members for representation to be relatively accurate.[15]

In majority systems, on the contrary, the smaller the constituency size, the more accurate the representation. But, even with single-member districts, large parties are at a premium, while those whose support is thinly and evenly spread can be grossly under-represented, a state of affairs from which the British Liberal party has suffered markedly, given that what counts is the size of the support in each constituency; on the other hand, for the same reason, a relatively small party whose support is clustered geographically can achieve satisfactory representation (as was the case in Britain with the Scottish National Party in the 1970s).

Furthermore, even among the major parties, a marked unevenness in the distribution of votes across the country will result in substantial distortions: a party which comes second in every constituency will not obtain a single seat, even if it obtained a substantial proportion of the votes, as what counts is the existence of clusters of strength. For the representation of the major parties to be relatively accurate, two conditions have therefore to be fulfilled. First, the distribution of the support has to be statistically 'normal' across the country.[16] Second, the overall strength of the major parties needs to be relatively close, as, even if this strength is distributed 'normally', a large imbalance in votes will result in a much larger imbalance in seats: both in Britain and in New Zealand, the disparity has been found empirically to be expressed in the form of a 'cube law', by which the ratio of the seats of the two major parties varies as the ratio of the cubes of the votes going to these parties, a ratio which seems independent from the number of 'observations' (i.e. from the number of seats in the country).[17]

Relatively accurate results (among the major parties) depend therefore on the 'normal' distribution of the parties across the nation; they depend also on the absence of biases in the distribution of these parties among large and small constituencies. Though constituencies of equal size are preferable, this is not an imperative, provided the distribution of smaller and larger seats among the main parties is random. Given a large number of constituencies and given boundary changes operated by impartial commissions, this condition is likely to be achieved.

Single-member majority systems can therefore produce a relatively good representation of voting patterns provided that these are based on a (small) number of relatively balanced parties, that these parties are spread evenly across the nation, and that the constituencies are drawn in an impartial fashion. Homogeneity is a prerequisite; a small number of parties is also a prerequisite and, consequently, a two-party system is preferable. It is not surprising that these systems, whose operation depends on somewhat peculiar socio-economic characteristics, should often distort results; nor is it surprising that they should have drawn politicians in many countries to move to proportional representation which, by comparison, constitutes a simple piece of 'machinery' which is less likely to 'go wrong'.

The dynamics of electoral systems and party systems

The influence of electoral systems on party representation at a given election naturally leads to the suggestion that electoral systems might also have a dynamic impact over a number of elections and over the party system as a whole. Not surprisingly, this question has exercised political scientists for a long time, although analyses have tended to be limited to the examination of the possible influence of party systems on the number of parties, rather than on their relative strength, their ideology, their structure, or their social basis. Almost certainly, the impact of electoral systems on party structure and social base has not been fully explored because, as was seen in the last chapter, systems of more than one party have lasted only for short periods outside the Atlantic area. Moreover, where parties are not legitimate mass, even if they have existed for a long time, the conditions of the competition are such that the mechanical effects of electoral systems over time are likely to be minimised.[18] Yet it seems to be the case that, because large or larger constituencies are a prerequisite of proportional representation, this system is more likely to nationalise the confrontation than the single-member majority system: in France, for instance, proportional representation was introduced for a time as a weapon against sectional electoral politics, though this system was not maintained for a sufficiently long period to assess whether it was to have a deep 'deparochialising' effect.[19] Where communal politics plays a large part, however, proportional representation might contribute to the integration of the various communities – though such an effect has not been very apparent in Northern Ireland or in Guyana. Overall, the evidence from countries outside the Atlantic area is too scattered to provide support for the view that electoral systems have a long-standing effect on the basis and the structure of parties.

There is, on the other hand, enough evidence drawn from within the Atlantic area and from a few other countries to test the view that electoral systems have lasting effects on the number of significant parties. This relationship has been stated for a long time in terms of the proposition that single-member first-past-the-post systems lead to two-party systems while proportional representation encourages multi-party systems. This assertion, which had been repeatedly made at least since the beginning of the twentieth century, was more systematically taken up by Duverger in the 1940s, though the first really rigorous test was made by Rae in the 1960s.[20] In a general and impressionistic manner, the relationship appears close: four of the five two-party systems of the 1950s and 1960s had a first-past-the-post electoral system (the fifth being Austria), while only one of the Atlantic countries (Canada) had the first-past-the post-system but not a two-party system. Further impressionistic evidence is provided by the fact that the large majority of the two-party systems outside the Atlantic area consists of countries which have adopted the first-past-the-post system. The systematic analysis conducted by Rae, which was based on the examination of the relationship between electoral systems and party systems over a series of elections, mainly in Atlantic countries, confirms the broad thrust of the argument: there is a strong positive association between single-member first-past-the-post systems and two-party systems, though there are some exceptions.[21]

While this relationship does exist, questions of extent of influence and of interpretation of the causal direction still arise. Earlier analyses manifestly grossly exaggerated the extent of influence. For instance, the victory of Nazism in Germany was attributed to proportional representation because it was argued that this electoral system led to unstable government, a proposition which will be examined in Chapter 18.[22] The argument followed the sequence: proportional representation, number of parties, instability of government. It is because the presence of a large number of parties is attributed to PR that the instability of government is in turn linked to this electoral system: it should simply be noted at this stage that the evidence suggests only that two-party systems are likely to be associated to single-member first-past-the-post systems.

The extent of the influence of electoral systems was further attributed by Duverger to the assertion that 'all polities' tended 'naturally' towards dualism if they were not 'hampered' by the electoral system.[23] This is an interpretation of the electoral and political evolution of societies (in effect of Western societies) for which no evidence is provided. Indeed, the (admittedly somewhat circumstantial) evidence which exists seems to suggest that no such tendency exists. First, when analysing systems of more than one party in the previous chapter, there was no suggestion of any movement towards the two-party system (except for a short period in West Germany); however, polities were seen to move in the other direction (for example, Britain, Germany in the 1980s, and indeed Austria). Moreover, if the question is considered historically (as it was by Duverger), it can be seen that the Scandinavian countries and Germany, which had a single-member majority system before World War I, did not move at all towards a two-party system and that the Belgian two-party system lasted for a long period and was broken by the arrival of socialism *before* the introduction of PR. Finally, Duverger's proposition is in part based on the proposition that PR leads to party splits, a point for which there is only scattered and inconclusive evidence.[24]

If one is looking for broader 'tendencies' and societal trends, moreover, it should be noted that both the single-member first-past-the-post system and the two-party system are common only among Anglo-Saxon countries. Of these, only Australia and Ireland (as well as Guyana in the Third World) do *not* have a first-past-the-post system. Conversely, no country outside this group has a first-past-the-post system, though some (such as France and Japan) have other types of majority systems. While the two-party system is not a preserve of the Anglo-Saxon world (and while several Commonwealth countries do not have a two-party system), the relationship is close: the degree of association between two-party systems and single-member first-past-the-post systems is as high as the degree of association between two-party systems and Anglo-Saxon political culture. There is thus good reason to suggest that the 'cause' may not be entirely found in the electoral system.

This leads directly to the question of the interpretation of the causal direction of influence. In examining this, it is worth remembering that the major factor which characterises two-party systems in contrast with two-and-a-half and multi-dominant party systems is that the two parties are balanced – at least to the extent that, over a period, they tend to be relatively equal. It was noted earlier that the single-member first-past-the-post system could produce a fairly good representation of parties only if parties were relatively equal in strength and if they were distributed in the country in a statistically normal fashion. Proportional representation, on the contrary, appears to correspond to polities in which party strength is often structurally unbalanced and the number of significant parties is large.

It seems therefore that a plausible hypothesis is not so much that the single-member first-past-the-post system 'causes' a two-party system but, rather, that only polities which naturally produce structural balance among the parties can 'afford' this electoral system and consequently that polities which over a period do not come to be structurally balanced do not find the single-member first-past-the-post system satisfactory. The only clear examples of countries which have maintained the single-member first-past-the-post system without having a balanced party system are Canada and India, though Britain itself came close to a similar situation in the 1970s and 1980s. In the Canadian case, the complexity of the party system is compounded by the existence of different configurations at the provincial level: this appears to reduce the call for change, at any rate as long as the third main party, that of the New Democrats, does not make a breakthrough in Quebec (traditionally because of its low popularity among French-speaking Canadians): the New Democrats are thus not real contenders for 'major party' status.[25] In India, the dominance of the Congress party has been such that there is normally little alternative. An alternative did emerge only as a result of the discontent resulting from the 'Emergency' measures of Mrs Gandhi in the mid-1970s and, second, in 1989, also as a result of discontent with the policies and leadership of Rajiv Gandhi; however, in this last case, the opposition to the Congress party was divided and Congress remained the largest party. In Britain, on the contrary, pressure for a change in the electoral system was strengthened as a result of the growth of the Liberal party since the late 1960s: the pressure always becomes weaker when the centre party (or parties) fare less well at the polls.

The question of the influence of electoral systems on party systems has probably over-occupied the minds of political scientists in search of 'laws' appearing to account mechanically for the development of party systems.[26] It is not possible to modify the whole of a country's party system through the operation of a device such as an electoral system. In the first place, opponents of change would be likely to resist such a form of 'engineering', as they have done in Britain. Moreover, even if the system is changed, the defenders of the existing system will simply try to return to the old electoral arrangements as soon as possible; this has happened in a number of occasions in France, including in the 1980s.

Conclusion

It is far from certain that electoral systems are anything more than the most adequate reflection of the kind of party configurations which members of a polity rightly or wrongly think is 'their own' and which expresses them best. This is not to suggest that members of the polity are in a position to decide impartially what the best party configuration should be; but it is to state that structurally unbalanced systems and multi-party systems may be favourably regarded in some polities. Contrary to a view commonly held in both political and academic circles, unbalanced party configurations appear to be acceptable and are indeed accepted in many countries. People adjust to the situation; indeed, some may prefer it, on the grounds that different shades of opinion are given a chance to be represented. One way of ensuring that such a situation obtains is to devise an electoral system which maintains the configuration which is in existence and which is broadly accepted. Thus the relationship between electoral systems and party systems may not be unidirectional. Electoral systems can be viewed as mechanisms designed to strengthen and maintain an equilibrium among the parties and among the social groups which relate to the parties; they may not be 'rules of the game' invented in advance to produce an ideal form of party system. Ultimately, it is the party system, not the electoral system, which really counts.

Moreover, the parts of the electoral system which count most are perhaps not the provisions relating to the allocation of seats, but those which were examined at the beginning of this chapter and which relate to the exercise of the right to vote and to campaign. If it is felt that liberal government is more likely to flourish under a system of more than one party, it is through the development of these conditions that systems of more than one party will develop, not through the accidents of a particular system of allocation of seats.

Notes

1. Although the literature on electoral systems is vast, much is descriptive rather than systematic. A comprehensive description of types of electoral systems can be found in W.J.M. Mackenzie, *Free Elections* (1958). But the main problem which has attracted attention has been the question of the effects of majority and proportional systems on party systems. The controversy in this field has lasted many decades: in the 1930s and early 1940s, it was sometimes argued that proportional representation was responsible for the coming to power of Hitler (see F.A. Hermens, *Democracy or Anarchy?* (1940)). In his classic on *Political Parties*, M. Duverger attempted to develop what he described as a 'law' of the relationship between two-party systems and the single member single ballot system on the basis of both psychological assumptions and the examination of a number of cases. The question was first truly systematically examined in the late 1960s by D.W. Rae in *The Political Consequences of Electoral Laws* (1967). See also A. Lijphart, *Democracies* (1984), pp. 150–69.
2. This is precisely where progress was made by D. Rae, as this author, unlike his predecessors, took each election, and not each country, as the unit of analysis: the

number of cases is thereby markedly increased and the problem of the relationship between electoral systems and party systems can be subjected to systematic statistical treatment.

3. In the 1980s, the question has begun to arise as to whether citizens of European Community countries living in a country different from their own can vote in their country of residence.

4. In Belgium, for instance, abstention is between 5 and 8 per cent, despite the fact that voting is compulsory.

5. The question of campaign finance began to be studied in the 1960s. The subject became increasingly popular, both among scholars and among politicians, as a number of proposals were presented and laws were passed. See A.J. Heidenheimer (ed.), *Comparative Political Finance* (1970) and H.E. Alexander (ed.), *Comparative Political Finance in the 1980s* (1989). For the United States, see H.E. Alexander, *Financing Politics* (1984).

6. For a descriptive summary of the types of electoral systems, see W.J.M. Mackenzie, *op. cit.* (1958). See also V. Bogdanor, *What is Proportional Representation* (1984) and V. Bogdanor and D.E. Butler (eds), *Democracy and Elections* (1983).

7. Proportional representation was strongly advocated by J.S. Mill in *Representative Government* (1861) in its single transferable vote form. The system which gained ground at the end of the nineteenth and early twentieth centuries was the list system: it was adopted gradually throughout most of Europe before World War II. Various forms of proportional representation are in use in Latin America. Commonwealth countries generally kept the majority system (with some exceptions, such as Guyana); the countries which adopt the single-party system generally also adopt the majority system: the Soviet Union, for instance, had traditionally adopted the single member majority system. With the introduction of pluralistic systems in some Communist countries, proportional representation is also being introduced, at least to an extent: this has been the case in Hungary for the 1990 election.

8. The question of the number of seats in each district has not typically been given considerable importance in the literature, except in the context of the distinction between single- and multi-member systems. The question is systematically examined by D. Rae, *op. cit.* (1967), pp. 19–21, however.

9. The formula $V/(S + 1) + 1$ was adopted as it gives the smallest figure necessary for the election to produce a number of candidates equal to and not larger than the quota. If full proportionality was the goal, the formula V/S would have to be adopted.

10. The single transferable vote is the one which is always discussed in Britain when the question of introducing proportional representation arises; it has indeed been introduced in Northern Ireland for the European elections.

11. See G. Hand, J. Georgel, and C. Sasse, *European Electoral Systems Handbook* (1979) and A. Lijphart, *Choosing an Electoral System* (1984).

12. This ordering is given here only as an indication: minimum percentage clauses can have different effects depending on the size of the minimum percentage, for instance; moreover, the Sainte-Lague system can come very close to proportionality, but only provided the 'divisors' are adjusted with respect to the particular type of party distribution.

13. The decrease in constituency size can affect markedly the proportionality of STV. The question was examined in the Irish case (which is the only national case in existence) by J.F.S. Ross in *The Irish Electoral System* (1959), in particular pp. 3–9.

14. A number of mathematicians were interested in the question of the 'best possible' electoral system throughout the nineteenth and twentieth centuries, the first being the Frenchman Condorcet.

15. The condition of size is gradually beginning to be appreciated. The electoral system

adopted in Spain after the end of the Franco regime, for instance, gives a marked premium to the larger parties, as most constituencies are rather small (about five seats). The same was true of the formula adopted in France for the 1986 General Election. By contrast, district size is very large in Germany and Italy and sizeable in Sweden.

16. Support would not be normal if it was spread in such a way that the second party was *always* or nearly always second in all the districts. This is statistically more likely to happen if there are only few seats to fill: this is why, at the local level in Britain, for instance, results sometimes lead to the overwhelming dominance of one party in seats although the difference in the proportion of votes may not be very large.

17. Controversies about the 'cube law' have taken place, not so much in relation to the law itself, but about the way in which biases intervene. The problem has been studied of course mainly in connection with Britain. See D.E. Butler, *The Electoral System in Britain Since 1918* (1963), pp. 194–204.

18. Where party support is primarily based on the allegiance to groups, changes are not likely to take place in the pattern of voting competition.

19. France adopted proportional representation only between 1919 and 1924, between 1945 and 1956, and for the 1986 election. Thus contrary to what is often believed, proportional representation is not the cause of the large number and undisciplined character of French parties. This situation has been earlier ascribed to the two-ballot system which was deemed to have the same effect as proportional representation (see M. Duverger, *op. cit.*, pp. 239–44). As a matter of fact, the re-introduction of the two-ballot system in France in 1958 coincided with a reduction of the number and a streamlining of the parties, in particular at the 1962 General Election and at subsequent elections.

20. M. Duverger claimed in *Political Parties* that this association was clear-cut: see pp. 216–28. The stricter test was administered by D. Rae, *op. cit.*, pp. 87–103.

21. D. Rae, *op. cit.*, pp. 93–05.

22. F.A. Hermens, *op. cit.*, *passim*.

23. M. Duverger, *op. cit.*, p. 215.

24. Such splits are in fact rather rare, although they did occur in Denmark and Norway among socialist parties (in large part as a result of the question of the adhesion of these countries to the European Community).

25. See D. Rae, *op. cit.*, pp. 94–5, on the part played by linguistic and ethnic differences in Canada in ensuring that some parties are not truly national.

26. Perhaps one of the major difficulties with Duverger's 'law' was that the relationship which was found was assumed to indicate that electoral systems had an effect on party systems, and not vice versa.

14 | Parties, party systems and the political system

Most countries have parties and nearly all countries have had parties for some of the time in the course of the last few decades. These organisations are thus a major feature of contemporary societies, but this does not mean that they are all strong and that they influence markedly the political life of the countries in which they emerge and develop. Party leaders often talk, in a somewhat grandiose manner, about the way in which parties guide political life. They may not all claim, as in Communist states, that parties are at the 'vanguard', but, in different terms and with a different emphasis, they usually hold the view that their organisations shape society in a significant manner. How far can these claims be sustained and, since the part played by parties manifestly varies, how far can one discover these variations both between countries and at various points in time?

It is not possible as yet to provide a precise answer to these questions, given the current level of development of the instruments at one's disposal. Neither the empirical knowledge nor the conceptual tools to undertake such a task are currently available. Studies of the 'impact of parties' have begun to appear, especially with reference to Western countries, but these cover only one aspect of the problem by attempting to ascertain how far policy-making differs if one party is in power rather than another.[1] They do not assess how far parties shape societies and thus modify the overall framework within which politics take place. This is not surprising, as such questions raise the type of difficult problems which were examined in Chapter 1. Parties are institutions which are embedded in a certain social structure; the extent of their effect must in some way be related to the nature of the society. Thus the parties which are apparently most effective are probably also those which are most closely related to the characteristics of their society; they are therefore as likely to reflect the society as to shape it.

Yet parties surely have an effect, and this effect is likely to vary from society to society. If, rather than trying to answer the matter fully, an attempt is made to obtain merely an impression of this varied effect, two indicators can be used. The first is the extent of stability or, more precisely, of durability of organisations:

191

without postulating that a party or a party system which lasts for a long period is necessarily more effective than a party or a party system which has been in existence for some years only, it is surely reasonable to claim that, as a group, relatively durable parties or party systems are likely to have more impact than parties or party systems which remain in existence for short periods only.

The second indicator relates to the extent to which parties achieve, in different societies, the three levels of activities which were listed in Chapter 9. At the level of the society as a whole, they should provide a link between people and government; at the level of the political process, they should help to formulate decisions; and they should contribute significantly to the recruitment of the 'political class'. On the basis of the examination of cases which have been studied in greater detail, one can obtain at least an impression of the variations of the role of parties with respect to these three aspects, and thus begin to have an idea of the extent to which they influence political life in contemporary societies.

Stability and instability among party systems

Variations in party systems

Parties and party systems which are durable and are therefore relatively stable can be assumed to have at least a greater potential to exercise influence on their society than those which are not. If one concentrates in the first instance on party systems, the picture appears rather mixed. Only in a small majority of countries (87 out of 163, or 53 per cent) has the polity been ruled throughout the post-World War II period or from the time of independence by the same broad type of party system, that is to say it had either a continuous one-party system (38 cases, including six Communist states which became single-party in the late 1940s) or a system of more than one party (49 cases). On the other hand, 12 countries never had any parties at all (all of these were traditional regimes), while in the remaining 64, the polity changed at least once from one form of system to another: 14 of these countries were without parties in 1989 (all but two of a military type), 26 were one-party systems, and 24 were systems of more than one party (see Table 14.1).

As might be expected, the spread of stable and unstable party systems is rather uneven. While all the countries which became Communist after World War II continued to be ruled by a single-party system until 1989, and while nearly all the Atlantic countries were continuously ruled by a system of more than one party, party systems were markedly more unstable in the Third World, and the proportion of one-party systems and of systems of more than one party among them has varied from region to region. Overall, 54 Third World countries (out of 125) have had stable party systems since World War II or since independence, as against 59 unstable systems and 12 systems which were continuously without parties. South and South East Asia and Latin America have had the highest proportion of stable party systems (about half) and, coincidentally, of systems of more than one party. In

Table 14.1 Stable and unstable party systems (1950–89)

	No party		Single party	More than one party	Total countries
	Traditional	Military			
Stable	12	0	38	49	99
Unstable	2	12	26	24	64
Stable and in existence since 1970	10	0	29	40	79

Black Africa and in the Middle East and North Africa, only about one-third to two-fifths of the party systems were stable; in Black Africa, the large majority of these were of the one-party variety; in the Middle East and North Africa, both types were distributed evenly, but the main characteristic of the region is the large proportion of systems without parties (eight out of 22, all but one in the Arabian peninsula) (see Table 14.2).

Table 14.2 Stable and unstable party systems in the Third World

	Stable	Unstable	Total including countries which have never had parties
Middle East and North Africa	7	7	22
South and South-East Asia	13	7	24
Africa south of Sahara	18	28	46
Latin America	16	17	33
Total	54	59	125

Yet the picture must be further qualified in two ways. The first qualification relates to Latin America and in particular to the proportion of stable party systems of more than one party in that region. While the proportion of stable party systems of this type is relatively large overall, this is primarily due, not surprisingly in view of the findings described in Chapter 12, to the large number of relatively new and very small Commonwealth states in the Caribbean: only three countries of this group – Brazil, Colombia, and Costa Rica – are Latin American in the strict sense. Meanwhile, three of the four stable single-party systems of the region were from Spanish America (Mexico, Nicaragua, and Paraguay, the fourth being Antigua). Thus, among Latin American countries in the strict sense of the word, the proportion of stable party systems is as low as it is in the Middle East (six out of twenty countries, or 30 per cent) and these stable party systems are, as in the Middle East, distributed evenly among single-party systems and systems of more than one party. South and South-East Asia are thus the only region outside the Atlantic area where older and populous stable systems of more than one party exist in substantial numbers.[2]

The second qualification relates primarily to Black Africa and to single-party systems in that region. So far only those countries in which the party system remained the same throughout the whole period have been considered, though one exception was made for the six Eastern European countries which became single-party shortly after 1945. However, there are also countries which have been nearly as stable, either because the party system changes which affected them occurred early (in practice in the first five years after independence) or because they have been ruled by the same system for two decades (1970–1990). While the first group is small, with only four countries, the second includes thirteen polities; however, three of these overlap with the first group (though there are some doubts about how to categorise a small number of them).

Only two of these fourteen countries (the Dominican Republic and Venezuela) were ruled by systems of more than one party, while the other twelve were one-party systems in 1990. Thus if these cases are added to those which have been examined so far, the number of stable single-party systems increases to fifty and becomes almost equal to the number of stable systems of more than one party (fifty-one). The inclusion of these single-party systems also has the effect of increasing the stability of party systems in Black Africa, as eight of these 'relatively stable' single-party systems can be found in that region. Contrary to what is often believed, therefore, the polities of Black Africa can be regarded as having been relatively stable; they are about as stable as the polities of South and South East Asia and more stable than the continental countries of Central and South America and the Middle Eastern countries.

Thus, while Communist and Atlantic countries had truly stable systems of one party and of more than one party respectively, only about half the polities of Black Africa and South and South-East Asia have had stable party systems, in the first case of the single-party variety, in the second case of the more than one party variety. Stable party systems of Latin America proper and of the Middle East and North Africa have emerged in only about a third of the polities of these regions.

Borderline cases and variations among parties

A picture of only relative stability of party systems thus emerges, with little to choose in this respect between single-party systems and systems of more than one party. Yet it was already noted in Chapters 11 and 12 that there were borderline cases between single-party systems and systems of more than one party (in particular where there was a strongly dominant party) and between systems without parties and systems with parties. To these cases must also be added those where some change occurred in the basis or nature of the party or parties as well as in the nature of competition or of party configurations. Beyond or below the apparently 'exogenous' stability of the party system, there is an 'endogenous' instability among the parties themselves; this tends to further diminish the overall level of stability in contemporary political systems.

The borderline between single-party systems and systems of more than one party

A substantial number of countries of the Third World (twenty-one in 1990) are difficult to classify, as they are based on a strongly dominant party which allows for some element of pluralism. One-third of these are not classified as stable party systems as they had been at some point full single-party systems before or after being of the more than one party variety (Egypt, Senegal, Syria, or Zimbabwe, for instance). The remainder are so classified. Yet, in some of these cases, there has been a move, however slow and gradual, towards pluralism, as in Mexico in the 1980s; it therefore becomes difficult to claim with any assurance that these systems have been stable, although, of course, it would be rather arbitrary to select a precise point at which the major party ceases to be so dominant that the country should be viewed as being ruled by a system of more than one party. Such changes are not apparent, as yet, in all the countries of the group: little had happened in Taiwan, Singapore, or Madagascar by the late 1980s to suggest that an evolution was taking place at all. But there is a borderline area and the existence of such an area does tend to diminish further the proportion of stable systems, especially since to these countries must be added those in which the Communist system collapsed in 1989.[3]

The borderline between party systems and systems without parties

Such an evolution takes place because, while the same party remains in power, its character, and in particular its ideology and its social base, may be changing. A similar evolution may be occurring from another direction, as when a system without parties becomes a party system and in particular when a military regime sets up a party. There are few traditional regimes in which a somewhat artificial party of this type is organised in this manner (it did occur, however, in Iran, towards the end of the Shah's rule, as well as in Lesotho). These somewhat artificial single parties come into existence, as was seen in Chapter 11, in the hope that they will provide a stronger base for military rulers. The majority of the examples are from Black Africa, for instance Benin, Burkina Faso, Burundi, Chad, Rwanda, Somalia, Sudan, Togo and Zaire, but there have also been cases in the Middle East (Egypt, Libya) and in Asia (Pakistan, Bangladesh). Some of these parties have lasted long enough to be regarded as 'stable' according to the definitions given earlier, but this is not always the case.

What is at stake is whether these systems are truly different when the party is set up; moreover, if they *become* different in character, they are unlikely to be so at the beginning. Thus the situation is analogous to the one encountered earlier at the border between single-party systems and systems of more than one party. Systems which are 'military-cum-party' are true borderline cases which may or may not evolve, which probably take some time to become true party systems, and which may also collapse before this point is reached.[4]

Changes within single-party systems

Furthermore, it is questionable whether all the single-party systems or all the systems of more than one party which remained in existence throughout the post-1945 period can be regarded as having been genuinely stable, as some profound changes may have occurred. Some countries have been ruled continuously by a single-party system for substantial periods, but the party in power may be different – indeed so different that the bases of the regime are entirely transformed. Extreme examples of such 'instability' within single-party systems are Cuba and Nicaragua, which moved from the rule of a (dominant) authoritarian–inegalitarian single party to that of an authoritarian–egalitarian single party in Cuba and to that of a dominant authoritarian–egalitarian single party in Nicaragua. Less extreme forms can be found in Black Africa, when a leader replaces a single party by another, or in the Middle East (Iraq, Syria, South Yemen) where coups have occurred within the context of what is ostensibly the same single party. For instance, the Baath party has been the dominant organisation in Iraqi and Syrian politics for decades, yet changes in leadership have been sufficiently important to come close to approximating a change of regime. Indeed, the changes which occurred in Eastern European states in the 1960s and 1970s, as in Czechoslovakia in 1968–9, or in Poland and Hungary in the 1980s before the events of late 1989 led to a collapse of Communist rule, might also be deemed to have constituted forms of real instability.[5]

Thus a substantial number of single-party systems are stable only in the somewhat formal sense that a single party remains in power for decades. Differences in the characteristics of the party or of its leadership may be such that one should regard the change as close to being a change of regime. With single-party systems, problems of succession are often considerable: coups or palace revolutions constitute a common, if not a normal means of 'changing the guard'. As these succession periods are also often major turning points and sometimes lead to major political uncertainties, they have also to be regarded as constituting a hiatus in the stability of at least some single-party systems.[6]

Changes within systems of more than one party

Changes also occur within systems of more than one party; indeed, they occur in two ways, corresponding to two different types of situations. One type is somewhat related to the cases which have just been encountered among one-party systems. Thus Brazil moved from a truly pluralistic party system to a contrived two-party system which was brought about, between 1964 and 1984, by the action of the military; the country then returned to a pluralistic party system in 1984. The Indonesian party system also went through at least two sharply distinct periods during which there were different forms of imposition, since the ideologies of Soekarno and Suharto were vastly different.[7] The King of Morocco also put varying degrees of pressure on the political parties at different points in time, with the result that the party system and the parties themselves varied markedly in relative strength and in overall influence. These cases amount therefore to forms of instability of parties within systems of more than one party which resemble those encountered among single-party systems.

There is another way in which instability occurs within systems of more than one party: this results from changes in the electoral performance of parties which affect the configuration of the party system to such an extent that they amount to a difference in kind. This type of change is likely to occur when the country undergoes a traumatic experience, as Germany did between 1933 and 1945; the experience which France underwent in 1958 was also sufficiently dramatic to transform what had been an ill-organised multi-party system into a multi-party system with a dominant party.[8] However, the increased changes in the relative strength of parties which result from the apparently greater independence of voters is sometimes also sufficiently large, as was seen in Chapter 12, at least to raise the question of the stability of these systems. This has been the case in particular in Belgium and Denmark; the British party system also seemed, at least at some points in the late 1970s and early 1980s, to be on the verge of a profound transformation, and a return to a similar uncertainty cannot be altogether ruled out.

Parties and party systems of the contemporary world are thus not very durable. First, the party systems are unstable, as nearly half the polities which have had parties have moved at least once from a single-party system to a system of more than one party or, more often, vice versa as well as from and into systems without parties. Moreover, in a number of countries at the borderline, movements are taking place which may also change the nature of the party system. This type of instability, originally confined to the Third World, has extended to the Communist area as well. Meanwhile, the party systems of the Communist and Atlantic countries, as well as those of the Third World, have also been somewhat affected by another type of instability which results from internal changes within the system, either because the character of the ruling party is profoundly transformed or because the configuration of parties is so altered that the 'rules of the game' become different. It therefore seems that most contemporary parties and party systems are not very solid, including many of those in the Atlantic area and those in the Communist world which have not collapsed altogether, and that the potential for strength and influence is consequently rather limited.

The weight of parties in contemporary political systems

The durability of party systems is clearly an indication of the strength and impact of parties in the different polities, but it is at best a rough indication. Ostensibly at least, some parties which collapsed and were never reconstituted, such as Nkrumah's Convention People's Party in Ghana, or parties which were reconstituted after a long period during which they were banned, such as the Peronist party in Argentina, had a considerable impact on their country. Conversely, parties which were in existence continuously or at least for a long period, such as those which the military set up and maintained in a number of Black African countries, appear to have had little influence.

Parties and the recruitment of national decision-makers

Although no general measurement of the weight of parties in different political systems has been undertaken so far, it seems possible to draw tentative conclusions by considering the role of parties at the three levels at which they are expected to play a part in political systems. Let us first look at the impact of parties on the recruitment of national decision-makers. If parties are the main agencies through which these are recruited, the role of the parties is likely to be significant in society. Although no study has as yet examined comparatively the extent to which governmental leaders and ministers are selected through parties, some broad conclusions can be drawn.

By and large, top national decision-makers tend to be recruited through the party machinery where the party system is stable, both in single-party systems and in systems of more than one party. For instance, by and large, they have traditionally been drawn from the parties in Atlantic and Communist countries. The same applies to Third World states which have had a stable party system, but, as has been explained, these constitute a minority.

This generalisation needs to be qualified in three ways, however. First, while on the whole unstable parties play little part in the recruitment of national decision-makers, this is particularly the case where they are artificially created and sustained, for instance by military rulers. On the other hand, those unstable parties which emerge naturally may, during the years in which they are in existence, be an important source of recruitment of national leaders: this is typically the case in Latin America during periods in which civilian rule prevails. This means that, overall, in a given country, national leaders may not be primarily drawn from parties, but some may be. It is the artificial character, rather than the lack of continuity, of the party which is the critical factor.

Second, even in stable parties, highly personalised leaders may be able to circumvent party activists and bring to the top of the political system men and women who have not moved up the party hierarchy. They may for instance be able to appeal to specialists and to technicians whose ties with the party were small or even non-existent. This type of situation occurs relatively frequently in some Western European countries.[9]

Third, the institutional framework may provide leaders with greater or lesser room for manoeuvre. Parties are likely to be less critical in the recruitment of national decision-makers where the executive is located at some distance above the rest of the institutions. This is of course the case when the leader is a national figure who is above the political system as a whole, for instance because he or she has saved or wholly reconstructed the country. This naturally also occurs in the few remaining polities where a monarch is able to dominate political life. Moreover, it also arises in presidential systems, as (both according to the constitution and in practice) the executive is not linked closely to the legislature. Thus, in presidential systems in general and in the United States in particular, the part played by party in the recruitment of national decision-makers is smaller than in Western European parliamentary systems, though, even there, differences exist which arise from the fact that the leader and the government as a whole may be regarded as somewhat distant from the legislature.[10]

Thus, even in stable party systems, a proportion – and often a large proportion – of national decision-makers does not emerge from the parties. Yet, by and large, the role of parties is important in recruitment: they have almost a monopoly of selection in a sizeable number of countries, both single-party and of more than one party, and they are a substantial factor in recruitment in many other polities. To this extent at least, parties have a considerable weight in the fabric of many contemporary polities.

Parties and national decision-making

It is more difficult to be so definite with respect to the role of parties in national decision-making itself, for the measurement of this role is more problematic. If parties are decentralised, for instance, their impact is likely to be more diffuse. Moreover, party influence on decision-making probably varies everywhere according to the fields of governmental activity; they are less involved, at any rate in a continuous manner, in foreign than in domestic affairs. Finally, parties may be more concerned with short-term gains than with long-term developments.

Distinctions can be made, however. At one extreme, some parties play a substantial part in the definition of governmental programmes and even in the solution of conflicts over specific issues. This occurs especially in parliamentary systems where there are coalition governments, though it happens also when the government is of one party. This suggests that parties will be more influential where the party system has been stable for a substantial period, though they may occasionally play a substantial part even if they are in control for short periods only. By and large, the areas in which this type of party influence has prevailed most are the Communist and Atlantic areas.[11]

At the other extreme are the situations in which the party or parties are too inchoate to have a clear decision-making impact. This can be because a party is emerging very slowly from a large communal group and its local leaders are in such control of the organisation that they can take whatever decisions they wish, irrespective of other participants; this situation has become relatively rare. A more frequent form of limited party influence can be found in the cases of parties which are recent creations of a leader, especially of a military leader; the main national decision-makers are then the leader, the entourage of the leader, and the bureaucracy. Thus, in Black Africa, in the Middle East and North Africa, as well as to a lesser extent in Asia (in South Korea and Taiwan, for instance), the role of the party as such in the national decision-making process appears limited.

These situations are not rigid, however; even parties in which the leader was originally fully in control can gradually acquire influence with respect to at least some aspects of decision-making. Conversely, parties which are typically relatively influential can become, perhaps only temporarily, so dominated by a leader that his or her policy may prevail whatever the party may have wished. This has been the case in some Western European countries, Mrs Thatcher's Britain being an example. The result is a combination of relatively small areas of party influence and of large areas in which the leaders and their entourage (often with the help of the national bureaucracy) are in charge of decision-making. But there are also intermediate cases which are more stable, in that the institutional arrangements favour a dissociation between party and governmental decision-making; this is the case in presidential systems in general and in the United States in particular, where parties appear to play more the part of pressure groups than that of central elements in the elaboration of the policy framework.[12]

Parties thus seem to play a major part in decision-making in only a minority of polities. Indeed, even in these cases, they probably help to define only the broad options within which governments operate, though they sometimes follow through these options at the level of specific decisions, which can be very contentious, for instance in coalition governments. It is principally in Western Europe and, in a different manner, in Communist countries that parties have played this role. Elsewhere, the role of parties is vaguer and more peripheral: they are unlikely to be closely involved in the solution of national conflicts even if, in a large number of polities, they are involved in some manner in the presentation of problems or in the setting-up of at least some elements of the public agenda.[13]

Parties and the link between rulers and the population

The impact of parties is often also considered in terms of the strength of the link which exists between rulers and the population. This link can be of two kinds, as was seen in Chapter 9: it can move downwards and constitute an attempt to 'educate' or 'mobilise' the population in the direction of the goals which leaders wish to pursue, or it can move upwards and result in the representation of the population's desires by the political elite. It can also be of both types within the same party.

Western political systems are deemed to be 'representative'; the constitutional framework is based on this principle and parties have often been set up to achieve this goal. However, Western parties – or at any rate many of them – also aim at mobilising and educating the population. This has traditionally been the case with parties of the left, in which large elements often claimed that the status quo was maintained because large numbers of electors did not realise where their 'true' interests lay. This characteristic also applies to many parties of the right, who often act on the assumption that they need to modify the views of electors who may be misguided, for instance as a result of what is sometimes described as 'liberal' or 'Socialist' propaganda. Thus there is an underlying desire to mobilise the electorate on the part of Western parties, while the representative function is clearly also present; this leads to ambiguities and tensions which are particularly noticeable at election times.

Communist systems and the more 'progressive' regimes of the Third World have traditionally emphasised mobilisation rather than representation as their goal. Representation is typically viewed as tending to favour forces of conservatism rather than the development of the economy and of the society; it is regarded as being primarily concerned with the present and as leading to a neglect of long-term improvements. The mobilising goal has been given considerable prominence in some cases, for instance during the cultural revolution in China; but, even when it has not been pressed so strongly, it has remained profoundly embedded in the philosophy of the parties which propose authoritarian–egalitarian and populist ideologies. This stance also enables leaders to justify their policy of pressing ahead with their goals irrespective of opposition and to regard as wholly unacceptable any move designed to distract the population away from these goals.

It is because of the need to enlist the support of the population in this way that parties have been critically important to these authoritarian–egalitarian and populist leaders. Many leaders have often been less concerned with the other aspects of the role of parties: they are not anxious to see the organisations they created or inherited from their predecessors become markedly involved, or involved at all, in decision-making. Such an involvement would tend to diminish their influence and can therefore be regarded as leading to representation rather than mobilisation. The purpose of the party is essentially to provide an instrument through which the views of the leaders can be communicated to the population in a sufficiently forceful and convincing way for that population to be ultimately prepared to follow.

This hope has rarely been fulfilled, possibly because the overall goal, which might entail a complete transformation of mentalities, is truly impossible to achieve. Such a goal requires the build-up of extremely extensive and extremely active organisations at the devotion of the ruling elements of the party: this means a deployment of resources which Third World countries, at least, do not have at their disposal and which even Communist countries have found difficult to muster. Thus the experience of the second half of the twentieth century suggests that this type of mobilisation effort is based on an illusion; by and large, single-party systems which originally had this aim have come gradually to redefine the purpose of the party whether consciously or not and whether in an outspoken manner or not. This purpose has come closer to the administration of existing arrangements than to a striving towards new structures. Consequently, there has been an element of representation, in effect, in these parties, at least in terms of a part of the membership of the party itself: parties have become self contained organisations in which there is greater stress on the placement of colleagues than on the provision of a link designed to influence the population on behalf of the rulers.[14]

This does not mean that no mobilisation effort can ever succeed; but it clearly indicates that the amount of mobilisation which takes place must be related to the ability of the leaders to set up and maintain a large organisation able to engage effectively in the education of the population. This also means, however, that such an educational effort must not attempt to push the population too far away from the desires and expectations which it holds at the time, as, otherwise, the effort will be viewed as propaganda and will have no impact at all on the attitudes and behaviour of the broad majority. The experience of the second half of the twentieth century clearly points to the fact that the amount of psychological change which can be obtained by parties in a voluntaristic manner is small, that it is markedly smaller than party activists suppose, and that it is probably truly long-lasting only if it is accompanied by changes in life-styles which parties cannot achieve unless these changes occur in the context of marked economic transformations.[15]

Thus mobilising parties mobilise and educate appreciably less than they would wish – and claim – to achieve; the amount of mobilisation which is undertaken by Western parties and by pluralistic party systems in general is also appreciably less than some of their active members would wish. Indeed, many of these parties seem gradually to have recognised the limits of their potential for mobilisation, particularly since the 1970s. Western Socialist and other parties of the left have reduced markedly their proposals for change; few of their members, at any rate in the top leadership, appear to believe that they can any longer go appreciably beyond the desires which are currently expressed by the population.[16]

This self-denying ordinance can be considered a victory for the representative model of the political system. Yet, while the mobilising philosophy has lost ground, both in the reality of party achievements and in the minds of party leaders, the representative capability of parties appears also to have been eroded. By and large, the representative-cum-mobilising model which some Western parties tended to espouse was based on the general assumption that parties were the channel of communication *par excellence* between people and government in the contemporary world. Chapter 9 showed why there are indeed grounds for believing that this view could be correct; but the emergence of many new groups, covering a variety of interests and cutting across the traditional divisions between parties, especially in the West, has tended to undermine the representative character of these parties, in that they do not seem to many supporters of the groups to be able or even willing to defend their interests. This has been the consequence of the increased strength of such bodies as feminist, ecological, or regional organisations. Some of these groups have created parties; the 'Greens' are a particular example. Others have remained marginal to the political system, though they have occasionally played a key part in the decision-process. But these new organisations have not succeeded in replacing the old parties: at best, they have eroded them somewhat; more importantly, they have not transformed the framework within which political life operates, for instance by making parties in general more participatory.[17]

Thus parties in Western countries appear to float somewhat above the population rather than be truly drawn from it and be closely tied to it. This state of affairs coincides with a development on the basis of which parties compete in a market and attempt to sell their products to an increasingly independent electorate. But such an interpretation also means that these parties are not representative of the population in the true sense of the word: they may be representative in the global sense that the party system as a whole, by way of the operation of the electoral 'market', provides the population with at least a rough mechanism through which to express their desires; but each individual party fails to fulfil a strongly representative role.

It can therefore legitimately be asked whether the linkage between rulers and ruled is achieved satisfactorily by political parties, whether of the 'mobilising' or of the 'representative' varieties. Some parties are manifestly so artificial that they have scarcely any contacts with the people; but even those whose tentacles plunge deeply into the population at the local level seem to remain relatively distant from 'the people', whether because they cannot implant their goals on the majority or because other bodies seem to be better able to catch the public's imagination. It would be exaggerated to claim that parties have no impact on society, but it is surely highly unrealistic to suggest that the societal role of parties is achieved in more than a limited manner, even in the best of circumstances, in the contemporary world.

Conclusion

The general impression that parties have not been able to provide a strong link between government and people leads to the question of the future of these organisations. It could be that parties were characteristic of and well-suited for a particular phase of the modernisation process, but that they are not equally suited to providing the link which is needed when societies acquire a complex but disparate set of needs; groups might be a better channel in such a situation. Developments in the United States, where parties seem to have markedly declined in strength, especially in California, suggest a possible demise of parties in the future; while such a point has not been reached in Western Europe, the reduction in the solidity of traditional parties and the corresponding increase in the volatility of the electorate may constitute a move in the same direction.

Yet the practical way in which parties could be replaced is unclear, not only with respect to the recruitment of the political 'class' or to the process of national decision-making, but with respect to the provision of a satisfactory linkage between government and people. This linkage cannot take place through groups, as these are specialised and are in marked competition; an aggregative element has to emerge if the political process is to function effectively. Parties are therefore probably here to stay, for at least many decades, not just in the Third World, but in the developed countries as well. It is not surprising, however, that there should be periodic worries about the problems which they pose, nor is it surprising that they should be less stable and less effective than they have typically been expected to be by their faithful supporters.

Notes

1. The question of whether parties 'matter' has begun to be examined systematically for Western Europe in the 1970s and 1980s. See in particular F. Castles (ed.), *The Impact of Parties* (1982). For a spatial analysis of programmes of Western European parties, as well as a few others, see I. Budge, D. Robertson, and D. Hearl (eds), *Ideology, Strategy, and Party Change* (1987).

2. This is largely because, as was seen in the previous chapter, India, Sri Lanka and Malaysia have had pluralistic party systems throughout the period.
3. Somalia became a system of more than one party again in the early 1990s.
4. See Chapter 21. See also J. Blondel, *The Organisation of Governments* (1982), pp. 126–34.
5. Since the pluralistic party system has not been in existence for a substantial period in Eastern Europe, it is of course impossible to assess to what extent the developments which begun in these countries in the late 1980s can be regarded as stable.
6. The coming to power of Gorbachev in the 1980s (and indeed of Kruschev in the 1950s) can indeed be regarded as having constituted forms of changes of regimes within the context of the single-party system.
7. The first leader was on the left, the second on the right of the political spectrum.
8. Yet some characteristics of the French party system did remain or periodically returned to the surface, in particular among the centre parties, which never succeeded, throughout the Fifth Republic, in uniting and being truly disciplined. These divisions did indeed help successively the Gaullist party (up to the mid-1970s at least) and the Socialist party (during the 1980s).
9. A number of ministers have been non-party in Western European parliamentary systems, in particular on the Continent. See Chapter 18.
10. In the United States, while the President is recruited through the parties (and indeed broadly through primaries within the parties), many of the national decision-makers (ministers and presidential aides, for instance) do not have a clear party background.
11. See F. Castles (ed.), *op. cit.*, and I. Budge (ed.), *op. cit.*
12. This is due in large part, as in the case of recruiting national decision-makers, to the institutional structure of the United States. The parties, including the parties in the legislature, lack the means of ensuring that their views are directly implemented.
13. The role of some parties in decision-making in the Third World needs to be noted, however. See, for instance, the part played by a number of important ones in V. Randall (ed.), *Political Parties in the Third World* (1988).
14. The failure of the 'cultural revolution' in China provides at least circumstantial evidence of the inability of parties to change mentalities and to fully mobilise the population. Indeed, the return to a pluralistic system which has been manifest in Eastern Europe in the late 1980s also suggest that even less dramatic attempts at introducing major changes in the economic and social structure cannot easily, if at all, be implemented.
15. See Chapter 8 on political communication. The effects of propaganda on the mobilisation of population have clearly been over-estimated, both by those who initiated such propaganda efforts and by outside observers.
16. The Socialist left in Western countries has often claimed that the failures of its parties were due to a lack of popular mobilisation. There is of course a sense in which this view has never been fully tested, but there is little evidence to suggest that this standpoint is correct and there is indeed some evidence to the contrary: Socialist parties have not tended to lose votes to the left to a significant extent while moving to the right in the 1980s in several Western European countries, in particular France and Spain.
17. Traditional parties have been eroded somewhat by the 'Greens' in Western Europe, as was noted in Chapter 12. By and large, the effect of new groups has been more to change the agenda somewhat (for instance by giving more importance to feminist, ecological, and regional issues) than to alter radically the configuration of the party system, although this may happen in the long term. The emphasis on greater participation which has characterised many of the new groups has not apparently led to a marked change in the structure of parties, although 'representativeness' can be said to have increased somewhat as a result of the fact that the views of the new groups tend to be listened to by the parties. In this respect, American parties can be considered to be at the extreme end of the continuum, since a substantial proportion of the issues raised by the parties or by

members of parties in the Federal and State legislatures come from interest groups; meanwhile, relatively little comes from within the parties themselves, in turn because these parties are so decentralised that a uniform policy has little chance of being adopted. In this context, the 'democratic' way in which candidates are selected (through primaries at which many electors participate) militates against the possibility of a uniform 'programme' being adopted by the parties.

Part IV

Governmental structures

15 | Constitutional and non-constitutional rule

The effect of constitutions on the governmental process

So far the nature of the relationship between people and government in different types of political systems has been examined. The discussion must now turn to the structure of governmental institutions and to the processes of public decision-making. Such an analysis is rendered complex, however, since it is not sufficient to describe structures of government as they are; one must also take into account the part played by constitutions in prescribing how these structures should be organised and how governmental bodies should behave. Indeed, for a long time, the analysis of governmental structures was almost entirely confined to the examination of the constitutional provisions regulating these structures. For the reasons which were discussed in Chapter 1, modern political science has deliberately emphasised the analysis of patterns of behaviour alongside the examination of constitutional arrangements, indeed occasionally at the expense of constitutional arrangements. A truly realistic approach entails that both prescription and behaviour be examined in parallel, as the prescriptions put forward by constitutions both influence behaviour and are, in themselves, behavioural statements about the characteristics which governments are expected to embody.

Yet it is difficult to combine the analysis of patterns of governmental organisation and the examination of prescriptions of constitutions, in part because the two elements are intertwined and, more important, because they are not intertwined to the same extent in each polity. On the one hand, while governments exist everywhere and are therefore necessarily organised in a certain way, constitutions have introduced ideas and precepts about their organisation which have deeply affected both theory and practice, even where there is no constitution. The constitutional developments which have occurred since the end of the eighteenth century have resulted in a universal debate about the principles of the organisation of governments and about how best to implement these principles. On the other hand, constitutions have been distorted and even set aside in many parts of the world at many points of time; they are indeed distorted to an extent everywhere. It is no longer the case that one can divide countries into those which have a constitution and those which do not. Few polities do not have a constitution now; those which do not are the remaining traditional states (principally located in the Arabian peninsula) and those countries which the military has taken over and in which the basic law is temporarily set aside; sooner or later, the military has to leave office or feels the need to proclaim a new constitution. The problem is not even to distinguish between countries which implement their constitution and those which do not, though many constitutions are deliberately set aside in practice while being extolled in theory. The real problem is that constitutions are implemented to a degree, and to a different degree, in various countries, and that the reasons why constitutions are implemented to a greater or lesser extent range from, at one extreme, the existence of customs and traditions which the constitution cannot break to, at the other extreme, a deliberate desire not to implement on the part of the rulers of the day.

Thus the analysis of the structures of government raises complex matters. It entails looking at these structures as they are as well as at the extent to which these structures follow the precepts of the constitution. This is why, before examining the various aspects of the organisation of governments in the contemporary world in subsequent chapters, this chapter will be devoted to the examination of the character and impact of constitutions. This will be done, first, by looking at the general way in which constitutions can affect the structure of government, second, by examining the question of constitutional change in the light of changes in society, and third, by outlining the main elements of the content of constitutions.

The nature of constitutional rules and the impact of these rules on governmental life

All governments are organised in a certain way. This organisation results from the combination of a number of elements, of which constitutional arrangements are only one, the others being a large number of traditions and customs, which are in turn the product of a variety of forces, among which long-standing institutions, on the one hand, and rulers, on the other, play a substantial part. Even in the best of circumstances, constitutional provisions will therefore only with difficulty change patterns of behaviour, with the corollary that they will tend to be most effective if they do not depart markedly from existing practice.[1]

Conventions and customs

Constitutions aim at structuring the operation of government on the basis of a number of principles. Rarely, however, do constitutions operate on a *tabula rasa*; in most cases, if not always, they are introduced against a background of strongly established conventions and customs. As a result, even where there is no constitution, other rules are likely to shape governmental arrangements. These rules may include laws which do not have constitutional status but in practice play the same part. There is no constitution in Britain, as Britain has no document with this title; but there are many laws which have a *de facto* constitutional character, as they organise the governmental institutions.[2] These conventions and customs are no less stringent for not being written. This is the case in Britain, as is well known, and it is also the case in other countries, whether or not these conventions are recognised as such. Their absence would mean that current leaders can operate in a wholly arbitrary manner. Such a situation is rare, even in very authoritarian systems; it tends to occur only at the interstices of political systems, so to speak, for instance when a country or a regime is being established (though, here too, conventions have often existed in the past and they continue to play a part) or when a popular leader comes to power (though such a leader will quickly come to 'routinise' his or her rule). In most polities most of the time, on the contrary, there are rules, both written and unwritten, on the basis of which the government comes to power, is organised, and relates to the rest of the polity. The constitution is part, but only part, of these rules – and it may not be the most important part.

The three meanings of the word 'constitution'

Even when constitutions are, so to speak, overwhelmed and almost set aside by conventions and customs, they none the less retain a special character in that their aim is to prescribe, on the basis of some principles, arrangements which are expected to benefit the polity. Principles, detailed arrangements and effective patterns of behaviour have to be examined jointly and result in the words constitution and constitutional having three distinct meanings. First, the constitution refers to a series of *prescriptive* arrangements; this is summarised in the expression 'constitutional rule', which tends to refer to a form of government which is liberal, emphasises restraint in the operation of government, and gives maximum freedom to the citizens. Second, the word constitution refers to a *document*, written at a given point in time; this document establishes institutions and procedures, which may or may not be in conformity with the principles of 'constitutional rule' – yet it is the document which prevails in practice, not the principles. Third, constitution also relates to the *actual organisation* of the polity: to this extent, the constitution is simply a description of the institutions.

In this last sense, all countries have a constitution. The descriptive meaning of the constitution applies to all types of government, as all states are organised in a certain way. It is only by reference to the first two meanings – 'constitutional rule' and the existence of a document – that some states can be said not to have a constitution. As was noted earlier, in the contemporary world, the large majority of states have a constitutional document; on the other hand, probably only a minority can be said to be 'constitutional' in the sense that the government abides by truly 'constitutional' rules. But the third meaning, that of the descriptive organisation of the state, is the one which provides an impression of the conventions and customs on the basis of which the government operates. Moreover, by comparing this description with the 'constitutional principles', one can see whether the principles are put into practice. One may then discover that some of the norms which prevail in a state may not be embodied in the constitutional document, while other norms which the document prescribes are not applied. Moreover, the document may even specify arrangements which have little to do with the overall organisation of the state and are inserted simply because constitutional documents are usually relatively difficult to amend.

Types of constitutional principle

So far the discussion has covered the extent to which states implement their constitution and examined under what conditions governments can be said to abide by 'constitutional' principles. Yet these constitutional principles themselves vary noticeably. As was suggested earlier, the words constitution and constitutional have traditionally referred primarily to a form of government which is based on restraint. This is because, from the end of the eighteenth century and throughout the nineteenth, constitutions were viewed as the main way of combating tyranny and introducing freedom. As constitutions were primarily aimed at bringing about a liberal system, they essentially related to what was defined in Chapter 3 as the dimension of 'means' of government, rather than to participation and even less to substantive policies. They emphasised procedures more than the substance of governmental activity. Yet such an emphasis has been regarded as unsatisfactory by those who felt that the state should not merely promote freedom, but also bring about greater equality. An effort in this direction has taken place in constitutional documents drafted from the end of the nineteenth century: some view such an effort as intrinsically unsatisfactory as they feel that, by their very nature, constitutions can only deal effectively with questions of procedure.

One can identify four phases in the development of constitutions. The first wave, which includes the American Constitution and those of Central Europe in the early part of the nineteenth century (though not of all French constitutions before 1815), exemplifies what can be regarded as a pure 'constitutional' approach. The emphasis is almost exclusively placed on restraint on the executive.[3] Towards the end of the nineteenth century, interest in greater popular participation led to the introduction of provisions relating to the extension of the suffrage and to more electoral equality. In Western Europe after World War I and in some other parts of the world after World War II, constitution-makers became concerned with the underpinnings of democracy and listed a number of 'positive' rights, mainly social and economic, alongside traditional individual rights; these 'positive' rights were viewed as a necessary extension of the liberal protection provided in earlier texts.[4]

The first three types of constitution were therefore based on liberal restraint, although some provisions for participation and substantive policy goals were gradually introduced. The fourth wave of constitutional development, characteristic of Communist states and of some 'progressive' Third World countries, went markedly further by wanting to give precedence to egalitarian goals over liberal restraint. Based on Marxist ideology, which emphasises the primacy of the economic substructure over the political superstructure, they called for policies designed to achieve 'positive' freedoms, for instance by stipulating stringent conditions under which traditional freedoms could be exercised and by ascribing to the single party (often the Communist party) the task of guiding the nation towards these goals (in theory during a period of transition during which the conditions for these concrete freedoms would be established).[5]

Such an approach contrasted sharply with the standpoint of previous constitutions. In the Communist model, problems of the organisation of government tended to be regarded almost as technical matters while the main focus seemed to be on ensuring that society moved towards social and economic equality. In practice, however, the evolution of Communist societies in the 1970s and 1980s constituted a retreat from the earlier 'orthodox' Communist position: this evolution appears to lead increasingly to traditional ('bourgeois') freedoms being given greater recognition and to matters of state organisation being given greater prominence, partly through constitutional change, but partly by other means. Even in Communist states, the main purpose of constitutions seems no longer to be to press for socio-economic change but to ensure, as in liberal democracies, that the boundaries of governmental action are limited by procedural means.

Constitutional supremacy, rigidity and the question of constitutional change

In a perspective which views constitutions as setting out the basic rules under which the government is to operate, it is logical to declare that the constitution is supreme – that is to say, that it takes precedence over all other rules, written or unwritten. The case of the supremacy of constitutions is therefore watertight from a juridical standpoint. It is less strong in practice, however: this is in part because, as was seen earlier, constitutions have to be related to the context within which they come into existence. The constitution may still be viewed as supreme, but only in relation to other legal documents. As political life may be governed by customs and conventions which differ widely from the constitutional prescriptions, the scope of this supremacy may be narrow and, at the extreme, almost non-existent.

Constitutional supremacy is thus undermined by conventions and customs. It is also likely to be undermined over time, as constitutions are somewhat rigid documents. They are rigid by virtue of the fact that they stipulate rules and prescribe detailed arrangements; they are also rigid, often at least, in the technical sense that their provisions can be legally altered only with difficulty and on the basis of special procedures.

This rigidity is usually considered valuable and even normal: the constitutional provisions need to be preserved because they embody the most 'sacred' norms of the polity. Thus, naturally, the extent to which the constitution will be made rigid depends on the extent to which the framers of the constitution are confronted with challenges to the system which they introduced. In countries in which the political evolution has been gradual, the constitution does not need to be rigid. Hence there is a paradox: where the constitution could be rigid because there is limited challenge to its norms and even its detailed provisions, it is unlikely to be rigid because it is not necessary that it should be so; where, on the contrary, the constitution is challenged by sections of the society who do not approve of the norms which it embodies, the constitution is likely to be rigid, but this in turn increases the extent of opposition to the constitutional provisions, which are viewed as maintaining by a variety of procedural devices the status quo which opponents reject.

The rigidity of constitutions may well be justified in the eyes of the drafters of these documents, both on the legal grounds that they are supreme and on the political grounds that only if they are rigid will they be likely gradually to affect behaviour. Yet, as constitutions are difficult to alter if they are rigid, they will also adapt with difficulty to changes in the social and political context. The reasons which militate for rigidity in the eyes of the framers of the constitution are also those which risk provoking problems of implementation as time passes. This is particularly the case where the constitution is very detailed; such constitutions may include many provisions which come to be regarded not merely as contentious or outside the field of constitutions altogether, but as cumbersome as well. Thus the constitutions of many states of the United States and of a number of Latin American countries describe the organisation of governmental institutions in great detail and include financial and other provisions which may be widely regarded as not being part of the framework of the organisation of the state which is the normal province of the constitution. The more such topics are introduced in the basic law, the more opportunities there are for problems to occur as time passes.[6]

The legal supremacy of constitutions can therefore raise serious political difficulties. Thus the problem of constitutional change is often posed; but, as the rigidity of the document may render the process of amendment arduous and even frustrating, it is not surprising that constitutions should often be altered by other means, namely by what might be called customary change, when they are not purely and simply overthrown as a result of a coup or of a revolution.

Constitutional amendments, customary change and the revolutionary overthrow of constitutions

Constitutional *amendments* lead to changes taking place according to the procedure devised by the constitution. This procedure varies from maximum flexibility, when the constitution can be amended in the same way as any piece of legislation, to maximum rigidity, when no amendment is allowed at all. Some constitutions, such as those of Britain, New Zealand or Israel, are wholly flexible; no constitution is wholly rigid, as 'extra-constitutional' change would topple the system, but some constitutions are very rigid indeed.[7]

Constitutions may be rigid 'in bulk' or 'in detail'. The whole constitution may be made rigid in order to maintain a system which is challenged or in order to perpetuate a compromise between contending forces. Rigidity is achieved by requiring special majorities of the legislature (normally between three-fifths and two-thirds), by electing special conventions (as in Belgium and some of the US states), by making popular approval by referendum necessary, or by combining this last condition with one of the previous two (as is the case in many Western countries). Special rigidity is achieved by entrenching some clauses which can be amended only if there is concurrence, unanimous or in a majority, of the group or groups which are to be protected, whether ethnic minorities (as in Lebanon), geographical bodies (typically states in a federation), or even institutions (as in the case of the French Senate, which may not be abolished if it does not concur). Entrenchment can even be total, as with the 'Republican form of government' in the French Constitution of 1946. Levels of rigidity have frequently been imitated from one constitution to another. Constitutional amendments are, on the whole, rather infrequent.[8]

Constitutions are also modified by *customary* practice, and indeed this often occurs. Sometimes this is even formally recognised and may be partly helped by judicial action. Such changes are strictly 'unconstitutional' and, perhaps as a result, are somewhat understudied. They increase as time passes, but the rate at which they occur is not known. The matter of 'customary' change is mainly examined in the context of the English constitution, which is formally unique, not because it is flexible (as has been seen, the New Zealand constitution is also flexible), but because it cannot be found in a single document: yet the question of customary change is one which occurs everywhere. For instance, the American constitution has been *de facto* amended with respect to the behaviour of the members of the Electoral College – contrary to the document, which wished them to be free to decide among the presidential candidates, they have in reality become pledged to vote for the one with whom they have associated themselves during the election campaign.[9] Similarly and even more importantly, the American constitution was *de facto* amended when the Supreme Court declared itself competent, in 1803, to quash federal legislation, a matter which will be examined again in Chapter 22. It is because of the incidence of customary change that it is often difficult to decide how far a constitution is being 'truly' implemented. There are slow gradations ranging from minor twists given to the spirit of the text or simple *de facto* abandonment of provisions to clear and outright flouting of a positive command. No constitution is fully applied; indeed, it is probably because they are slowly modified by customary change that many constitutions can survive. Customary change is one way of by-passing formal provisions, quietly and step by step, and thus a means of reconciling the rule of law and the supremacy of constitutions with the fact of social and political change.[10]

Revolutionary overthrow is the third way in which constitutions come to be altered, in this case a drastic measure, as the basic law is purely and simply set aside.

Despite the 'supremacy' of constitutions, lawyers have always recognised, rather realistically, that a coup or a revolution means the end of the previous constitution – the new rulers can make an entirely fresh start. This view is not illogical, as a revolution means a major change in the configuration of norms in the polity. However, such a brutal overthrow will have consequences for the political strength of any subsequent constitutional document which the leaders of the new regime may wish to promulgate. A constitution born under these circumstances may have little support and may in turn be rapidly overthrown; examples have been numerous in nineteenth-century France as well as in several Latin American countries up to the present day.[11]

The content of constitutions; declarations of rights and the setting up of institutions

Constitutions are based on general principles which they attempt to embody. Often the most solemn way in which they do so is by means of 'declarations of rights' which are typically listed and expounded in the early part of the document, though this is not always the case: the American Bill of Rights took the form of a series of ten amendments to the Constitution. On the other hand, constitutions are mostly concerned with the setting-up of the institutions of government which are expected to regulate the operation of the polity in the future. Although declarations of rights are probably the most solemn parts of the documents, the institutions which are set up are the most practical elements. Constitutions would have little impact on the organisation of the state if they did not prescribe the institutional arrangements under which the polity is expected to be ruled in the future.

Declarations or bills of rights

Declarations or bills of rights pose many problems of implementation, as they are increasingly concerned with matters of social and economic policy as well with the expansion of individual liberties. In earlier versions, these declarations were almost exclusively related to individual liberties. This was the model of the American Constitutional Amendments of 1791 and of the French Declaration of Rights of 1789, a model subsequently followed by a number of liberal constitutions. Rights covered freedom of speech, of religion, of the press and of meetings; they usually included a reference to property, which was, in Locke's interpretation, the protection of free men. These rights were firmly and clearly expressed as 'natural, sacred, and inalienable, in order that this declaration constantly in front of all members of the social body should always remind them of their rights and duties', to use the expression of the French Declaration of Rights of 1789. Rights were 'expounded'; they were 'absolute' (at least in the French version), 'general', and individual.

Modifications arose from a critique of these characteristics. Marxists suggested that declarations were purely formal. It was claimed that rights were not absolute, but relative to a particular society, since they existed only where a society existed and in relation to that society. Rights should not be deemed to be general, but should be given to a degree and an extent appropriate to each individual; they were not truly individual but affected the community and should be granted appropriately; finally, they should not be viewed as 'expounded', but conceived dynamically in relation to the structure of the community, to the education of the people and to the general needs.[12]

This critique led to the concept of 'new rights', both in Communist and non-Communist states, as, for instance, in France (1946 and 1958), Italy (1946) and West Germany (1949); indeed, the United Nations Declaration of Rights of 1948 and the European Declaration of Rights of 1955 also mentioned these new rights. These include education, the right to work and the right to strike, social security, and restrictions to private property, even in Western countries, in the form of suggestions for the nationalisation of monopolies. These new rights were placed alongside the old rights but, in Communist states, emphasis was also placed on the dependence of old rights on specific policy conditions to be met; this was the case for instance in Article 125 of the Soviet Constitution of 1936, though some change is likely to occur as Communist states become increasingly concerned with the protection of individual liberties.[13]

The new rights entail a positive state function; this distinguishes them sharply from old rights, which had only to be protected by the courts. New rights involve positive action on the part of the government and the public administration. These new rights also entail the setting-up of expensive services, which means, in turn, that such rights cannot be granted quickly, let alone immediately, and that there is always a danger that they may not be met in full. Thus constitutions could not simply 'declare' these rights and expect that they would be implemented. In practice, limitations had to be introduced; these have tended to be of two kinds. Either the right is mentioned, but the same or the following sentence includes a reservation about conditions of implementation,[14] or declarations are given merely a programmatic character, as in the case of the 1946 and 1958 French Declarations which are classified as 'preambles' and do not have therefore a clear constitutional status. Indeed, some of these limitations came to be extended to old rights, possibly because constitution drafters became aware of the conditions under which rights could be properly implemented.

This meant a loss of authority for declarations of rights. Yet there is a dilemma: should no mention at all be made of rights on the grounds that they cannot easily be implemented, or should they be mentioned with the corresponding danger that discrepancies will occur between the ideal and reality? A 'preamble' is perhaps the best way of ensuring that the underlying ideas gradually permeate the polity: principles are mentioned, but it is also suggested that it is unrealistic to treat these declarations as being full parts of the constitution. Preambles tend to be exercises in socialisation as much as provisions of the basic law. In fact, these rights are implemented to an extent, especially in Western Europe, but also elsewhere; declarations serve as reference points for both the national and the international community.

By moving into new policy fields, declarations of rights have attempted to move constitutions beyond their original domain. Difficulties of implementation are unavoidable. Constitutions are essentially instruments designed to establish institutions and procedures: it is overambitious to expect them also to guide the activity of governments in a detailed manner. It is therefore perhaps surprising that they should have had, legally as well as politically, the relatively large impact which they have come to have, at least in some parts of the world.[15]

The organisation of governments

The area in which constitutions are usually expected to be most effective is the organisation of government. Since the eighteenth century, constitutions have been regarded as the main mechanism by which the ideas of such political theorists as Locke, Montesquieu, Rousseau, and others could be translated into specific institutions and procedures. Not surprisingly, however, since differences of opinion exist among these theorists, differences also arose among the constitutions as far as the principles which they were to embody were concerned. There have also been differences, at the practical level, about the way in which these principles could best be operationalised. At the level of principles, for instance, not all constitutions believe that power should be given to 'the people'; nor do all constitutions believe that considerable power should be devolved to regions and localities. At the level of the operationalisation of principles, some constitution-makers may have felt that 'popular sovereignty' could be better achieved by a sharp division between executive and legislature, while others, with the same aims in mind, may have come to a different conclusion on this point. It may also have been felt that the powers of localities would be better preserved in the context of a federal system, while other constitution makers may have believed that it is preferable to maintain a unitary state, even if this meant fewer powers for the localities.[16]

Differences relating to the operationalisation of principles stem primarily from differing views about the effectiveness of given institutions and procedures. Constitution-making is a form of 'political engineering'; it attempts to change behaviour by setting up institutions and procedures. There will naturally be differences of opinion about the effectiveness of particular pieces of political engineering, especially since constitutions tend to be written without a systematic analysis (often impossible to undertake) of the consequences of certain provisions. Moreover, the effectiveness of provisions is likely to depend, not only on the intrinsic value of these institutions and procedures, but also on the extent to which they fit a given context. Most constitutional provisions emerged out of theories which, for the most part, were developed in the eighteenth and early nineteenth centuries in Western Europe and North America. It is perhaps not surprising that they should often prove somewhat ineffective when they are applied many decades later to societies which are vastly different; it is perhaps more surprising that they should be, by and large, as effective as they are.[17]

The main fields of governmental organisation

The structure of the executive
Constitutions have to cover three main areas of governmental organisations, as these are the three areas on which an answer must be given in all governmental systems: if they do not provide an answer, an answer will be provided by the practice of political life. First, they have to specify how the central decision-making body is to be organised: is the executive to be a pyramid with one person at the top or is a group to share the overall responsibility? In other words, is there to be one ruler or is there to be a cabinet? This question is closely related to views about the best way to achieve both reasonable and speedy action; it is also closely connected to the crucial role of leadership in political systems. Ideas have differed markedly, both about the principles and about their operationalisation. Monarchical rule was based on the principle that the executive should be led by one ruler. Some constitutions inherited this tradition; others proclaimed that the executive should be collective. The first principle led to a variety of forms of presidential rule, while the second resulted in various types of government by committee, the best-known and probably the most effective of these types being cabinet government. There are also intermediate arrangements, either stipulated by constitutions, or resulting from practice, not merely because rulers have not wished to implement the constitution, but because the provisions of the constitution may turn out to be ineffective in a particular context.

Representation
The second area to which the organisation of government relates is that of the links between the executive and various types of 'councils', the most important of these being legislatures or parliaments. As constitutions have typically attempted to limit the powers of executives, as they have also attempted to introduce (or reinforce) the principle of representation, the question of the role and powers of legislatures or parliaments is central to constitutional documents. Here too, however, both principles and operationalisation vary from one basic law to another. Perhaps the most important – and surely the best known – distinction is that which distinguishes between separation of powers systems and parliamentary systems. The first type of arrangement stipulates that legislature and executive are to be elected independently while, in the second, the government needs the confidence of parliament to remain in office, though the government may be allowed to appeal to the people by dissolving the chamber. Some constitutions have also proposed a further model, in which the chamber appoints the government but cannot be dissolved by it, but this system so weakened the executive that it proved generally unworkable. As a matter

of fact, executive–legislative relationships have often been different in reality from what the models suggested, both in liberal and in authoritarian countries. In most polities, the role of the legislature came to be markedly reduced, in part because of the influence of strong parties. Though constitutions had a key role in developing the idea of representative government, the forms which constitutional engineering has taken have often led to a marked *de facto* distortion of the principles: legislatures and parliaments officially designated as sovereign have in reality a less exalted position.

Centre–periphery relations

The third area in which government has to be organised is that of the relationship between centre and periphery, that is to say, the extent to which public decisions are to be taken at a number of different levels and therefore decentralised. Decentralisation is sometimes put forward by constitution-makers in the name of citizens' freedoms; it is often also a necessity because the burden of decision-making at the centre would otherwise be very heavy. Experience in the Eastern Communist states since the 1960s showed that some decentralisation had to take place, whatever the principles of Soviet Communism may have suggested. The question of decentralisation is therefore one which every state (and, consequently, every constitution) has to address. In practice, however, in Western Europe at least, many constitutions (especially the older ones) said little about the problem and have left ordinary laws and perhaps traditions free to handle the matter. In other cases, such as the United States, constitutions have put forward a model of centre-periphery relations based on federalism; this stipulates that central and regional bodies must be separated in order to ensure that the regional bodies retain maximum power. In practice, however, federalism has not always achieved its stated aims and, by design or by accident, the degree of decentralisation which has resulted has not matched the ambitions which were expressed in the constitution.

Conclusion

The coming chapters will therefore examine central–local relationships, the nature and role of representative bodies, and the characteristics of the executive, as well as the nature and role of leadership, since these are problems which all polities have to face and which therefore pose universal questions. They will also investigate the extent to which various types of constitutional arrangements have attempted to modify and indeed have modified in practice the ways in which these problems are being tackled in the different political systems of the contemporary world. Constitutions have been and continue to be important elements in the fabric of modern government, even if they have to be considered in context and even if they have often been overthrown or only implemented in part. 'Constitutionalism' is one of the ways in which governments are being shaped: only by examining governments both in a constitutional and a non-constitutional context can one assess the impact which constitutional principles and constitutional arrangements have on the characteristics of the composition and life of governments.

Notes

1. The limits of the extent to which behaviour can be changed by constitutional and institutional means are now better appreciated. One of the best and clearest presentations of the problems posed by constitutions is to be found in K.C. Wheare, *Modern Constitutions* (1966). See also V. Bogdanor (ed.), *Constitutions in Democratic Politics* (1988).
2. There is no constitution in Britain in the sense that there is no single document – see below. On the question of the meanings of the word constitution, see G. Sartori, 'Constitutionalism: a preliminary discussion', *Am. Pol. Sc. Rev.*, 56, (1962), pp. 853–64.
3. It has been argued that the characteristics of these constitutions resulted from the nature of the society and of its ruling elite. See in particular, in the case of the United States, the celebrated study of C. Beard, *An Economic Interpretation of the Constitution of the United States* (1913).
4. This was the case in particular with the constitutions of Continental Europe which were promulgated after 1918 (Weimar Germany, for instance) and after 1945 (France and Italy).
5. The archetype was the Soviet Constitution of 1936, which was superseded by the Constitution of 1975. The emphasis was on what was regarded as 'concrete' rather than 'abstract' 'bourgeois' freedoms. Thus Article 125 of the 1936 Constitution read:
   > In accordance with the interests of the workers and in order to strengthen the socialist system, the law guarantees to the citizens of the USSR: a) Freedom of speech; b) Freedom of the press; c) Freedom of assembly and meeting; d) Freedom of street processions and demonstrations. These rights of the citizens are ensured by placing at the disposal of the workers and their organisations, printing works, supplies of paper, public buildings, streets, posts and telecommunications and other material prerequisites of the exercise of these rights.
6. Some of the constitutions of the states of the United States are very long and have extremely detailed provisions; the same applies to many Latin American constitutions.
7. Strictly, the English Constitution is no longer flexible since the Parliament Act of 1911 requires, in respect of the duration of the House of Commons, the concurrence of both chambers.
8. There have been, for instance, only twenty-five amendments to the United States Constitution, the first ten of which were approved in 1791 as they formed the Bill of Rights. The same applies to European constitutions, which tend to be amended on average at most once per decade.
9. The American Constitution viewed the members of the Electoral College as 'independents' who would make up their minds freely: in practice, the members of the Electoral College consider themselves normally (indeed practically always) pledged to vote for a given candidate. This ensures that the views of the people are translated into the mechanics of the presidential election; but this development does amount to a 'customary' amendment to the Constitution.
10. There is a clear need for a systematic analysis of 'customary' amendments and of the periods at which they occur.
11. The view that a successful revolution automatically abrogates the previous constitution was never seriously in doubt in the nineteenth century in Continental Europe (a period during which this type of situation occurred frequently); it was accepted in particular in

France, which had many constitutions between 1791 and 1875. This view is also accepted in Latin America.

12. Critiques of the traditional conception of rights were made by Marxists in particular, on the ground that these rights were 'abstract' rather than 'concrete' and helped the bourgeoisie to maintain their power. An expression of the classic Communist view in these matters can be found in A. Vyshinski, *The Law of the Soviet State* (1948). These views have been put aside or toned down, not just in the states which have abandoned Communist principles, but also in those, as in the Soviet Union, which have remained Communist and yet have moved markedly in the direction of reform.

13. See note 5, above.

14. An example is given by the Preamble of the French Constitution of 1946 (maintained in the 1958 Constitution): 'The right of strike is exercised within the framework of the laws which regulate it.' This kind of expression leads to the legal difficulty as to whether, if there is no such regulation, the right in question is granted in full or not at all!

15. There has been a resurgence of the part played by rights in the 1970s and 1980s. In the Western European context, the European Declaration of Rights has been implemented to a considerable extent by the courts, including the European Court. In the broader European context, the Helsinki Declaration has led to considerable pressure being put on Eastern European Communist countries, and has contributed to the changes which occurred in the 1980s.

16. See K.C. Wheare, *op. cit.*, (1966) for a more detailed examination of these matters.

17. There have been several examples of the extension of constitutional arrangements to other countries in the past. In the early nineteenth century, many European countries imitated the English constitution, though with various modifications. The newly created Latin American countries, at about the same period, imitated American, British, and French practices. In the twentieth century, the 'decolonisation process' was often accompanied by the introduction of constitutions, based on the European model, before independence was granted. The result was often unsuccessful, except with respect to the Commonwealth, many of whose members adopted constitutions on the British model, kept them in existence, and indeed applied them.

16 | Centralisation, decentralisation and federalism

No government, even the most authoritarian, can ever take all public decisions at the centre. Some power has therefore to be given to authorities below the national level to take the decisions which the centre cannot take. From this general remark emerges the idea of decentralisation, an idea which can of course take many forms and vary markedly in extent. In its principle, however, the concept of centralisation and decentralisation can be formulated simply: if one were to list all the decisions taken in a country by all the public bodies, that country would tend to be centralised if the proportion of the decisions taken by the central authorities was large to very large and tend, on the contrary, to be decentralised if the proportion was small to very small.[1]

While the concept of centralisation is relatively simple to define, it is complex to measure. Indicators of the extent to which decisions are taken at the centre or below the centre are impressionistic and therefore unsatisfactory. However, the problem of measurement is complicated by the fact that the question of centralisation and decentralisation, which relates to the extent to which various agencies are responsible for decision-making, is confronted with the concept of federalism which, in its various forms, is a *constitutional* answer to the problem of decentralisation. Yet, since decentralisation is difficult to measure, the relationship between federalism and decentralisation is encumbered by a number of obscurities. If one is to attempt to discover under what conditions states can be regarded as decentralised and whether federalism is an adequate means to bring about decentralisation, it is necessary first to determine some general criteria of decentralisation, then to consider how far the federal 'blueprint' meets these criteria, and, third, to assess, at any rate in broad terms, whether in practice federal states can be regarded as more decentralised than those other states which are defined as unitary.

Centralisation and decentralisation

A general analysis of centralisation and decentralisation must answer two main questions. First, what general societal conditions lead to centralisation or to decentralisation? Second, by what criteria can one assess whether a state tends to be centralised or decentralised? Once these questions have been answered it will be possible to see whether the federal model provides a realistic answer to the question of decentralisation.

Norms of government, efficiency and the question of centralisation

In the contemporary world, patterns of centralisation and decentralisation often appear well-established. Although, especially in recent years in Western Europe, pressure for decentralisation has increased, long-standing traditions exist and these account for the fact that some states are centralised while others are decentralised. Thus France has long been a country of centralisation, to a large extent because of the policy of the kings who wished to extend their hold on the country against the local aristocracy. On the contrary, in America, Britain and indeed Germany, decentralisation has a long history: no ruler was able for long to ensure that most major decisions were taken in the capital.

Yet history alone does not explain trends towards centralisation or decentralisation; more precisely, historical traditions can be explained in terms of political ideologies and of political forces. By and large, liberalism appears to lead naturally to decentralisation. It is more difficult for a liberal polity to justify high levels of centralisation – which accounts for the fact that France, so long a centralised country, has made moves towards decentralisation in recent decades and that Spain has in the late 1970s established regions and given them considerable autonomy.[2] However, liberals may become champions of centralisation – though perhaps more uneasily than supporters of authoritarian systems – when their system is under attack. Thus regimes which come to power with the aim of promoting radical new policies and whose leaders fear (or suspect) that these policies will encounter substantial opposition are likely to support centralisation. Moreover, decentralisation means the acceptance of differences – of variations from one part of the country to another. This suggests that regimes which propose to bring about equality are likely to be uneasy about decentralisation. This is why, by and large, the left has tended to centralise more than the right, though there are interesting exceptions – either on the left (as with French or Spanish Socialists who felt that their country was too centralised to be truly liberal) or on the right (as with, of course, the authoritarian right but also those Conservatives who believe that only a dose of centralisation can stop the 'excessive profligacy' of left-leaning local authorities).[3]

Overall, therefore, a relationship exists between ideology, the degree to which the regime is accepted, and centralisation. Liberal regimes which are well accepted will tend towards decentralisation; authoritarian regimes are likely to promote centralisation, except where they are so well-accepted and so traditional that they do not propose to put a new mark on their polity. But most authoritarian systems and those liberal systems which are not well-accepted are likely to veer towards centralisation, though to a varying degree and with greater or lesser consistency.[4]

Areas, fields and techniques of decentralisation

Assuming that a state tends towards centralisation or decentralisation, what instruments will it use to achieve its policies? These instruments are numerous, but they can be classified under the following seven broad headings:

1. Centralisation may naturally concern the *fields* of government: certain matters may be dealt with centrally, others locally.
2. These fields can be given *en bloc* to the same authority or be divided into a number of *ad hoc* authorities.
3. The authorities can be divided into two or more *levels* (region, county, city, or village, for instance).
4. All these authorities may *share the same powers*, or these powers may be markedly distinct at the different levels.
5. Each authority may or may not be entirely free to *appoint its decision-makers* (for instance elect all its rulers).
6. Each authority may or may not be free to *set up its own administration*.
7. The centre alone may or may not be free to *decide on the allocation of these various powers*: it may have to share with others the power to settle who is entitled to do what.

While it is manifestly difficult to assess in every case where a state is to be located with respect to these criteria, it is at least possible to gain an impression of the extent of decentralisation by using these criteria. This is also the way in which it is possible to assess, first, what federalism aims at and, second, whether federal states are truly decentralised.

The federal model and its distortions

Federalism was conceived partly *a priori* and partly empirically, on the basis of what seemed to be relatively successful solutions. As it is a constitutional model, its main impact is likely to be on procedures rather than on substantive policies. Since the setting-up of the United States as a federal government by the Constitution of 1789, federalism has been presented as the answer to the problem of the division of labour between central government and other authorities in a way which could maximise decentralisation and yet avoid the break-up of the polity: expressions such as 'unity within diversity' have sometimes been used in this context. However, specific institutional arrangements needed to be devised; consequently, there have been disagreements as to which of these arrangements would be 'truly' federal. These discussions are sometimes beside the point, however, as what is at stake is not so much whether a country is truly federal but whether specific arrangements lead to more or less decentralisation.[5]

The principle of the federal blueprint

This section will therefore examine the blueprint of federalism in relation to the questions which decentralisation raises and which were listed earlier. Federalism should give answers to each of the seven dimensions and these answers should logically stem from the basic principle of federalism. This can be stated in the following way: in order to optimise the two prerequisites of decentralisation and of national unity, rule-making authorities should be divided into *two sets of authorities independent of each other within their own sphere*. It is not appropriate here to try to assess whether this is indeed the optimum solution. This model happens to have been elaborated and little purpose would be served by inventing another model which has not been so far in existence.[6]

If the principle of the federal blueprint is applied to the seven dimensions which were identified earlier, the following conclusions should follow:

1. Fields of government should be divided, but the principle of federalism does not give any guidance as to which fields are to go to which authority.
2. Federalism states that each authority has to have all the power, or none at all, in each sphere.
3. There are to be only two levels of government which are to be given 'independence': one could have imagined that there might have been more, but federalism stops at two levels.
4. Each of these levels should be organised on the basis of one authority only: federalism is not 'functional' and there are not as many independent authorities as there are fields of government.
5. Each level should be completely independent in the appointment of its decision-makers.
6. Administrative agencies should be entirely distinct.
7. On the question as to who is to have the power to decide how the allocation of powers is to take place, the federal principle gives little guidance.

Thus the federal blueprint gives precise answers to only five of the criteria. It is unsatisfactory on the fundamental question as to who makes the allocation: as will be seen, this is not surprising, as no clear-cut solution can be given in this respect. Nor does the federal blueprint give any real guidance about the important matter of the allocation of fields of government: it merely states that there are to be two 'boxes', without saying what ought to be in each box. In reality, the federal blueprint emerged accidentally, in too haphazard a manner, to have been able to meet these points. It resulted from the search for a middle point, a 'half-way-house' between two extreme positions, that of the unitary state and that of the confederacy. In a unitary state, only the central body is legally independent and the other authorities are subordinated to the central government; in a confederacy, on the contrary, the central government exists only because member-states are prepared to keep it in existence. Thus the British Parliament is 'sovereign' and can regulate absolutely the division of labour between authorities within the United Kingdom;[7] on the contrary, the United Nations or the Organisation for African Unity can only do those things which the individual polities are prepared to let it do and as long as those polities concur in letting it do those things. Historically, the concept of the 'half-way house' represented by federalism emerged at a time when earlier confederacies seemed (possibly wrongly) to have been ineffective. Thus the United States was a confederacy before becoming federal; the same happened to Switzerland and to Germany (despite the fact that Switzerland remains a confederacy in name, it is a federation according to the blueprint).[8]

The characteristics of federalism and its unavoidable problems

Thus federalism developed to some extent by accident; it did not confront systematically all the problems posed by decentralisation, though it did meet a number of these problems. This is why it is somewhat artificial to condemn as 'quasi-federal' states which do not follow all the precepts of the federal blueprint. This is why, too, as will be seen, even states which are deemed to be 'truly' federal have evolved in directions which tend to diminish markedly the extent to which they are decentralised.[9]

The discussion will now turn to the characteristics of the blueprint and the consequences which it entails. First, no state can be federal unless it has a constitution. More specifically, this constitution needs both to be rigid and to include provisions aimed at setting up a body with powers to control and adjudicate between the two levels of organisation. Second, federalism determines a number of characteristics of the polity. It suggests a sharp separation between two types of authorities, but, as it leaves unanswered two major problems posed by decentralisation, that of the distribution of the fields of government and that of the 'power to allocate powers', substantial differences are likely to occur among federal countries and a ranking will be found among them. Indeed, the characteristics of the same federation are also likely to change over time. If the powers of the two types of authorities have been defined with precision in a given federation, but if, over time, the relative importance of these powers varies, the real extent of decentralisation will also vary. Furthermore, as new fields of government will emerge from time to time (for instance as a result of technical change), the relative position of the two types of authorities will vary. This will also affect the extent of decentralisation in the country.

The question of the 'power to allocate powers' also leads to theoretical difficulties. Strictly, there should be consensus, and indeed this should exist at two levels, between the authority and the regions and among the regions, since, if this does not obtain, it is not strictly true that each component is independent, even in its own sphere. Yet this result is not likely to obtain, as the idea of total consensus defeats the very suggestion of the 'half-way house' which federalism purports to embody: some form of majority principle has therefore to be introduced, even if major safeguards have also to be included. It follows that there will be degrees of approximation of federalism in this respect as well: arrangements which exist in practice will be in the nature of variations away from the blueprint. As these variations exist, the situation which obtains on these points is the same as on the allocation of policy fields: the rules will differ from country to country.

Difficulties and problems of implementation are therefore particularly acute in relation to the authority which decides on allocation and with respect to the division of powers between authorities. They are summarised below.

As the federal principle requires consensus and this requirement cannot be met, a combination of three types of arrangements have been devised in the allocation of the supreme authority. These are as follows:

1. The overall principle of complete rigidity is abandoned and replaced by a majority (normally a qualified majority) principle.
2. Day-to-day implementation of the division is left to a supreme court which controls both types of authorities and is indeed above them.
3. A representation of the component bodies takes place at the central level (through a second chamber) to compensate for the fact that the central authority can force at least a minority of component bodies to agree.

However – and the situation becomes one of detailed arrangements – the problems are still not entirely solved, since the question of appointments to the supreme court should also require unanimous agreement by all the component authorities and in practice such a requirement cannot be met either. The implementation of the basic federal principle is thus open to major variations.[10]

The same remarks can be made about the second area of difficulty (the allocation of fields). It is stated that authorities are supreme within their own sphere, but that powers are to be circumscribed in a number of ways. The principle of federalism being mute on the fields which 'should' go to each authority, one would expect that it might at least suggest a *principle* of division. Even this is not achieved, and a number of solutions obtain. There can be an allocation of powers to the regions, to the centre, or to both. In the first two cases, the centre and the regions respectively have residual powers; in the third case, it must be decided also that one or the other wins in cases of conflict as any other arrangement would lead to partnership, not to sovereignty of each within its sphere. It is normally suggested that if the residual power is left to the regions, the system is 'more' federal, since new powers go to the decentralised bodies; but this is a question of degree and the actual extent of federalism clearly depends on what these new powers come to be.[11]

The situation has, moreover, a third effect. Since the application of the federal principle does not lead to strict arrangements, either on the overall power to decide or on the allocation of policy fields, it follows that the other aspects of the federal principle lose much of their value. As one can envisage federations which might be 'empty' in relation to these two major areas, the adoption of a rigid principle on appointments, for instance, ceases to be very important.[12] It also follows that it is incorrect to consider that federations which do not rigidly embody the federal principles on, for example, appointments or rule-application are necessarily 'less federal' than federations which do. The problem is transposed from a constitutional analysis of the implementation of the blueprint to the examination of behavioural levels of decentralisation. Whatever is said about the all-or-nothing character of federalism, the allocation of the supreme authority comes to be based on criteria of an incremental character, such as the percentage of regions involved in constitutional change, the role of the supreme court, or the composition and powers of the second chamber.

The distortion of the federal blueprint and degrees of federalism

There were seventeen federations at the end of the 1980s. One-third of these were in the Atlantic area (the United States, Canada, Australia, Switzerland, Germany, and Austria), four in Latin America (Mexico, Venezuela, Brazil, and Argentina), three in the Communist area (the Soviet Union, Yugoslavia, and Czechoslovakia), two in Asia (India and Malaysia), one in the Middle East (the United Arab Emirates) and one in Africa south of the Sahara (Nigeria).[13] Three of the four largest countries in the world were federations (the USA, the USSR, and India – the fourth country of the group being China): as a result, while only 10 per cent of the world's polities are federations, over a third of the world's population live under a federal form of government. It is on the basis of the four early federations of the Atlantic area, namely the United States, Switzerland, Canada, and Australia, that the federal blueprint was first developed and later systematised;[14] but, even if only these four are considered, the ideal of a perfect equilibrium between federal and regional authorities is not fully maintained. Not surprisingly, the other federations are further away from the blueprint. One can easily establish this point by assigning scores to all the federations on the basis of the extent to which their constitutions adopt the federal blueprint with respect to the different criteria which were identified earlier. Only the United States and Australia score very highly; although Switzerland and Canada are also long-established federations, they obtain lower scores (in the first case because of the limited role of the supreme court, in the second because of the 'non-federal' character of the second chamber); Latin American federations are even less federal; so is the Soviet Union.[15]

In general, the following variations can be found. First, the principle of constitutional amendment by component regions *as well as* by the centre is not universally adhered to. There is thus no substantial difference between the constitutional amendment procedure in the Soviet Union and the amendment procedure in the constitutions of many unitary states. Moreover, only on the rather legalistic ground that the West German Constitution of 1949 is a provisional basic law due to be changed when the country is reunited can it be justified, from the point of view of federalism, that the principle of amendment by the people is not enforced. Admittedly, it is only in federal states that one finds provisions allowing for popular majorities in individual component units to be taken into account;[16] but, as the amendment procedure is rigid in many unitary states and as many federal states do not adopt the principle that amendments must be approved by a majority of the component units, the difference between federal and non-federal states is not very marked in this respect.

Second, and perhaps more importantly, the distribution of powers has given rise to many formal variations and resulted in an erosion of the distinction between federal and unitary systems. One of these variations consists in creating the category of 'concurrent' powers, whereby, in some fields, *both* the central government and the regions can intervene, but with the further proviso that 'federal law breaks state law':[17] this amounts to suggesting that some fields of government belong to the regions only as long as central government decides not to intervene. The regional area of competence is thus conceived by the constitution itself as a gradually shrinking area, an interesting example of a constitution being concerned with change and development, but in one direction only. Furthermore, the principle of equality between the two levels of government is sometimes eroded by various powers of veto or of 'federal intervention' and, indeed, in the case of the Soviet Union, of positive ratification: the budgets of the Republics must be accepted by the USSR government before they can be put into force; in India and Malaysia intervention within states is allowed by the constitution; in Latin American countries, particularly in Venezuela, the power of the central government includes that of appointing the heads of provincial governments. Finally, the principle of the separation of administrations is not always maintained: the federal administrative system of Germany is based on a single administration, appointed by the *Länder*, which runs all the services, federal as well as regional, on behalf of the two levels of government.

The safeguards provided for by both the judiciary and the second chamber are also modified in ways which may limit or even almost wholly abolish the federal principle. Supreme courts do not always exist or, when they exist, they do not necessarily have the power to intervene in disputes between the central government and the regional governments.[18] Second chambers exist, but they are usually not composed on the basis of parity between the component bodies and a weighting is given to take into account the population size of these bodies; this is the case in practically all the new federations, and particularly in the Soviet Union and West Germany.[19]

Thus the concept of *quasi-federalism* has been developed by some authors in relation to some of the more recent federations.[20] It is not only in practice that, for instance, the Soviet Union is 'quasi-federal': it is the constitution itself which gives the federal government powers of intervention, of amendment, of veto and approval which clearly place the country at considerable distance from the principle of equality between centre and regions. The same conclusion can be drawn for West Germany and Austria, for Malaysia and India, for Brazil and Venezuela. Thus 'pure' or nearly pure federalism appears to characterise only a very small number of countries: given, as was noted earlier, that federalism is not strictly applied in Canada and in Switzerland, perhaps only the United States and Australia can be described as truly federal. A category which leaves on one side practically all the polities of the world may be considered to have only limited significance.

Centralisation, decentralisation and federalism in practice

In order to compare federal and unitary states, the component bodies of unitary states which can be said to approximate to regions in federal governments need to be identified. This examination reveals two general points. First, the component bodies of federal states are also normally divided into sub-units, urban or rural, which have some powers and are involved in rule-making: the cities and counties of states within the United States have powers and these powers must be distinguished from those of the states themselves. Second, the regional components of federations are normally rather large, at least in relation to the size of the whole federation. The United States has by far the largest number of component units of any federation in the world, with fifty states. No other federation has more than twenty-nine components and some have fewer, the average being sixteen. Variations in population between the component bodies are, of course, vast. Some of the larger regions are truly large: the Russian Republic has over one hundred million inhabitants, the states of California and New York about twenty million and the state of Sao Paolo over ten million. Thus, in terms of both the absolute size of some of the larger component bodies and the average size of all the component bodies, these are large units and this contributes to an extent to the power of these units.

The overlap between unitary and federal countries

It is only on average that unitary states have fewer 'decentralising' characteristics than federations: there are many cases of overlap between federations and unitary states, especially in relation to appointments, the organisation of administrative authorities, and even the allocation of functions.

As a number of unitary states have created second chambers which in some fashion represent component bodies within the state (the French Senate as well as the senates of several Latin American countries, for instance) even these polities ensure some form of protection for regions. Courts – often administrative courts – also guarantee, to some extent, the powers of these bodies. Regions in unitary states are not entrenched as much as in the older federations, but the result compares, sometimes not unfavourably, with the relative lack of protection which characterises some federations if the component units are not always involved, even on a majority basis, in constitutional changes (the Soviet Union for instance), if the supreme court is not empowered to adjudicate in these matters, or if the second chamber is not organised on the basis of equality (as in a majority of cases).

Even in federations, the appointment of rule-makers in the component units is often subjected to forms of control, at least of a negative kind, by the central organisation. This is not only because some federations, such as India, envisage powers of federal intervention in cases of emergency; powers of veto can be exercised over the appointment of governors or other executive agents of federations as well. Conversely, a number of unitary states are based on principles of local autonomy. The central government has no control over the appointment of the personnel in charge of local decision-making in Britain, France, or the Scandinavian countries, for instance.

Administrative authorities overlap or are combined, rather than being separated in a number of federations. The best-known example is that of West Germany, as was noted earlier, where, in sharp contrast to the United States, Switzerland and Britain, the central government relies on the regional administration to implement the decisions of the federal authorities throughout the country, the provision having been inserted in the Constitution of 1949 in order to avoid duplication. This could mean that the central government is in the hands of the regional authorities, if these refuse to comply: thus the constitution gives the federal government a power of intervention known as 'federal execution' which, if frequently used, might result in close supervision and detailed control of the actions of regional administrations. This form of association – which is reproduced elsewhere, and in particular in the Soviet Union – suggests that the separation of authorities leads to administrative costs and to inefficiency, a point which is often raised against extreme forms of decentralisation. It does suggest that, in this area as well, the distinction between federal and unitary government is far from clear-cut.

Partnership and the increasing centralisation of powers in federal states

An organisation of administrative authorities on the West German or Soviet model suggests that a form of partnership is created between two sets of authorities. However, partnership extends further, especially, as could be anticipated, in the area in which the federal principle is the vaguest, namely the allocation of powers. First, sometimes by constitutional amendment and more often by customary change, the scope of the powers of federal authorities has increased.[21] In the economic field, a 'liberal' interpretation of clauses such as those on interstate commerce in the United States enables the Federal government to legislate in a wide number of fields. Rearguard battles did take place in this respect, especially in the United States in the mid-1930s, when a number of texts were quashed by the

American Supreme Court, one of the grounds being that the Federal authorities were interfering in matters which came within the jurisdiction of the states.[22] In various social fields, changes have also gradually increased the scope of federal activity in all federations, so that social security, housing and education, are covered by federal legislation, even in those polities, such as the United States, where federal legislation is still relatively less developed. Differences still exist, not so much between federations in general, but between the older ones, primarily the United States, and unitary countries; however, they are reduced to an increasingly narrow front. Less energy is now required on the part of proponents of federal intervention: a constitutional amendment was needed to introduce federal income tax in the United States, but the Supreme Court later desisted from its role of defender of the states after its effort against the 'New Deal' legislation in the 1930s. Central intervention in socio-economic affairs is now no longer seriously challenged. As a result, differences are more pronounced in matters pertaining to private law (especially in the United States), though, in this respect too, these differences have decreased.[23]

Yet the most 'revolutionary' developments which occurred in the socio-economic fields concern the emergence of a 'partnership' between federal and regional authorities as well as, in some cases, between federal authorities and cities or counties, with the result that the state authorities are thereby by-passed. By a number of means, whether financial (through grants-in-aid), administrative (through the issuing of circulars, model by-laws, and even model laws) or socio-psychological (through meetings of technical experts), federal authorities succeeded in inducing states to adopt policies conforming to those of the federal government. The success is not universal: component authorities of federal states may be better placed than those of unitary states to resist central encroachments of this type. But these moves have taken place on a wide scale. Federal authorities do what the governments of unitary states do: they cajole, press, and, where they are not obeyed, warn or use sanctions. In order to avoid having to use sanctions, however, they engage in partnership activities, whether with decentralised units in a unitary state or with states in a federal polity. The basic principle of the division between the two types of authorities is thus flouted. While the constitutional organisation often makes for two sets of bureaucracies and two distinct 'power structures', the practice in all federations amounts to a situation which is little different from the one which the West German constitution recognises, namely a partnership between authorities.

Centralisation and decentralisation in unitary and federal states

It was noted earlier in this chapter that there was still no way of measuring accurately the extent of centralisation in a given polity: it is therefore not possible to demonstrate rigorously that federal countries are more decentralised than unitary states. Federalism has moved towards greater centralisation in a number of ways, as was seen; but centralisation has also increased in unitary states. If the rate of increase in centralisation in unitary states is the same as that in federal states, one might conclude that increases in centralisation are characteristic of contemporary societies, but one should also conclude that the difference between federal and unitary states still continues to obtain.

Centralisation did increase in unitary states. Socio-economic legislation is new, administrative partnership is new; while model laws are a recent practice of federations, model 'by-laws' are also recent in unitary polities. Yet, if the tools of analysis do not allow for a definitive answer, two considerations are likely to give indications. First, the sizes of the average and largest component units and of the whole polity have to be taken into account. Large authorities are more powerful than small ones. It was noted in Chapter 9 that parties are more decentralised if the second level of party administration is large; states which have relatively large provincial or regional authorities are equally more likely to be decentralised than states which are divided into a large number of small authorities.[24] Large cities are more powerful than villages: to take only one example, the weakness of French local government is related to the fact that the basic local authority, the commune, is very small.[25] Federations are at an advantage here, as the average number of regional units is smaller in federal than in unitary states (sixteen units instead of twenty-two) and as the average population of these sixteen units is about five times larger than the average population of the twenty-two units of unitary states (five million instead of less than one). As a result, the component units of federal states are likely to be more powerful than the component units of unitary states, whatever the structure of govenment in these two types of polities: the state of New York, the Russian Republic, the West German *Land* of Nordrhein-Westfalen are thus more powerful than the average English or Swedish county, irrespective of the politico-administrative structure imposed by the constitution.

Second, however, the problem of centralisation versus decentralisation and the traditional contrast between federal and unitary states have to be viewed in terms of the sum of the decisions which characterise rule-making. In particular, administrative practices need to be assessed alongside state powers. Constitutions may decide on the bodies which are to take decisions; but the dynamics of administrative behaviour remain independent of these constitutional decrees. Some centralisation is necessary, particularly in a complex polity: traditional federalism was probably so much below this level that the blueprint had to be by-passed. The extent of centralisation of many unitary states was also probably superior to the level which societies, particularly complex societies, can easily tolerate. It was noted earlier that the use of sanctions against local authorities is often politically inadequate, though more so when the authority is large than when it is small; administrative sanctions are also inadequate, because the system can be clogged and the machine may then not render the services for which it was created. Centralisation cannot therefore go beyond a certain point without considerable costs. The administrative problems of the Soviet Union and other advanced Communist states have repeatedly pointed to the difficulties resulting from the centralising ideology of these regimes; various decentralising techniques have had to be adopted. Thus it follows that, given a general increase in public services in the course of the last decades, the rate of centralisation cannot have been the same in highly decentralised polities, of which federal states form a number, and in highly centralised polities, most of which are unitary. It also follows that the more centralised unitary and federal states are likely to have become less different from the other unitary and federal states which have moved faster towards centralisation.

Evidence for the existence of such maximum levels of centralisation can be found not just in Communist states (whether federal or not) but in other polities, particularly Western ones. The movement towards regionalism which characterised Western Europe since the 1960s, in France, Italy, and Spain in particular, was not merely ideological; it was also the consequence of the increasing difficulties experienced by central governments in coping with the management of the country. Thus federalism has become a technique which unitary states imitate to some extent in order to find administrative techniques which will reduce centralisation when it appears to be too high.

Supra-nationalism

Federalism has sometimes been said to be transitional because some polities moved from confederal to federal status.[26] The question of the development of confederacies still remains alive in connection with moves towards 'federalism by stages' or 'functional federalism' which have occurred in the last decades, in particular in Western Europe. Such a federalism covers only some fields of government; states which belong to the new unit remain independent for the rest of the decision-making process, as only a few powers are transferred (often slowly) to the central authority. These transfers are also combined with safeguards for state independence, such as the representation of the component governments in Councils of Ministers as well as vetoes allowed for certain types of matters. This type of 'minimum' federalism, known as 'supra-nationalism', is in turn a half-way house between the idea of a confederacy and the 'full' federalism in which all the powers are formally divided.[27] Supra-nationalism has been used in particular in Western Europe with respect to the six, then twelve countries of the European Community (France, West Germany, Italy, Belgium, the Netherlands, Luxemburg, Britain, Ireland, Denmark, Greece, Portugal, and Spain); it has also taken place elsewhere, for instance among Central American countries which are joined in a Common Market. Furthermore, since supra-nationalism is an intermediate arrangement, other arrangements, in turn intermediate between confederacy and supra-nationalism, have also been devised, so as to allow decisions to be taken in certain circumstances without unanimity. The United Nations itself represents a move from the position of outright confederacy which characterised the pre-1939 League of Nations to a position which is somewhere on the road to supra-nationalism.[28]

Conclusion

The problems of centralisation and decentralisation have exercised the minds of many in relation to many types of organisations: both efficiency and freedom appear to be at stake. Not unnaturally, authors of constitutions were pressed to provide techniques to meet the requirement and, not surprisingly too, these techniques proved too imprecise to achieve the desired results. Federalism succeeded in a number of contexts, but it has been to an extent by-passed as a result of modern state intervention: a degree of cynicism arose as a result. Neither exaggerated hopes nor an exaggerated cynicism are justified. In early periods of development, when a polity moves from a confederacy to a state of greater unity, the federal blueprint and indeed the intermediate technique of supra-nationalism are likely to achieve substantial results, provided the norms of the polity are such that liberalism, rather than authoritarianism, tends to prevail. This was not the case in the Soviet Union;[29] nor was it the case in many states of the Third World. What re-emerges then is the underlying problem of the maximum amount of centralisation which a country can countenance. This maximum is lower than many political leaders might hope for; *de facto* decentralisation is then likely to occur through laxity in grass-roots implementation. In parallel, the movements, ostensibly away from the federal blueprint and towards greater centralisation, which characterised older federal states, as well as the apparent tendency towards centralisation in other complex societies, suggest that in advanced countries the margin between maximum and minimum levels of centralisation is relatively narrow. A more precise assessment of these limits is urgently required, as it is useless and wasteful for polities to engage in experiments of extreme centralisation or extreme decentralisation which cannot be fully implemented.

Notes

1. The concepts of administrative centralisation and decentralisation will be examined in Chapter 20. The case for political centralisation and decentralisation is somewhat distinct in that there are normative (for instance ideological) reasons, as well as administrative reasons for wishing to centralise or decentralise a nation. But the case for or against federalism is a subset of the case for political centralisation and decentralisation. For an analysis of the general aspects of the problem, see T. Fleiner Gerster, *Federalism and Decentralisation* (1987).
2. 'Regionalism' is a form of decentralisation which stops short of declaring that the nation is no longer unitary, that is to say that the regional units are set up by the central government and, theoretically at least, that they can be abolished by the central government as well, though this is more theoretical than practical. The first development of regionalism in Western Europe took place in Italy (where the move was completed in the early 1970s). Spain and France followed suit. There was also a move in the 1970s, which was unsuccessful, to give regional status to Wales and to Scotland.
3. It is somewhat paradoxical that the left should move towards regionalism in France at the time when, in Britain, the Conservative party under Mrs Thatcher should have moved

towards greater centralisation (including the abolition of the largest urban authorities, London in particular).

4. The extent to which a regime is accepted plays a large part in the degree to which the leaders of this regime feel able to allow a high level of decentralisation. France is a good example: centralisation has been high in large part because successive governments felt that their rule was somewhat insecure; thus the revolutionary governments of 1789–91 started to decentralise and quickly moved back towards a strongly centralised state.

5. The real question is the level of decentralisation: federalism is a means by which a given level of decentralisation can be achieved. See T. Fleiner Gerster, *op. cit.*, (1987).

6. For a further examination of the federal principle, see K.C. Wheare, *Federal Government* (1963), pp. 1–14. See also D.J. Elazar, *The Federal Polity* (1974) and M. Burgess, *Federalism and Federation* (1986). There is indeed some argument as to what federalism truly is, but unless a precise definition is given, there is no way of distinguishing federal from unitary states: federalism simply becomes then a form of decentralisation.

7. The sovereignty which is referred to here is that of the British Parliament within the United Kingdom. It can of course be argued that, since Britain joined the European Community, the British Parliament is no longer truly sovereign. The matter is somewhat academic, however.

8. Confederacies have indeed probably been unjustly criticised for their 'impotence', in large part because, in the American case, considerable pressure was exerted by some to strengthen the links between the states after a few years of independence. On the other hand, not only the Swiss Confederacy, but also the Dutch United Provinces (which were a confederacy until the French Revolution) were successful arrangements.

9. The expression 'quasi-federal' is used by K.C. Wheare, *op. cit.*, *passim*, in particular in order to define the constitutions of a number of countries which do not meet the requirement of 'equality' between centre and regions. See in particular pp. 18ff.

10. On supreme courts, see Chapter 21. On second chambers, see Chapter 17. The representation of regions is not the most commonly held view of the purpose of second chambers. Moreover, if there is to be 'equality' between centre and regions, there is no logical reason for the representation of the regions to take place at the centre: the real reason is political. It stems from the fact that the centre is expected to be powerful and the regions therefore want to have a say at that level.

11. This is of course a practical way of ensuring a greater degree of decentralisation: strictly speaking, the matter does not affect the federal principle since, as was noted, federalism has nothing to say about the distribution of the fields of activity between centre and component states.

12. It is at this level that it is often suggested that Latin American federations are not 'real' federations. See for instance K.C. Wheare, *op. cit.*, pp. 21–3.

13. Belgium became a federation, though of a special kind, in the early 1990s, as a result of the division between Flanders and Wallonia (as well as Brussels).

14. K.C. Wheare, for instance, argues that only these four countries are truly federal. See K.C. Wheare, *op. cit.*, pp. 15–34.

15. Changes which have begun to take place in the Soviet Union since the late 1980s may result in the country indeed becoming 'truly' federal.

16. In the United States, three-quarters of the state legislatures must approve a constitutional amendment if it is to become law. In Australia and Switzerland, amendments need the approval of the majority of the population in a majority of the component units if they are to pass.

17. As stated for instance in West German Basic Law of 1949, following previous German tradition.

18. The powers of the Swiss Constitutional Court are more limited than those of a 'full' supreme court.

19. Equality of representation of component units in the second chamber is achieved in the United States, Australia, and Switzerland; in most federations, on the other hand, there is some weighting in favour of the larger component units.
20. On 'quasi-federalism', see note 9, above. See also K.C. Wheare, *op. cit.*, pp. 18ff.
21. For the part played by customary change in modifying constitutions, see Chapter 15.
22. See Chapter 22 on the American Supreme Court.
23. While private law varies from state to state in the United States, this is not the case, for instance, in Germany or Switzerland. Conversely, Scottish private law differs from English private law, although the United Kingdom is a unitary state.
24. Federalism does in many cases provide a base for the recruitment of national politicians. American presidents have typically been drawn from among state governors; three German chancellors (Kiesinger, Brandt and Kohl) were drawn from among *Länder* politicians. This is not always the case, however, and this situation may have more to do with the presidential system than with federalism (West Germany being an intermediate case in this respect).
25. Large cities can be very influential, on the other hand. Indeed, many national French politicians have started from a local base, although France is somewhat exceptional among Western European countries in this respect.
26. This view was put forward by Laski.
27. Supra-nationalism is a half-way house between confederal and federal government as there is some delegation of powers from the component units to the centre, but only in some fields and with a variety of safeguards.
28. The Assembly of the United Nations can thus take majority decisions which are regarded as binding.
29. Indeed, problems multiplied in many Republics of the Soviet Union when, in the late 1980s, the strong dominance of the centre was gradually reduced.

17 Representation and the role of legislatures and parliaments

No country is fully centralised. The question of the extent of centralisation and of decentralisation thus arises everywhere. In parallel, the question of representation also arises everywhere, even though the extent of representation varies markedly from country to country and, where representative institutions formally exist, their role also varies markedly. No government can make rules wholly in isolation from the sentiments and even the pressure of at least some segments of the polity; a degree of representation, however limited, has therefore to exist.

The forms which representation takes obviously vary, however, and, here too, as with respect to decentralisation, constitutions have provided different formulas. Indeed, it is on representative institutions that constitutions have placed the greatest emphasis. Perhaps as a result, it is also in this context that the effectiveness of constitutions has given rise to most disappointment. Through constitutions, efforts were made to establish, often for the first time, powerful representative institutions, yet in many cases authoritarian habits and the need for rapid decision-making markedly reduced the role of these bodies. The success has been greatest where, as in the United States, a tradition of representative government anteceded the promulgation of the constitution. Where, on the contrary, as in France at the end of the eighteenth century or in Latin America in the course of the nineteenth, parliaments and legislatures were granted major powers at the time they were established, their development was difficult and gave rise to repeated false starts. The story of the many failures of constitutions with respect to representative assemblies suggests that it is unrealistic to expect these rapidly to take on a central role in the national decision-making process, if it is possible for them ever to play such a part. Before examining the structure, activities and influence of legislatures, it is therefore necessary to look at the general 'problem' posed by these bodies. Why is the role which they have in reality so often much smaller than the one which constitutions grant them?

239

Formal powers and the effective role of legislatures in the contemporary world

In the overwhelming majority of countries, constitutions state that the 'legislature', the 'parliament' or the 'congress' is the expression of popular sovereignty and either that it is the top decision-making body or, at least, that its status is on a par with that of the executive. The reality is different, however. To simplify, one might say that there are four broad types of situation along a continuum. First, in a minority of cases the legislature is abolished or suspended. Second, in a substantial number of countries the legislature is wholly manipulated; this type of situation prevails in most authoritarian states. Third, there are many cases of legislatures which are controlled, more or less tightly, by the executive; this occurs in many liberal countries, including many Western European countries, though to a varying degree. There are only few polities in the fourth category, that of legislatures which constitute a key element in the national decision-making process. It is therefore not surprising that the subject of representation should have led to disquiet and pessimism: from the late nineteenth century at least, comments have repeatedly been made about the 'decline of legislatures'.[1]

This is only one aspect of the picture, admittedly: almost every year, some legislatures are abolished by military coups, but, almost every year, too, some legislatures are established or re-established. Moreover, the existence of national representation has great symbolic value. Many regimes attempt to ensure that the legislature is limited to being a symbol; modern single-party systems have been most sophisticated in this respect. Yet these legislatures do survive and, by surviving, keep alive the idea of representation. When the regime relaxes its domination, the legislature can come to life, as has been the case in some Eastern European countries since the late 1980s.[2]

The relative weakness of most legislatures

Thus representative assemblies perform at the very least an important symbolic function, but they rarely exercise to the full the effective powers which are granted to them by the constitution. These are typically very large and, as will be seen, include the power to legislate and, in many cases, to oversee and even overthrow the government. It is indeed argued that such parliaments are 'sovereign' or at least embody popular sovereignty.[3] If it were possible to divide legislatures into just two groups – the powerful assemblies of liberal countries and the purely symbolic bodies of authoritarian states – the fate and characteristics of these bodies would be easier to understand. In reality, although legislatures are weaker in authoritarian than in liberal polities, the difference is not sufficiently sharp to allow for a clear-cut division. Governments of liberal countries allow legislatures to debate major issues and representatives to voice criticisms, admittedly, but they also generally succeed in ensuring that the policy-making process is not markedly affected as a result. This is largely the consequence of the fact that, in Western European systems at least, governments can normally control the assembly because of strong party discipline. As a result, they can see to it that laws are passed in the shape which they wish these to have. In such a case, the effective influence of parliaments is so reduced that these can scarcely be said to exercise the powers which are constitutionally theirs.[4] Indeed, one can go further: when parliaments have exercised a real power of control over the government, as in France until 1958, the effect appears to have been negative, as the assembly seemed to undermine the legitimacy of the regime by its inability to pursue a consistent policy line.[5]

Legislatures of Western European parliamentary systems are thus often rather docile; those of presidential systems appear to be less so, because, as is sometimes argued, they are not closely tied to the executive. The Congress of the United States is strong; occasionally at least, the congresses of some Latin American countries appear also to be strong. Yet even the United States Congress is not truly determinant in policy-making: its main strength consists in scrutinising, delaying, and from time to time blocking presidential proposals, but its positive role is less obvious. In Latin America, the congresses which have been powerful have sometimes generated such conflicts with the executive branch, as in Chile between 1970 and 1973, that a major trial of strength ensued, in turn giving rise to opportunities for military takeovers.[6]

Representative assemblies thus encounter major problems. Not only do dictatorships often abolish them, but they domesticate those which they do not abolish; not only do many liberal governments succeed in markedly limiting the effective powers of legislatures, but, when these powers are fully exercised, the result seems to be a considerable loss of prestige for the regime and indeed for the assembly itself. Is it then that the formal powers given to legislatures by constitutions are unrealistically large? Are these powers ill-suited to the characteristics of modern government? Has representation to be given only limited scope for the machinery of government to be able to function?

Representative assemblies and the changing character of legislation in the contemporary world

The difficulties experienced by the legislatures of even the most liberal states suggest that these bodies may not be able to deal with the role which is assigned to them. Indeed, the main problem relates to the fact that, as the name of these bodies indicates, one of the major functions of legislatures, if not their main function, is that of law-making, yet representative assemblies do not appear equipped to generate and develop modern legislation.[7] This is because the scope and character of laws have changed markedly since legislatures were devised by liberal theorists. In the eighteenth century, laws were primarily concerned with the regulation of the private activities of citizens; they dealt mainly with the family, property, and crime. It seemed natural that such laws should be debated by an assembly if the system was to be liberal. The aim was to protect the citizen; laws were to 'declare' in a solemn manner what the relationships between citizens were to be.

With the development of state intervention in the society and the economy, most laws have taken on an entirely different character. They are no longer primarily designed to regulate private relationships among citizens. The main goal is to establish services, such as education, housing, social security; these services are highly technical, and they have also a dynamic character. Moreover, unlike the traditional 'declarative' laws of the eighteenth and nineteenth centuries, modern laws entail high levels of expenditure as well as the training of large numbers of specialist staff who also have to be paid. Economic life too is regulated on a daily basis and is helped and promoted by a whole series of dynamic governmental actions. Locke and Montesquieu realised that the need for continuity and the urgent character of decisions in the realm of foreign affairs made it impossible for an assembly to take key decisions in this field; this was to be the province of the executive power.[8] The current role of governments in economic and social matters stems from similar needs for continuous action and for urgent decisions.

It is therefore not surprising that parliaments should have to concede to governments the function of preparing legislation, including that of deciding when this legislation could be prepared. Interestingly, legislatures often continue to exercise substantial influence in the field of private law.[9] Moreover, governments are also markedly constrained with respect to many aspects of modern legislation, as they, too, have to contend with a 'situation' which results in only some proposals being realistic. Thus, first, it is simply impossible for assemblies to be 'sovereign' with respect to modern social and economic legislation; they can only *participate* in a general process of decision-making. The real question is therefore how large their influence is in a given country at a given point in time. Second, the constitutional emphasis on the legislative function of assemblies has had the paradoxical effect of leaving aside a number of other ways in which legislatures can – and often do – exercise influence, for instance with respect to the scrutiny of administration, although, in these matters too, they can only participate in an overall decision-making process.

Such a conception of the role of legislatures has consequences for the structure of these bodies and the attitudes of their members. On the one hand, the procedures designed to pass laws are not equally well adapted to the other types of activities which legislatures can exercise; on the other hand, members of parliament canot fulfil their tasks adequately if they are generalists. They need to specialise if they are to grasp the intricacies of social and economic problems and thus exercise influence.[10]

Only within this framework does it become possible to assess the real 'weight' of legislatures in the contemporary world. Clearly, such a 'weight' will vary from country to country and from period to period. The 'symbolic' legislatures of authoritarian systems are unlikely to exercise the type of generalised influence – even to consider exercising the type of influence – which legislatures of more liberal countries can aim to exercise. However, the need to examine generally the extent to which legislatures participate in the national decision-making process means that one must consider these activities – and the activities of members individually – in the broadest possible way. Certainly one needs to look at the effect of assemblies on bills, but one must also look at all the fields in which legislators intervene. This effort has only begun to be undertaken in recent years and it is far from complete.[11]

The general characteristics of contemporary legislatures

Before considering the activities of legislatures, however, it is necessary to look briefly at the general framework – the structure, the powers and the composition of contemporary representative bodies. There are naturally wide variations even in this context since, for the first time in the history of mankind, nearly all countries have, or have recently had, a representative assembly. Only a few traditional monarchies, mainly located in the Arabian peninsula, have never had any elected legislature. The exact number of legislatures varies from year to year, however; because of military coups and revolutions, as many as 20 or even 30 legislatures, mainly in Latin America and in Africa, may be closed or suspended in any given year. At the end of 1989, the number of parliaments effectively in existence was 142 out of 163 countries, a high achievement, indeed one of the highest ever achieved; the return to liberal democracy of many Latin American countries in the 1980s accounts in large part for this result.[12]

Structure

Two aspects of the structure of legislatures are particularly relevant. One of these has been repeatedly discussed and indeed has often been held to be critical: this is the question of the division of representative bodies into two chambers. It was variously claimed that the possible excesses of lower houses needed to be counterbalanced by the 'wisdom' of more sedate upper houses and, alternatively, that if a upper house was different in composition from the lower house, the system would be undemocratic because the popular will could then be frustrated.[13] The debate has lost much of its strength, in large part because governments can rely on parties to control the legislature, whether it is based on one or two chambers, and in part because second chambers have also lost many of their powers. In several countries they can only delay legislation (for example Britain and France); they are more powerful in federal countries, for reasons which were discussed in the previous chapter, but, even there, they are not always equal to the lower house (as in West Germany and Canada).

There are now about as many legislatures which have just one chamber as there are which have two chambers; it is difficult to detect any major differences between the two situations. Some truly liberal countries, Sweden, Denmark, and New Zealand, in particular, abolished their upper chamber without any apparent deleterious effect. On a world-wide basis, the number of two-chamber parliaments is diminishing, but only slowly. Two-chamber parliaments are mostly found in South America and the Caribbean (but not in Central America) and in Atlantic countries; they are rare in Black Africa and in Communist states (unless these are federal).[14] Apart from federalism, one of the factors which appears to account for the existence of a second chamber is the size of the country's population. Overall, it is therefore questionable as to whether there is any longer a real case for a second chamber, except in countries where there are sharp geographical cleavages (this is the reason for their value in a federal context).[15]

Perhaps a more important aspect of the structure of representative assemblies is their overall size, although the question is less often discussed. There are parliaments of 1 000 members (as in the USSR up to 1988) and parliaments of about 50 members (for example Costa Rica, Luxembourg and Iceland). The size of the legislature is related to the size of the country's population, but not closely. Legislatures of small countries are relatively larger than those of large countries: there is thus one representative for every one million inhabitants in India, one for every half a million inhabitants in the United States (and one senator for every two million inhabitants), one Soviet deputy for 250 000 inhabitants. In France, West Germany, Britain and Italy there is one member of parliament for approximately every 100 000 inhabitants, in Belgium one for every 50 000, in Switzerland and Sweden one for every 25 000, in Ireland and Norway one for every 20 000. This means a double advantage for smaller countries: since the legislatures are smaller, representatives have more opportunity to participate in the activities of the chamber; since each MP represents fewer constituents, the links between people and parliament are closer. Thus the legislatures of smaller countries probably function better, other things being equal, than those of larger countries.

Powers

The framework within which legislatures operate is of course also characterised by the range of their formal powers, though the relationship between formal powers and influence must not be exaggerated. Traditionally, the most fundamental distinction has been between *legislatures* – assemblies which do not have the power to force the executive to resign and which, as a counterpart, cannot be dissolved – and *parliaments* – which can censure the government but, in many cases at least, can be dissolved.[16] This distinction remains valid and constitutes the basis of the differentiation, in liberal countries, between presidential systems (the United States and most Latin American countries) and parliamentary systems (most of Western Europe, Japan, Israel, and many Commonwealth countries). However, this distinction does not apply to most Third World states where there is a more authoritarian form of presidentialism, as the president may dissolve the assembly, while the legislature does not have the right to censure the government. Nor does it apply to Communist states, which in theory have a form of 'assembly' government, that is to say that the chamber can legally force the executive to resign without being threatened by dissolution: this system so weakens the government that it only exists in Communist states because the reality does not conform to the theory. Nor does the distinction between presidential and parliamentary systems characterise even all liberal states, as there are also intermediate systems, either semi-presidential, like those of France or Finland, or which subject the vote of censure and/or the power of dissolution to stringent conditions (as in West Germany, for instance). Indeed, in some cases (such as Norway) there is no right of dissolution at all. There is, moreover, the special case of Switzerland where the members of the Federal Council are elected by the two houses of the legislature, but for a fixed term; they cannot be dismissed, nor can the chamber be disssolved. Since, overall, the existence of parties markedly reduces the extent to which the chamber can effectively exercise its power of censure, the distinction has perhaps more importance for the structure of the government, which will be analysed in the coming chapter, than for the power of the legislature.[17]

Whether they are legislatures or parliaments, representative assemblies have two main legal powers – making laws and voting the budget. However, these are not always given in full, even in theory. Budgetary powers are restricted, both in fact and in law, even in liberal countries. For instance, parliaments may not have the right to increase expenditure or reduce income, as in France (as a result of the constitution itself) or in Britain (as a result of the standing orders of the chamber). The power to legislate can also be restricted. First, there is a slow, but gradual increase in the use of the referendum. It is now no longer merely Switzerland, Australia, and a number of (primarily Western) states of the United States which use this technique; it has been adopted by many other liberal countries. The prejudice against referendums, which prevailed in the past, is being gradually overcome.[18] Thus there have been referendums in about half the Western European countries since 1950, specifically in Italy, Denmark, France, Sweden, Ireland, Belgium, Norway, Finland, Britain, Spain and Portugal, on such matters as the ratification of the Common Market treaties, nuclear energy policy, or 'conscience' problems, for instance divorce or abortion. The power of the legislature to legislate is consequently reduced. Second, and again even in liberal countries, the executive is sometimes given legislative powers, either because the legislatures may be asked to pass 'outline laws' which the government is entitled to fill in (as in France in particular) or because the government can promulgate decrees which are to be ratified subsequently (as in Italy and France). Furthermore, the constitution (as in France) or the standing orders of the assembly (as in Britain) may either give the government the power to restrict debates or allow it to force a vote to achieve this effect. Thus, even in theory and even in some liberal states, let alone in authoritarian systems, the power of the legislature to pass laws or decide on the finances of the state can be restricted, while the powers of parliaments to censure governments (whether or not this is coupled with the right of dissolution) are also sometimes limited.[19]

Composition

Structure and powers establish the framework within which legislators can exercise their tasks. Legislatures are also naturally affected by the background of their members; an assembly composed of lawyers is not likely to behave in the same way as an assembly composed of manual workers. In general, legislatures tend to be primarily male, middle-aged, and drawn from the middle class. Women are a tiny minority (5 or 6 per cent or even less) almost everywhere: only in Scandinavian countries and in some Eastern Communist states do they form a substantially larger group, though still not a majority. Legislators are normally middle-aged, though they are younger in African legislatures than in Latin America or in the West: this means that the world's representatives are elected only after having held another job, often for many years.[20]

This previous occupation is likely to have been a middle-class job. Farmers are rare, and particularly rare in the Third World where they are most numerous in the population at large; in Western countries, the number of farmer representatives comes closer to the proportion of farmers in the population, but only because the farming population has markedly declined. Manual workers are a small minority, even in countries where Socialist parties are strong, as in these parties white-collar employees and managers are gradually replacing trade unionists. Only in Communist states has the proportion of workers in the legislature been rather larger (one-quarter to one-third), but there, too, it has diminished.

Thus the large majority of legislators are lawyers, teachers, managers or civil servants. In the United States and Canada, lawyers alone form the majority; in Western Europe, they represent about a quarter of the total. Teachers are more numerous in Western Europe, while businessmen, managers and civil servants often form a third of the legislature. This distribution is fairly close to the one found in the Middle East, in Asia, and in Latin America (though two-thirds of the Colombian Congressmen were found to be lawyers). In Communist states, on the other hand, most representatives have tended to be manual workers, teachers, and white-collar employees: there were very few lawyers among them.

These distinctions suggest that there are three types of representation in the contemporary world. In North America, the stress is on representation in the legal sense: legislators are spokesmen; they act 'for' the people. In Western Europe and most Latin American countries, this view competes with another model, that of 'social representation', especially with respect to Socialist, Christian, and Agrarian parties, in which different groups are represented. This is particularly the case in Scandinavia and Central Europe. In Eastern Communist states, while some groups are represented, the main stress has traditionally been on a third model, that of the 'vanguard' in which an 'intelligentsia', composed mainly of teachers and managers, leads the rest of the population, the aim being to mobilise rather than to represent. A similar model is also adopted in the more 'progressive' Third World countries, especially in Africa and the Middle East.

Does being a legislator mean being part of a profession in the strong sense of the word? This is debatable, both because the background of members is diverse and because some of them are part-timers; in addition their stay in the legislature is usually rather short (less than ten years on average), as the result of a variety of political 'accidents', and of traditions, at least as much as of electoral vicissitudes. In some countries, the military may close the legislature. In others, especially in Latin America, legislators are not permitted to stand again, at least immediately. In single-party systems, representatives are sometimes not re-nominated for a variety of reasons: this is for instance the case in Kenya or Tanzania. Thus American and Western European legislators, who remain in the chamber ten years or more on average, tend to be, paradoxically, more secure in their jobs than legislators from many non-competitive systems; indeed, in Atlantic countries, disappointment and frustration with the parliamentary experience lead to many resignations, quite apart from electoral defeat. There appears to be a tendency for the average duration to grow longer as time passes, as analyses in countries as diverse as the United States, Switzerland, and Colombia have shown. However, so far at least, even in these cases the 'career' in the legislature remains relatively short; it begins as a second job and it is typically followed by a third, or a return to the original occupation.[21]

The broad framework of the activities of legislators

Frequency of meetings

The powers of legislators can only begin to be exercised if the framework of activities allows members to discuss and debate a large variety of problems. This means, first, that the chamber needs to meet rather frequently. Yet there is a sharp contrast in this respect alone: some legislatures meet almost every day throughout most of the year (as in the United States, Britain or Canada, for instance); others scarcely meet at all and they more closely resemble party conferences than debating chambers – many parliaments of Communist states have traditionally had this character.[22] The number of days during which chambers meet can thus range from upwards of 150 a year to not more than a handful. In between, many parliaments meet only for two or three weeks in the year; most Western European parliaments meet on about 75–100 days a year.[23]

Yet the fact that the chamber meets frequently does not mean that members can participate often on the floor of the house, especially when the legislature is large. For instance, British MPs can only speak for about an hour and a half a year on average, despite the fact that the House of Commons sits almost every day; a similar situation characterises other Western European countries. Members of African parliaments have even less time to speak from the floor, while those of Communist parliaments, except perhaps Polish and Hungarian representatives in recent years, have typically had almost no opportunity at all to do so. Thus individual legislators are unlikely to exercise substantial influence through speeches and debates and, consequently, committees are likely to be a significantly more effective platform.

Activities on the floor of the house

The activities which take place on the floor can be of four types – legislation, discussion of financial provisions, general debates, and questions. This last activity is mainly developed in Britain and in a number of Commonwealth countries, though there has been a tendency in recent years for the procedure to spread to an extent to the continent of Europe.[24] The discussion of legislation occupies most of the time of most representative assemblies; indeed, some never have general policy debates, probably under government pressure – this is the case in many African parliaments, for instance.

Legislative debates can be rather formal, lead to limited discussions and result in few or even no changes to the government text. Moreover, the overall importance of the bills presented to parliament varies greatly. In the West, parliaments discuss and approve between fifty and a hundred bills a year, some of which are truly important and may lead to long debates; this is also the case in several Latin American countries or in India. In many Third World countries, on the other hand, the bills presented by the government appear to relate primarily to matters of private or commercial law. There are opportunities for discussion with respect to these bills, but broader economic and social matters do not come to parliament and are dealt with by other means. This has been the case in Tunisia, Senegal, Kenya, Madagascar, or Singapore, for instance. In Eastern Communist states, the inner body of the chamber, the 'Presidium', is empowered to approve bills between sessions of parliament. As a result, only very few bills have traditionally been presented to the full legislature; indeed, there was practically no debate. Only in Poland, Hungary, and Yugoslavia did more prolonged discussions occur, especially during the 1980s.[25]

One can therefore divide legislatures into three broad types from the point of view of the characteristics of the debate on the floor. First, in Western Europe, as well as in most Latin American countries and in a number of Commonwealth states, much time is devoted to (essentially governmental) legislation, but the final outcome is rarely in doubt. The main exceptions are the United States and, in some cases, Latin American congresses, where government bills are not only debated at length, but frequently rejected or markedly amended. Second, in most Third World countries, some debates do occur, but they typically concern bills of relatively limited importance. Third, in Communist states, traditionally at least, legislation did not lead to debates in the real sense of the word. Leaders made speeches about broad governmental policy. Some change has begun to occur, however, and, in Eastern Europe and in the Soviet Union after the 1989 election, legislatures have started to engage in real discussions on a number of issues.

Committees

Since activities on the floor can scarcely give legislators an opportunity to exercise influence, major attention has moved to committee work. Legislative committees have markedly increased in number over the last decades in Atlantic countries, even where, as in Britain, there was a great reluctance on the part of the government to allow them to develop. France is somewhat exceptional in this group of countries as the number and power of its parliamentary committees were reduced by the Constitution of 1958, on the grounds that the activities of these bodies had been detrimental to the efficiency of previous regimes. Outside Atlantic countries, the committee system is usually not well-developed. In many Third World states few committees exist and those which do meet infrequently. Committees do play a part in the legislatures of Communist states, where they have multiplied since the 1960s; even at that early period and even in the Soviet Union, amendments to legislation have occasionally been adopted.

Committees have a two-fold function, to examine legislation and scrutinise administration. Britain is rather exceptional in having established two different types of committee for the two purposes. Elsewhere, the same committees are normally involved in both types of activity, in part because, historically, the scrutiny of administration emerged in the context of the examination of bills or of financial discussions. The United States Congress is the legislature in which activities of inquiry are by far the most developed, with representatives of the executive and other witnesses being grilled in the sharpest manner; major scandals have been uncovered as a result. Moreover, while the United States Congress cannot censure the government as such, the appointment of members of the executive gives rise, in the Senate, to 'confirmation' debates which are also extremely searching. In Western Europe, committees are less forceful, although they have been engaged in recent years in more systematic inquiries, in particular in Britain, and these have had an impact on governmental policy.[26]

Committees are thus very important in giving legislatures and their members an opportunity to exercise influence, not just because bills submitted by the government may be modified in the process, but because policies and administrative practices can also gradually be altered. Consequently, committee work has an impact in boosting the morale of legislators who can see that they are not reduced to mechanically supporting – or opposing – government. However, the influence of members is also a function of the extent to which they become more specialised – a move which committee work naturally fosters. While committees do not by themselves shift the initiative in policy-making from the executive to the legislature (a shift which is, as was pointed out, rather unrealistic under present conditions), the legislature can and probably always does acquire a greater say as a result of the development of committees.

The influence of legislatures

Influence at the level of specific issues

The influence of legislatures is complex to measure, as one needs to take into account the effect which these bodies have in a variety of ways. Indeed, alongside their role in the legislature, whether in the chamber or in its committees, individual legislators can exercise some influence. An overall impression of the influence exercised can be obtained by examining a number of different levels at which it takes place. The first of these levels is that of specific, detailed and individual matters, for instance personal requests from electors or sectional demands from groups and associations. Members of every legislature are subject to this type of pressure, though to a varying degree. In many countries, representatives have to open 'surgeries', more or less regularly, to handle requests. Delegations from associations may also come and meet parliamentarians, though this happens primarily in Western countries. Most complaints are probably made by correspondence which can be bulky – a hundred letters a day for the average American Congressman, fifteen to twenty letters a day for the average British MP – although the flow is almost certainly lower outside Western countries.[27]

To deal with these requests, members typically first raise the matter with the appropriate government department; if this approach is unsuccessful, the legislator may put the matter in the hands of an official in charge of examining complaints (the *ombudsman*): in some countries, for instance in Britain, this civil servant can be approached only through an MP.[28] Alternatively, members may raise the issue somewhat more formally, especially if it has general implications, by way of written or oral questions (especially, as was noted, in Britain and Commonwealth countries), and even through private members' bills[29] – in the United States specialised bills are often drafted by members of Congress. Budgetary debates may also provide opportunities to present specific cases.

The real influence of these activities has not so far been generally assessed, but legislators give them some prominence, as their personal standing with electors may depend on showing concern for constituency matters. They have to do so, not merely where elections are competitive, but even in single-party systems, as their re-nomination may be at stake.[30] The influence cannot be measured only by the number of successes, however: overall, these pressures may have the effect of forcing the administration to be less casual and more responsive to the public at large. The impact of these individual and concrete activities may therefore be relatively wide: the relationship between government and citizens is probably somewhat modified as a result.

Influence at the intermediate level

Above concrete questions are 'intermediate' matters which have a general character but which remain within the framework of a policy which is not being challenged. Such matters may consist, for instance, of the determination of groups to whom a measure is to be applied, of the detailed fields which may be included or excluded in a measure, or of the conditions under which the measure will apply. The influence exercised by legislatures in this way may not be well-publicised and may not even take place in the open, yet it may have a considerable effect on certain categories of citizens.

Committees are the arenas *par excellence* where such an influence can be exercised – an influence which is related both to the extent to which legislators have access to information (which they may be able to obtain from groups) and to the extent to which they are specialised. The part played by committees is especially large in relation to bills, though it should not be exaggerated. While some amendments are accepted by the executive even in Communist states, as was seen earlier, this is a relatively rare occurrence. On the other hand, the number of amendments accepted by liberal–democratic governments, for instance Western European governments, is relatively small: government bills tend to emerge out of the committee stage in their original shape.[31]

Yet the influence of legislators should not be measured only in terms of successful amendments passed, although these are the most obvious indicators of influence. There may be greater influence resulting from pressure exercised over a period of time, as this may induce the government to modify its views and present different proposals. One area in which this influence may take place is the scrutiny of administration which normally occurs in committees. There are also other ways in which, at least in liberal countries, legislators can begin a process as a result of which changes may eventually take place: questions, short debates, or budgetary debates provide mechanisms which enable members to press points on their colleagues, on the government, and to an extent on the public at large.

The measurement of the overall influence of legislators over matters of 'intermediate' importance is imprecise; this influence depends on the readiness of the government to allow both debates to take place and committees to develop. The influence of legislatures of authoritarian states in these matters is therefore likely to be relatively limited, but, on some issues at least, it can take place even in these regimes. In liberal countries, this type of influence remains diffuse. It does depend, in most of these countries, on the readiness of the government to concede points as well as on the level of the research support which members can enjoy. It is because the American Congress benefits on both counts that it appears to be able – and almost certainly is able – to exercise greater influence than Western European parliaments on matters of intermediate importance.

Influence at the broad policy level

It is at the level of broader policy influence that the role of legislatures is normally assessed, however; it is also at this level that pessimistic comments about this role are typically made. If one considers legislation, social and economic policies which do not need the sanction of the legislature, or financial provisions, legislatures appear to be primarily ratification bodies and even the few representative assemblies, such as the United States Congress, which can appreciably modify governmental proposals, only do so to a limited extent and, in most cases, by means of delaying rather than overturning the requests of the executive. Legislatures do not initiate: they follow. The difference is that some may be able to follow grudgingly and by dragging their feet.

If one is to appreciate fully the influence of legislatures in these matters, however, and if one is to differentiate between legislatures from the point of view of their impact, it is necessary to examine their activities in a rather broader context. Two general characteristics need to be taken into account. First, while legislatures may not be able to affect markedly the bills which governments present, they do often play a part in preventing governments from launching certain policies. The precise measurement of the extent to which the executive self-censors itself in this fashion is of course difficult, indeed strictly speaking impossible. However, there is evidence of occasions in which, in Western European countries, for instance, the government refrained from putting forward proposals because of anticipated difficulties in the legislature. A number of celebrated cases occurred in Britain, for example over trade union legislation in the late 1960s; similar situations almost certainly occurred in other countries. This is less likely to take place in authoritarian states, however, where, by and large, policies are accepted without question or even, as was noted, implemented without any reference to the legislature.

Thus the more powerful legislatures do at least have a part to play in circumscribing the area within which the government can intervene; they play a more positive part as well. By and large, legislatures are not in a position to initiate: they do not have the technical competence to do the necessary preparatory work which the civil service, advised by a variety of organisations, can undertake. The real role of legislatures is different. They should not be concerned with governmental proposals only when they are presented as fully developed bills to the chamber; this can be much too late, as many discussions with interested parties will have taken place. Legislators should be involved earlier, namely by launching suggestions and, in effect, by starting 'great debates' in the nation. Such debates will go beyond the confines of the chamber and of the (specialised) public; this may oblige the executive and the civil service to become concerned with the problem and make specific proposals. Committees of inquiry can therefore be crucial, especially if these include members of the interested public alongside legislators. The legislature then provides a forum which can play the part fulfilled by Royal Commissions in Britain and by Presidential Commissions in the United States; a process of this kind occurs in Sweden, where members of the legislature are involved in a significant manner in this 'pre-preparatory' phase of policy development.

So far, however, legislatures are involved in the early stages of policy preparation to a relatively limited extent, even in Western Europe, in part because the potential of such activities does not seem to have been fully perceived. This type of involvement is none the less growing, as legislatures become more specialised and have better research support. These opportunities are probably open almost exclusively to the legislatures of liberal countries, not merely because, in authoritarian states, the pressure of the government is strong, but also because the institutional infrastructure is likely to be unsatisfactory.[32] One can therefore in this way rediscover some of the differences among legislatures which seemed to be elusive when the only criterion used was the character of the bills which were passed. While Western European representative assemblies do not reach the level of open and apparently direct involvement in policy-making of the United States Congress, they can play a 'subterranean' part in determining the national agenda; the potential exists, although in practice these legislatures are not always using all the opportunities which are offered to them.

Conclusion

A general survey of the activities of legislatures suggests that these bodies, while far from reaching the levels of influence which constitutions suggest that they should have, can none the less play a part even in the elaboration of broader policies, at least in liberal countries, although this part remains limited and somewhat concealed. It is concealed because governments wish to present legislation as theirs:[33] this is probably justified because they, alone, have the means of preparing legislation in detail. It is limited because legislators often are not – and in some cases have only recently become – sufficiently specialised to be competent to discuss the technical questions which general policies raise. The influence of legislatures exists in these matters as well at the level of more detailed questions and concrete individual problems; but the influence on broader issues is probably confined to liberal systems and in particular to Western countries. It is particularly marked in the United States, though the fact that it is more apparent there does not necessarily mean that it is greater in the long term. Thus, overall, both potentially and in reality, provided they adapt to the conditions of policy development in modern societies, legislatures can play a part at all levels while being able to exercise a significant role in scrutinising governmental and administrative action.

Notes

1. The idea of a decline in legislatures was suggested by Bryce as characteristic of the development of late nineteenth-century legislatures, because of both a decline in personnel and an increase in governmental control. See Lord Bryce, *Modern Democracies* (1921), vol. 1, pp. 367–77. See also J. Blondel, *Comparative Legislatures* (1973), pp. 5–7.
2. This has been the case in particular in Poland and Hungary as well as in the Soviet Union after the 1989 election.

3. Rousseau argued for instance that the British Parliament was truly sovereign and that the people could play a part only during a short period at election times (*Social Contract*, Book 3, Chapter 15).

4. The effective influence of some Western European legislatures seems to have somewhat increased in the course of the 1980s, in part because of the increased role of committees, in part because party systems have become less rigid. See below.

5. The French Third and Fourth Republics (from 1875 to 1958) were characterised by weak governments as a result of the rather inchoate character of the party system. This led to a considerable influence of the legislature, though typically of a negative kind (in particular to overthrow bills and governments).

6. It is of course in order to ensure that the legislature would be powerful that the Founders of the American Constitution wanted it to be separated from the executive: the view was that the British King could manipulate the British Parliament through the government. Some of this strength of the US Congress has manifestly remained; however, it is also the case that the President does take a lead and that, to a very large extent, Congress is responsive rather than initiating. In this context, the Congress can be regarded as negative, as the congresses of Latin American countries are often regarded as negative. Conflicts often result from this situation, and are, at least in part, at the origin of military intervention in many of these states. In the Chilean case, the period of the Allende presidency (1970–3) was characterised by very strong conflicts between President and Congress.

7. Both Locke and Montesquieu put forward the view that laws should be passed by the legislature and were in a sense the function *par excellence* of a relatively large body, representing the people, and discussing matters in a serene fashion. This view was indeed fully realistic in the eighteenth century, when legislation was primarily concerned with personal affairs.

8. Indeed, Locke suggested that there be a 'federative' power dealing with external relations (from the Latin *foedus* which means treaty).

9. In Britain, for instance, many aspects of the personal status of individuals are still dealt with by private members' bills, while MPs have free votes on questions of conscience.

10. Indeed, with the conception that the law was general, members could be 'amateurs'; this is no longer appropriate with complex social and economic legislation and with the need to scrutinise the activities of the civil service.

11. The development of legislative studies since the 1970s has been substantial, both on a country and on a comparative basis. Models of the role of legislatures have gradually developed. See the bibliography at the end of this volume and in particular M.L. Mezey, *Comparative Legislatures* (1977).

12. The number of legislatures in existence was very substantial in the early 1960s, which was the time when many Black African states became independent. The number then declined, as many legislatures were closed as a result of military coups. For the evolution in the 1960s and early 1970s, see J. Blondel, *op.cit.* (1973), pp. 7–10.

13. The literature on the subject is substantial, particularly in the earlier period. See for instance K.C. Wheare, *Second Chambers* (1963). On the role of the United States Senate, see D.R. Matthews, *US Senators and their World* (1960).

14. The second chamber (Senate) was re-established in Poland in 1989.

15. The debate on second chambers was very heated before World War II. There appears to be less interest at present.

16. The juridical distinction between presidential (or separation of powers) systems and parliamentary systems has traditionally been regarded as the *summa divisio* with respect to legislatures, governments, and government–legislature relations. For a systematic *exposé* of the distinction, see D.V. Verney, *The Analysis of Political Systems* (1959), in particular pp. 17–97. In practice, the distinction does not have the sharpness which the juridical

contrast suggests. In particular, the importance of party discipline in reducing the real power of legislatures has already been noted.

17. It used to be argued that the right of dissolution was absolutely critical and the case of pre-1958 France was typically mentioned as an example of the dangers for governmental stability resulting from the absence of a right of dissolution. Indeed, it is true that the dissolution has played a significant part in the life of the Fifth Republic in streamlining the party system (in 1962, 1968, 1981, and 1988). However, this situation has to be seen in the context of the fact that the French party system is still less well-structured than the party system of other Western European countries. The absence of a right of dissolution has not led to instability in Norway; nor has the fact that the right of dissolution has been limited in West Germany appeared to lead to instability.

18. See Chapter 23.

19. Limitations of the right to censure the government have been introduced since World War II in both France and Germany in order to reduce instability; it was felt in particular in Germany that a mechanism had to be devised in order to ensure that a combination of extremist parties would not result in the fall of governments. There has indeed been less instability, though it is not clear how far these mechanisms have contributed to the result.

20. See J. Blondel, *op. cit.* (1973), pp. 77–80.

21. *ibid.*, pp. 85–91.

22. There have been significant changes in this respect in Hungary and Poland: in both countries the legislature does debate laws and indeed passes amendments. This has also been the case, though to a lesser extent, in Yugoslavia since the 1970s. It was still not the case in the majority of Communist states until 1989, however, and only the collapse of the Communist regime has led to an awakening of the legislature in East Germany, Czechoslovakia and Bulgaria (but not in Romania).

23. See J. Blondel, *op. cit.* (1973), pp. 56–62.

24. Question time, which originated in Britain, has been to an extent imitated in other Commonwealth and Continental countries: on the Continent, however, the formulas adopted are appreciably more formal. One should also note that, despite its importance, question time does not have perhaps the impact that is sometimes attributed to it. See J.W. Marsh, 'Representational changes' in P. Norton (ed.), *Parliament in the 1980s* (1985), in particular pp. 83–5.

25. See J. Blondel, *op. cit.* (1973), pp. 62–6.

26. Britain was one of the last countries to adopt a system of truly effective committees: these have unquestionably markedly increased the ability of MPs to scrutinise the activities of the administration. The committees of the American Congress are notoriously very powerful. See J.D. Lees and M. Shaw (eds), *Committees in Legislatures: A comparative analysis* (1979). For Britain, see S.J. Downs, 'Structural changes' in P. Norton (ed.), *op. cit.*, pp. 48–68. For the United States, among the vast literature, see S.C. Patterson, 'The semi-sovereign congress' in A. King (ed.), *The New American Political System* (1978), pp. 125–77.

27. See J. Blondel, *op. cit.* (1973), pp. 94–6. For Britain, see A. Barker and M. Rush, *The Member of Parliament and his Information* (1970).

28. See Chapter 20.

29. The fact that MPs present private members' bills does not mean that they expect these bills to be passed. In many legislatures, vast numbers of such bills are being presented and quietly buried. In presenting them, MPs may have a variety of aims, ranging from satisfying their constituents to attempting to place an issue on the agenda.

30. It has become common practice in several Third World countries (especially in single-party systems) not to re-nominate retiring MPs or to subject them to what in effect are primaries within the constituency. This has been the case in particular in Tanzania. See J.D. Barkan, 'Legislators, elections, and political linkage' in J.D. Barkan and J.J.

Okumu (eds), *Politics and Public Opinion in Kenya and Tanzania* (1979), pp. 64–91. On Tanzania, see R.F. Hopkins, 'The role of the MP in Tanzania', *Am. Pol. Sc. Rev.*, 64, (1970), pp. 754–71.

31. There have been some changes in this respect in some Western European countries: in Italy, for instance, committees are very influential and do change the shape of some legislation.

32. One should not understimate the part which this infrastructure support plays: one reason why US Congressmen are more active is because they have a truly large staff at their disposal. The matter is also associated with the pay of legislators: if the pay is low, many legislators will be tempted to take on another job.

33. There are some exceptions: in the 1970s and 1980s in particular, the Danish government has tended to rely markedly on the legislature; occasionally at least, Italian governments do the same.

18 | The national executive

National executives are universal. Every country has an executive, a 'government' in the strict sense of the word, as indeed in every other social organisation, from the most simple to the most complex, there is always a body, normally relatively small, though varying in size, which has the task of running that organisation. The executive is also manifestly a key point, if not *the* key point of political life. This remains true even if doubts are sometimes expressed about the ability of executives to affect markedly the course of events, let alone to alter drastically the social and economic structure of their country. At least they have, more than any other body, an opportunity to shape society; it is indeed their function to do so.

National executives are at the centre of political life: unlike almost all the institutions examined so far, they are also rather compact bodies, whose views and pronouncements are usually well-publicised. Parties and even legislatures are more amorphous. Their 'will' is less clear – if these institutions can be said to have a collective will. Because national executives are relatively small and very visible, it is easier to think of them as groups which have a common goal and indeed act as teams. In reality, admittedly, they may well not be united and their differences may even come out in the open. However, the notion of a united government is not wholly unrealistic; it is indeed a characteristic to which many executives aspire. The aim is to give an impression of a well-oiled and efficient machine which can lead the country towards its future.

Governments may exist everywhere and may be, on the whole, rather small and compact bodies. Yet within this framework, major distinctions exist between them. They vary in composition, in internal organisation, in selection mechanisms, in duration and in powers – both formal and informal. There are autocratic governments and governments which emanate from the people or from its representatives; there are egalitarian governments and hierarchical governments; there are governments which seem to last indefinitely and ephemeral governments; there are strong and weak governments. As one examines the characteristics of national executives, therefore, differences among these appear to be as large as differences among groups, parties or legislatures.

Indeed, as one analyses executives further, even the idea that they always constitute truly compact and circumscribed groups ceases to be axiomatic.[1] The exact limits of the set of individuals who form part of the government cannot always be clearly marked, as there are many men and women around the government whose status in relation to that government is not well-defined. Many national executives include under-secretaries or junior ministers, for instance: in one sense, these are members of the government, as they are appointed by the ministers and leave office at the same time as them, but many other officials fulfil the same conditions, for instance the personal staff of ministers. Meanwhile, junior ministers are normally excluded from the process of elaboration of general governmental policy, but there are also cases where some ministers are excluded from this process, especially in hierarchical executives in which leaders take the most important decisions and are free to choose whom they wish to advise them. Moreover, especially in such cases, members of the personal staff of leaders may play an important part in decision-making – a more important part even than ministers – although they are not part of the official structure of the executive: should they be deemed to belong to the government, while some ministers and most junior ministers are excluded? Is this not the case with many of the counsellors of the American President, for instance? Is it not also the case with the members of the Politburo of the Communist party of the Soviet Union, and indeed even of the Secretaries of that party, although these may not belong to the Politburo? Thus, while governments may have a clear nucleus, composed of the leaders and at least many ministers, a 'grey zone' whose boundaries are not precise forms, so to speak, the 'tail' of these governments.

It might seem easier to define a national executive in terms of the functions which it fulfills; indeed, it is only by reference to these functions that one can determine whether junior ministers or members of personal staffs should be deemed to belong to the government. Yet these functions are also somewhat unclear. In a general way, the government is expected to 'run the affairs of the nation', but it does not run these affairs alone or it runs them only up to a point, since it is 'helped' or 'advised' by groups, by parties, by the legislature, and, above all, by the very large bureaucracy which all states have now developed. It is therefore necessary to examine these functions first, before turning to the differences which exist in the structure, composition, and duration of national executives in the contemporary world, and before turning to the difficult and currently controversial question of the real impact of governments on the life of the nation.

The functions of national executives

To 'run the affairs of the nation' simply means that the government is formally at the top of the pyramid of decision-making. In practice, however, the government is at the junction between two processes which characterise this decision-making. As was described in Chapter 2, the government 'converts' inputs into outputs, that is to say turns demands into policies.[2] This process of 'conversion' is not automatic, however. Governments choose among inputs; they may indeed discard some demands which are strongly supported and select others for which there is little support. Yet, at the very least, governments need to take into account demands which are expressed, even if only to oppose them. No national executive totally 'invents' the policies which it formulates: ideas for policies originate in the public, including in this context the entourage of the government itself, and if these demands arise, they have to be handled by the government in some manner. This is true even where the system is authoritarian, though the 'reactions' of the government are then likely to be different form the 'reactions' which characterise a pluralistic system.

Thus, while the government has to show imagination in the development of policies, this imaginative effort relates mainly to the discovery of the practical means by which 'solutions' can be found to problems with which the government is faced. The process of elaboration of public policies therefore has two characteristics. First, 'realistic' policies have to be developed – realistic in the sense that the policies can be physically implemented and in the sense that they are politically acceptable (if necessary by using compulsion). An agricultural, industrial, or social policy will be elaborated on the basis of the perceived 'needs' of the country as well as on the basis of an impression of what the citizens are prepared to 'live with'. Second, however, policy elaboration cannot be divorced from the implementation process, that is to say from the discovery of the mechanisms through which governmental policy can become reality.

Thus, while the government has a function of *conception* which is linked to the demands which exist in the polity, it has also a function of *implementation*, at least insofar as it must find the means by which policies can become reality. It must therefore appoint and supervise a bureaucracy which is able to put the policies in operation. This two-fold function is crucial for governments. Tensions arise as a result, as conception and implementation are related to different psychological attitudes, which are reflected for instance in the conflict between those who 'dream' and those who 'manage'; they entail that members of the government have a combination of different skills. While the function of conception requires creative imagination based on a certain vision of society (whatever the level of the policy which is being discussed), the implementation function requires an ability to manage individuals and groups; the same men and women may well not possess both types of skills. Admittedly, this distinction seems to correspond to the division between 'leaders' and their 'helpers' (the word 'minister' refers etymologically to someone who 'helps'); in practice, the two functions cannot be separated, even if only because it is not very useful to conceive ideas which cannot be implemented. Thus the two aspects are closely linked and it would be dangerous not to organise at least some links between those who conceive and those who are at the head of the implementation process. A government must turn this combination into reality, both as a group and through its members.

The link between these two functions is further strengthened by the existence of a third function, which may be viewed as intermediate, that of *co-ordination*. An important element of the process of policy elaboration consists in ensuring that the policies do not go against each other and, ideally, that they develop harmoniously. Moreover, policy elaboration entails making choices or at least establishing priorities, both for financial reasons and because of constraints in human resources. Since everything cannot be done at the same time, a timetable has to be drawn up, but such a timetable must take into account the inter-relationships between policies and the internal logic of policy development.

Co-ordination can be successful only if close ties exist among members of the government both at the level of policy elaboration and at that of policy implementation: a housing policy entails a school building policy, which must be expressed not merely in general, but in detailed terms; the same applies to an industrial policy, which must lead to a housing policy, and so on. The natural tendency of branches of the public service to operate independently from each other must be corrected in order to ensure that distortions, contradictions, and ultimately policy failures be minimised. This is the role of co-ordination, though there are limits on the extent to which it can effectively take place. Thus administrative and political centralisation cannot go beyond a certain point without reducing overall efficiency, as many examples drawn from the Soviet Union and Eastern Europe make abundantly clear. Even where centralisation does not go too far, co-ordination remains a major problem: it must be at the centre of the government's preoccupations if the process of implementation of public policies is to be efficient.

Conception, co-ordination, and direction of implementation are therefore the three elements of governmental action. These elements are analytically distinct; it is the government's duty to combine them. However, this combination inevitably raises problems. Depending on circumstances, conception, co-ordination and implementation will be given greater emphasis. It is not surprising that the development of governmental structures in the contemporary world should have been the result of a variety of *ad hoc* experiments which have been more or less successful. Not surprisingly, too, the conflict between the three goals or functions of government has only been solved to a rather limited extent.

The forms of governmental organisation

The evolution of governmental arrangements

Contemporary governmental arrangements reflect the diversity and increasing complexity of the tasks which are being undertaken by executives. However, the variations in the structure of these executives are not a new phenomenon. The oligarchical arrangements of Italian republican cities of the Renaissance were at great variance from those of the absolute monarchies which began to emerge in the sixteenth century, without mentioning the theocratic and despotic governments which have existed for instance in the Moslem world.

Nineteenth-century developments have endeavoured to 'domesticate' governmental arrangements and to give these a less haphazard and more rational character.

Two constitutional systems, which were encountered earlier in the context of legislatures, have tended to dominate the European and North American scene for a century. On the one hand, the *cabinet system*, which originated in England and also in Sweden, is based on the notion that the head of the government, the prime minister, has to operate in the context of a collegial system in which a group of ministers fully participates in the decision-making process while being also in charge of the implementation of the decisions in a particular sector. Cabinet government extended gradually to Western European countries; in Central and Eastern Europe, meanwhile, the remnants of absolutism were gradually undermined, to the extent that the cabinet system seemed likely at one point to replace old absolutist and authoritarian governmental structures everywhere.[3]

In contrast to the cabinet system, the *constitutional presidential system* was first established in the United States and then extended gradually to the whole of Latin America. In this model, the executive is hierarchical and not collective. Ministers (often named secretaries in this system) are subordinates of the president and only responsible to him. Although this formula is closer to that of monarchical government than that of the cabinet system, it does mean some demotion for both the head of state (who is elected for a period and often is not permitted to be re-elected indefinitely) and for the ministers (as these typically have to be 'confirmed', as was pointed out in the last chapter, by the legislature). The formula was rather unsuccessful in Latin America, however, as many presidents have been uncomfortable with the limitations on their position and many coups have taken place, as a result of which authoritarian and even 'absolute' presidential governments have been installed.[4]

At least one of the two constitutional formulas was therefore encountering difficulties before 1914. The problems multiplied after World War I, with the emergence of the Communist system in Russia and authoritarian governments of the Fascist variety in Italy and later throughout much of Southern, Central and Eastern Europe, and after World War II, with the emergence of a large number of absolute presidential systems, civilian and military, in many parts of the Third World. These developments were characterised by the emergence or re-emergence of the role of the strong leader, which constitutional systems had sought to diminish, and the consequent decline of the idea, fostered by cabinet government, of collective or at least collegial government. However, the period was also characterised by the 'invention' of a new form of executive structure, which was consequential on the development of parties but which had not been brought to its ultimate limits in either of the two constitutional systems: this was the intrusion of parties and, in authoritarian systems, usually of the single party, in the machinery of government.

For the proponents of constitutional systems, whether of the cabinet or of the presidential type, the executive was regarded as the apex of the national decision-making process; the question of sharing this position with any other body was not even conceived. Admittedly, with the emergence of parties, the recruitment of the governmental personnel and the determination of the broad lines of policy were gradually but informally influenced by these organisations. Yet this development was not regarded as having profound consequences for the character of the government.[5] With the coming to power of the Communist party in Russia, however, a new idea emerged; it was felt that it was the function of the party to ensure that the top organs of the state (that is to say the government) were kept under control. From this view developed the concept of a dual structure of 'party' and 'state': the top party body, the Politburo, achieved as a result a status equal to or even superior to that of the government. Such a model naturally extended to Eastern European Communist states after 1945; it came to be adopted also in some single-party states of the Third World, particularly in Africa, especially those which were of the 'progressive' variety. By a process of imitation, the formula was also used by some military rulers who established 'military' or 'revolutionary' councils alongside the regular government.[6]

Thus the notion of a two-level or 'dual' form of governmental structure developed in the course of the twentieth century and in particular in its second half. But this formula was not merely an ideological accident; it also corresponded closely to the functional division between 'conception' and 'implementation', which was outlined earlier. The increased complexity of governmental tasks (particularly in Communist and other centralised states, but also in Western systems) seemed to justify such a dualism. Indeed, the latter seemed to be affected, to an extent at least, by similar developments; the growth of the office of the President since the 1930s suggests a *de facto* division of the United States government into two layers.[7] Conversely, the difficulties experienced by Western European cabinet systems in maintaining the collegiality of the government are also an indication of a certain inability of executives to operate effectively if all functions are concentrated in the same hands.[8]

Types of governmental structure in the contemporary world

While every state has a government, it is only in the third quarter of the twentieth century that *independent* governments rule practically the whole of the planet. This means that the number of national executives has more than doubled since the 1940s. Meanwhile, as governments became more 'modern' – being increasingly concerned with a large variety of aspects of social and economic life – their size increased substantially. While national executives had about a dozen ministers on average in 1950, they had on average about 18 posts in the 1980s. Globally, there were under 1 000 ministers simultaneously in office after World War II; there were over 2 500 thirty years later.[9]

The rate of increase in the size of governments has not been the same across the world, however. Atlantic, Latin American, and Asian countries have seen the smallest rate of increase, while Communist, Middle Eastern, and African states have had the largest increase. There are also substantial absolute variations. Communist governments are large, even if one adopts a rather restrictive definition of governments. Thus the Soviet executive – which is the largest of all – had seventy-five members in the 1980s. Not surprisingly, perhaps, efforts have been made in the late 1980s to reduce this number; the prospect may not be good, as the Chinese government increased in size again after having been substantially cut for a while in the 1970s. The size of these executives is in large part commanded by the traditional concern of Communist systems to direct the economy in great detail, thus making it necessary to establish specialised ministries relating to various industries.[10] However, other governments have also tended to increase, to a greater or lesser extent, in response to various demands or desires for interventionism. Thus developing countries, expecially those of the 'progressive' variety, typically have fairly large governments. Only in those executives which have been regulated by legal or even constitutional rules has the number of ministries remained relatively small, alongside those of countries whose population is very small indeed, such as Luxemburg or Iceland. This is why constitutional presidential executives – and, therefore, Latin American governments as well as the United States government – have relatively few members (twelve to fifteen, as against twenty to twenty-five in many Western European cabinets).

Collegial governments

Cabinet governments are in principle collective and egalitarian. Decisions have to be taken by the whole cabinet;[11] neither the prime minister nor any group of ministers is formally entitled to involve the whole government. The counterpart of this provision is 'collective responsibility', which stipulates that all the ministers are bound by cabinet decisions. In its most extreme form, this rule suggests that ministers are also bound to speak in favour of all the decisions.

These principles are markedly eroded in practice in nearly all the countries which operate on the basis of cabinet government, that is to say in Western European countries (except Switzerland) and many Commonwealth countries (Canada, Australia, New Zealand, India, Malaysia, Singapore and most ex-British Caribbean and Pacific islands), as well as Japan and Israel. In the first instance, in many of these countries, following British practice, collective decision-making only applies to members of the cabinet in the strict sense: the government can be much larger because of the appointment of substantial numbers of junior ministers (especially in Britain, where it includes, in its widest definition, a hundred members or more).[12] These junior ministers are bound by the principle of collective responsibility, but do not share in the decision-making process. Second, the number and complexity of decisions are such that the cabinet cannot physically, during what are normally short meetings of two to three hours each week (in some cases twice a week, admittedly), truly discuss all the issues which require decisions. As a result, while the cabinet formally ratifies all the decisions, many of these are *de facto* delegated to individual ministers (when they come within the purview of their department), to groups of ministers sitting in committee (the number of these has markedly increased in many cabinet governments), or to the prime minister and some of the ministers.[13] Cabinet government is at most collegial government and it is, in some cases, even hierarchical.

One can in practice distinguish between three broad types of cabinet arrangements, although there is strictly speaking a continuum between truly collective and egalitarian cabinets (of which there are very few) and hierarchical governments, sometimes labelled prime ministerial cabinets. The more *collegial* cabinets are those in which, often because of the existence of a coalition but also because of political traditions, the prime minister has to rely on a high degree of interchange with colleagues before decisions are taken. As a matter of fact, although (or perhaps because) Switzerland does not have cabinet government but instead has ministers elected for a fixed duration on the basis of a permanent coalition of the major parties, its executive is probably the most equal in Western Europe – though, even there, full collective decision-making does not occur. Scandinavian cabinets are more collegial than those of Central and Western Europe, despite the fact that, especially in Sweden, single-party government occurs fairly frequently.[14]

The second model is that of the *team*, which is more common in single-party governments, as in Commonwealth countries, including Britain. The ministers, who have often worked together for a number of years in parliament, have broadly common aims and even a common approach. Much work is delegated to individual ministers, to committees, or to the prime minister, but there is a spirit of understanding which results from the relatively long joint experience of government members. While the prime minister appoints and dismisses ministers, the pool from which these are drawn – mostly the parliamentary party – drastically limits the opportunities for selection.[15]

There is a third model, however, which is sometimes described as *prime ministerial*, in which ministers are noticeably dependent on the head of the government, for instance because he or she has considerable popularity. This arises from substantial and repeated election victories or from the fact that the head of the government has created the party, the regime, or even the country. Such cases have been frequent in the cabinet governments of the Third World (in the Caribbean or in India, for example); they have also occurred in Western Europe, at least occasionally (in West Germany, France or even Britain). The relationship between ministers and prime minister is then hierarchical and resembles that which prevails in presidential and indeed in traditional monarchical systems.[16]

Hierarchical governments

The large majority of the other governmental arrangements are, formally at least, hierarchical, in that ministers – and any other members of the government – are wholly dependent on the head of the government and head of state. They are appointed and dismissed at will; their decisions are taken by delegation from the head of the government; formally at least, they play no part in policies which do not affect their department. These arrangements were traditionally those of monarchical systems; as was pointed out, the constitutional presidential system did not alter this model. The many authoritarian presidential systems which emerged in the Third World after World War II adopted a similar formula; while about fifty governments are of the cabinet type, as many as eighty countries – mainly in the Americas, Africa, in the Middle East – have governments of this variety.

The extent to which these systems are hierarchical in practice is not always the same, however: a number of moves suggest that they may be closer, in some cases at least, to cabinet systems, for the head of the government may not be able to select or dismiss ministers at will or may have to pay attention to their views. Heads of government may be obliged to appoint some ministers because, in traditional monarchical regimes, members of certain families are very influential, or, in civilian or military presidential regimes, because some individuals may have helped the successful head of government to come to power. The American president is freer in this respect than most other constitutional presidents, who are more closely dependent on party support to achieve power.[17] Second, the complexity of issues, especially economic and social, obliges many heads of government, not merely to appoint some well-known managers or civil servants, but to pay attention to their views to such an extent that they may exercise influence well beyond their own department. Moreover, individual ministers are often closely linked to the officials of the departments of which they are in charge; as a result they acquire some autonomous power and the head of government may have some difficulty in controlling them.

This situation is particularly noticeable in the constitutional presidential executive which is the largest of all, that of the United States. It is difficult to regard this executive as any longer truly hierarchical: it is more accurately described as atomised. Departments are vast and therefore naturally form self-contained empires. Moreover, any vertical relationships which might exist between departmental heads and the president are undermined by the horizontal relationships existing between each department and Congress, and especially by relationships with the committees of Congress relevant to the departments, as the departments want to ensure that they obtain the appropriations which they feel they need and the laws which they promote. Finally, the links which develop between departments and their clientele (the various interest groups which gravitate around each department) tend to reduce further the strength of the hierarchical ties between departments and president.[18]

Thus the American government tends naturally to be atomised; to remedy this defect, presidents since F.D. Roosevelt in the 1930s have appointed increasingly large personal staffs whose aim is to supervise and co-ordinate the activities of the departments in order to ensure that presidential policies are carried out.[19] This has meant, however, as was noted earlier, that it has become difficult to discover what constitutes the 'real' government of the United States. Beyond the formal hierarchical structure of president and secretaries, the government seems to have two levels, with the 'upper level', formed by the White House office, having some degree of collegiality while the 'lower level' has little unity. By becoming gradually a government at two levels, the American government thus resembles in part the dual arrangements which prevail in some countries and in particular in Communist states.

Multi-level governments

For the historical reasons described earlier, the party structure and the state structure led to the emergence of divided governments in the Soviet Union and, after World War II, in the other Communist states. Indeed, this division goes beyond duality: the Politburos of the Communist parties have traditionally been helped by large secretariats, whose heads constitute the personal staffs of the First Secretaries, the latter being generally regarded as the 'true' leaders of their countries.[20] On the other hand, the state 'half' of the governmental structure has traditionally been divided into a 'Presidium' and a Council of Ministers proper, the Presidium being composed of the most important ministers as well as of some representatives of the regions, at any rate in the Soviet Union. In the full version of the model as it has traditionally existed in the Soviet Union, there are four distinct bodies. One of these, the Politburo, is primarily in charge of policy elaboration, and is helped by the Secretariat, while the Presidium is in charge of co-ordination and the Council of Ministers deals with implementation. The links between these bodies are achieved because of the fact that some of the more important ministers and the prime minister (normally a different person from the First Secretary of the party) belong to the Politburo, to the Presidium and, of course, to the Council of Ministers at the same time. These traditional arrangements have been put in question as a result of the Soviet Union's move towards presidentialism, however, while most Eastern European countries have abolished their Communist structures altogether.

Multi-level governments have existed for decades in Communist states; comparable systems have developed in some non-Communist single-party systems and in a number of military regimes. Supreme Military Councils or Committees of National Salvation have thus been created to ensure that the regular government (often composed of civil servants) carried out the policies of the military rulers. This formula, which started in Burma in 1962, was adopted by many African states (Nigeria for instance); it also existed for a period in Portugal after the end of the dictatorship in 1974. These arrangements have had a varying degree of longevity and apparent success; they have typically been less systematically organised than in Communist states.[21]

Members of governments

Social and career background

During the period 1945–90, about 20 000 men and women have been members of national governments. These ministers have similar backgrounds to those of members of legislatures: they are mostly male, drawn from middle-class groups, and middle-aged. The numbers of women in government have been growing since the 1970s, however; in Scandinavia women have come to be a substantial minority and, in the late 1980s, they formed a majority in the Norwegian government. Manual workers, white collar employees, and farmers are relatively rare in governments. The proportion of manual workers, once substantial in Communist governments (about one-third) declined markedly in proportion in the 1970s and 1980s. Ministers are mostly lawyers, teachers, civil servants, managers, or, in military regimes, military men, while business leaders are under-represented, as in most parliaments. Public sector managers and civil servants are numerous, not just in Communist and Third World states, but in many Western countries as well.[22]

The routes to office

Ministers are rarely young and usually join the government in their late forties; they come to office by one of three main routes – politics, the civil service, and the military. The political route, through parliament and a political party, is the most common of all, especially in Western countries (though not in the United States, where the proportion of ministers coming directly from business is large). This route is naturally important in cabinet systems, since there is a formal link between government and legislature in that system. In the Third World, the proportion of politicians among ministers varies appreciably: it is substantial in South East Asia (where there are a number of parliamentary systems) and in Latin American civilian governments. In Communist states, as well as in some Middle Eastern and Black African countries, it is sometimes difficult to distinguish the political from the administrative routes to office, as ministers often have a party background while also being civil servants. Businessmen and lawyers usually come to office through the political route.

Alongside the political route, the civil service route provides a way of reaching the government for a substantial minority of ministers. It is sometimes combined with the political route, as we saw, but this is far from being always the case. Indeed, the civil service route is the most traditional of all: monarchs always chose those who helped them from among administrators because they had the necessary knowledge and at the same time could be expected to remain loyal. Thus the traditional monarchies which remain in existence appoint many civil servants to the government; so do other non-party systems (primarily led by the military) and even some single-party systems. In Communist countries, particularly in the Soviet Union and China and to a lesser extent in Eastern Europe, a ministerial position has often traditionally been the apex of a long career in a department. Despite the fact that, as was noted earlier, the cabinet system creates strong links between executive and legislature, the civil service route plays a substantial part even in some Western European countries, not only in France, where civil servants (and managers of public enterprises) started to be appointed to the government with the advent of the

Fifth Republic in 1958, but in Austria, the Netherlands, Finland and Norway.

The third route to ministerial office is the military, a route which plays a substantial part in the Third World as a result of the existence of many military regimes: this is particularly the case in Central and South America (though not in the Caribbean), in Black Africa (especially in West Africa), in the Middle East and in North Africa. Yet the extent to which military men come to office varies markedly among military regimes, while, in civilian governments, ministers in defence departments are often (as in Western Europe in the nineteenth century) members of the military. As will be seen in Chapter 21, the military route is significant since it constitutes an alternative to the party route in countries where parties are too weak to prevent the occurrence (or recurrence) of military regimes.

The ministerial career proper

A long preparation is usually needed before one becomes a minister, despite the fact that there are examples of ministers who achieve office suddenly, for instance after a military coup. Yet a minister cannot normally expect to remain in office for more than a few years and, in many cases, for more than a year or two. Admittedly, a position in the *cabinet* often follows a post as a junior member of the government – which may have been held for four or five years. Even if one adds these positions together, however, the average duration remains low: to the four or five years as a junior minister can be added perhaps three or four years in the cabinet proper.[23]

There are of course marked variations around this average. Some are ministers for a decade or more, though usually not in the same post, and often not in succession, while a substantial proportion, indeed almost a third, are in the cabinet for only one year.[24] There are also variations from country to country. The ministerial career has traditionally been longest in Communist states (six years on average), especially in the Soviet Union; it is shortest in Latin America and in the Middle East (two years or less); ministerial duration is relatively long in Atlantic countries (about four years), in Black Africa, and in South and South-East Asia.

A number of factors lie at the origin of these variations. The instability of regimes in the Third World and, in liberal systems, the alternation of parties in power are important contributory elements. Ministers were more stable in Communist states because these phenomena, traditionally at least, did not occur; these countries have, in a sense, kept the same 'government' in power for decades, though, in those in which some instability has occurred, as in Poland, ministerial duration has been affected.[25] These factors also partially explain why ministerial duration tends to be higher in traditional monarchies (as in those of the Arabian peninsula) and in some Black African states in which a 'charismatic' ruler has been in power for long periods (the Ivory Coast, for instance).[26] Similarly, ministerial duration is longer in those Western countries where the alternation of parties in power has been relatively infrequent (such as Canada and Sweden) or where at least one of the parties has been in office for many years, if not permanently, in a coalition context (as in Germany or Austria).[27] An indirect effect of these factors can be found in the fact that, by and large, ministerial duration is shorter in constitutional presidential systems than in parliamentary systems; in the former, newly appointed presidents tend to select new ministers, while in the more collegial cabinets of parliamentary systems the departure of the prime minister often does not provoke that of the ministers as well.

Variations in ministerial longevity are also due to cultural factors alongside institutional characteristics and changes of regimes or of parties in power. There appear to be different traditions with respect to the extent to which cabinets are periodically 'reshuffled'. The contrast between Sweden and Japan is particularly sharp in this context, since in these two countries the same party has been in power for decades and yet differences in average duration are considerable: Swedish ministers of social democratic governments have been in office for over eight years on average, while, in Japan, the average duration is little over a year; in Japan, many ministers and indeed almost the entire cabinet are replaced every year. Cultural characteristics of this type, though less pronounced, account in part for variations between Austria or Germany (where reshuffles are rare) and Britain or France (where reshuffles are more frequent). They also account for variations among other systems. In Chile, for instance, both during the period of constitutional rule up to 1973 and during the period of military rule of the 1970s and 1980s, the turnover of ministers was so high that the average duration of ministers was also scarcely over one year, while, in Mexico, reshuffles are rare and ministers remain in office on average for about four years.

The averages which have been discussed so far relate to the total longevity of ministers in office, not to their duration in individual posts. For the majority, the figure is the same, as most government ministers only ever have one post; but a substantial minority holds two or more posts in succession. This sometimes occurs after an interruption, though such interruptions are rare in presidential systems, military governments or Communist regimes; they tend primarily to occur in parliamentary systems, in part as a result of the alternation of parties in government. Reshuffles leading to ministers moving from one position to another in succession are also more frequent in parliamentary systems.[28]

The fact that many ministers move from one post to another is sometimes linked to political traditions (the prime minister may feel that someone who changes positions is less likely to be a danger); but it also relates to different conceptions of the role of ministers. Where the emphasis is on implementation, there will be a tendency to appoint specialists to direct departments and not subsequently to move them to another post. This is the practice commonly followed in Communist states, a practice which also prevails in many Third World regimes, in many presidential systems, and even in some parliamentary systems, especially in Central Europe. Where, on the contrary, the emphasis is on office-holders being concerned with policy elaboration and co-ordination in a collegial manner, ministers are regarded as having a primarily political role; they are often described as being 'amateurs', rather than as specialists. This view is widely held in parliamentary systems, particularly in those which came directly from the British tradition; the proportion of ministers having held more than one post in succession is naturally largest in this group of countries.[29]

The career of ministers is short; it is almost an accident for most ministers – indeed it is truly an accident for a substantial number of them. It is perhaps surprising that such a career should be sought after, as it seems to be, even in countries where the duration prospects are low. Admittedly, the rewards are substantial while in office; there may also be rewards after leaving office (in business and public enterprise, and in international positions), though there are also dangers, including physical dangers, admittedly mostly in the Third World. In many cases, an attempt is made to marry political skills and administrative skills, but the duration is so short for most and the preparation so limited that the question does arise as to whether governments can truly have a profound impact on the countries which they rule.

The impact of governments

It is extremely difficult to measure the achievements of governments or even to gain a satisfactory impression of their extent. The contrast is sharp between rapid comments frequently made about the potential achievements of executives and the slow progress of systematic analyses designed to determine what governments can and do realise, as there are major problems at several levels. First, to assess the role of governments, one must distinguish the developments which would have occurred 'naturally' as a result of social and economic change from those which can be said to have occurred because the government decided on them. Comparative analysis can help in this respect, as it is possible to discover whether different policies have a different impact. Thus, while unemployment was widespread in Western Europe throughout the 1980s, it was very low in some countries, such as Sweden, Austria and Switzerland. Yet, even by comparing nations, it is still difficult to be certain whether a particular effect should be attributed exclusively or even primarily to governmental action.

Second, it is often not possible precisely to relate particular outcomes to particular governments. Sometimes the duration of governments is too short for valid conclusions to be drawn. Little can normally be said about the impact of governments which last a year or less; yet, as was seen, many ministers remain in office for one year or less. Moreover, governments often 'slide' into one another, so to speak, as a result of reshuffles. The British Conservative governments of the 1980s were almost entirely reconstructed, although the same leader remained in office; on the other hand, Italian prime ministers change fairly frequently, while ministers may stay or return to office after a few years. What then constitutes a government becomes a debatable point. If one takes a narrow definition and considers that a government has to remain truly identical to be genuinely *one*, then almost no national executive remains in office for more than a year or two; if one relaxes the condition and decides for instance to discard partial reshuffles, the problem arises as to which cut-off point to adopt. One may for instance suggest that a government is the same if it has the same prime minister or president, is composed of the same party or parties, and corresponds to the same parliament. Such a definition may be valid for some purposes (and for countries in which elections matter); but it is clearly a 'compromise' definition, since such a 'government' will have been modified in composition, perhaps markedly, during the period.

It is because of these numerous reshuffles as well as because the problem is almost exclusively confined to Western Europe that the question of the relative duration of single-party and coalition governments, though technically very interesting, probably does not deserve the prominence which it was once given. As was indicated in Chapter 13, it has sometimes been suggested that proportional representation has the effect of leading to executive instability because it results in greater party fractionalisation in parliament. Yet minority governments and coalitions, which are indeed numerous in Continental Europe, are not all weak and unstable; the difference in duration between these and single-party governments is substantial overall, but only if one does not take into account the incidence of reshuffles in single-party governments. Moreover, types of coalition are varied: there are small coalitions and 'grand coalitions', 'minimum size' coalitions and 'oversized coalitions', as well as minority governments, and conclusions about the longevity of these different types are not identical. It is at any rate wrong to claim that coalitions (and even minority governments) are necessarily or even generally weak and ineffective, as the German, Austrian and Dutch examples indicate.[30]

There is a further difficulty, which is particularly serious since governments normally last for short periods: it takes time for governments to elaborate policies and perhaps even more time for policies to be implemented. There is therefore necessarily a lag between the moment at which an executive comes to office and the moment at which policies have an impact; this point is true, even if, as is sometimes claimed, new governments and new leaders may benefit from a 'state of grace'.[31] Since there is such a lag and indeed a lag which varies from policy to policy, results should often be attributed to preceding executives rather than to current ones. As, moreover, governments normally have little room for manoeuvre since the large majority of expenditure (90 per cent or more) relates to matters which cannot be altered (salaries, maintenance of existing activities, etc.), the determination of the real impact of a given government is often speculative and is likely to be highly controversial.

Not surprisingly, conclusions in this respect have remained rather vague: they are more concerned with certain broad characteristics of whole classes of executives than with individual cabinets. Thus it has been possible to establish that social democratic governments have, at least in many respects, an impact on social and economic life, despite the view which is sometimes expressed that no difference can any longer be detected among governmental parties.[32] It also seems established that, contrary to what some had claimed, Third World military governments do not perform better economically than civilian governments.[33] Other generalisations often made about governments have not so far been confirmed; in particular, it is not established that instability of ministerial personnel has the negative consequences for social and economic development that it is often said to have (though it may have a negative impact on the regime's legitimacy).[34]

The firm conclusions which can be drawn on the impact of governments on economic and social life are therefore limited. Yet it seems too narrow to assess executives solely on the basis of this impact. The broader cultural and ideological values which governments foster may modify the general climate within which political, social, and economic life develops. Such an effect is even more difficult to assess, however, since the nature and extent of a change of climate cannot usually be measured adequately, let alone be closely related to the activities of a particular government. This difficulty does not constitute sufficient ground for excluding any impact, however, let alone for deciding not to consider impact at all. Only with patient efforts and on the basis of the general hypothesis that governments do matter somewhat, though probably less than is readily assumed (especially by those who wish to criticise a particular cabinet), can progress be made in the measurement of the role of national executives.[35]

Conclusion

It may seem paradoxical to ask the question of whether governments matter when so much emphasis is placed on national executives by the media, the organised groups and large sections of the public. This paradox is only one of the many contradictory sentiments which governments appear to create. Perhaps such contradictory views are understandable: governments both attract and repel because they are at least ostensibly powerful and give those who belong to them an aura of strength, of *auctoritas*, which fascinates, tantalises, but also worries and, in the worst cases, frightens the subjects and the spectators of political life. Yet there are also other contradictions and paradoxes of governments, from the great complexity of the tasks to be performed to the often ephemeral character of their members, from the many ways in which they can be organised to the ultimate paradox – namely that, in the end, it is almost impossible to describe precisely who is in the government. If one adds the particular role of leaders, to which the discussion now turns, it seems legitimate to conclude that the central part of the political machine, the national executive, is also one of the most elusive elements of the political process.

Notes

1. Indeed, the idea that they are a compact body is not altogether very old. The concept of a government as such did not exist in republican Rome and, in absolute monarchies, there were individual ministers helping the King, not a government.
2. This is the process suggested by systems analysis, as was described in Chapter 2.

3. See Chapter 17. For a reference to the sharp distinction between parliamentary and separation of powers systems, see D.V. Verney, *The Analysis of Political Systems* (1959), pp. 17–97.

4. The only country in which constitutional presidential government has truly succeeded is the United States; the difficulties which this system has encountered elsewhere (essentially in Latin America) can be attributed to the rigidity with which it sharply distinguishes between legislature and executive.

5. The consequences of the involvement of parties are large, even in Western Europe, even though they are not typically considered systematically: the involvement of parties does mean that they have a large part in the agenda-setting for the government (programmes, for instance) as well as in the decisions which governments take on a daily basis.

6. The Nazi and Fascist models also gave prominence to the party. However, the leader dominated the scene in both cases to such an extent that the problem of the relationship between party and government, in these regimes, took second place. The same occurred in the Soviet Union under Stalin: only since his death has the question of party–state relationships become truly important.

7. One can consider the Office of the American President as being a kind of government. See for instance J. Blondel, *Organisation of Governments* (1982), pp. 154–8. See also C. Campbell, *Governments under Stress* (1983), *passim*.

8. The difficulties experienced by Western European cabinets in matters of collegiality are well established and discussed in country texts. See G. Smith, *Politics in Western Europe* (1972), pp. 217–22. See also J. Blondel and F. Muller-Rommel (eds), *Cabinets in Western Europe* (1988), *passim*.

9. See J. Blondel, *Organisation of Governments* (1982), pp. 175–7.

10. The maintenance of the reduction in the number of ministries is thus dependent on the ability (and desire) of Communist governments to diminish their direct intervention in various sectors of the economy (thus making it unnecessary to have ministries of light industry, heavy industry, etc.).

11. Cabinet government has of course developed from parliamentary government, and it is the parliamentary origin and basis of the cabinet which accounts for its collegial characteristics. The idea was expressed in the nineteenth century by Bagehot in *The English Constitution* in terms of the government being a 'board of control chosen by the legislature, out of persons whom it trusts and knows, to rule the nation' (Fontana edn, p. 67).

12. The practice of appointing junior ministers has extended throughout Western Europe and indeed to cabinet governments outside Western Europe. The British (and Italian) governments are among those which have appointed the largest numbers to these positions.

13. Given the load of cabinet meetings, committees have become increasingly important, almost everywhere, both to prepare and indeed (at least in practice) to decide on many matters on behalf of the full cabinet. See T.T. McKie and B.W. Hogwood (eds), *Unlocking the Cabinet* (1985).

14. Coalition governments are a feature of cabinet governments. Only occasionally do such governments exist in other systems, in part, of course, because of the large number of single-party systems. Continental European governments are nearly always coalition governments, although these coalitions can be small or large (and may include almost all the relevant parties); on the other hand, British and Commonwealth governments tend to be of the one-party variety, while Scandinavian governments oscillate to an extent, except in Finland, where coalitions are the rule. One-party governments can also be either majority or minority, of which there are a sizeable number, in some countries at least (Denmark in particular). The nature and size of coalitions has been the object of many studies as these vary appreciably; among the explanations which have been brought forward have been in particular the 'minimum size principle' (Riker) and the 'ideological

proximity' (De Swaan). For a general presentation of the analysis, see E.C. Browne and J. Dreijannis (eds), *Government Coalitions in Western Democracies* (1982); see also A. Lijphart, *Democracies* (1984), pp. 46–66.

15. Although such governments are team governments, the prime minister is more able than in coalition governments to appoint and dismiss ministers, as in a coalition government the partners of the coalition tend to have a large say in the appointment of the individual office-holders.

16. The idea of prime ministerial government developed primarily in Britain: R.H.S. Crossman suggested that this was what British Cabinet government had become. See his Preface to Bagehot's *English Constitution* (1963) (Fontana edn, pp. 48–57).

17. The other constitutional presidential systems in existence tend to be more party-based. Indeed, in Venezuela, there was even a coalition arrangement in the government for a period in the late 1950s and early 1960s.

18. For a description of the character of the relationship between departments and Congress, see for instance H. Heclo, *A Government of Strangers* (1977), pp. 166–8.

19. See C. Campbell, *op. cit.*, p. 19, for an analysis of the size of the Executive Office of the American President.

20. There is some tendency to move towards a form of 'presidentialism', perhaps on the Mexican model, in the way Gorbachev and Jaruzelski became 'strong' presidents in the late 1980s.

21. See J. Blondel, *op. cit.* (1982), pp. 78–93 and 158–73.

22. See J. Blondel, *Government Ministers in the Contemporary World* (1985), pp. 29–54.

23. *ibid.*, pp. 90ff.

24. *ibid.*, pp. 90ff.

25. The duration of ministers in office was always relatively low in Poland, even before the 1980s; this is due to the political difficulties which Polish governments experienced long before the arrival of Solidarity on the scene.

26. Ministerial turnover is very high in South America, but not in Black Africa, despite the incidence of military coups, as some regimes remain very stable.

27. But not in Japan, as will be seen.

28. One of the reasons why ministers are more likely to return to office in cabinet systems is because they can remain in parliament during the intervening period. This opportunity scarcely exists in other systems.

29. These ministers can be regarded as 'amateurs' in that they do not have a technical background and are selected to governmental posts not because of their specialist ability, but because of their political skills.

30. On the duration of cabinets and governments, see A. Lijphart, *Democracies* (1984), pp. 78–84. The duration of cabinets given on p. 83 exaggerates markedly differences between single-party and coalition governments as reshuffles are not taken into account. British ministers do not remain in office as long as West German ministers, for instance; Japanese ministers are reshuffled almost every year. Moreover, Austrian governments are not truly 'minimum winning' during the period 1945–66, but, in reality 'oversize', as there were 'grand coalitions' of the two main parties. These points illustrate the difficulty of using 'governments' or 'cabinets' as a basis for the calculation of duration: the longevity of ministers is a markedly better indicator.

31. This point was made strongly by V.E. Bunce in *Do New Leaders Make a Difference?* (1981).

32. The role of parties has been studied more systematically than that of governments, because the duration of given parties in office is typically longer than that of individual governments. The points which have been made have tended to be negative, for instance with respect to the limited role of transient ministers as well as in relation to 'overload'. See for instance R. Rose, *Understanding Big Government* (1984). On the effect of parties,

see F.C. Castles, *The Impact of Parties* (1982). See also Chapter 14.

33. See R.D. McKinlay and A.S. Cohan, 'A comparative analysis of the political and economic performance of military and civilian regimes', *Comp. Pol.* (1975), October, pp. 1–30.

34. The question of the serious consequences of rapid reshuffles was viewed with particular concern in Britain in the 1970s. See for instance P. Kellner and Lord Crowther-Hunt, *The Civil Servants* (1980), pp. 211–12.

35. It is equally difficult to measure the impact of individual ministers, a subject which has only just begun to be considered.

19 Political leadership

Political leadership is highly visible, much talked about, and complex to assess. The visibility of leadership has been markedly enhanced by the mass media, and in particular by television, but it was always large. The great leaders of antiquity, of the Renaissance, and of the modern period were all well known to their contemporaries, despite the fact that they could only be seen and heard by relatively small numbers. Their qualities and defects were probably the object of many conversations; at any rate a considerable amount of scholarly work was devoted to them. Indeed, studies by historians were primarily concerned with describing the actions of leaders, and subsequently the concept of leadership itself began to be analysed.

Yet the literature on leadership has scarcely led to the development of what might be regarded as an established theory on the subject.[1] Uncertainties litter the field. To begin with, there have always been controversies about how to assess leaders from a normative standpoint: qualities and defects co-exist to such an extent that little guidance can be provided. There are heroes and there are villains, but many – perhaps most – leaders are both heroes and villains and their performance can be assessed only in a sharply contrasted manner. Except for a few mythical rulers, such as Cincinnatus, who returned to live an entirely ordinary life after having shaped Roman society, there are few leaders who have not made citizens suffer and die as well as prosper and live harmoniously. Leadership seems double-edged: for this reason alone, it is difficult to pass straightforward judgements.

Indeed, the number of villains has been such that many efforts have been made to reduce the powers of leaders. Constitutional developments since the eighteenth century were the clearest manifestation of this trend, though attempts were made earlier, in Greece and in Rome, in Italian cities and in medieval England, to ensure that rulers were unable to abuse their powers and become tyrants. These moves had only limited successes in the past, as did many constitutional endeavours of the twentieth century, a period which saw the emergence of some of the most ruthless rulers whom the world has ever known. Thus leadership often had a bad name, and analyses have consequently more often been devoted to finding means of reducing the power of leaders than to discovering ways of fostering their positive role.

Meanwhile, it proved difficult to determine the relative role of leaders and of the environment in which they emerged. Similar difficulties were encountered with respect to governments and to parties: do their achievements depend primarily on the efforts of those who run them, or on the environmental conditions in which they develop? Leaders seem ostensibly powerful, but their emergence, their subsequent actions, even their opportunity to remain in power are markedly helped by the context in which they operate. This question led to inconclusive debates between those who believed in the primacy of social and economic forces and those who believed in the influence of individuals. The paradox is that Marxist regimes have also been those in which individual leaders have played the most obvious part, both as heroes and as villains, from Lenin to Mao and from Stalin to Castro, to mention only the best-known among the Communist rulers.[2]

As a result of these conceptual and empirical difficulties, the study of leadership remains relatively underdeveloped. There is still no generally agreed framework on the basis of which leaders can be classified and assessed.[3] Despite the obvious importance of the topic, much of what can be said about it has therefore to remain somewhat tentative. The exploration of the problem will be undertaken here, first by examining ways of classifying types of leadership, second by considering the institutional framework within which constitutions have attempted to 'domesticate' leaders, third by investigating the personal qualities which appear to play a part in fostering leadership, and, finally, by looking at the conditions which are likely to maximise its impact.

The nature of political leadership and how it can be identified

Definition of leadership

Leaders seem to be good or bad, heroes or villains; but leaders seem also to be more or less successful, more or less effective. The distinction has been made, in this respect, between *leaders*, in the strong sense of the word, and 'mere power-holders' or, perhaps more accurately, 'office-holders'.[4] It seems intuitively correct to claim that many rulers – probably the large majority – are not very influential, as they appear to do little to modify the course of events, while some are great 'stars' who, ostensibly at least, profoundly affect the destiny of mankind. A distinction has therefore seemingly to be made between those who are leaders and those who are not: this means that, to begin with, a definition of leadership has to be given.

To say that leaders have to be distinguished from office-holders means that leadership does not automatically follow from the holding of certain positions. Leadership may be helped by the holding of positions such as those of prime minister or president; indeed, efforts made to 'domesticate' leadership have concentrated on attempts to regulate the powers connected with these positions. But leadership operates on a different plane. It relates to the ability to make others do what they presumably would not have done otherwise; it is a form of power, a special form of power, admittedly, as it is exercised by one individual over a large group and, in the case of the national political leadership, over a very large group. Leadership is therefore intrinsically a highly inegalitarian relationship. This relationship may be accepted for a number of reasons, ranging from 'natural' recognition to pressure and even compulsion, by those who are led, who are thus induced to act in the direction which the leader suggests. One can therefore define national political leadership as the power exercised by an individual (or, in some cases, two or a few individuals acting jointly) to direct members of the polity towards action in a particular direction.[5]

Scope of leadership

It is thus possible, at any rate theoretically, to distinguish leaders from non-leaders: those position-holders who do not succeed in making others act in the direction which they choose are not leaders. One needs to go further, however, and differentiate among various categories of leaders. To do so, specific criteria have to be discovered: two of these are particularly important. One involves distinguishing between leaders on the basis of their goals, of the type of 'project' which they have in mind. There are 'great' leaders, who shape their society entirely, who 'transform' its character; there are other leaders who are primarily concerned with the functioning of the society and who make compromises and 'transactions', while accepting the framework within which economic, social, and political life takes place.[6]

Such a distinction should not be viewed as a dichotomy, but as the two poles of a continuous dimension dealing with the 'extent of change' which leaders wish to bring about, this change being orientated either towards 'progress' or towards a return to the past. One should indeed go further, as there are in reality two dimensions; leaders do not merely exercise their power by attempting to bring about more or less change, they also exercise their power by attempting to achieve more or less change over a broader or narrower area. One can be a revolutionary in the full sense of the word – Lenin or Mao wished to transform their society completely, for instance – but one can be a revolutionary over a limited area as well, as one may wish to transform the educational system, or the system of central–local relationships, or the system of labour relations. The scope of leadership should therefore take into account both the extent to which leaders wish to 'transform' or change the existing system (a change which can be either 'progressive' or 'regressive') and the breadth of the governmental area over which this desire for change is manifested.[7]

Origins of leadership

One criterion of classification is thus the scope of leadership; another criterion is the nature of the bond between leaders and society. This type of classification was primarily explored by Max Weber who identified three 'ideal-types' of such relationships, based on tradition, a bureaucratic–legalistic ethos and charisma. The idea of charismatic leadership has subsequently been widely used, although in his original presentation Weber had construed it rather narrowly around a religious connotation. As a result, instead of being 'a certain quality of an individual personality' . . . 'endowed with supernatural, superhuman, or exceptional forces or qualities', charisma came to be reduced to an idea of 'personalisation' of power.[8]

It is perhaps not accidental that the notion of charisma should have been 'devalued' in this manner, for, as with the scope of leadership, the bond between leaders and led should be viewed as based on continuous dimensions, rather than on a number of mutually exclusive, well-defined types. Indeed, Weber's ideal-types can be turned into dimensions. The distinction between traditional and bureaucratic–legalistic leadership can be regarded as identifying two opposite poles of one dimension ranging, at one end, from a communal society in which relationships are based on long-standing loyalties to, at the other, an associational society in which relationships are based on contracts. Real-world leaders can be expected to be located in many cases somewhere between these two extreme positions.

Ostensibly at least, charismatic leadership is less able to give rise to a dimension if it is considered in its pure religious form – a form which, in Weber's view, tends to emerge when there is a total breakdown of the social and political institutions. However, Weber himself envisaged situations which could give rise to charismatic leadership where there was not such a total breakdown.[9] More realistically, there are undoubtedly cases when a degree of personalisation of leadership occurs, as a result of which the led associate directly with the leader, even when the society is not breaking down or indeed even when the system functions regularly. Such a bond may exist at whatever point the leader is located on the dimension of traditionalism versus bureaucratic legalism. Thus leaders should be classified with respect to two dimensions in terms of the bond which links them to the population. Overall, there are therefore two main ways in which leaders can be categorised, in both cases on the basis of two dimensions: they can be categorised according to their goals and achievements, and they can be categorised according to the nature of the bonds which tie them to the population.[10]

The institutional bases of leadership

If positions do not constitute leadership, they foster its development by giving those who hold them opportunities to achieve power. This is indeed why those who have wished to restrain leadership have attempted to reduce the opportunities open to position holders to exercise power by limiting the scope of their activities. These efforts have only been relatively successful, since, in this respect as with representative institutions or with governmental arrangements, constitutions have often been by-passed or set aside; indeed constitutions have sometimes not achieved their desired effect at all. Thus, although there are very few formally wholly unrestrained leaders in the contemporary world, there are many rulers whose scope for action is in practice not markedly limited.

Prime ministers in cabinet systems

The scope of activities or rulers is strongly regulated in the context of two types of rulers only, the prime ministers of parliamentary or cabinet systems and the constitutional presidents, while a third category, the constitutional monarchs, now usually have a purely symbolic role. The position of prime minister is, ostensibly at least, less prestigious than that of president. It exists normally in conjunction with that of a symbolic monarch (as in Britain, most Scandinavian countries and the Low Countries) or of a symbolic president (as in West Germany, Italy and India). Although these heads of state have few real powers, they exercise ceremonial functions which contribute to giving them some authority which is denied to prime ministers;[11] this is indeed the reason why a number of Third World prime ministers, in particular in Black Africa, brought about constitutional changes a few years after independence as a result of which they became presidents (for instance in Kenya, Zambia and the Ivory Coast).

The power of prime ministers is ostensibly limited because it is exercised in the context of a cabinet which must concur in the decisions. Indeed, prime ministers were traditionally regarded as being only 'first among equals'; the role of the leader was 'domesticated' because of the collective character of the policy-making process. In the contemporary world, there are considerable variations in this respect, however. In some cases, often because of the divided character of the party system, prime ministers are not markedly superior to their cabinet colleagues. They do not have enough political power nor enough longevity in office to dominate the scene.[12] There are cases, on the contrary – and especially where there is a two-party system, as in Britain and many Commonwealth countries, let alone a single-party system or a near-single-party system, as in Singapore – where prime ministers are truly strong leaders. They control their party and the parliamentary majority and, if electoral support is maintained (or unnecessary, as in single-party systems), exercise control for long periods. Thus, in Canada, Australia, West Germany, Sweden, or India, some prime ministers have dominated their country's politics for a decade or more, Mrs Thatcher being the only British prime minister in the twentieth century to have enjoyed a similar record. On the other hand, some prime ministers are mere 'office-holders' (as were most of the French prime ministers before 1958). Some countries, such as Belgium, Austria and even Britain, have oscillated between 'strong' and 'weak' prime ministers. Thus the model is inherently flexible. The general political conditions, the specific situation, and the qualities of the office-holders are the factors which appear to account, more than the institution itself, for the extent to which prime ministers play a limited part or, on the contrary, become truly great leaders.

Constitutional presidents (and effective but constitutional monarchs)

The 'domestication' of leadership is more systematically achieved by constitutions in which the powers of the monarch or president are strictly limited. Constitutional monarchs rarely exercise effective functions any longer as, in the large majority of cases, these have been transferred to prime ministers; Morocco and Jordan are among the few examples of countries in which the monarch really shares power with the prime minister.[13] Constitutional presidencies, on the other hand, are relatively numerous; they tend to be located in the Americas, Latin American countries having modelled their constitutions on that of the United States. The powers of such presidents are markedly restricted, both because the legislature has an independent base – since it cannot be dissolved – and because the president is elected for a limited period only and may not be re-elected immediately or, at most, may be re-elected only once, as in the United States. Thus American or constitutional Latin American presidents cannot achieve the longevity achieved by a Swedish or even British prime minister.[14]

Yet this constitutional arrangement has only been moderately successful; indeed, its only real success has been in the United States, as no other constitutional presidential system has lasted uninterrupted since World War II. The limitations imposed on leaders by the constitutional presidential system appear to be too strong; the conflicts which occur between president and congress cannot be solved by forced presidential resignation or by appeal to the people, as in a parliamentary system, since the congress cannot dismiss the president nor the president dissolve the congress. Moreover, the fact that the president cannot be re-elected more than once and often not at all results in extra constitutional attempts to remain in power. The scenario which occurred in France in the early 1850s, when the elected president, who was the nephew of Napoleon, maintained himself in power by a coup (and subsequently became the Emperor Napoleon III) was to be repeated in many Latin American countries. Since the 1950s, admittedly, presidential succession has been regular in Costa Rica, Colombia, and Venezuela;[15] the 'domestication' of leadership may thus become gradually accepted in the region. In Mexico, a regular handover of power has also taken place for many decades, but, in this case, because of the near-single-party system, the president has traditionally been subjected to few limitations and in particular has not been markedly restricted by Congress, which is continuously dominated by the same party.[16] As long as this situation obtains (there are signs that it might change), the Mexican ruler plays a part which resembles that of the authoritarian presidents to which we now turn.

Authoritarian presidents and monarchs

In large parts of the Third World, leaders are constrained very little, or not at all, by constitutional rules designed to 'domesticate' their power. This is of course the case in absolute monarchies but, as has already been stated, these have become rare and their numbers are shrinking. This is also the case in military regimes, but these tend to have only a short duration, as will be shown in Chapter 21. Indeed, military rulers often introduce some form of civilian structure in order to prolong their tenure; the regimes which these then establish are forms of authoritarian presidencies, which are subjected to few formal constraints and to even fewer informal limitations.

Authoritarian presidents often devise constitutions designed to suit their ambitions. They are thus allowed to be re-elected indefinitely (and are sometimes even appointed for life as in Malawi and earlier in Tunisia); they are allowed to dissolve the legislature, and the government depends entirely on them. The spread of these absolute presidencies has coincided with the arrival of many countries to independence, especially in Africa, for, in Asia, leaders often remained constrained, to an extent at least, by the limitations imposed on prime ministers.[17] Many authoritarian presidents were the first leaders of their country: they were able to build political institutions and to shape these in the way they wished. Some were close to being 'charismatic' leaders in the full sense delineated by Weber. They relied on strong popular support, in the main, as well as on authoritarian practices; they were the 'fathers' of their countries and often remained in office for two decades or more, thereby forming a disproportionately large number of the leaders who have been in office for a very long period in the contemporary world.[18] The successors of these first leaders generally found it more difficult to rule in such a 'paternal' and absolute manner: in many cases (in Tunisia and Senegal, for instance) the result has been a more 'domesticated' presidency, albeit still rather authoritarian.

Dual leadership

Political leadership is usually regarded as being naturally exercised by one person only: the image is that of the pyramid, with a single leader at the apex. A majority of states are indeed ruled by a single leader, especially if one does not take into acount the symbolic heads of state of parliamentary systems. Yet there are also many cases where single-leader rule does not obtain. There are examples of government by council, to which the cabinet system is only partly related, because of the role of the prime minister; this exists also in a 'purer' form in Switzerland (with the Chairman of the Federal Council rotating every year) and in Yugoslavia. Council government also existed in Uruguay for a period. There are 'juntas', in particular among provisional Latin American governments, in which a small number of military officers (often drawn from the three branches of the services) rule the country for a period. But there are, above all, a substantial number of cases of dual leadership.

Dual leadership has existed at various moments in history: republican Rome was ruled primarily by two consuls, for instance. Its modern development arose in the first instance from the desire (or the need) of kings to devolve a part of their burden onto a first or prime minister. This did not merely occur as a result of popular pressure, as tended to be the case in Western Europe in the nineteenth century, following British example. It also took place in highly authoritarian states, such as in early seventeenth-century France with Richelieu, in nineteenth-century Austria with Metternich and in Germany with Bismarck. Thus the development of dual leadership is a much wider phenomenon than simply an instance of the transition from 'monarchical' to 'popular' rule. It appears often to result from legitimacy difficulties, to be sure (as when the king needs to associate a 'commoner' with his power); but it is also the consequence of administrative necessities or of the need to combine the national legitimacy, which the head of state embodies, with a more specialised administrative or technocratic legitimacy, which the head of the government represents.[19]

The existence of a wide variety of grounds for dual leadership accounts for its spread in the contemporary world in countries as diverse as France and Finland, Communist states, the kingdoms of Morocco and Jordan and the 'progressive' states of Tanzania, Algeria, or Libya. There are thus both liberal and authoritarian dual leadership systems (though liberal dual leadership systems are rarer), conservative and 'progressive' dual leadership systems, Communist and non-Communist dual leadership systems.

In Communist states the distinction between party secretary and prime minister has traditionally corresponded to the division between party and state which has also traditionally characterised these countries;[20] but, interestingly, most party secretaries have (sometimes only after a time) also become presidents. This has placed them in a position relative to prime ministers not unlike that which is found in presidential systems where there is also a prime minister or in monarchies where the monarch is still markedly involved in government. The Communist party secretary-cum-president embodies (or wishes to embody), like other heads of state, the 'permanent' legitimacy of the nation.[21]

It is sometimes argued that dualist systems are transitional, as if it were more 'natural' for leadership to be held only by one person. While it is true that more systems have a single leader at the top, there are enough cases of dual leadership having lasted for many decades to raise doubts about the 'natural' character of single leadership. If one includes Communist states, the many authoritarian African presidencies in which there is a prime minister, the few monarchies in which the monarch shares with a prime minister the running of the affairs of the state, as well as the scatter of liberal semi-presidential countries, such as France, Finland, or Sri Lanka, to which Peru should perhaps be added, one finds that between one-quarter and one-third of the nations of the world are ruled by a system of dual leadership and that in most of these the system has operated in a stable manner.[22] A dualist system does not entail that the two leaders be equal, indeed quite the contrary, as is suggested by the distinction between a leader embodying the national legitimacy and a leader embodying the administrative legitimacy; but the complexity of the modern state is such that it is far from surprising that leadership should often have to be shared in order to be effective.[23]

Leadership and the personal qualities of leaders

The role of the environment in helping or limiting leaders is more than just apparent: it is there for all to see. The role of personal characteristics also appears intuitively to be large, but it seems to elude precise measurement and even broader assessment. There are, first, difficulties stemming from the relatively under-developed character of studies of personality in general and of the personality of leaders in particular. Indeed, there are still many controversies surrounding the concept of personality itself, since personality refers to what is permanent, and yet slowly changing, in the characteristics of an individual.[24] Assuming that one can speak of *the* personality of a leader, however, there is still as yet no generally accepted list of attributes constituting that personality, let alone any understanding of the way in which each of these attributes 'should' be mixed in order to produce a 'well-balanced' or 'forceful' leader. One can suggest a number of elements which seem important, such as energy, courage or intelligence, but one can scarcely go beyond an enumeration of this kind. Psychologists and social psychologists have attempted to determine a number of 'traits', but the many studies which have been conducted in a large number of organisations have resulted in widely differing conclusions. As many as forty elements have thus been found by scholars to be relevant to leadership, covering physical appearance (such as age, but also energy), social background, intelligence, 'personality' in the narrow sense (including adaptability, enthusiasm, resourcefulness, self-confidence) and task-related charac-teristics as well as social characteristics (such as administrative ability, popularity, and tact). While these elements were not found to play the same part in every case, at least intelligence, dominance, self-confidence, achievement, drive, sociability, and energy have appeared positively correlated with leadership in a substantial number of studies undertaken by experimental psychologists.[25] Overall, therefore, leader-ship seems associated with many, if not all aspects of human personality.

The second problem posed by the determination of the personal qualities of leaders stems from the fact that these qualities need to be related to the situation with which the leader is confronted. Psychologists have shown that different types of leadership are appropriate to different situations.[26] A more 'task-oriented' leader will be satisfactory where problems are relatively simple, a leader more concerned to establish a 'rapport' with the led will be more appropriate where the questions to be solved are complex. Such a conclusion seems to apply to national political leaders, though the size of the problems which these leaders face is such that it may not be valid to extrapolate from observations relating to leaders supervising small groups engaged in rather simple operations. Yet national 'office-holders' who are exaggeratedly concerned with the details of the work (i.e. who are closely identifying themselves with the tasks, such as President Carter, for example) seem less successful 'leaders' than those who have a wider vision and who are concerned with the impact of their actions on both their immediate subordinates and on the nation at large (such as President Reagan).[27] This point needs to be tested systematically, however, before a general conclusion can be drawn.

Because of these difficulties, studies of the personal qualities required of national political leaders tend to focus on certain types of rulers and on certain types of situations. Many earlier analyses concentrated on the 'pathology' of leadership, as a result of the extreme worry felt in the 1930s and 1940s at the emergence of leaders whose psychological balance seemed to be in doubt. However, this meant that it was difficult to develop a general model, though it was claimed by one author that the number of severely mentally disturbed leaders had been extremely large across the centuries.[28]

Special attention has been paid more recently to another group of leaders, the revolutionary leaders, in order to assess whether these can be regarded as forming a class from the point of view of their personal characteristics. Rejai and Phillips have made most progress in this direction by examining generally the personal and situational conditions under which these leaders emerged, although, as there is no control group of non-revolutionary leaders, it is difficult to know how far the characteristics found in the revolutionaries apply exclusively to them. They have been shown to have a number of traits in common, such as vanity, egotism and narcissism as well as nationalism, a sense of justice and a sense of mission; they are also characterised by relative deprivation and status inconsistency.[29] It was found in addition that these leaders had marked verbal and organisational skills. Admittedly, it is also pointed out that 'no single motivation or dynamic is sufficient to explain the formation of all revolutionary personalities'.[30] The analysis thus remains somewhat inconclusive, but it does at least present a picture of a whole class of leaders and it does identify elements which are of significance among members of that class.

Political scientists have also attempted to identify 'basic' elements in early socialisation which could account for the behaviour of leaders. If it could indeed be proved that these factors played a major part in decisions subsequently taken by leaders, it would appear to follow that personal elements – indeed the most durable aspects of these personal elements – are highly significant. One might not be able to state, at any rate as yet, which elements were most instrumental in the development of leadership; but one could at least conclude that personality characteristics, as moulded at an early age, made a difference to the way in which national decisions were taken. Too few studies of this type have been conducted, however, for a general panorama to emerge, though the classic study of US President Wilson did at least provide a clear example of the role of early socialisation in explaining subsequent decision-making trends.[31]

A general model of the characteristics and role of personality will probably need to be simpler, however, if fairly robust conclusions are to be drawn. A step in the direction of simplicity has been provided by Barber whose analysis of the personal characteristics of American presidents is based only on two factors, drive or energy (labelled 'activity' or 'passivity'), and satisfaction with the job (a 'positive' or a 'negative' approach).[32] 'Active–positives' enjoy what they do and do it with considerable gusto; F.D. Roosevelt, Truman, and Kennedy are classified in this manner, while, at the opposite extreme, those who are 'passive–negative', like Eisenhower, 'are in politics because they think they ought to be'.[33] Even if one leaves aside the question of the way in which individual presidents are characterised in this model, there are difficulties with such an approach, since it is not stated why these characteristics, rather than others, are particularly instrumental in helping to describe given leaders. There should also be rankings among leaders within each category: not all the 'active–positives', for instance, are likely to be equally strong or equally successful. Yet this categorisation has the merit of helping to discover some broad personality types and to relate these types to the way in which leaders take decisions.[34]

It is thus still not possible to state with assurance whether leaders behave in the way they do because of their personality, let alone to rank leaders in terms of the extent to which particular aspects of their personality are likely to account for the results which they obtain. On the other hand, it seems that leaders are markedly helped or hindered by the characteristics of the political and administrative system. Groups, parties, legislatures and the government itself, as well as the bureaucracy, make it possible for leaders, to a varying degree, to elaborate and apply the policies which they favour and to mobilise the population in support of these policies. Yet these structures are not givens; leaders can and do create or alter them. For instance, at least in new countries or in those which have been in turmoil, leaders have set up parties and groups;[35] moreover, most leaders are also able to appoint to the government men and women of their choice, at least within a certain range; many leaders can also play some part in shaping or remoulding the bureaucracy. What is difficult to assess is the extent to which, under different conditions, leaders can thus modify the instruments which they need to exercise their power. The part which they play in this respect is often overshadowed by the durable and even ostensibly permanent character of these instruments. Overall, therefore, it is not surprising that it should be difficult to determine the role of personal factors in the development of leadership: more sophisticated methods of analysis need to be elaborated before it becomes possible for political scientists to give a satisfactory answer to this fundamental question.[36]

How much does leadership matter?

Related to the problem of the role of personal factors in leadership, but distinct from it, is the equally complex question of the impact of leaders on political life. It seems clear that leaders have *some* impact and that a few leaders have a very large impact, despite the fact that it has been claimed that the environment could account for the behaviour of leaders. The immense role of some leaders is manifest, whether

Napoleon or Lenin, Bismarck or Churchill, to quote only from among the dead: it is up to those who deny this role to sustain their claim.[37]

The difficulty therefore concerns not so much the large part played by some leaders, but the smaller impact of the great majority of leaders. It is also difficult to assess the extent to which circumstances contribute to help a number of rulers and to frustrate the endeavours of others. 'Great' revolutionaries appear to achieve markedly more than leaders whose actions take place within the context of a political, social and economic system which existed when they came to power; but a comparative assessment is not that simple, since revolutionaries are helped by the fact that the demand for change in their society is strong and thus provides opportunities which are denied to those who rule a society where the members are satisfied with the status quo. Thus the efforts of Lenin or Mao were helped by the turmoil prevailing in Russia and China at the time. These leaders turned the situation to their benefit, to be sure; they also developed policies which were truly their own and which the 'situation' in no sense demanded, but they were able to start remoulding their society as a result of events which were not (primarily) of their making. Such an opportunity is not available to a leader who emerges in a country where levels of discontent are low.

The impact of leaders must therefore be assessed not only by examining the policies elaborated and implemented by these leaders, but by relating these policies to the demands made by the population and in particular by its most vocal elements.[38] Ideally, the impact of leaders should be measured by assessing the extent to which they are able to change the framework within which the population approaches public policy problems, as well as by the concrete reforms which they bring about. This is why it is important to take into account the two dimensions which were described earlier and which help to distinguish between the extent of change and the scope of that change. Rulers who administer the system as it is and do not aim at altering policies may be regarded as having very little impact, though even these rulers may be influential if there was a substantial demand for change which they succeeded in thwarting. Meanwhile, rulers who introduce changes on a relatively narrow front do not necessarily have less impact than those who embark on policies designed to alter their society fundamentally. The assessment depends on the extent to which that society was predisposed to undergo change. Such a predisposition often follows periods of great uncertainty and in particular defeat at war: the new ruler can then point to the failures of the previous regime and proclaim that radically new policies need to be adopted. In such a situation, the collapse of the institutions and of the political system as a whole enables the new leader to emerge as the only fixed element to which the population can refer. Not surprisingly, such a leader is often 'charismatic' in the truly Weberian sense and can make a major impact on the society.

The role of leadership must therefore be assessed by relating the rulers to the ruled and the characteristics of personalities to the climate among the population. The measurement of the influence of leadership is rendered more complex as a result, since the role of 'obviously' great leaders is partly reduced while that of other, less dramatically prominent statesmen may appear more substantial. The impact of leaders must also be assessed over time. When examining government, it was noted that there is a 'lag', often a substantial lag, between elaboration and implementation in national policy-making.[39] A similar lag exists with respect to the role of leaders and it may extend over many decades. Indeed, the impact of leaders may never be fully determined, as it may be exercised on generations as yet not born; it can also fluctuate, as what has been done by a leader can be undone by his or her successors. Mao's policies have thus been substantially modified, even overturned, by those followed him. Thus the impact of the founder of the Communist regime in the world's most populated country may not be as large in the 1990s as it was in the 1970s.

The impact of leadership has still not been measured adequately and there is still no means of ranking the role of various leaders. But it is probable that this role is larger than is often recognised in the case of many rulers, while it is perhaps smaller than is often claimed with respect to the best-known leaders. The difficulty of the measurement is no justification for the extreme view that leaders do not matter, nor should it suggest the desperate conclusion that an adequate measurement can never be achieved. The assessment of the impact of leadership will become more precise as the personal qualities which are essential for leadership become better known, for here lies the most important key to the understanding of the link between the rulers and the ruled.

Conclusion

Views about leadership have been, to say the least, markedly ambiguous. By and large, political theorists of the past have regarded leaders with considerable suspicion, with the exception of a small cohort of scholars anxious to give prominence to highly romantic values such as energy and personal strength. Attitudes have changed somewhat since World War II, despite the brutal manner in which some leaders ruled both their own country and the countries which their armed forces occupied. This attitudinal change resulted from a better recognition of the positive (indeed probably unique) part which leaders can play at the time of the birth of nations – a part which Weber emphasised by singling out the unique characteristics of charismatic rulers. Since the second half of the twentieth century was exceptional in giving rise to so many new nations, leadership as a result almost automatically obtained a prominent position. Yet leadership is not only important in the context of new nations; nor is it important only in the context of older nations when these are in turmoil, for instance after a war and especially after a defeat. Leadership plays a part in every situation, even though this part is rendered less obvious by being less dramatic. This is indeed the area where further analyses need to be undertaken and are in fact undertaken, as the problem is not only to contrast a few charismatic leaders with a mass of grey and indistinct office-holders, but to see under what conditions these 'office-holders' can truly become leaders.

Notes

1. The literature on individual leaders is vast, whether in the form of biographies or autobiographies; so is the psychological literature on middle-level leaders and on managers. But the comparative literature on political leadership remains limited, although there has been a remarkable increase in the interest in the field, especially in the United States, since the mid-1970s. See the bibliography for a number of titles. See also the bibliography at the end of J. Blondel, *Political Leadership* (1987).
2. The question of the influence of individuals on the course of events has been and continues to be highly controversial. For a presentation of the possible role of some great leaders, see S. Hook, *The Hero in History* (1955).
3. Various conceptual frameworks have been developed, in particular that of J. McG. Burns in *Leadership* (1978). This framework is discussed below.
4. Burns, *op. cit.*, p. 5.
5. See J. Blondel, *World Leaders* (1980), pp. 11–15. See also K.F. Janda, 'Toward the explication of the concept of leadership in terms of the concept of power' in G.D. Paige (ed.), *Political Leadership* (1972), pp. 45–64.
6. Burns' model is based on the fundamental distinction between 'transforming' and 'transactional' leadership. See Burns, *op. cit.*, *passim* and in particular Parts III and IV.
7. For a development of this model, see J. Blondel, *op. cit* (1987), pp. 87–97.
8. M. Weber, *Economy and Society* (1968 edn), vol. 1, p. 214.
9. Weber himself stretched the concept of charisma somewhat and used it to describe a number of contemporary situations. See J. Blondel, *op. cit.* (1987), pp. 54–7.
10. For a general presentation of the problems posed by Weber's tripartite distinction, see J. Blondel, *op. cit.* (1987), pp. 51–4.
11. The fact that the head of state is purely ceremonial (or mostly ceremonial) in cabinet systems does not mean that he or she plays no fundamental political role. In the British case, for instance, the role of the monarch as head of the Commonwealth is manifestly very significant. On the other hand, in Sweden, since the 1975 Constitution came into force, the role of the monarch is extremely limited. In some countries, such as Belgium and the Netherlands, monarchs play some part in the process of selecting the prime minister.
12. In coalition systems, prime ministers are frequently chosen because they are good compromisers and not because they are, in the conventional sense of the word, 'leaders'. There seems to be some change in this respect, however, as developments in the 1980s in the Netherlands and Belgium suggest, as well as to an extent in Italy.
13. The head of state remains clearly 'above' the prime minister, however; occasionally, the post of prime minister has even been dispensed with in Morocco.
14. The longevity of constitutional presidents is reduced precisely in order to ensure that the president does not become too powerful. This has sometimes led to difficulties, however, as it is not always clear that the president should stay as long as, and no longer than, the pre-determined term.
15. In the 1980s, presidential succession has also begun to be regular in Argentina, Ecuador, and Peru.
16. See Chapters 9 and 11 for an examination of the very special character of the Mexican PRI.
17. The cabinet system still plays a major part in South Asia because, as was seen in Chapter 12, the liberal–democratic system was maintained in a number of Commonwealth countries of the region and in particular in India, Malaysia and Sri Lanka.
18. See J. Blondel, *op. cit.* (1980), pp. 217–56, for an examination of the characteristics of 'long leaders'. Founders of countries have been found to be those most likely to remain in office for ten years or more, alongside traditional monarchs and

Communist rulers. This situation explains why leadership has tended to be relatively durable in Black Africa.

19. Despite its importance, the phenomenon has still not been systematically examined. For a preliminary analysis, see J. Blondel, *op. cit.* (1980), in particular pp. 63–73.
20. See Chapter 18. In the case of Communist states, there is both divided government and dual leadership.
21. The assumption of a national role has been noticeable in the case of many First Secretaries of Communist parties in Communist states, from Tito to Gorbachev.
22. Sri Lanka introduced a strong presidency system in the 1970s, following the French example (1958). Peru is the only Spanish American polity where there is a prime minister alongside the president.
23. The distinction between party and state reflects this distinction in Communist states. *Mutatis mutandis*, this distinction is also valid elsewhere.
24. See F.I. Greenstein, *Personality and Politics* (1969), in particular Chapter 1, pp. 1–30.
25. B.M. Bass, *Stogdill's Handbook on Leadership* (1981), pp. 43–96.
26. See F.E. Fiedler, *A Theory of Leadership Effectiveness* (1967).
27. Jimmy Carter was very successful as Governor of Georgia, and yet less effective in the broader context of Washington: the difficulty may have had to do with Carter's interest in detail. See G.M. Fink, *Prelude to the Presidency* (1980).
28. R.L. Noland, 'Presidential disability and the proposed constitutional amendment', *Amer. Psychologist*, 21 (1966), pp. 232–3.
29. M. Rejai with K. Phillips, *World Revolutionary Leaders* (1983), p. 37.
30. *ibid.*, p. 38.
31. A.L. George and J.L. George, *Woodrow Wilson and Colonel House: A personality study* (1956).
32. J. D. Barber, *The Presidential Character* (1977), pp. 11–14.
33. *ibid.*, p. 13.
34. For a further discussion of the approach, see J. Blondel, *op. cit.* (1987), pp. 126–8.
35. See Chapters 11 and 14.
36. See J. Blondel, *op. cit.* (1987), pp. 189–93.
37. See S. Hook, *op. cit.*
38. See J. Blondel, *op. cit.* (1987), pp. 97–107.
39. See Chapter 18.

Part V

Implementation and control

20 Bureaucracies and their role in government

While governments and assemblies deal with the elaboration of laws and other general rules, bureaucracies and the military, as well as the judiciary, are expected to be concerned exclusively with their implementation. This, at least, is the traditional democratic view, which stipulates that the fundamental decisions must be taken by politicians. This is also the view which prevails in many authoritarian states, in particular in single-party systems; there, too, administrators are regarded as having to conform to the decisions of the political rule-makers.[1]

Yet the distinction between rule-making and rule-implementation is not always clear-cut, nor is the distinction between the role of politicians and that of administrators always precise. This is partly because a sharp separation does not always exist at the level of personnel; governments often include civil servants and members of the armed forces, as well as judges. To a greater extent it is because what constitutes implementation is often rather obscure, especially in the contemporary world, where bureaucracies are large and have become involved in a vast array of activities. The concept of implementation may have a definite meaning when one is concerned with a set of rather simple rules which have to be enforced; it is less easy to circumscribe when rules are numerous and complex, indeed at times contradictory. To 'apply' them no longer means to ensure that a given pronouncement is put into practice; it means exercising choice and judgement, even discretion, among a number of different rules.

Nor can administrators be regarded as solely concerned with implementation, even when this is viewed in the broadest possible manner. Rules are not merely complex and difficult to implement; attention needs to be paid to the concrete way in which they can be implemented in a given context. Politicians, as well as the public at large, have become increasingly aware of the political, social, and economic circumstances which have to be taken into account if laws and regulations are to be effective. Moreover, politicians need technical advice which administrators and specialists have at their disposal. These are therefore necessarily involved in the policy development process. This is particularly true in the general field of economic 293 and social management. In practical terms, evidence has to be collected before legal documents are drafted; this means, in other words, that 'advice' has to be taken on a broad front. Administrators and technicians are those to whom one has to turn in order to obtain this 'advice'. Thus members of the bureaucracy and in particular those at the highest echelons are naturally involved in the crucial phase of preparation of parliamentary legislation and of the governmental documents which flow from this legislation. Needless to say, those who give such advice are closely involved in the reality of decision-making. 'Implementation' and 'rule-making' are thus difficult to distinguish.[2]

Meanwhile, the wide involvement of the modern state in the life of each country has resulted in administrators being concerned, not just with the implementation of rules, but with the management of services. Yet only remotely can management be regarded as a form of 'implementation'. It consists of actions designed to ensure that a service or a corporation is run as effectively and as productively as possible, not of applying a number of rules more or less mechanically. There are of course general goals, such as the 'public interest' – in itself a vague and elusive concept – which managers are expected to follow, but this is not implementation. As a matter of fact, the relative independence of managers in this respect comes close to another tradition, which formerly prevailed on the continent of Europe and stems from the old monarchies. This tradition suggests that civil servants are the agents of the state rather than of the government; it further entails that administrators should obey general principles of 'rationality' and that they therefore remain somewhat autonomous from politicians.[3]

The relative independence of managers has come to pose serious problems as their numbers have increased in all types of political systems. Managers of course play a part in the industrial and commercial undertakings of the state, which are numerous, at least in many countries. They also play a part in many social services, such as education, health, or housing, as these are now often large enterprises. They even play a substantial part in the more traditional governmental activities, both because these are concerned with the supervision of economic and social undertakings and because, with the growth of civil service employment, it has become necessary to pay considerable attention to personnel management to ensure smooth administration as well as to reduce costs.

Given that many civil servants are deeply involved in management, and given that they often have to give 'advice' in the preparation of laws and regulations alongside their traditional role in implementation, it is not surprising that the question should be asked whether, in modern government, they should not be regarded as having taken over much of the reality of political power. It is thus occasionally suggested that bureaucrats and technocrats have replaced or are gradually replacing politicians, directly or indirectly. Some of them may belong to the government itself; but even when this does not happen, they may have become so indispensable that they can in effect dictate decisions and shape the general character of the political process.[4] This view may be exaggerated or mistaken, at least in so far as it is held to correspond to a general trend, but it is sufficiently widespread to deserve to be discussed. This chapter will therefore examine first the problems which governments face in attempting to ensure that administrators 'obey' their decisions; it will then consider the extent to which managerial activities give administrators and technicians special responsibilities and even a degree of independence. Finally the general question of the overall role of bureaucracies will be discussed: are these truly able in some cases to take over the functions of rule-making and to install an 'administrative' or 'technocratic' state?

How far can governments count on administrative 'obedience'?

Public services have grown in scope everywhere. In many, if not most, countries they employ a substantial proportion of the workforce.[5] This means that the problems faced by governments in attempting to ensure obedience are becoming increasingly serious. Admittedly, the public service at large includes more than just administrative services; many industrial and commercial undertakings often belong to the state. Moreover, in many countries large numbers of people are employed by regional and local authorities; these employees belong to the public sector at large, but they do not form part of the same administrative hierarchy as that of civil servants who work for central government. There are substantial variations in structure in this respect; these correspond to the marked differences in the extent and forms of decentralisation which exist around the world.[6] However, even if one considers only the civil service in the strict sense, that is to say the set of bodies which are directly run by central government, the numbers of employees are now such in most countries that size alone poses problems of organisation and of control which are likely to affect implementation, irrespective of the broader decision-making implications which are closely associated with the question of implementation.

Difficulties resulting from the structure of the administration itself

The question of personnel competence

Civil servants are likely to implement rules more efficiently if they are competent and well-trained. These conditions will be better met where the bureaucracy is small than where it is large, as, when it expands, the state will have increasingly to recruit personnel of lesser ability and with less extensive training. Thus, inevitably, the level of competence of the administration will decline as manpower requirements increase. This can only be offset in the short run if the state can employ some of the talent which would otherwise have gone into the private sector. However, this is not without negative effects, since the private sector, being staffed with relatively less skilled employees, is likely to be less effective and indeed to implement less quickly and less well the decisions of the administration. An improvement can take place in the long run, but only if there are improvements in education and the competence of the candidates for the civil service increases as a result.

All countries face these difficulties, but those which attempt to expand the public sector rapidly as well as those in which the fund of competent personnel is limited are likely to be most affected. This is to say that many developing countries, especially in Africa, suffer from this problem, although, in relative terms, the bureaucracies of these nations are often smaller than those of developed states. Programmes of technical aid of various kinds, such as loans of personnel or training schemes, fill only a limited part of the gap. It follows, on the other hand, that countries, especially developing countries, in which there is less 'interventionism' on the part of the state are likely to have higher levels of implementation. Putting it differently, there are diminishing returns, in terms of implementation, in attempting to increase the size of the civil service. No state can escape this general constraint, but those states in which educational levels are low are particularly exposed to the danger of over-extending their administrative personnel, especially since, in the contemporary world, these countries often wish to pursue populist policies which require continuous government pressure if they are to be applied. In practice, these policies may not be implemented because the competent manpower is not large enough.[7]

Size and implementation

Levels of implementation are also affected by the size of the bureaucratic organisation. Despite some benefits of scale, which tend to relate more to management than to implementation, the greater the distance between the top and the bottom of the pyramid, the greater the likelihood that the rule-application process will distort the 'intentions' of the rule-makers. Admittedly, the efficiency of the bureaucratic machine can be improved in various ways; techniques of organisation in public and private administration have helped to improve communication networks and in particular the relationship between 'staff' and 'line', the span of control of each administrator, and so on; but a loss will take place as the size of the bureaucratic pyramid increases. Large organisations reach a point beyond which rates of implementation are likely to decline. Hence the general development of 'delegation' practices;[8] hence, too, the case for federalism and for other forms of decentralisation which were discussed in Chapter 16.

As administrative organisations in developed polities are likely to be larger than those in less developed polities, the advantage of developed societies in terms of competence and training of personnel is likely to be somewhat offset. In practice, however, the relative effect of organisational size and personnel competence is difficult to measure, as processes of decentralisation, through federalism or otherwise, have to be taken into account.

Control of the administration

Naturally enough, the dangers resulting from lack of implementation have been perceived from the early period of development of bureaucratic organisations; various control mechanisms have therefore been devised, but these in turn raise further problems.

First, as control can be operated only through controlling agencies, these are affected by problems of competence and size as are the controlled agencies; in particular, the larger the controlling agency, the less likely it is to exercise its control effectively. It follows that, where the agencies to be controlled are large, control is also likely to be less efficient.

Second, the distance between the controlling and the controlled agency is important. However, it is not possible to maximise both tightness of control and a good knowledge of the operations of the agencies to be controlled. Controlling agents are under the close supervision of rule-making agents only if they are somewhat distant from the agencies which they have to control; however, they will then not be truly familiar with what these agencies do. Conversely, controllers who know what implementing agencies do have to remain close to these agencies, but are then unlikely to control the controlled agencies effectively, as they are closely involved in the activities of these bodies.

In concrete terms, controlling agents must both recognise the authority of rule-makers and have access to the activities of the implementing agencies. 'Access' means real access, and not merely being taken around on a special occasion; the controlling agents must 'understand' the attitudes and behaviour of the controlled agencies. Yet controlling agents will only be able to do so if they are 'at one' with the controlled agents, from which it follows that the controlling agents would probably take the same decisions. Thus a very close knowledge of controlling agencies may lead the controlling again to control the deviants only; 'accepted' patterns of behaviour may not be questioned or even scrutinised. Consequently, if rule-making agencies want to change the behaviour of the administration, they will have to create controlling agencies which are distant from the agencies which are being controlled; correspondingly they will have to be prepared to accept that these agencies will be less knowledgeable about what actually goes on at the grass roots. The controlled agencies will be able to undertake activities which the controllers may simply not discover or may discover only in part.

Control is therefore likely to take a number of forms corresponding to the particular conditions of a given polity. At one extreme, inspectors and controllers can be recruited from among the employees of the agencies to be controlled, in order to maximise the knowledge of the patterns of behaviour which characterise these agencies. At the other extreme, they can be recruited from among politicians who have no previous experience of the civil service. In between, they can be selected from outside bodies, which can be expected to have 'some' knowledge of what goes on in the agencies to be controlled but which are expected to be less close to the agencies than inspectors drawn from among civil servants who previously worked in the agency itself.[9]

These differences in the type of recruitment of inspectors and controllers are related to the extent to which rule-makers – the politicians – feel that they can trust the members of the civil service. The more they suspect that these agents are not loyal, the more they will tend to appoint controllers from outside. This will arise particularly when a state is relatively new, after a revolution, or even after a change of government, when those who come to office attempt to put forward markedly different policies. Thus control will tend to take place from inside the civil service in those polities in which governmental norms are generally accepted by the whole polity; it will tend to be from outside where goals tend to be imposed. Intermediate solutions or a combination of different arrangements are in force where goals are in part imposed.

The effectiveness of control is not affected only by the characteristics of the controlling agencies and by the background of the controlling agents, however; it also depends on the authority of the rulers: a regime which needs to impose outside controls may therefore be unable to reap the benefits of these forms of control, if its leaders have little or no authority independently of the implementing agencies. This raises the question of the 'administrative state' which will be examined in the last section of this chapter.

Next, however, types of control in different political systems will be examined. In developing countries, the bureaucracy is likely to require a large proportion of the skilled personnel existing in the polity; moreover, if the government wishes to impose new goals, which is often the case, the problem of control is likely to be serious. Overall, rates of implementation are therefore likely to be relatively low. In developed liberal democratic polities, on the other hand, problems are likely to be less serious, despite the relatively large size of the bureaucracy. There are differences among them, however, as there are among developing countries. For instance, controls are more likely to be internal in Anglo-Saxon countries, where the government has traditionally been better accepted, than in Continental countries, where acceptance of democratic norms is more recent or less widespread. This is why, in this last group of states, control tends to be achieved through groups of the bureaucracy which are distinct from the groups to be controlled and through groups which are directly attached to the political personnel – hence the development of what have been known as 'ministerial cabinets' in France and some other Western European countries.[10] This is a dimension, however, and not a dichotomy. Anglo-Saxon countries will develop controls of the intermediate type (from other corps, for instance, as with Treasury control in Britain) as well as internal controls; conversely, Continental countries will also tend to develop internal controls and these will increase as regimes become better accepted. There will then be an increased reliance on internal controls, or a gradual 'internalisation' of the personnel coming from outside groups. Thus the 'ministerial cabinets', once composed of politicians, have come to include civil servants. In the process, 'ministerial cabinets' have somewhat changed their character. As they have gradually included more civil servants, they have come to be in part a liaison mechanism between ministers and the regular bureaucracy. Yet an element of control remains to the extent that ministers still need or want to satisfy themselves that their policy directions are being followed.[11] In other polities, outside the West, the more the policy is imposed, the more outside controls play an important part, as has been traditionally the case in Communist states. When imposition decreases (as it has more recently in Eastern Europe), the same movement as the one described above for Western Europe is likely to take place. Control also involves a variety of bodies, either judicial, such as administrative courts, or quasi-judicial, such as ombudsmen's offices; these will be examined in Chapter 22. These act on behalf of citizens but, in the process, they also tend to be part of the mechanisms of control of the bureaucracy.

The status of managers and administrators

Questions of control are more complex, however, since administrative bodies are not merely asked to implement rules, but are increasingly managerial enterprises which have their own goals and thus follow a somewhat autonomous development. In such a case, the relationship between politicians and administrators becomes somewhat different. One cannot just send inspectors; the government has to use different means to ensure that managers remain basically loyal and indeed are at one with the aims of the rulers.

Management, technical skills and the notion of implementation

The development of administrative bodies in the twentieth century has given prominence to a characteristic of state bureaucratic organisations which remained somewhat hidden under nineteenth-century concepts of implementation.[12] With state intervention becoming common, a conflict appeared between the 'positive' activities of officials and the principle of 'rule-application'. State intervention implies 'autonomous' action and indeed missionary zeal on the part of administrators; this development has consequences in terms of the profile and occupational background of the personnel. Rule-implementation in the narrow sense entails placing great stress on lawyers; management results in giving prominence to specialists or technicians. This does not just mean that a different type of personnel is recruited; it also means that there is at the top a different breed of people who, while they may be imbued with the view that they should promote the interests of the state, do so in quite a sectional manner. What concerns them is their service, whether it is roads, power stations, hospitals, or housing. They wish to develop the undertakings which they run; they are not so much concerned with problems of rule-application as with problems of development.

These technical services need not be directed by technicians, admittedly, but, if they are not, the government runs the risk that the service will be less efficient, because decision-making will be slower and clumsier; there may also be a loss of efficiency as specialists feel a sense of frustration. Moreover, as these technical services need to take technical decisions, the most that can be decided is that the specialists will be 'advisers' of the 'generalists' – that they will be 'on tap' rather than 'on top', to use the distinction which has been made in the context of the British civil service.[13] Yet this arrangement is not likely to solve the problem. Specialists will also experience difficulties with respect to general administration, as there is a fundamental contradiction between the desire to promote services and the effort to achieve co-ordination. What the existence of different arrangements suggests is that there are profoundly diverging views about the nature of the state and about the role of politicians. Where it is felt that the state's permanent function is to 'develop' society, along the lines of eighteenth-century enlightened despotism, as is the case in France and in many Continental countries, specialists tend to be in charge of the services in the name of the state. Where, as in Britain and other Anglo-Saxon countries, civil servants are viewed as being appointed to apply decisions taken by politicians, generalists will tend to be on top.[14]

While the dichotomy between the desire to develop services and the need to co-ordinate policies and to establish priorities exists everywhere, and while the structure of the organisation may result in a greater weight being given to one or the other of these goals, a special emphasis on strong state economic and social intervention tends to exacerbate difficulties. Thus the problems posed by management are particularly serious in countries where the public sector has traditionally been large. This is true in Communist states; it is also true in those developing nations in which political leaders press for populist social policies and for rapid economic development. In such cases, the autonomy of technicians may be very substantial; alternatively, strong forms of control have to be exercised in order to curb this autonomy.

The control of managers and specialists by political and social means

The problem of the control of technicians and managers is thus of great importance for governments; but, given the fact that this type of public servants can truly dominate the services they run and are, in effect, indispensable, ordinary administrative controls will probably be insufficient to stop the sectional demands they are likely to make. Controls have to be deeper and must aim at ensuring a profound loyalty, indeed ultimately they must ensure that specialists and managers share the ideology of the politicians. This means that controls have to be political and even social, rather than merely administrative.

Political controls stem typically from a variety of standpoints about the relative role of politicians and public servants which will be encountered again in the next chapter in relation to the military. These controls emphasise the positive value of furthering the goals of the political system. Where the political system is liberal, political controls result from socialisation – technicians, together with the rest of the population, accept the values and processes of the polity. Political control is therefore effected through a respect for procedures. This is particularly true in the older democracies, and especially in Anglo-Saxon countries, where, by and large, technicians recognise the constitutional view according to which ministers, and not the experts, are responsible for the most fundamental decisions, even if these experts often feel that decisions may be too slow or even wrong. Thus the principle of ministerial responsibility which exists in particular in parliamentary and cabinet systems helps to maintain a degree of cohesion in public administration and to reduce somewhat the power of specialists.[15]

Where the political system is less widely accepted, there can be serious difficulties in ensuring that managers and specialists in general remain under the control of the government, particularly if considerable emphasis is given to economic and social development. It is therefore inevitable that politicians should use more artificial means to maintain their control. The single most common means of control is the party within which managers and technicians are expected to join politicians and thus to appreciate and indeed endorse governmental ideology. This practice was particularly developed in Communist states in which, especially until the late 1980s, managers and specialists were expected to be members of the party. Other single-party states have been less successful in giving real life to the party; indeed, it has become questionable whether even Communist states have been truly able to use the party as an effective means of ensuring the loyalty of technicians.[16]

In fact, technicians can be maintained in a situation of 'dependence' by using strong political pressures only for a period. Tensions can be more effectively reduced when specialists are divided into a number of organisations which have separate goals. Thus the division of capitalist societies into a private and public sector, the division of public sectors into 'nationalised' forms and 'administrative agencies', and the division of administrative agencies into central, regional and local, probably tends to reduce the ability of specialists to exercise control.

The division achieved in this way among technicians is counterbalanced by two factors, however. First, technicians may acquire a common outlook and a sense of solidarity by being trained in technical schools, particularly prestigious ones. These promoted the development of technical skills on the continent of Europe, and in particular in France, in the nineteenth century, but they also fostered technical influence. It is significant that the first theories of social and political 'engineering' were developed by Frenchmen who taught or had been otherwise associated with some of these schools and in particular with the *Ecole Polytechnique*.[17] Where such schools do not exist, on the contrary, solidarity will be lower: in Britain, the absence of such schools, the fact that the training of technicians takes place in universities rather than in specialised schools, and the tendency which universities foster to create social links cutting across professional disciplines have contributed to a reduction in the status and power of technicians. Second, associations of technicians may also cut across divisions and foster at least a limited level of 'mobilisation' of technicians. The effect may not be as strong as with technical schools, but common goals may develop among the various categories of specialists through these associations.[18]

The structure of a society and of its political institutions may reduce the ability and even the desire of technicians to challenge overtly the basic rule-making processes. However, these mechanisms are not everywhere sufficient to constitute effective barriers against the spread of influence of technicians. In a number of Continental European countries, for example, administrators and to a greater extent technicians have traditionally had a degree of autonomy. In France, for instance, up to 1958, when the Fifth Republic was set up, they exercised great influence.[19] France was therefore often regarded as a country where the opportunity for a 'technocracy' to emerge, in the strict sense of government by technicians, was not an entirely remote possibility, especially since, after the advent of the Fifth Republic, a number of specialists came to be appointed to the government itself. What, then, are the situations, if any, in which administrators and technicians can be fully in control?

The idea of the administrative state

To an extent, all modern polities are 'administrative states', since a number of decisions of importance are in the hands of administrators and of technicians;[20] governments have to accept that their decisions are only implemented in part. Furthermore, technicians have also some scope to develop their own ideas of excellence in the context of the industrial and commercial undertakings which they manage. Yet an administrative state does more than give administrators and technicians the opportunity to share power; it is a polity in which a very large percentage of decision-making is in the hands of the administrators and in which the authority of the administrators is openly recognised as being established over a wide area of policy. At the extreme, such an authority would extend to all governmental decisions.

Conditions which must be fulfilled for the development of an administrative state

To go beyond the conditions favouring administrative and technical influence which have been examined so far, a number of conditions need to be met. First, the political system must be unable to produce strong patterns of authority. This may occur for a variety of reasons. The rule-makers may lack authority as a result of 'accidental' circumstances (war, defeat, a natural calamity); alternatively, divisions between leaders may be such that the system cannot act efficiently or at least is thought incapable of acting efficiently. In the 1940s and 1950s the Fourth Republic of France was 'accepted' but was unable to generate leaders with genuine authority; it was therefore open to forms of bureaucratic rule. Second, the technical and administrative groups must be large enough to constitute a pole of attraction; a country which develops slowly and where the number of technicians and specialists also increases slowly will not be open to administrative rule. Third, there must be an accord between the 'ideology' of the technicians and the prevailing ideology of the country. This ideology must be one of progress, of development, more along technical lines than along social or even economic lines. This is likely to occur relatively rarely. Such an ideology will be widespread if some development has already taken place, but this will occur only if political leaders (other than technicians) have helped to push it forward; this means that these political leaders must have had substantial authority. Thus technicians and administrators will only be in a position to acquire control if the authority of the politicians decreases, or if, as was suggested earlier, dissent occurs among leaders within the general framework of a recognised authority. In summary, administrators and technicians can take over only at relatively advanced states of development and only if those in authority, having previously been able to impose (or push forward) an ideology of progress, start to lose their authority.[21]

This means that technicians are unlikely to take power by themselves early in the development of the society; indeed, at that point, technicians (particularly indigenous technicians) are probably not sufficiently numerous.[22] Admittedly, because of the lack of technical skills in new countries, international technical assistance programmes and governments of developing countries appoint administrators and technicians from developed nations, usually on a temporary basis, but these obviously cannot put the same amount of pressure on the political leaders of the states in which they work as technicians would do in their native countries. As a result, nations at early stages of development are unlikely to move towards a form of administrative or technocratic rule.

The basic instability of an administrative or technocratic state

An administrative state will also rarely emerge because the ties linking the people to the technicians are relatively weak. First, as was previously noted, technocratic rule is essentially sectional in character; each group of technicians is concerned with the development of its service and with the solution of the problems which concern its profession. A political system run by technicians would thus be a kind of 'confederacy' of groups running different services, these being 'trailed' by bodies of 'users' of the services acting as interest groups. Aggregation being low, such a system would find it difficult to solve problems of co-ordination and of resource allocation.

Second, as resource allocation and co-ordination can ultimately only be achieved by non-specialists, an administrative state might therefore appear more viable than a full technocratic state; but such an administrative state would also suffer from major handicaps. If the ideology is one of 'progress' and 'development', administrators are not as well placed as technicians to embody such values; criticisms can be levelled at administrators in terms of excessive bureaucratic rule, exaggerated caution and lack of drive. Moreover, as sectional demands are likely to be large, the non-technical sections of the administration will need to have considerable authority on their own, independently from the technicians; they must be able to rely on the support of the population, and such a support is not likely to be forthcoming.

Thus an administrative state is unlikely to be stable if there are many specialists and if goals of development and progress are prominent. One situation remains, however, namely that of a 'pure' administrative state, in which technicians would play relatively little part and where the administrators are in control. This situation corresponds to that of a traditional and indeed closed polity. It is conceivable that, in such a circumstance, a form of government by administrators might be maintained. Some states, such as Ancient China, have approximated such a model; the fact that almost no nation can at present remain truly closed makes this type of political system rather theoretical in the contemporary world.[23]

The modified administrative or technocratic state

What is more likely to occur is an intermediate situation resulting from a combination of administrative or technocratic rule and other patterns of authority. If an administrative or technocratic state is one in which rule-making is not only in the hands of administrators and/or technicians but also recognised as such, a 'modified' or mixed administrative or technocratic state can be defined as one in which part and only part of the rule-making is in the hands of the administrators and/or technicians and only *some* recognition exists of the power of the administrators.

The conditions leading to the emergence of a 'modified' administrative or technocratic state are the same as those which would have to obtain for the 'pure' version of such a polity to exist. First, an ideology of progress must be widespread for technocrats to have some authority among the population. Second, other patterns of political authority need not have completely ceased to exist; it is merely necessary for them to have diminished sufficiently for a *modus vivendi* to be agreed by the holders of the legitimacy (the politicians) and the technocrats or administrators. This may well occur at early stages of development; it may also occur under military rule, as will be seen in the next chapter. A similar situation may even be found in more developed societies, if politicians have some limited authority and divisions among them are such that they find it difficult to exercise power in a stable or durable manner (as was the case in France before 1958). Such cases are exceptional, however.

A 'modified' form of administrative or technocratic rule is more likely to occur when the political leaders themselves decide to share power with civil servants. Some rulers may be uninterested in the details of social and economic development and may be concerned only with results, preferring for example to devote their activity to foreign affairs. They might then delegate decision-making in the economic and social fields to specialists in whom they have confidence. 'Charismatic' leaders have often taken such a stand in the contemporary world, in both developed and developing polities. In post-war Western Europe, De Gaulle was the ruler closest to this model, though others also gave technicians considerable scope. Such an arrangement is more likely to be stable than that in which a leader is forced to ally himself with the technicians rather than choosing to do so; this is often the case in military regimes, whose rulers sometimes inherit a difficult economic situation combined with strong pressure for development. In the long run, however, all types of modified administrative rule encounter difficulties, either because the leader who made the arrangement is replaced by another who is less well disposed towards civil servants, or because specialists do not achieve the kind of economic development which had been expected.

Conclusion

'Modified' administrative or technocratic rule is somewhat more widespread and somewhat less inherently unstable than 'pure' administrative or technocratic rule, but even 'modified' administrative rule is unlikely to last for very long. The circumstances under which it develops are peculiar; they either correspond to an intermediate stage of development or depend, somewhat unpredictably, on the presence of a charismatic leader. Bureaucrats are thus in a constant dilemma. Their ultimate 'goal' may be to 'make' the rules and take the decisions, in particular when they are specialists and are concerned with managing a public service. Yet, because of their special interest in some and only some aspects of policy, they come into conflict with other specialists and lack the authority to communicate directly with the people. Their ideology is too 'abstract'; they do not produce leaders who will embody this ideology. Bureaucratic hierarchies therefore almost always ultimately depend on the authority of political leaders, although they raise problems for many leaders and for all types of political system, even if only because the morale of administrators is affected by the position of dependence in which they find themselves and because the efficiency of the governmental machine is affected as a result. No simple solution to this problem can be found; there is no recipe which will make administrators and specialists fully adopt the ideology and the approach of politicians. Efforts must be made none the less to find an optimum level of mutual acceptance and understanding, as all polities, developed or developing, may otherwise suffer losses which might reduce appreciably the strides which they can make towards achieving greater socio-economic development or greater political participation.

Notes

1. The theory of the political responsibility of ministers is at the root of democratic theory, particularly in the context of cabinet systems. The question is not so much whether the theory corresponds to the reality of the responsibility, but whether, as a practical arrangement, it makes it possible to emphasise the special role of politicians and thus enables the administrative structure to remain when governments change. From this practical point of view, the theory has undoubtedly had considerable value.

2. Indeed, many civil servants are expected to give advice: this is indeed formally the case with top civil servants in Britain. Britain is perhaps the country in which the question has been debated most thoroughly, both within the civil service and among politicians. The sharpness of the distinction arises principally in cabinet systems; in presidential systems, for instance in the United States, there is more of a gradation and there is a larger number of 'political' appointments within the departments. See E.N. Suleiman (ed.), *Bureaucrats and Policy-making* (1984).

3. The characteristics of this 'philosophy' of management have been most marked in France since the beginning of the nineteenth century, but the idea has spread as bureaucracies have become increasingly involved with economic and social development.

4. The question of the take-over by administrators is an old one: the danger has often been mentioned in the French case, but the problem is general. Given that the duration of ministers in office is generally rather short, it is not surprising that the problem of civil service dominance should be widespread; moreover, as was pointed out in Chapter 18, many ministers are themselves civil servants. See for instance E. Strauss, *The Ruling Servants* (1961), in particular Chapters 2–5, pp. 23–92, and, for the French case, M. Crozier, *The Bureaucratic Phenomenon* (1964); for Britain, see P. Kellner and Lord Crowther-Hunt, *The Civil Servants* (1980).

5. It is difficult to evaluate precisely the size of the public bureaucracy: this is partly because one has to decide whether industrial undertakings should or should not be included, and also because it is questionable whether local authority services should be viewed as part of the state bureaucracy in the strict sense. On average, the civil service proper includes between 5 and 10 per cent of the employed population and the public sector in general employs a quarter or more, even in Western countries.

6. The difference can be very large as, for instance, teachers are regarded in some countries as state employees (France) and in others as local authority employees (Britain).

7. See for instance J. La Palombara (ed.), *Bureaucracies and Political Development* (1963).

8. Delegation suggests that a public authority (often local) does the work which another is legally asked to handle. A different arrangement consists of asking a private firm to undertake the work under contract. This practice has long been common in many Western countries, though its value has been extolled once more in the 1980s with the desire to decrease the role of the state.

9. The question of the control of administrators has exercised students of public administration for long periods. See Chapter 22 on administrative courts and tribunals. The question of control in developing countries is particularly acute, but cross-national studies are still relatively abstract; see J. La Palombara (ed.), *op. cit.* (1964), *passim*.

10. These ministerial 'cabinets' (who constitute the personal staffs of ministers and prime ministers) must be sharply distinguished from cabinets which are governments.

11. Although the members of the 'ministerial cabinets' were originally constituted of friends of ministers and, therefore, primarily of politicians, there has been a marked tendency for civil servants to be appointed within them, largely because only civil servants are expert enough to be able to discuss technical problems. As a result, the problems of control which were mentioned above reappear.

12. These nineteenth-century developments did follow ideas of 'enlightened despotism' which had prevailed in many European countries in the second half of the eighteenth century.

13. The expression 'on tap' rather than 'on top' has been traditionally used in Britain, where technicians are not in charge of services in the central administration, but are merely advisers (while, in local government, they are in charge of services).

14. This view is being modified slowly and the difference is less sharp. Yet it continues to exist, despite suggestions made periodically by a number of bodies that the civil service should be less 'amateurish'. See G. Drewry and T. Butcher, *The Civil Service To-day* (1988), pp. 46–8. See also P. Kellner and Lord Crowther-Hunt, *op. cit.* (1980), pp. 23–45.

15. See note 1 above. The 'collective' responsibility of the cabinet must be distinguished from the 'individual' responsibility of ministers; in the case which is discussed here, it is individual responsibility which is at stake.
16. The question will arise increasingly in the states which were Communist, as the Communist parties' hold on these nations continues to decline.
17. The French *grandes écoles* play a major part both in the appointment of senior civil servants and in the general higher educational structure of the nation. It is worth noting that the idea of the French administrative state was in part developed by Saint Simon (1760–1825) who was a teacher at the *Ecole Polytechnique*, one of the oldest and most prestigious of the engineering schools.
18. Associations of specialists across the private and public sectors can also help to offset decentralisation. See Chapter 16.
19. With ministerial instability, which was very high in France before 1958, the dominance of civil servants was naturally very large.
20. The 'administrative' and the 'technocratic' state will be examined together, though an administrative state would be one where generalists are in control, while a technocratic state would be one where the specialists take the decisions.
21. The question of the rule of bureaucrats has been the object of many studies. See for instance F.W. Riggs, 'Bureaucrats and political development: a paradoxical view' in J. La Palombara (ed.), *op. cit.* (1964), pp. 120–67.
22. Nor do they have enough sheer strength, unlike the military – hence their association with the military in many situations. See Chapter 21.
23. The systems of the Incas and, indeed, of the Roman empire in the second and third centuries AD were of a bureaucratic 'stable' and perhaps even 'static' type. The static character of such regimes renders them open to invasion or unable to survive technological change.

21 | The role of the military in the political process

While the influence of bureaucracies in government tends to be covert and therefore remains relatively unnoticed, the participation of the military in politics is a well-documented and often painfully overt experience. Yet the picture which emerges at first sight is somewhat confusing. Take-overs of governments by the military – as well as attempts at take-overs – appear to occur almost exclusively in Third World countries. Both Western democracies and Communist states seem protected, by and large, from the phenomenon, though there have been, to limit the discussion to the post-World War II period, incidents bordering on takeovers or attempted takeovers in France, Spain and Portugal, and indeed an actual takeover in Greece.[1] On the other hand, even in Western countries and in Communist states, armies make themselves felt; in the United States and in the Soviet Union, to mention only the superpowers, the military is known to exercise various forms of pressure. These pressures are designed either to prevent the government from carrying out policies which the military does not like, or to induce the policy-makers to pursue some policies more strongly than the civilians might have wished. Thus the role of the military in politics appears to be widespread with respect to some types of activities, and to be by and large concentrated in some types of polities with respect to other types of activities.

The picture is thus somewhat confusing in terms of the manner in which the military tends to intervene. It is also somewhat confusing with respect to the extent to which military and nation appear to relate to each other from the point of view of overall values. Traditionally at least, it seemed possible to distinguish between countries which could be regarded as 'militaristic' (such as Germany or Japan) and nations which could be viewed as having a more 'civilian' outlook and in which the military was not given a prominent position (such as the Anglo-Saxon countries). Some countries such as France appeared to stand between these two extremes, with the military and the civilian regime locked in what appeared to be a permanent conflict. This contrast seems to suggest a distinction at the cultural and ideological levels, while the first distinction seems to refer more to the means which the military is prepared or able to use.

308

Prentice-Hall

SIMON & SCHUSTER INTERNATIONAL GROUP
66 Wood Lane End, Hemel Hempstead, Hertfordshire, HP2 4RG, England
Telephone: Hemel Hempstead (0442) 231555   Telex: 82445   Fax: 55618
Registration: London 714516   VAT Registration No. 490 5885 08

JOHN MC MORROW
NEWTOWN COLLEGE OF F E
WHITEABBEY
CO ANTRIM
N IRELAND

REFERENCE
IU047417

Date and
Tax Point
16/10/90

INSPECTION COPY

SBN	TITLE	AUTHOR	PRICE	STK NO
8600 3-719-3	INTRO COMPARATIVE GOVERNMENT	BLONDEL	£ 12.95	013806

This book is being sent to you for 60 days examination following YOUR REQUEST BY TELEPHONE

When you have had the opportunity to examine the book, please complete the details below and return this form.

☐ This book will be recommended for purchase as a main course text for my course on: ....

.... (Subject)

Beginning on: .... Student Numbers: .... I am therefore retaining the book as a desk copy.

Which bookshop will you inform of your students' requirements?: ....

Will the decision on textbook adoption for this course be a committee decision? If so, please supply us with the
names of your colleagues on the committee:

Books currently in use on this course: ....

.... the book herewith.

Payment should be

☐ I am retaining the book and wish you to debit my credit card account with the amount of

My Access/American Express/Visa/Diners Club No. is

| | | | | | | | | | | | | | | | |

Expiry Date

Name

Home Address
Required by Credit Card Companies

☐ I am retaining the book and require an invoice.

Comments on the book (Academic quality, course applicability etc.)

PACKED BY

22

We would be grateful for the names of colleagues whom you think might be interested in this book:

Signed

Telephone No.

Ext

Date

PLEASE QUOTE REFERENCE WHEN REPLYING

These two levels can be brought together, however, as connecting links are provided by two considerations. There is first the question of the tension between the values universally held by the military, though at a greater or lower level of intensity, and the values which are widely spread throughout the society; there is, secondly, the question of the extent of the support which the civilian regime and government enjoy in the population. This means that one must consider the nature of the values of the military and look at these values in relation to the conditions, both societal and specific to the armed forces, which are likely to affect the propensity of the military to intervene in politics. The first section of this chapter will therefore be devoted to this matter. It will be possible in the second section to demonstrate how these conditions lead to various levels of military intervention. The third section will then be devoted to the strongest form of military intervention, that which results in the establishment of military regimes, and to the difficulties which these face.

Conditions favouring military intervention

The military profession and its special characteristics

The military is a branch of the 'bureaucracy' in the broad sense. It has to fulfil specialised functions and is, in relation to the government, one of the services which, in the same way as others, makes calls on public resources. Like other specialists and indeed all administrators, military men can be expected to do more than merely be concerned with implementation; indeed they are likely to be fairly autonomous, as they exercise a unique function and have means of coercion which no-one else possesses. The military are entrusted by the state with the role of defending the existence of the nation and, to achieve this goal, they are equipped with a vast array of weapons; even in the case of small and less developed countries, they can therefore control society in a way which no other group can. Indeed, they are even called by the civilian authorities to use this power, not merely to defend the nation externally, but also to quell major outbreaks of internal resistance. Even police forces do not come close to having the strength of the military; moreover, in many countries, at least a substantial proportion of the police force is part of the army.

The military is therefore likely to develop special features as a result of its unique function. Indeed, because of the difficult and dangerous character of the tasks which members of the armed forces may be asked to fulfil as part of their duties, they have to receive a specialised training; this training naturally develops an *esprit de corps* which is stronger than anywhere else in the public sector. Not all the branches of the armed forces share this spirit to the same extent, admittedly: technical units of the army and, partly because of the technical character of their job, large sections of the navy or the air force may hold somewhat different attitudes. The cohesion of the armed forces may be reduced as a result; thus, occasionally, some branches, for instance of the navy or of the air force, have opposed moves made by the army to oust civilian governments. Yet, by and large, members of the armed forces share a number of values, as these stem from the nature of the military profession. These values are essentially founded on an emphasis on discipline and hierarchy, the need to prepare for an activity – warfare – which is almost never undertaken, and the belief in the magnitude of the potential dangers which face the polity.[2]

The first characteristic does not need to be described at length, as discipline ('which is the basis of army strength', according to the French army rule book) and hierarchy are obvious imperatives of military organisations. However, these virtues are likely to cause friction between military and civilian power, as they are seldom extolled to the same degree outside military establishments. The emphasis on these values is thus likely to lead to a relative isolation of the military from the rest of the community; furthermore, this isolation will be deliberately fostered as the military is unlikely to display the necessary qualities of discipline and hierarchy unless it is at least partly isolated from society.

Second, the military profession is geared to fighting wars; yet the fulfilment of this ultimate *raison d'être* of the armed forces is conceived as an unlikely occurrence and indeed is expected to be unlikely because of the very existence of the military. Members of the armed forces tend therefore to have an ambivalent attitude towards war, as can often be detected in the advice given by general staffs to civilian rulers. As Huntington noted, the military typically feels unprepared and continuously asks for more resources in order to achieve the state of readiness which it feels is required and yet is never achieved.[3] This ambivalence is particularly marked in the contemporary world and especially in relation to nuclear weapons. These are regarded as providing a deterrent – that is to say that they exist in order not to be used; the defence potential is deployed on such a scale that war becomes impossible. Yet some of the same ambivalence exists with respect to conventional warfare as well. Thus most military men prepare most of the time for an activity which occurs occasionally and may indeed never take place. While other public servants are appointed to fulfil the goals which they are employed to achieve, the military is asked to be ready for an eventuality which is to be avoided rather than pursued. Not surprisingly, this state of affairs creates frustrations and may more than occasionally place army and civilian government on a collision course.

Third, the need to be prepared derives from the view that external dangers are both very real and very large. This suggests that the military have a Hobbesian conception of society rather than a belief in co-operation and brotherhood among nations. This underlying ideology explains why general staffs are typically cautious when advising about starting a war; but it also leads more broadly to the demand that the nation be prepared, not just from a material, but from a psychological point of view. The military are deeply concerned with the 'morale of the nation', as success against potential enemies depends on citizens and leaders being ready to defend the country. They are consequently likely to support some ideologies and be suspicious of others; more than any other branch of the public service, they tend to believe that it is their duty to look at the possible consequences of governmental policies and to try to stop those which are viewed as undermining the moral fibre of the nation.[4]

Conditions favouring military intervention in politics

These characteristics of the military, together with the physical force which the army possesses, are thus important elements accounting for a general propensity to intervene in politics.[5] What makes intervention take place in concrete situations, however, is the combination of these characteristics with particular features of the polity. Four elements are essential in this respect – the degree of professionalisation of the military, the extent of legitimacy of the political system, the level of complexity of the society, and the type of ideology which prevails in the polity.

A high degree of professionalisation fosters military intervention, for, the more the army is composed of professionals, the more it is set apart from the rest of the society and, consequently, the more it tends to develop attitudes which are both idiosyncratic and deeply felt by its members.[6] Those who belong to a professional army will have few occasions to meet informally with other groups in society; they will therefore rarely have to defend their ideology or be subjected to the views of others. Their isolation is often reinforced by the tendency of the military to marry within their own group and thus to belong to families in which particularistic values are passed from generation to generation. Conversely, the potential for intervention is reduced where the army is drawn broadly from the population at large and where the bulk of the military have widespread contacts with the rest of the society; the same is true where the technical side of the military is large and powerful, as members of technical corps are likely to have links with colleagues in other walks of life and may even move from a position in the army to equivalent employment in civilian life. The argument is the same as that discussed in relation to sectionalism in Chapter 7: where cross-cutting cleavages are low, sub-cultures tend to develop; where sub-cultures tend to develop, tension between the sub-cultures increases. A high level of military professionalism is a particular instance of sub-cultural development.[7]

The probability of military intervention also increases as the legitimacy of the political system decreases. When legitimacy is low, the military are unlikely to be inhibited in putting pressure on the government or in escalating demands. Moreover, a low level of legitimacy of the political system also indicates to the military that the regime has limited support and, therefore, that the country is unlikely to be morally ready to defend itself with vigour in the event of armed conflict. Finally, a polity in which the legitimacy of the political system is low is likely to be characterised by periodic outbreaks of civil disorder: the army may therefore be called to play a part in internal political life. It may thus already have a foot in the door and further intervention against a weak government may come to be regarded as a logical next step.[8]

Conversely, the probability of military intervention is low when the political, social and economic system is complex, which is particularly the case with developed societies. This is in part because cross-cutting cleavages tend to increase as the complexity of the society increases. This is also because direct intervention by the military becomes difficult to bring about. Although the army's equipment may be highly sophisticated, the network of state and other public institutions is so vast and so diffuse in an advanced society that military intervention would have to take place simultaneously at too many points to allow success. Moreover, in these societies, the military are likely to be incorporated in the governmental machine, for instance through the interpenetration of civilian and army personnel in the ministry of defence as well as in many other organisations, both central and regional.

The probability of military intervention increases if the prevailing ideologies of the polity differ sharply from the values which the military characteristically hold. This is why there are underlying problems between military and civilian values in regimes which emphasise jointly or separately democratic participation goals, liberal means and egalitarian ends. These values tend to clash with the notions of discipline and of hierarchy which the army upholds. The problem is particularly acute when societal norms change abruptly with a new regime or a new government coming to power; on the contrary, slow modifications of goals may be easily accepted by the military. Moreover, potential conflicts between military and civilian authorities are reduced when a democratic government takes a nationalistic posture. Typically, the values of such a regime are associated with an emphasis on universalistic ideas of social and economic development rather than on a traditional conception of the national interest. However, if the polity is faced with strong opposition from its neighbours because of its policies, the military and the civilian government may come closer to each other, as was the case during both the French and the Russian revolutions.

Civilian control and its limits

There is thus a high probability that the military will intervene in various types of polities. The theory of civilian control of the military, which has typically been presented as a model, is therefore likely often to remain a hope rather than a reality.[9] It seemed realistic, admittedly, in nineteenth-century Europe, but this was because, somewhat accidentally, societal conditions combined to reduce the opportunity for or the desire of the military to intervene in that part of the world. First, the professionalisation of the army was slow; the officer class of the traditional European monarchies continued to be drawn from and to remain closely linked to the aristocracy, except in France as a result of the Revolution of 1789. Not surprisingly, France was one of the countries where problems of civil–military relations were most acute.

Second, again with the exception of France, European countries did not typically experience a regime break in the nineteenth century. Liberalism emerged under the cover of the monarchical systems, to which the military remained loyal, because of the traditions embodied by the King or Emperor. There was indeed a system of 'dual' legitimacy, not just in Imperial Germany but elsewhere, whereby military men felt that they owed their allegiance directly to the head of state. They could at least have the impression that their traditional status in the nation was protected by the part played by the institution of the monarchy.

Third, in the case of France and, later, of Soviet Russia, potential civil–military conflicts were reduced to an extent as a result of the incidence of international conflicts. The armies of the Revolution were given the task of defending the regime and the nation. Difficulties were not altogether avoided, as the history of nineteenth- and twentieth-century France was to show; but the potential for an army takeover was none the less reduced by the 'nationalistic' tradition of the Republic, as it was later also to be reduced in the Soviet Union for the same reason.

Thus, by and large, the theory of civilian control of the military seemed to be broadly valid in Europe, especially until 1918. After that date, when many traditional monarchies collapsed, problems began to grow; this was the case in Europe, and especially in Eastern and Southern Europe. Thus the reality of military intervention appeared to be increasingly large. This is not, however, because the theory of civilian control was any less valid than it had been before World War I: indeed, military coups had taken place frequently in Latin America during that period. It is merely that the conditions which had minimised the potential for military intervention in Europe before 1914 ceased to apply to the same extent afterwards.

Levels of military intervention

The four levels of military intervention

The potential for military intervention in politics thus depends on a number of social factors. In practice, this means that it will take a number of forms which will make it be more or less severe; following S.E. Finer, these forms can be described as influence, blackmail, displacement, and supplantment.[10] At the lowest two levels, the role of the military is not very different from that of an interest group. Influence is used, for instance, when members of the military attempt to increase the resources at their disposal or attempt to shift policies by lobbying politicians; there is no attempt at modifying the relationship between, let alone the positions of, the 'players' in the game.

Blackmail activities are designed to achieve more, for example to alter policy on a more general front, in particular in foreign affairs or on territorial matters. The means include a variety of threats, in particular threats of resignation designed to show the civilian authorities that they cannot maintain the line on which they have embarked as implementation may be impossible. A typical blackmail operation was that conducted by a number of British officers before World War I who intimated their opposition to the proposed policy of the Liberal government regarding Ireland by threatening to resign.

If blackmail does not succeed, the next step which the military may take is to displace the existing government and replace it with one which would be expected to be more amenable to their aims. Displacement can vary in severity. At one end of the continuum, it can merely aim at exchanging one civilian group for another; it is then a form of arbitration, as in the case of the *poder moderador* exercised by the military in some Latin American countries and in particular in Brazil in the past. The army did not have any particular inclination towards a specific political group; it merely believed that its function was to prevent the excesses of some civilian elements. But the military may want to go further and bring to power groups which it supports ideologically, often by revitalising them: the return of De Gaulle to power in 1958 in France is a case of this type, since Gaullism had lost practically all its strength during the preceding years.[11] The intervention of the military on behalf of traditional conservative parties in Latin America also constitutes an instance of the same type of displacement, as the strength of these bodies had typically markedly declined. Perhaps the most extreme case of displacement occurred in Uruguay in the 1970s when the military imposed a civilian president on the country. This was indeed very close to supplantment.

Supplantment is overt military rule. The civilian government is replaced by members of the armed forces who act as a group and take the government over. It is a *collective* action of military men and not merely the action of the military on behalf of an individual, even if this individual is a soldier: Napoleon's coup of 1799 was not a case of supplantment, but an extreme form of displacement.[12] With supplantment, the military become the structure of power; in particular, they typically abolish parties and extend their direct control at the regional level.

Levels of military intervention and the structure of society

These levels of military intervention need to be related to the four types of societal characteristics (professionalism, lack of legitimacy, complexity of the society and character of the ideology) which were identified earlier as likely to have an effect on the link between the army and the nation. Influence being the lowest level, it is likely to be characteristic of countries in which the professionalisation of the army is low, regime legitimacy and the complexity of the society high, and the ideology of the civilian government close to that of the military. A country in which the opposite characteristics prevail is likely to be open to supplantment. Countries at intermediate positions will be subjected to blackmail and displacement.

The relationship between levels of military intervention and these societal characteristics can be stated more precisely if consideration is given to the role of the army at four stages of socio-economic development, namely those of under-development, take-off, early development, and mature development. First, the complexity of the society grows with socio-economic development. Thus, the more a society is advanced in socio-economic terms, the more it is difficult for the army to take it over. Second, however, the professionalisation of the army is likely to be low at the under-developed stage and higher at other stages of development, though perhaps not at its highest point at the most advanced stages.[13] Third, the ideology of traditional political systems is likely to be close to that of the military; it is less close at other stages of development, with the added problem that, at the take-off and early development stages, a new democratic or egalitarian ideology may be suddenly pressed on the polity, for instance at the time of independence. Finally, legitimacy is likely to be at its highest at the stages of under-developement and of mature development, while countries at the take-off and early development stages are characterised by high levels of conflict about regime goals and about the bases of the political institutions.[14]

Countries at the under-development and mature development stages are thus likely to be marked by the lowest levels of military intervention. In developed societies, on the whole, the military uses influence and acts as an interest group. Where, as in the United States, the legislature is powerful and is able to act either to initiate or at least to veto governmental legislation, the military operates on the legislature as well as on the executive. In societies at the under-development stage, such as traditional monarchies, associational groups are weak and communal groups such as tribes or ethnic groups are strong;[15] the military will also use influence and perhaps blackmail, but the pressure which is exercised takes place through these communal groups. Gradually, however, as traditional societies begin to change, the military begin to acquire a sense of corporate identity; it starts to be, as was noted in Chapter 7, an institutional group. Meanwhile, conflicts over ideology and regime also increase, with some groups supporting modernisation while others defend traditional values: the legitimacy of the political system declines. The army becomes increasingly concerned with the future of society and wishes to play a part in shaping this future. As a result, the probability of displacement and even of supplantment becomes high, although supplantment is more characteristic of countries at the take-off stage while displacement is characteristic of countries at the early development stage. This is a stage at which the society begins to be too complex for an army coup to succeed easily, though instances of supplantment do occur, and these can be severe and even brutal, as were the cases of supplantment in Chile and Argentina in the 1970s and 1980s. The intensity of military intervention is thus related to the development of societies in the form of a bell-shaped curve, with the mildest forms of army action being at both ends of the range and displacement and supplantment being characteristic of the intermediate positions. Given that, in the post-World War II period, many countries moved from the traditional to the take-off and early development stages, it is not surprising that there should have been many military coups and many military regimes in the contemporary world.

Military regimes and their fate

The emergence of military regimes in the contemporary world

Military regimes thus tend to occur when societies are at the take-off and developing stages; they occur as a result of the decrease in the legitimacy of the traditional forces, and especially of the communal groups, which exist in undeveloped societies. At that point, a legitimacy vacuum occurs, so to speak, and the military often embodies the hopes of those who are looking for a transformation of the country. As the armed forces have physical strength, they can carry out a coup successfully in the context of state organisations which are relatively simple; as they have a hierarchical organisation which is likely to extend into the provinces, they can be a substitute for parties and communal groups in providing a chain of command through which decisions at the centre may be implemented at the periphery.

It is therefore not surprising that military regimes should have been established in Latin America on numerous occasions since the early part of the nineteenth century and in Eastern Europe between the two world wars; nor is it surprising that half the Third World countries (52 out of 104) in existence before 1970 should have had at least one military regime, together with one Western European country (Greece). Indeed, a number of these countries (Ghana, Nigeria, Sudan and Argentina in particular) have more than one military regime (see Table 21.1).

Table 21.1 Military regimes and military-dominated regimes

	Total countries in area	Number of countries which have had military regimes since 1945	Number of current military regimes	Number of current military-dominated regimes
Atlantic	23	1	–	–
East Europe and North Asia	15	1	–	–
Middle East and North Africa	22	7	–	3
South and South-East Asia	24	7	1	1
Africa south of Sahara	46	22	9	10
Latin America	33	14	2	2
Total	163	52	12	16

Although military regimes are numerous, they have not emerged at random throughout the post-1945 period. To begin with, as might be expected, successful coups tend to occur after a few years have elapsed since independence, and not immediately. Thus while most Black African countries became independent in or around 1960, military regimes occurred in that part of the world in the second half of the 1960s, as in Ghana, Nigeria, Benin (then Dahomey), Burkina Faso (then Upper Volta), Mali, Mauretania, Zaire and Burundi. Not surprisingly, therefore, only countries which became independent in the 1980s have not been affected by military takeovers.

Moreover, the number of these regimes declined sharply in the 1980s: the majority of the Latin American countries which had had military regimes or regimes strongly based on the military from the late 1960s or the 1970s turned to civilian governments in the 1980s; this has been the case in Ecuador, Peru, Bolivia, Argentina, Brazil and Uruguay. A similar tendency can also be noticed in the rest of the world, though it is appreciably less marked and it has given rise to the development of mixed military–civilian regimes rather than pure civilian regimes.[16]

The decline in the number of pure military regimes in the 1980s has been sometimes regarded as a sign of a long-term decline in the sharpest and most 'naked' forms of military intervention in politics, in part because all societies have become more complex – the trend throughout the world would follow a similar evolution which took place in Southern Europe, where liberal democracy has been regarded as undergoing a process of 'consolidation'.[17] Yet the decline in the number of military regimes in the 1980s may only be part of a cyclical trend. There were indeed previous periods during which the incidence of military rule was also relatively small, for instance in the late 1950s and early 1960s when, in Latin America, civilian regimes emerged in many countries, among which were Venezuela, Colombia, Ecuador, Peru, Bolivia and Argentina; but civilian regimes survived the 1960s in Venezuela and Colombia only, while Brazil and later Chile and Uruguay joined the list of the countries under army rule. Indeed, such cycles of civilian and military regimes correspond to the fact that tensions in developing polities – as well as the ineffectiveness of the bureaucracy in these countries – create conditions for army takeovers. However, the cycles result also from the difficulties which military governments experience in maintaining themselves in power for long periods. Thus some developing countries are able to avoid army takeovers if, for instance, party and group structures, both tribal and associational – such as trade unions – are legitimate because they are well implanted in the population. This has been the case in most Commonwealth countries, only six of which (among over thirty) have experienced successful coups.[18] On the other hand, when these structures are not strong enough and a military regime emerges, this regime is unlikely to establish strong political institutions and well-developed social groups; it is therefore also unlikely to acquire the legitimacy which it requires to maintain itself for a long period.[19]

Weaknesses and failures of military regimes

While observers are accustomed to note the strengths of military regimes – and, to begin with, the fact that they can physically coerce opponents – the weaknesses are less apparent. They are, none the less, real and they impede the long-term maintenance of these regimes.[20] Military rule lasted only six years on average in the post-1945 period, and this average is almost the same for each of the regions of the developing world (Middle East and North Africa, South and South East Asia, Black Africa, and Latin America).[21] Only in ten cases did military regimes last more than a decade, the longest being those of Chile (seventeen years up to 1990), of Ethiopia (fifteen years up to 1990), of Pakistan (fifteen years) and of Bolivia and Nigeria (thirteen years). Conversely, military rule lasted two years or less in thirteen cases and between three and four years in eighteen cases. Thus most military regimes are short-lived and even those which last for a long period are transient by comparison with civilian regimes, not merely Western liberal–democratic, but also Third World liberal–democratic, as in India, Malaysia, or Sri Lanka, Communist, or even those based on the leadership of a charismatic president whether or not supported by a single party, as in many African states, for instance Senegal, Ivory Coast, Kenya and Zambia.

Military regimes are thus normally transient: this is because they suffer from structural weaknesses which counterbalance their strength and which both affect the ability of the military to run the government effectively and prevent the armed forces from providing linkages between rulers and people equivalent to those provided by parties and groups. Members of the armed forces are not trained to fulfil the functions of party leaders, namely to elaborate, co-ordinate, and supervise the implementation of policies, except with respect to those matters which pertain directly or indirectly to the military.[22] The military men who occupy ministerial positions therefore quickly find themselves in difficulty, both from a technical point of view, since they do not have the specialised answers, and from a broader political point of view, since they uphold rather simple philosophies which are unlikely by themselves to provide a framework for policy-making.

Military rulers therefore have to rely markedly on the bureaucracy to give them solutions to the problems which they face. These problems are particularly serious as coups typically take place in order to speed up social and economic development. Yet, as was pointed out in the previous chapter, the bureaucracy is handicapped by its sectionalism and its relative lack of legitimacy. Military rulers have therefore to be able to co-ordinate and indeed elaborate policies and also to impose them, occasionally at least, on branches of the bureaucracy.[23] In many cases, they are unable to do so, both because they do not have the necessary technical competence and because they are unable to acquire sufficient support among the population. The army does have 'tentacles' in the provinces, since it has a territorial structure of garrisons and outposts, but these tentacles do not normally have the 'length' and the flexibility of the local organisations of parties or interest groups. Indeed, such 'tentacles' may not always exist, as the armies of most Third World countries are often very small; the few thousand soldiers who constitute them may be able to carry out successfully a coup in the capital and subsequently to control that capital and a few urban centres, but their numbers are not adequate when what is needed is an effort to educate and mobilise the population, particularly in the countryside and in the small cities. The military rulers may therefore be unable to reach the mass of the population and thus acquire a large following.

Moreover, the army is less flexible and versatile than a party or a group as a result of its disciplined and hierarchical character. Members of the military may occasionally engage in activities designed to educate the population, in particular in matters of communication or of land use and especially at times of emergencies; but they are less able to engage in a continuous process of mobilisation, since they typically operate as units and have to maintain a degree of internal cohesion which results in them remaining somewhat apart from the population.

Thus, not surprisingly, military rulers become confronted after a few years with the emergence of a gap – a zone of silence – between themselves and the people. They then face a dilemma. They may be unable or unwilling to fill this gap, in part in order to remain relatively 'pure'; they then have to start the process by which they will transfer power back to civilians. Alternatively they may want to remain in power, but they then need the help provided by other institutions. They often use the bureaucracy for this purpose, but this is not sufficient. They have therefore to start building around themselves a political party and associations dependent on that party, such as trade unions. In this process, the military regime begins to 'civilianise' itself and becomes transformed into a mixed military–civilian government.[24]

Mixed civilian–military governments

While the number of 'pure' military governments declined appreciably in the course of the 1980s – the peak being in the mid-1970s – there has been a corresponding and substantial increase in the number of mixed civilian–military regimes during the same period.[25] As a result, by 1990, over one-sixth of all the Third World governments belonged to this category, as against only 10 per cent of 'pure' military regimes.

Mixed military–civilian rule is a relatively recent phenomenon. In the past, the few governments of this type were essentially based on a military executive acting in combination with (and imposed on) traditional rulers. The Thai government had this character from the 1930s to the 1970s. Contemporary mixed military–civilian regimes are rarely associated with traditional rulers, however; military regimes often overthrew this type of government, as was the case in Syria and Iraq in 1958, in Libya in 1969, in Afghanistan in 1973 and in Ethiopia in 1974. By far the most widespread form of mixed civilian–military rule prevailing since the 1970s is therefore that which takes the form of an association between the army and a single party; that party is typically created by strong military leaders, some of whom succeed in obtaining a personal following among the population and want to capitalise on this following through a party.[26] While such a development has become characteristic of the 1970s and 1980s, it is not entirely new. It began in Latin America and was particularly successful in Mexico with the setting up of the

PRI in the 1920s; a similar move took place at the same period in Turkey under Ataturk and in the 1950s in Egypt under Nasser. From the 1960s, a substantial number of military rulers attempted to maintain their rule in this way in the Middle East, parts of South Asia, and above all in Africa. In particular this has been the basis of the evolution of Zaire, Sudan (until the 1980s), Somalia, Ethiopia and Burma, in which a single party was set up after a period during which parties had been banned.[27] In Syria and Iraq, the relationship between party and military has been more complex, as the Baath party is not the creation of the armed forces; however, these have been so influential in the development of that party since the 1960s that it can be said to have been to a large extent the tool of the military rulers.[28]

Parties created by military rulers are often highly artificial, however, especially in the early period. At worst, they may have a symbolic existence only. Yet the situation can change gradually if the leader does have a genuine personal following and is anxious to broaden the base of his power. This effort appears particularly characteristic of military regimes with a left-wing ideology, such as those which have emerged since the 1970s, especially in Black Africa, as in Ethiopia, Benin and Congo. The party is then set up along lines which are somewhat similar to those of a Communist party and it tends to play a substantial part in educating and mobilising the population.[29] However, such a development reduces still further the military character of the regime. Indeed, as has been the case in Mexico since the 1930s and in Egypt since the 1960s, the civilianisation process gradually becomes complete as the party and other groups acquire genuine autonomy. Thus mixed civilian–military regimes eventually give way to pure civilian regimes.

Military regimes thus last for relatively short periods. After a few years, they are likely to disappear, either suddenly, as has been the case in most Latin American countries, or through the longer process of civilianisation, as occurred in Mexico and in many African and Asian countries. Meanwhile, however, the disappearance of military regimes by one or the other of these formulas does not eliminate the reasons which originally accounted for military intervention. A new cycle then tends to begin, with further takeovers likely to occur in the future, at least as long as the polity fails to reach the level of mature development.

Conclusion

Military intervention in politics is thus a universal phenomenon, but this phenomenon takes many forms. At its lowest and most widespread level, it is characterised by types of pressure which scarcely distinguish the military from other bodies; at its highest and sharpest points, both because the military have special features and because many societies experience serious internal conflicts, military intervention can lead to a complete take-over of the government. Such take-overs result from the difficulties experienced by civilian governments in handling the problems which they face and in particular in reducing the tensions which erupt at the take-off and early development stages of societies.[30] Yet military supplantment does not lead to regime stability, largely because military rulers are typically ill-equipped technically to run complex societies and to develop deep-rooted links among the population. Thus they have in turn to retreat altogether or at least to ally themselves with other groups. Military intervention is therefore universal in its mildest forms; in its most manifest expression, it is symptomatic of the profound malaise which some societies experience. Yet military regimes do not provide a cure for the malaise which is at the origin of their existence. Where they take over power, they do not provide more than, at best, a temporary and often illusory solution.

Notes

1. In May 1958, the French army in Algeria ceased to obey the orders of the government: this was the direct cause of the collapse of the Fourth Republic and of the coming to power of De Gaulle. Parts of the military were restive in Spain after the return of that country to democracy in the mid-1970s and, on one occasion, a military officer stormed into the parliament. The military overthrew the Portuguese government in 1974 and it took over two years for a full return to civilian government to be achieved. In Greece the 'colonels' took over power in 1967 and democratic government was only restored in 1974.
2. These developments follow the analysis of S.P. Huntington in *The Soldier and the State* (1957), particularly pp. 1–97. Differences between the army, the navy and the airforce have sometimes led to the failure of a coup or to the end of a military regime. These differences are in part the consequence of variations in levels of specialisation; the navy and the airforce are more technical than the bulk of the army.
3. S.P. Huntington, *op. cit.*, p. 66.
4. *ibid.*, pp. 62ff.
5. As S.E. Finer points out in *The Man on Horseback* (1962):
   > Instead of asking why the military engage in politics, we ought surely to ask why they ever do otherwise. For at first sight the political advantages of the military *vis-à-vis* other and civilian groupings are overwhelming. The military possess vastly superior organisation. And they possess *arms*. (p. 5).
6. Hence the case is often made in favour of a conscript army by those who want to link the military with the nation. Yet paradoxically the development of conscription did constitute a reason for the growth of a professional officer corps.
7. See Chapter 7 on the effect of sub-cultures.
8. See S.E. Finer, *op. cit.*, pp. 72ff. on the 'opportunity to intervene'.
9. The theory of civilian control should be viewed as part of the theory of ministerial responsibility. See Chapter 20. On the peculiar conditions under which civilian control was able to function before 1914 in liberal societies, see S.P. Huntington, *op. cit.*, pp. 80ff.
10. See S.E. Finer, *op. cit.*, pp. 86–7.
11. De Gaulle returned to power after the army had effectively ceased to obey the Fourth Republic government in May 1958.
12. In 1799, Bonaparte came to power after the army overthrew the government of the Directory, but it was Bonaparte, rather than the army as such, who came to power.
13. Because the sub-culture effect of professionalisation plays less of a part at the advanced stages of development, the army is more closely linked to the rest of the population.
14. See Chapter 5.
15. See Chapter 7.

16. But a coup took place in 1989 in Sudan while various attempts at military intervention (admittedly unsuccessful) took place during the presidency of Alfonsin in Argentina (1983–9).
17. See G. O'Donnell, P. Schmitter, and L. Whitehead (eds), *Transitions from Authoritarian Rule* (1986).
18. Coups have taken place in Ghana (three times), in Nigeria, Uganda and Pakistan (twice), in Sierra Leone, and in Fiji.
19. Military regimes have difficulty in acquiring legitimacy except, indirectly, through the personalisation of the military ruler. See Chapter 5.
20. See S.E. Finer, *op. cit.*, on the weaknesses of the military, pp. 14–22.
21. See J. Blondel, *Organisation of Governments* (1982), pp. 126–7.
22. The military in Nigeria was a case in point. See O. Oyediran (ed.), *Nigerian Government and Politics under Military Rule* (1979).
23. See O. Oyediran (ed.), *op. cit.*, pp. 73–95.
24. See S.E. Finer, *op. cit.*, pp. 197–204. See also S.P. Huntington, *Political Order in Changing Societies* (1968), pp. 237–63.
25. See J. Blondel, *op. cit.* (1982), p. 100.
26. See S.E. Finer, *op. cit.*, pp. 198–204 and S.P. Huntington, *op. cit.*, pp. 237–63.
27. In Sudan, 'civilianisation' led to a return to the pluralistic party system which proved unable to end the civil war in the South; a coup occurred in 1989. In Somalia, the military ruler decided in 1989 to introduce a multi-party system, as had occurred previously in Turkey and Egypt, but, in these last two cases, it occurred only after the original leader had disappeared from the scene.
28. On the complex characteristics of the Baath party in Iraq and Syria, see M.C. Hudson, *Arab Politics* (1977), in particular pp. 251–80.
29. The actual extent of mobilisation appears low and spasmodic, except perhaps in Ethiopia, where the situation has been complicated in the 1980s by wars in both Eritrea and Somalia. For the examination of specific cases, such as those of Benin (formerly Dahomey), Togo, Congo and Uganda, see S. Decalo, *Coups and Army Rule in Africa* (1976).
30. One of the problems being that of corruption. See for instance O. Odetola, *Military Regimes and Development* (1982), pp. 37–49. The tensions which arose in Eastern Europe after the collapse of Communist regimes in 1989 gave some opportunities for the army to intervene. Problems seem to be larger in this respect in Yugoslavia and Romania, and indeed in the Soviet Union itself, in this last case because of the ethnic conflicts at the periphery of the country.

22 | Rule-adjudication and the role of judges in government

The notion of rule-adjudication

Bureaucracies (and armies) are the main instruments by which the rules made by executives and assemblies are implemented, although these institutions are also often involved in rule-making as well, even if they encounter difficulties when they attempt too conspicuously to take on the role of the politicians. Yet bureaucracies and armies are not the only bodies whose role is to implement rules. Alongside them are courts and tribunals which are also engaged in what is in essence rule-application, albeit of a special nature.

Rule application by courts is special, not just because these bodies have a formally solemn character, are staffed by a personnel whose career is governed by particular rules and operate on the basis of procedures which are highly distinctive. The activities of courts are special because the principle of operation is different from that of bureaucracies. Administrators typically move from general principles to specific cases; judges, on the contrary, start from specific cases which they then relate to one or a number of principles. This is why the operation has sometimes been described as 'rule-adjudication' rather than rule-application: judges 'adjudicate' among the rules which should be (or should have been) taken into account in a particular case. The operation which they conduct is thus the converse of a 'normal' operation of rule-application.[1] Yet it remains fundamentally a form of rule-application, as the aim is to discover what rule should be implemented in a particular context.

Two consequences follow. First, rule-adjudication has a somewhat 'passive' character. It is concerned with what has occurred (or what should have happened); it can therefore be set in motion only after the event. It does not provoke events, as does rule-application by administrators. Bureaucrats are often concerned with management, even when they apply rules; those who are engaged in rule-adjudication do not manage situations, but pass 'judgements' (in the ordinary sense of the word) on what has or has not happened.[2] Second, rule-adjudication is 323 necessarily immersed in detail and is concerned with establishing, obviously with various degrees of rigour and precision, what has or has not taken place, since the applicability or otherwise of a specific rule will depend markedly on the extent to which it is established that some events did indeed occur. Clearly, persons who are professionally engaged in rule-adjudication will become interested in the general implications of rules, but they are primarily concerned with the problem of establishing that some alleged happening did indeed take place. Rule-adjudication is not first and foremost an effort designed to discover the general consequences of rules; it has to deal with particular actions and with the extent to which one or more rules relate to these actions.

No society can avoid problems of rule-adjudication. All societies have norms, whether these are written into laws or are unconsciously passed on from one generation to the next. Whatever executives and bureaucracies may decree and try to implement, there will always be happenings which will not fit these decrees. Thus all polities need institutions which will carry out the operation (or in Almond's terms the function) of rule-adjudication. But societies differ in the degree to which rule-adjudication takes place. The judicial process may be more or less sophisticated, for instance. Some events may be 'judged' without considerable care for details, or some happenings may even be left 'unjudged' because courts are not allowed to deal with the problem. Thus, though the operation of rule-adjudication exists everywhere, there can be major variations in its form and extent. This is indeed a point where the norms of the political system, consciously or by custom, may have a major impact; an analysis of political life therefore entails an examination of the processes of rule-adjudication.

The norms of the political system affect all aspects of the rule-adjudication process. First, they affect the extent to which the institutions (the courts and the tribunals) are autonomous from the government and from the bureaucracy, not merely formally, but in fact. Liberal systems state that courts should be independent; authoritarian systems, on the other hand, try to control the courts. The norms of the political system affect rule-adjudication in terms of its content as well. Not only are the laws likely to be more favourable to the citizen in a liberal state, but in such a state, too, the judiciary is likely to be given greater powers to question the validity of the laws themselves. This means that constitutionalism plays a crucial part with respect to rule-adjudication, as it does with respect to assemblies and executives. Yet, as in the case of assemblies and executives, the characteristics of the courts and the extent of the involvement of these bodies in the defence of the rights of citizens can change markedly over time; this occurs particularly in the context of the scrutiny of the actions of the administration. While the growth of rule-adjudicating institutions – courts, tribunals, and other judicial bodies – is closely related to the spread of liberal ideas by way of constitutional arrangements, it is also related to the development of practices which may extend, or restrict, the provisions of the constitution.

The three dimensions of rule-adjudication

Polities are therefore likely to vary markedly in terms of the extent to which rule-adjudication is allowed and is able to take place. It is easiest to consider the matter in the context of a concrete case. If plaintiffs try to obtain redress (or alternatively, if being brought to court by another person or by the state, they attempt to defend themselves), three basic questions will arise. First, to what extent are judges really 'free' or 'independent' in the examination and eventual adjudication of the case? This question relates partly, but only partly, to the existence of separate institutions; it tends to be assumed that, where structures are differentiated, the 'hearing' will be fairer, but this assumption has to be tested. Second, to what extent are judges competent to consider the case? Is this one of the matters which they are entitled to solve or will they have to say that they have no jurisdiction, not because the plaintiff went to the wrong court, but because no court in the country has the right to adjudicate on the matter? This happens if the question is deemed 'discretionary' and the state has the final right to decide. Third, to what extent is the judge allowed to question the rules? Plaintiffs may not complain that they have been wrongly treated according to a specific rule, but that the particular rule is wrong, because it does not fit with the provisions of another, more general rule, which should have had precedence over the specific rule. Yet judges may have to say that they have no right to examine whether the specific rule was wrongly made and that they can only see whether plaintiffs were wrongly treated under that rule. The 'extent' of rule-adjudication has thus both a 'vertical' and a 'horizontal' meaning. The horizontal meaning relates to the degree to which questions can be discussed and adjudicated upon; the vertical meaning relates to the extent to which the judge can examine the whole sequence of rules on the basis of which the event is being supported or criticised.

We need therefore to examine three problems, namely the extent of independence of judges, the scope of rule-adjudication, and the depth of rule-adjudication. These problems are related to each other, but only in part. Judges may be highly independent and yet be severely restricted in the scope of their activities; moreover, they may not be empowered to scrutinise any of the rules to see whether they contradict higher norms – for instance the constitution. Thus three distinct aspects of the problem need to be examined; only by doing so can one assess the character and extent of rule-adjudication in a particular polity.

Rule-adjudication and the degrees of independence of courts

The first question to be considered is thus whether rule-adjudicating bodies are independent. However, independence is a matter of degree; it depends on both formal and informal arrangements, and it cannot go beyond a certain limit. One element is provided by the existence of separate bodies in charge of rule-adjudication. It is obviously important that there should be courts, recognised as such and entrusted with the duty to adjudicate on certain matters. Yet the fact that courts exist does not in itself guarantee independence, while, conversely, some tribunals and informal committees of inquiry may operate in a 'judicial' manner although they do not have the status of courts. Thus what needs to be assessed is not – or at least not merely – whether formal arrangements establish the independence of courts, but whether the methods of selection of the judiciary and the procedures which are in force guarantee the reality of that independence.

Such an analysis is difficult to conduct, however, because what is meant by independence is not entirely clear. Independence means lack of imposition; but from whom should the courts be independent? Is it just from the political leaders of the day and from their subordinates? This view has been that of the constitutionalists who asked for a separation of the judiciary from the executive and legislature.[3] Judges should be able to act without fear of what the government or bureaucracy might do. Yet independence may mean more than freedom from interference from the politicians; it may mean freedom from the norms of the political and social system itself. This is not what the liberal conception of rule-adjudication suggests; it claims that courts must protect and indeed uphold the rule of law. Yet some have claimed that this results in the courts being ultimately the defenders of the social order rather than independent bodies striving for justice or equity. By and large, even in the best cases and although there are some exceptions, judges tend to operate within the context of the principles on which the society is based; they are separate from the government rather than fully independent.

The extent to which judges are truly free from governmental interference naturally varies from country to country and over time; the precise amount and the exact character of the variation is so far not well-known. It is known that there are cases in which judges have been dismissed or harrassed, but the degree to which more subtle pressures are being exercised is uncertain.[4] No general investigation has been carried out in order to discover how far courts are able to pass judgements against the government of the day. Moreover, the question is typically considered primarily in the context of bodies which are legally defined as 'courts', but there is now a large and increasing number of semi-judicial organisations which deal primarily with matters relating to the relationship between the citizen and the bureaucracy.[5] These bodies have grown somewhat haphazard and their status is often less protected than that of courts. The extent of independence of these bodies should obviously be taken into account if a comprehensive picture of the characteristics of rule-adjudication in a given country is to be drawn, but the activities of these institutions is even less well documented than that of courts.

Legal arrangements designed to ensure independence

Like the constitutional arrangements designed to bring about decentralisation, the legal arrangements designed to ensure the independence of courts and other rule-adjudicating bodies tend to concentrate on procedural aspects. The principal aim is to ensure that the career is more secure than that of ordinary administrators; this is achieved by regulating appointments and promotions. There are difficulties, however. To begin with, someone has to select the judges. In order to avoid governmental interference altogether, they are sometimes elected directly by the people; this is the case with many state judges in the United States. However, the result is that the judges may not be technically competent; moreover, they may be anxious to please the majority who elected them or perhaps even more the few who nominated them for election. An alternative is co-option, but this has the effect of perpetuating certain traditions or attitudes and indeed of breeding nepotism. In practice, most countries have adopted a mixture of co-option and governmental appointment. First, the appointment of the *top* judges is often ultimately in the hands of the government; this might be reduced in practice by a customary form of co-option, even at the top, but this is not always the case, as is shown by the appointment of the United States Federal justices.[6] Second, entry to the corps of judges is often dependent upon successfully passing examinations and therefore showing some general intellectual as well as technical legal competence.[7] Thus appointment mechanisms do not – and cannot – establish complete separation between judges and government.

There are also difficulties with respect to promotion mechanisms. Someone has to promote judges and whoever has such a power can reduce markedly the independence of the more ambitious among them. In this respect as well, the choice has to be made between co-option and governmental decision. Liberal states opt for co-option, with the restriction that, at the very top, the government may be involved in the process to some extent. There is, moreover, a rule that tenure is fully protected, but this only means that judges can be fully independent provided they are prepared to face the prospects of a promotionless career.

These principles are in force in Western countries, but they are also enshrined in the constitutions of most other states and, indeed, by and large, they are applied in many parts of Latin America under civilian regimes and in the Commonwealth. Indeed, even in Communist states, a tradition of judicial independence gradually developed.[8] Only in a minority of countries are there frequent and blatant cases of formal restrictions to the independence of judges.

The question of the separation of judges from ordinary administration arises even more in relation to tribunals and other quasi-judicial bodies which deal with professional matters, technical questions and grievances of citizens against the bureaucracy. The members of these bodies often do not enjoy the type of protection which is given to judges. A good example is that of the French highest administrative court, the Council of State, whose members have no more security of tenure than other *higher* civil servants – in theory very little indeed – and whose career often consists of moving in and out of the court, either into other areas of the public sector or into private enterprise.[9] There is often no or very little security of tenure for members of tribunals and other quasi-judicial committees which have proliferated since 1900 with the growth of social and economic legislation, in particular in Western countries. The scope of rule-adjudication may have increased, as will be seen in the last section, but the legal arrangements designed to protect the independence of judges have often not been extended beyond the area in which they were originally applied.

The independence of judges: social and political pressures

Yet the limited evidence which can be obtained on new quasi-judicial bodies does not amount to an indictment of these courts any more than the legal arrangements relating to traditional courts suggest that these have been truly independent, not only in authoritarian countries but even in liberal polities.[10] Studies which have been conducted in a number of Western liberal democracies on the origins of judges and judicial behaviour show that members of the judiciary tend to be recruited, on the whole, from the better-off sections of the society. The same often obtains even for juries (or for magistrates in England, who, although they do not legally play the same part as juries, constitute, for relatively small crimes, a lay element which may fulfil the same social function). Members of juries are likely to come from a wider cross-section of the community than judges, but they are unlikely to be socially representative. If it is assumed that the political and social attitudes of judges and juries correspond to those of the social groups from which these come, they are unlikely to hold views which reflect those of a representative cross-section of the community.[11]

Thus, even in the absence of direct political pressure, members of rule-adjudicating bodies in liberal democracies are more likely to uphold the status quo than to oppose it. As, more often than not, governments of Western liberal democracies are drawn from among, and representative of, the better-off sections of the community, the judiciary of liberal democracies is therefore more likely to favour the government than the opposition. This may in part be the reason why the 'independence' of the judiciary is not really seriously questioned in Western liberal democracies. Only occasionally is there a major clash, and such clashes seem to take place typically (though systematic empirical evidence is lacking) when a left-wing government attempts to impose policies which do not appear to coincide with those of the status quo and which are therefore often regarded by judges as going against the rule of law. Meanwhile, courts appear to display a tendency to uphold conservative standpoints against more radical policies of governments. The case of Rooseveltian legislation of 1933–4 is one of the best known episodes – an episode to which the discussion will return in the next section – and examples can also be shown in relation to British radical governments.[12] These examples may not be typical, but the social basis of the judiciary would appear to constitute a reason for suggesting a built-in tendency towards conservatism among the judiciary.[13]

Political pressures are often blatant outside Western democracies, but there are also many cases where the most commonly used pressures are more subtle, even in authoritarian states. The predominant part played by the Communist party in the Soviet Union and other Eastern Communist states has traditionally constituted the basic framework within which the judiciary has operated in these countries. As this general political pressure reduced or indeed stopped the supply of judges who did not conform to the Socialist ideal, there has been relatively little need to use overt weapons of intimidation, at least since Stalin and before the major upheavals which these countries underwent in the 1980s.[14] In Latin America and even in Africa, where the pressures of the single party are smaller or less successful, social pressures may be exercised within a more confined political and social elite to ensure that judges do not exercise their independence in ways detrimental to the cause of the government.[15] Thus an equilibrium appears to be reached, as a result of which the level of anti-government utterances and of political opposition expressed by judges corresponds to the level broadly tolerated by the polity.

Judicial independence is therefore exercised within limits. At one end, in the large majority of countries, a minimum of independence exists; this is necessary if the administration of justice is to be conducted at all in civil, commercial, and criminal matters.[16] At the other end, independence does not go beyond a certain point, not just because courts have to uphold the principles on which the society is based but because they are themselves the products of their society and in particular of the more 'conservative' parts of that society. This trend is typically reinforced by the recruitment mechanisms in which co-option plays a very large part.

Maximum 'depth' of intervention; the problem of constitutional control

Even if judges are independent, they may not be entitled to intervene deeply in the rule-application process, let alone in rule-making, because they may not be allowed to question the validity of the rules which are being applied. The legal system is based on a hierarchy of rules. This means that judges can be asked to state whether a given document conforms to the parent and more general rules on which the document is based. If courts are allowed to decide on such a matter, the depth of rule-adjudication is obviously greater that if they are not. Moreover, this power may be more or less extensive. If it goes beyond the procedures and is concerned with examining whether the spirit of the dependent rule is consistent with the spirit of the parent rule, this control is truly comprehensive.

Ultimately, judicial supervision is at its deepest when rules are being assessed on grounds of their constitutionality, since the constitution is the most general rule which exists in a polity. The control exercised in depth by the courts can range all the way from the examination of the most specific bureaucratic order to the most general piece of legislation; the mechanism is the same as with the control of constitutionality, but constitutional control raises larger problems as the laws which are passed by the legislature can be put in question in the process.

This issue is particularly difficult to handle because, if judges can question the validity of statutes, they can be said, at least negatively, to be involved in rule-(un)making.[17] Strictly speaking, any interpretation given by a court with respect to the most detailed governmental order is a form of rule-making, but, at that level, the conflict between rule-making and rule-adjudicating agencies remains limited. When the laws made by the legislatures are being questioned, the potential political problem is large. If courts are allowed to define, interpret, and limit the operation of statutes in the name of the constitution, they seem to be in position to define, interpret, and limit the powers of all the rule-making agencies which exist in the polity.

The logic of constitutional control is, on the surface, convincing. If and when the organisation of the state is based on the 'rule of law', it seems consistent with the rule of law that no authority should be allowed to act against principles of the law, even if this authority happens to be the executive or the legislative branch of the government. Yet a difficulty soon arises because constitutions are concerned with general principles, which are of necessity described in rather broad terms. As was seen in Chapter 15, these broad statements cannot be implemented easily, let alone automatically.[18] Courts can therefore find grounds for stating that the constitution is not applied; more seriously even, they have considerable scope for changing their views about the extent to which the constitution is being applied in the case of a particular statute. This means that they (and in practice primarily the supreme courts) can adopt a posture which, in some respects, makes them the real government. Does liberal democracy then imply government by judges?[19]

The emergence of constitutional control and control of the legality of administrative actions

This is why there has long been some ambivalence, in liberal countries, about the extent to which courts should have the right to question the constitutionality of laws. Constitutional control and, more generally, the control of legality grew out of two practical situations rather than out of general principles. The first is the principle of arbitration. Where two or more authorities are in a position to demand the citizen's obedience, there has to be a body which decides which of the authorities is to be obeyed. This problem arises particularly in federal states, since there are in these systems two types of authorities which are deemed to be equal in status. Supreme courts have therefore been set up to adjudicate disputes between these authorities, as was seen in Chapter 16.[20] In particular, the American Supreme Court was created for this purpose; nothing in the Constitution itself suggests that the supreme court is more than an arbiter between the component states and the Federal government.[21] Yet this power of arbitration opens the way towards full constitutional control, since it has naturally the effect of prohibiting one level of authority from acting in some sectors in the name of the constitution. As a federal constitution distinguishes between fields of regional competence and fields of national competence, supreme court intervention in disputes between states and federal government leads naturally, if not automatically, to full constitutional control.

Second, the question of the legality of bureaucratic activities grew out of the need to redress errors of judgement made by individual administrators. This began simply as an extension of efficient government. It cannot be assumed that all the agents of the state act lawfully; there should therefore be some checking mechanism. Gradually, this type of control developed. It first covered procedures; next it considered the manner in which administrators had acted; eventually it looked at the legality of the rules passed by governmental agencies. At that point it became, in some countries at least, a general control in the name of legality. Constitutional control thus grew mainly in federal countries and in particular in the United States, while in other liberal countries, especially in those in which the state bureaucracy was relatively developed, such as France, the control of legality took form and expanded. A similar type of control has come to be adopted in many other countries.[22]

Constitutional control and the control of legality in practice

The American Supreme Court's battle with Roosevelt in the 1930s was the most dramatic example of the behavioural limits to which a court, even one endowed with great authority, can go without impunity. After the Court deemed part of the New Deal legislation to be unconstitutional, as was seen in Chapter 16, President Roosevelt threatened to ask Congress to pass a law which might have altered the composition of the Court through the appointment of new judges. This showed the limits of the extent to which the Court could be regarded as independent. In part for this reason, the Court desisted somewhat from its desire to quash federal legislation and began to follow another principle, known as 'legal positivism', according to which the Congress is given the benefit of the doubt, so to speak. The Court has concentrated its action on disputes between state and federation – directly or indirectly, as over matters of racial integration, or the drafting of electoral boundaries – and not on disputes between the federal government and an idealised version of the constitution.[23] This has not prevented the Court from being an object of controversy, however, as its judgements have often appeared to many conservatives to be too liberal, for instance on racial matters or on abortion.

This function of arbitration between states and regional bodies can extend beyond federal states, at least where regional bodies are given special status in the constitution. This is why it is in the logic of separation of powers systems to include a Supreme Court, even when countries are not federal, as happens in Latin America. It is equally in the logic of the Italian Republic to provide an arbitrating mechanism between the central authority and the regional bodies which were created gradually by the Italian government after World War II. In a parallel manner, it is in the logic of the French Fifth Republic to give a Constitutional Council powers of arbitration between government and parliament, since the President of the Republic is held to be, since 1958, as much an embodiment of the popular will as is the parliament. On the contrary, where the system of government is based on one line of authority stemming directly from the people, there has been considerable reluctance to set up a supreme court or a constitutional council: thus in Britain, the Netherlands, and the Scandinavian countries, the traditional view continues to be upheld, according to which parliament is sovereign and courts cannot question its decisions.[24]

The development of the control of legality has taken place in a less dramatic manner than the evolution of constitutional control, but the move has been similar. The French Council of State, for instance, was gradually given the right to examine the legality of regulations (and, in particular, of government decrees); this led to a marked increase in the scope of the intervention of what became known as administrative courts. However, the Council of State has been wary of too much intervention at the level of central government and has tended to concentrate its scrutiny on local bodies, perhaps because these bodies are, indeed, often guilty of breaches of the law, but perhaps also because major clashes with the top rule-making bodies needed to be avoided. It is helped in practice in this tendency by the requirement that plaintiffs must raise their objections against a decision within two months of that decision being taken. Overall, the Council of State appears concerned not to go too often, or too directly, against governmental action, any more than the United States Supreme Court wishes any longer to go too often, if at all, against federal rule-making.[25]

This is not to suggest that there is no difference in the 'depth' of intervention between courts which question the constitutional character of laws or the legal character of governmental regulations and courts which merely satisfy themselves that the correct procedures have been followed. The difference exists and it is often noted, for instance, that British courts, which adopt a restrictive view of their role, have tended to give less protection to the citizen. The point is made particularly in connection with civil liberties: this is indeed why it has been suggested frequently in Britain that there should be a Bill of Rights protected by a written constitution.[26] However, the difference is not always nor any longer as large as it once was.

At the time when some of the older constitutional courts were becoming somewhat less determined to restrict governmental powers, some newer courts, such as the French Constitutional Council, became more anxious to scrutinise executive and legislative action. At the time when some of the older administrative courts were becoming somewhat wary of undermining too openly governmental decisions, many courts which had been more restrictive in the field of administration, such as British courts, took it upon themselves to look a little more closely into the legality of administrative decisions. Indeed the matter may to an extent be by-passed as a result of the increased importance of the European Court of Justice, not just in matters concerned directly with European integration, but also in relation to human rights in general. This means that an equilibrium might be found leading to a middle position. It is being realised that courts cannot extend their role too far in the governmental process without challenging the rule-making process of executives and assemblies. This they did not wish to do, or could not do, or both; but they have helped to develop principles of arbitration between the organs of state and probably created greater respect for legality, particularly at the regional and local levels and in the bureaucracy. In the process, these ideas have extended to a large number of countries in which neither constitutional control nor the judicial control of administration had existed in the past.

The scope of rule-adjudication, the control of administrative action and the redress of grievances

While traditional liberal theory dealt with the independence of courts and paid some attention to the depth of judicial control, it made practically no effort to extend the scope of rule-adjudication. This is partly due to the fact that the liberal theory of the judiciary emerged before bureaucracies grew rapidly towards the end of the nineteenth century. However, the problem of extending the scope of rule-adjudication to all the fields of government existed before the growth of bureaucracies; yet traditional liberal theory did not seriously consider it. Naturally enough, solutions emerged gradually and often haphazardly; the institutions which were set up varied according to different countries' traditions and, more often than not, tended to take the form of councils, committees of inquiry, or tribunals, and, more recently, of ombudsmen's offices, rather than of formal courts.

The increase in the scope of rule-adjudication relating to administration has taken place along two dimensions. One dimension relates to the procedures and determines whether the bodies in charge of scrutinising the administration have (or are close to having) a judicial character. Procedures may take the following forms:

(I) At first, citizens are allowed to register complaints to an administrative authority about a decision.[27]

(II) A second type of procedure consists of allowing an enquiry on a specific case, where the committee of enquiry can only make a report and the political authority decides.

(III) Third, a general procedure is set up for future enquiries, though the administration retains the ultimate power.

(IV) Only with the fourth type of procedure, when a committee, tribunal, or court can reverse the decision, is a judicial body really set up.

The second dimension of rule-adjudication in administrative matters concerns the fields in which these scrutinising bodies can make investigations. Complaints and special inquiries naturally relate to specific matters only; a general procedure of inquiry relates to a whole branch of the administration. Administrative councils and tribunals cover the whole public sector, although, in all polities, some questions still remain unchallengeable, for instance questions relating to national security or foreign affairs, in part because it is assumed at least in liberal polities that the government is responsible politically for such matters.[28] The scope of administrative rule-adjudication thus tends to extend to the following areas:

(A) Matters relating to personnel, both in relation to conditions of service and to dismissals.
(B) The acquisition of property by public authorities (for instance compulsory purchase orders) and the control of procedures relating to the personal freedom of individuals being dealt with by criminal and not by administrative justice.
(C) Collective services, particularly at the local level.
(D) The widest form of scrutiny relates to all other state activities, but this is almost never achieved, though, in liberal countries, some development of judicial scrutiny over security matters has begun to take place, for instance in relation to the deportation of aliens or the granting of passports.[29]

Countries of the contemporary world can be ranked in relation to the extent to which the scope of activities of the bureaucracy is covered by means of the types of procedure listed above. For liberal countries, most of the activities coming under (A) and (B) are covered by procedures of at least type (III); only a limited number of countries include activities of type (C) within the ambit of courts of type (III); and only a small number of countries, mainly in Continental Europe, and in particular those which have followed the procedure which gradually evolved in France, developed a court of type (IV) to cover activities whose scope ranges from (A) to (C) and exceptionally comes under (D) (see Figure 22.1).

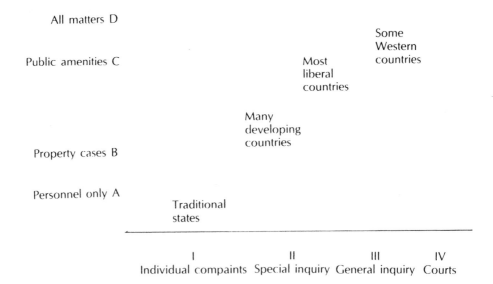

Figure 22.1 Scope of scrutiny of public administration

The gradual development of tribunals and courts dealing with administrative matters was slow, not merely because bureaucracies resisted the formalisation of the processes by which administrative problems were scrutinised or because there was no liberal blueprint of the scrutiny of the administration, but also because of the nature of the problems. The control of administration by courts faces the same difficulties as the control of administration by administrators: the further the controlling agency is from the body to be controlled, the more independent it remains but the less it is able to understand fully the conduct of the administration.[30] To be effective, enquiries aiming at redressing grievances have therefore to take place near the administrative agencies which took the decision. Hence, first, the value of committees of enquiry composed of persons engaged in similar activities and, consequently, the tendency for such committees to be created either *ad hoc* or within the administrative body; and second, a general tendency to staff committees with persons previously engaged in 'active' administration who have a thorough knowledge of administrative processes. The principle of structural differentiation which is at the root of rule-adjudication is therefore in part dysfunctional to the redress of administrative grievances.

Such a conclusion goes against the principles of the liberal doctrine, as it seems paradoxical to suggest that redress can be better achieved by setting up institutions which are closer to the administration. As a matter of fact, the point came to be valid only because the rapid increase in the growth of the bureaucracy was combined with an equally rapid spread in literacy and in living standards generally. Both conditions have to be met if there is to be at the same time a sizeable distance between controllers and controlled and a relatively large pool of aggrieved citizens who are also educated. Where the educated population is small, there is little demand for 'anonymous' procedures of rule-adjudication; the redress of grievances takes place on an informal basis, while the less educated part of the population lacks the contacts, resources, and skills to fight for the establishment of 'quasi-judicial' procedures in matters of administration. France was exceptional in having developed, almost by accident, a general administrative court in the nineteenth century; however, for a long period, that body did not function truly as a court and the redress of grievances was done on a more haphazard basis. Only gradually did the court expand its role and become the apex of a large network both of territorial administrative bodies which parallels 'ordinary' civil and criminal courts and of specialised tribunals dealing with particular sectors of administration.[31]

A similar move towards a greater scrutiny of administration occurred in most Western democracies, but the scope of the control of administrative decisions was extended, not necessarily by setting up general administrative courts on the French model, though this did take place in some Continental countries, but by other means, one of the most prominent being the establishment of ombudsmen's offices on the Scandinavian model.[32] Ombudsmen are not judges; they are in the nature of 'tribunes' of the people. Citizens communicate their grievances to them (though in Britain citizens have to go through their MP to be heard by the ombudsman). The ombudsman then investigates the case on behalf of the plaintiff and has access to the files and to the civil servants concerned. The action of the ombudsman is wholly informal. Thus where these decisions are authoritative, in fact, if not necessarily formally, they provide a simple, cheap and comprehensive means of redressing most types of grievances against the administration.

The increased scope of rule-adjudication is connected to the growth of the bureaucracy. Below a critical level, demands for control of administrative practices are too weak to be met, except in terms of a graceful 'petition' to the author of the decision who is asked to reconsider it. Because new countries emerged in the 1950s and 1960s with a larger bureaucracy than Western European countries had at a similar state of development, and because they could imitate models of administrative courts which appeared to be associated with modern forms of development, many of these polities created councils or tribunals on the European pattern. This situation resembles to an extent that of France in the early nineteenth century, where such a control was in a sense 'over-developed' in relation to the administrative system.

Overall, however, despite the fact that liberal theory did not directly consider the question of the control of administration, it played an indirect part in the process. The size of the bureaucracy and the level of education among the aggrieved population are the major variables, but liberalism provided a spur; it also provided a framework within which the judicial control of the administration could develop. Ultimately, although liberalism did not directly lead to the development of particular institutional arrangements, it is probably because the state is ostensibly liberal that the scope of rule-adjudication has been able to expand to such an extent in many countries of the contemporary world.

Conclusion

The extension of rule-adjudication to new fields is related to the increased scope of the bureaucracy in modern societies. The role of judges in the political system is therefore more extensive than in the past, even in authoritarian societies; citizens can thus be protected to an extent as the actions of the administration are double-checked. Constitutional theory went further and in a different direction, however; it attempted to introduce judicial control at all levels and to move towards universal constitutional control, but experience shows that rule-adjudication is too specialised, probably too slow, and not always sensitive enough to public opinion to be used so deeply. It is better and more practical that constitutional control should be exercised somewhat sparingly; it is unrealistic (and it was unrealistic in the past) to expect courts, whatever advantages may be gained in terms of guarantees given against the executive and even the legislature, to be substitutes for what the other institutions of the political system are set up to achieve. Courts must therefore continue to operate at the edges of rule-making and of rule-application: only in this way can a system of rule-adjudication be truly efficient and be effectively maintained.

Notes

1. 'Rule-adjudication' was the expression used by G.A. Almond. See Chapter 2.
2. See Chapter 20.
3. The separation of powers system entails a strict separation between the judiciary and the other two powers. This separation naturally refers essentially to the appointment mechanisms in the case of the judiciary, since judges have to deal with decisions of the executive or of the legislative. As we noted in Chapter 16, such a separation cannot be fully implemented, even in the context of appointments. In the parliamentary system, the 'separation' is far from complete. It is based on arrangements which give some autonomy to judges, but it is not a strict separation of powers.
4. Celebrated cases of tampering with the judiciary have taken place in a number of countries, for instance in Ghana and Nigeria. Covert pressure is more frequent, but remains undocumented.
5. See the discussion later in this chapter of the role of administrative courts and tribunals.
6. There are strong political considerations in the appointment of United States Supreme Court justices, though the result is often not the expected one. A number of justices appointed by conservative presidents have turned out to be liberal on many issues.
7. Britain is rather exceptional in appointing judges at superior courts from among barristers.
8. Even before 1989, there were marked differences among Communist states in this respect, as there were in other respects. There have also been cases of of strong judicial independence in Third World countries, particularly in the Commonwealth (for instance in India when Mrs Gandhi declared a state of emergency in the 1970s and attempted to assume full powers).
9. The paradox of the Council of State is that, despite – some might say because of – the absence of legal guarantees, members of this body succeeded in being gradually listened to and then 'obeyed' in the same way as the members of an ordinary court.
10. Attacks were made first against administrative courts (for instance by Dicey in Britain before 1914) and later against committees and enquiries (for instance by Lord Hewart in *The New Despotism*, 1929): these attacks proved erroneous. This is not because governments did not increase their powers, but because the protection given by administrative courts and tribunals proved satisfactory and even in many cases greater than the protection which ordinary courts could have given in the administrative field.
11. See, for Britain, J.A.G. Griffith, *The Politics of the Judiciary* (1985), pp. 25–31.
12. Examples of cases against the left can be found in J.A.G. Griffith, *op. cit.*, pp. 207–22. There have also been cases against conservative governments, though these are perhaps less celebrated.
13. The relatively conservative character of the judiciary can also be seen from results of elections to 'councils of the Judiciary' which exist in some countries (France, Italy). One should note, however, that, especially since the 1970s, groups of more 'progressive' judges have been constituted and indeed have put up candidates at elections to these councils.
14. The conception of the law traditionally put forward by Soviet analysts excluded the possibility of acceptance of what were regarded as 'bourgeois' rights of dissent (or, more precisely, stated that such rights did not need to exist, given the fact that Communist states represented the embodiment of working-class ideals). Views have markedly changed, at least in some Communist countries. See S. White, J. Gardner and G. Schopflin, *Communist Political Systems* (1982), pp. 222–62.
15. Yet there are cases of resistance by judges. In Latin America in particular, traditions of a liberal judiciary are strong; they are of course more pronounced when civilian governments are in power.

16. There is a minimum independence in the sense that most cases of private or commercial law must be decided in an independent manner if there is to be an administration of justice at all.

17. This is true whether there is 'case-law' or not. Case-law means technically that the courts are bound by precedents; where there is no case-law, courts are not legally, but behaviourally bound by precedents: this development has taken place all over Continental Europe, for instance, despite the absence of case-law.

18. See Chapter 15.

19. There was considerable worry at the time of the Roosevelt–Supreme Court controversy that there might be a 'government of judges', indeed a government by 'nine old men' (the number of justices on the Supreme Court), instead of a government by Congress and the President. These worries proved unfounded and have ceased to be voiced.

20. See Chapter 16.

21. The Supreme Court started to quash legislation in 1803, but it did not do so again until 1857. Only from the end of the nineteenth century was this 'customary' amendment to the American Constitution fully recognised by all, and by Supreme Court Justices in particular.

22. The French Council of State originally had a power of advice as well as, in parallel, that of listening to grievances against the administration. From this latter power the judicial functions of the council gradually grew; this was formally recognised by law in 1872.

23. The celebrated case *Brown* versus *Board of Education* (1954), which outlawed racial segregration in schools, is an example of such an action, in this particular case against a local authority.

24. There has been an increase in the number of constitutional courts and councils in the course of the second half of the twentieth century. Both the Italian and French Constitutional Councils, in particular the latter, have become influential. Specifically, while it was first conceived as a means of ensuring that the legislature did not overstep its powers (and, in this context, was not even an arbitrating body at the time), the French Constitutional Council became increasingly bold and began to scrutinise legislation from the point of view of its constitutional validity. It must be noted that the expression 'supreme court' is ambiguous: it is sometimes used simply to refer to the highest court in the land. In the present context, supreme court is meant to refer to those bodies which have powers to decide on the constitutional character of laws and other texts.

25. 'Decrees' can either be general and amount to rule-making on the basis of a legal text authorising the government to decide or specific and relate to individual cases (the equivalent of a British Order). The French Council of State is legally entitled to quash decrees, however general: in fact, it tends mainly to quash specific decrees or documents issued by local authority agencies.

26. It is suggested that British courts give perhaps less protection precisely because these courts are not fully accustomed to dealing with administrative matters. The situation may be changing somewhat. See J.A.G. Griffith, *op. cit.*, *passim*. Moreover, British citizens are also increasingly using the European Court of Justice to obtain redress.

27. The case is allowed, but only by 'gracious pleasure' of the government.

28. There is a running debate over what should be deemed to be political issues and what should be deemed to be judicial issues. One can argue that the government is responsible to parliament for its decisions (for instance on questions of compulsory purchase) and that courts cannot enter increasingly into such fields without effectively reducing the power of parliament. The problem is general; the power of parliament is necessarily reduced as rights given to citizens are increased and courts have to ensure that these rights are respected.

29. It is still not the case, however, even in Western countries, that governments have lost all discretion in such matters.

30. See Chapter 20.
31. The evolution of the Council of State was truly 'natural'. However, imitation led to the creation of administrative courts on this model in many countries, particularly on the Continent of Europe and in French-speaking Africa. These have not all had the same prestige *vis-à-vis* the administration as their French counterpart.
32. Ombudsmen originated in Sweden and Finland: these officers were charged with the duty of ensuring that grievances of citizens were examined in a wholly informal manner. The institution was given prominence in the 1950s and began to be imitated in Western Europe and later throughout the world. See D.C. Rowat, *The Ombudsman* (1968); G.E. Caiden (ed.), *The Ombudsman: An international handbook* (1983).

23 Government and people in contemporary politics

One of the most important questions of political life – perhaps the most important of all – is that of the nature, extent, and strength of the relationship between people and government, between the rulers and the ruled. Comparative government analysis is devoted to discovering the many ways in which this relationship takes place, while, by and large, works on political theory are devoted to the examination of the manner in which it *should* be established. The institutions and the processes which have been described in the previous chapters can thus be regarded as efforts at providing a solution to the question of the link between people and government.

This is true even for authoritarian systems although, in this case, much of the effort of the government consists in setting up bodies and establishing practices which attempt to prevent the people from being able to exercise direct influence; there is a relationship between the rulers and the ruled, but the rulers monopolise the public communication process and thereby endeavour to press upon the citizens the value of their policies and of their overall goals. Thus the flow of influence goes primarily and in extreme cases exclusively downward. Conversely, a 'perfect' democratic relationship would promote upward communication and, at the extreme, exclude any downward communication. This is so unrealistic a scenario that it need not be discussed further; indeed, while there is scope for increasing the flow of upward communication and influence everywhere, it is surely valuable, even in a democracy, for leaders to be able to propose programmes and policies to the people. Thus, except in the most extreme authoritarian systems where all or nearly all communication takes place in a downward direction, the relationship between the rulers and the ruled consists of a mix of downward and upward influences, with liberal–democratic systems including a greater proportion of upward influences, while downward influences prevail in authoritarian and imposed systems.

Whether it is upward or downward, however, the relationship between the rulers and the ruled has another universal characteristic, that of taking place on the whole indirectly, by means of institutions and of procedures; political systems need structures to perform the various operations (or 'functions') of articulation, of

340

aggregation, of rule-making and of rule-application, as was shown earlier.[1] The people are connected to the rulers – and the rulers to the people – through the structures analysed in this volume, namely groups, parties, governments and bureaucracies. As a result, all political systems have a 'representative' character, representative not in the technical constitutional sense that there are necessarily legislative assemblies which embody the sovereignty of the people, but in the more general political sense that the views and proposals of the population are communicated to the government and vice versa through intermediate bodies.

Not all relationships are indirect, however; three types of direct links can and do exist. First, in some countries and indeed to an increasing extent, at least in the West, there are mechanisms by which the people can express their views directly and make their influence felt on specific issues. Admittedly, referendums and other techniques of 'direct' or 'semi-direct' democracy are often regarded as rather unsuccessful and as likely to be manipulated by leaders; but these techniques exist, they are sometimes used, and they are not always manipulated.[2]

A second means of direct communication is provided sometimes by the parties themselves. If a party is large, if it is close to the aspirations of at least a majority of the population, and if the government is an emanation of that party, the relationship between government and people can be regarded as direct. This occurs for instance when a party is given a 'mandate' by the electorate to implement its programme – the election is then almost in the nature of a referendum in favour of the party. The parallel cannot be pushed too far, since the reasons why people vote for parties are complex and are in particular associated with general images rather than with specific issue-orientations, but whatever the motivations of electors, the relationship remains direct.[3] Indeed, more than with a referendum, that relationship has a broad base and can thus serve to sustain a general policy. A similar conclusion can be drawn in the case of some single-party systems, though the influence tends to go downwards. In such cases, leaders claim generally that the party's positions have to be supported because the party, by its very nature, constitutes the embodiment of the nation's future, a standpoint often taken by Communist rulers, at least until the late 1980s. Thus an institution which in principle mediates between people and government is elevated to become the means by which a direct relationship is established between the rulers and the ruled because the party is – or states that it is – the nation itself.[4]

In the third place, at the broadest possible level, albeit in a necessarily vague and diffuse manner, direct links also result from the general support which the people display for the political system. Such a support is often embodied in a feeling of popular allegiance for the leader, who, in turn, usually tries to benefit directly from the support. Yet the confusion between the support given to the rulers and the support given to the system has some virtue as, if leaders are popular, the support which they enjoy can be transferred to the political system and thereby contribute to the stability of that system. This has occurred in a number of newly independent countries since World War II, as was seen earlier.[5]

There are therefore three levels at which direct links exist between people and government. These direct links are more or less strong. They appear to an extent to be in competition with the many 'representative' ties which are built, for these ties are based on specific interests and issues and not on global support; thus the 'representative' links can undermine direct relationships between people and government. This can constitute a danger, as direct relationships provide the necessary framework within which groups and other institutions can develop and be able to press efficiently for the policies which they favour. It is therefore necessary to look at the ways in which both indirect and direct types of relationships between people and government can combine rather than oppose each other.

Institutions and the indirect relations between people and government

In the contemporary world, in many countries at least, the relationship between people and government takes place through specialised organisations. The number of these institutions has increased markedly, since one of the characteristics of socio-economic development is structural differentiation;[6] Western societies have thousands of associations dealing with specific issues and they continue to multiply. Meanwhile, the number of groups is increasing in Communist states, even in those which remain strongly authoritarian, as the leaders of these polities need to maintain their hold on the population by setting up bodies which are dependent on the party;[7] it is also increasing in the developing world in a context in which all-embracing communal groups are declining in strength. Even if the emergence of more diffuse and broader social movements, such as ecological, pacifist or feminist movements, occasionally gives rise to the impression, especially in the West, that 'narrow' interest groups are on the decline, the need to act at a variety of levels and in a number of sectors remains as strong as in the past. Bodies dealing with specific issues and interests are manifestly not in decline;[8] as a result, the web of these 'intermediate' bodies is increasingly large and complex. Not only governments and parliamentarians, but also parties and bureaucracies are 'advised' by groups and by their leaders; indeed, the larger groups are in turn 'advised' by smaller groups. For instance, trade unions and employers' associations are markedly under the pressure of specialised bodies. It therefore becomes difficult for the larger organisations and for the parties to develop policies independently. This is particularly true in the United States where parties have in large part abandoned their function of policy initiation to lobbies. It is also true even in countries where 'peak' organisations dominated the scene in the 1960s and 1970s, such as West Germany and Austria; groups with a narrow range of interests began to make their voice strongly heard from the late 1970s onwards. Furthermore, this trend is becoming universal. It began to occur in Eastern European countries even before Communist parties collapsed at the end of 1989; thus ecological groups had emerged in a number of these states in the early or mid-1980s. A similar movement is also taking place in the developing world, with variations of degree, admittedly, but it is evident to a marked extent in many countries.[9]

These changes can be regarded as signs that participation is on the increase and that the relationship between the rulers and the ruled is now developing in favour of the latter and against governmental decisions being dictated to the population from above. Indeed, the effect is not only to increase representation in general, but also to enlarge its scope by making it more probable that the views of the members of the public will be considered in some detail. Such a development tends to alter profoundly the traditional conception of representative government. This was based on the principle that the people were to exercise very broad choices only; indeed, the most extreme version of this theory entailed that parliamentarians should remain entirely unconstrained by their constituents, subject only to the condition that they might be defeated at the next election.[10] The idea became obsolete at the level of each representative with the development of parties, but these in turn have become constrained by the part played by groups. Thus the legal theory of representation has been superseded by one in which the official 'representatives' become spokesmen of groups or arbiters among groups.[11] As this model prevails in Atlantic countries and has only begun to be valid in other parts of the world, it seems that the West is characterised by *real* representation and that citizens of other polities only become truly represented as and when developments take place which are similar to those of the West.

Yet this interpretation of the role of groups can be regarded as over-optimistic. Decision-making in these bodies is often in the hands of tiny minorities. While oligarchical domination was regarded in the past as a widespread phenomenon, in parties for instance, this problem may ease as groups become smaller and more specialised. Yet it is still the case that the broad mass of the public is not involved in an active fashion in most organisations or that people are, at best, involved in an intermittent manner.[12] One can perhaps expect both participation and responsiveness to increase within the groups, precisely for the reason which led to the emergence of more specialised bodies, namely because of the dissatisfaction which resulted from the limited extent to which the larger bodies, as well as parties, take into account the desires of the public.[13] The process could thus be viewed as slow but real and as extending gradually beyond the Atlantic world to the rest of the globe. One might therefore expect, in perhaps two or three generations, substantially higher levels of participation, possibly triggered by the emergence of even smaller and more specialised groups.[14]

Such a scenario would therefore suggest a vast increase in the number of organisations, but it would also result in an atomisation of society. The corollary would be that the political system would have difficulty in functioning efficiently as too many demands would be made, in the same way as a pure technocracy finds it difficult to function because its elements are too sectional.[15] The society might be choked, so to speak; little 'aggregation' of demands 'articulated' by these organisations would take place, as there would be more groups whose views had to be reconciled and fewer bodies enjoying a sufficiently broad support to be able to undertake or promote this 'reconciliation'.

Moreover, the multiplication of associational bodies may not merely have the effect of increasing the capacity of members of the public to submit their views in a much larger variety of fields than was previously the case. It may also erode the support for the larger and more aggregative groups as the smaller organisations make their claims for the allegiance of members of the public. Although we do not know precisely how citizens distribute their support among the many organisations which make claims on them, the multiplication of groups tends to create conflicts of allegiance from which the broader groups – and the parties – will suffer somewhat.[16] The increase in the number of groups is thus one of the reasons which account for the decline in the allegiance of citizens of Western countries to parties, and in particular to the older, broad-based parties. The growth in the number of 'independent' voters in the United States in the second half of the twentieth century is one of the clearest examples of a movement which, in various ways, is affecting other liberal democracies, both with respect to parties and with respect to broad-based organisations such as trade unions and 'peak' employers' associations.[17]

If the development of representation by small groups is combined with the decline of support for parties and large groups, the problem of representation is not truly solved. On the contrary, the long-term trend might be towards an 'ungovernable' society because of the weakness of its centre and the large number of attacks made from its periphery. Ungovernability has become the subject of substantial concern, in particular since the 1970s, as was noted in Chapter 18,[18] but it becomes all the more probable as the lack of strong popular support for the centre is added to the technical difficulties of modern administration, these difficulties contributing in turn to erode even more the support which parties and larger groups enjoy among the population. Since these larger organisations appear somewhat ineffective and seem unable to listen to the detailed demands made by the population, it is not surprising that there should be concern with respect to a situation in which representation becomes increasingly specific. The question of whether direct relationships between people and government can continue to provide a strong link and can to an extent counterbalance the tendency for society to be 'atomised' as a result of the development of specialised groups needs to be examined.

Direct support for regimes and the role of leaders

The view that myriads of small groups undermine the support for the political system as a whole may be one-sided. Where these groups are most numerous, that is to say in Western liberal democracies, support for the regime seems as widespread as in the past. The norms of the political system are broadly shared both by the public at large and by the majority of the political elite. Indeed, the support enjoyed by groups takes place within the broader context of the values of the political system; these are regarded as superior to or more fundamental than the specific goals of particular groups.[19]

The precise effect of this support is difficult to assess, as the role of legitimacy in political life is not as yet measurable.[20] Yet one point is clear: while support for the regime is likely to be affected by the multiplication of groups, it is also likely to affect the level of following of these groups. Anti-system groups are likely to find it difficult to obtain a large clientele in regimes which enjoy strong support. Fascist and Nazi parties grew in Italy and Germany at a time when the regimes of these countries had limited legitimacy; conversely, anti-system parties have been either weak or contained after World War II in those and in other Western European countries, as the legitimacy of the regime was high.[21] Similarly, terrorist groups have had a limited following in Italy and Germany in the 1970s. Conversely, in those countries or regions in which support for the regime has been relatively low, for instance on nationalistic grounds, as in Northern Ireland or in the Basque country, terrorist organisations have survived much longer, as they have in some Latin American countries and in particular in Peru.[22]

Groups do not operate in a vacuum; on the contrary, the detailed demands of these organisations take place in the context of national values which, if broadly and deeply held, markedly constrain the ability of these bodies to press for their demands. This is indeed why Western liberal democracies have functioned effectively, by and large, despite the substantial development of groups whose claims were often contradictory, while, in Communist states and in the Third World, where support for the political system, the nation, or both is usually lower, groups created by the regime have not proved very effective. Thus the direct link between people and political system remains fundamental, even when groups multiply and the society is moving towards associationalism.

The lack of strong support for the regime may be due to considerable imposition on the part of the government; but it may also be due – and is often due in new countries – to a low level of support for the very idea of the nation. Where nation-building is not fully achieved, the political system depends markedly, if not wholly, on the support which broad communal groups are prepared to 'transfer' to the central government.[23] In these polities, support goes primarily to tribal or ethnic groups. Governmental authorities are obeyed only to the extent that their rules are acceptable to the leaders of the regional sub-units; they often attempt to counteract this by imposing some of their policies, but these authoritarian measures may not have the desired effect and risk, on the contrary, increasing 'separatist' tendencies rather than nation-building.

To be able to move out of the difficulty and achieve a 'nationalisation' of political life, the main solution has for centuries been to rely on the emergence of a popular leader. It is indeed naturally easier for populations to support an individual than to uphold sets of abstract values; at least it is easier for populations to support values if these are embodied in the person of a leader. This occurred with monarchs in the past, but, in the past too, generals and other types of usurpers have frequently received from the people strong demonstrations of support, even against apparently well-established monarchs. In the conditions which emerged after World War II, the role of leaders naturally became large: as new nations were set up on an unprecedented scale and as new values were imposed on some of the older nations, in particular through Communism, only strong leaders could hope to begin to 'nationalise' the sentiments of populations against traditional groups, tribal or ethnic, or against traditional values hitherto widely held.[24]

Indeed, the role of personalities has been marked in Western countries as well, perhaps even more than in the past. Many Western leaders have helped to strengthen the cause of their party; occasionally they went beyond party and adopted a national posture, for instance when the political system was reconstructed, as in West Germany in 1949 with Adenauer or in France in 1958 with De Gaulle. Leadership is thus a universal instrument by which links between people and government continue to be direct and are even more direct than they were in the past in many parts of the world.

Political parties as a means of providing direct links between people and government

Political parties appear to provide an indirect channel of communication, either because the people are able to express some of their views, albeit in a somewhat distorted or simplified manner, through the electoral process or because the leaders can use the parties – and especially the medium of the single party – to press their policies on the population. But large parties which are closely tied to the government can also provide a direct link between the rulers and the ruled.

This is true at one extreme with parties which aim at mobilising the people in the name of an overall goal; it is true at the other extreme with competitive parties which succeed in obtaining a mandate from the majority of the people for the policies which they propose to implement. Neither situation occurs frequently in its purest form, but they both exist sufficiently often in an embryonic manner to warrant being examined; more importantly perhaps, the absence of such direct links between parties and people seem to result in difficulties for the political system.

A party system can be described as having a direct mobilising effect if it enlists the active support of a very large proportion of the population. Many citizens may not be clear about the party's goals or about the ways in which these goals can be achieved; but, if large numbers of them believe that party action will improve society, the result is a close relationship not just between people and party but between people and government. This rarely occurs; a high degree of congruence has to exist between the party leaders and the population, such as may develop for instance at the time of the birth of a nation.

Indeed, this occurrence is particularly rare because it tends to require both strong personal leadership and the development of deep party roots. While personalised leadership was found to exist frequently in the developing world at the time of independence, the parties which these leaders have created and supported rarely had sufficient tentacles in the nation. Only in some countries, principally in the Commonwealth, has this model been approximated in practice, especially when the struggle for independence has been protracted and the national party has been given time to build its strength. The Congress Party of India and the Tanzanian African National Union are perhaps the closest examples of organisations which did mobilise large proportions of the population of their respective countries and were thus able to provide an almost direct link between people and government; yet the strength of these parties declined over time and their mobilising characteristics consequently declined.

Admittedly, many parties claim to be mobilising and to enjoy vast support among the population. This is particularly the case of Communist parties in Communist states; it is also the case with a number of single-party systems in developing countries, principally in Black Africa and in parts of Asia. Yet the hold of these parties over the population is usually more apparent than real; these organisations have consequently been primarily instruments by which downward pressure is exercised by the leaders over the people. In the process, the extent of true direct influence is reduced, first because, as we saw, these parties create dependent associations, such as trade unions, women's groups and youth organisations, in order to have a greater hold over the people and, second, because the lack of real support results in the population being affected by the party only in a minor way. Even the well-developed Communist parties do not appear to have had a profound effect on 'mentalities': the single parties set up in numerous African countries are usually so limited in extensiveness that they are likely to touch only a limited part of the (essentially rural) population.

There is another way in which the link between party and people can be direct, however, namely through competitive parties which succeed in giving the electoral contests a sufficiently tight programmatic character to approximate, in effect, a type of referendum. In this form of 'competitive mobilisation', the people are deemed to give the winning party a 'mandate' to put forward a set of policies. The notion of the mandate has been widely referred to in some countries, particularly in Britain, where the conditions of the political battles among the parties tend normally to simplify the choices which electors have to face.[25]

Competitive mobilisation can occur in this manner, but it occurs rarely, as the 'theory of the mandate' is predicated on four assumptions, none of which is validated in full. The first is that parties are disciplined, a situation which occurs in most Western systems of more than one party, but not in all; it does not even occur in all two-party systems – in the United States, party discipline in Congress is comparatively low. Second, voting has to be related to programmes, either on the basis of choices on major issues or through the ranking of issues. Yet voting studies show that legitimate mass parties are directly related to the electorate at large, as was seen in Chapter 9, but that this relationship often refers to images, rather than to issues.[26]

Third, the mandate theory assumes a party battle which is clear-cut. Yet, as was seen in Chapter 12, a large number of party systems are of a two-and-a-half or multi-dominant type and are profoundly unbalanced. Atlantic two-party systems are the most balanced: outside Western democracies, even two-party systems are often unbalanced.[27] When there are more than two parties or when one of the parties is at a permanent disadvantage (and this is reinforced when the situation is perceived in this way), the scope for 'competitive mobilisation' is markedly impaired. Typically, coalitions tend to take place and the 'will of the people' is mediated by the parliamentary leaders. Out of seventy-three countries with a system of more than one party, thirty-two have a party system in which there is only limited opportunity for alternation; greater opportunity does exist in forty-one countries or about a quarter of the polities of the world – and slightly more than half of those in which there is competition.

Finally, and most importantly, the mandate requires a clear-cut competition between party programmes. Yet the constraints of the systems of more than one party often lead to 'reconciliation' rather than to 'mobilisation'. There are times when clear divisions occur; but there are more occasions when this does not take place. The situation which has typically tended to prevail in the United States (except perhaps in the 1930s), in which the two parties do not differ markedly on broad issues while detailed policies are largely the product of interest group action, has extended to other liberal democracies. Admittedly, from time to time, as in Britain in the 1980s with the advent of Thatcherism, or in France in 1981 with the election of a Socialist government, polarisation occurs and a sharp division emerges between the parties. However, this situation is rare; it takes place in a few countries only and, even then, no more than once or twice in a generation.[28]

Thus, with competitive mobilisation being the exception, parties are more often vehicles for interest group demands than they are instruments of a direct link between people and government. Yet the potential for such a link does exist. Indeed, this potential is perhaps more important for the viability of the political system than might appear to be the case on the basis of the small number of occasions on which it occurs. Parties can become instruments of direct mobilisation if tension is high. The existence of such a reserve opportunity is crucial as it gives the people the chance, in the context of a competitive framework, to use the parties to express their desire for change and therefore to retain their overall support for the political system.

Referendums, popular initiatives, plebiscites and direct influence of the people on policies

While there may not be many cases when parties and party leaders embody directly the 'will of the people', there is an increasing number of situations in which citizens are asked to express their views on specific issues by means of referendums or popular initiatives or to support leaders through plebiscites. These forms of 'semi-direct' democracy are, in principle, constitutional techniques by which attempts are made to increase popular participation. While there was strong opposition to the introduction of these procedures in many countries on the ground that they could be manipulated, they have gained in importance and some of the criticisms proved unfounded.[29]

The methods themselves can give more or fewer opportunities for the people to participate. There is greater opportunity, for instance, with popular initiatives, by which a percentage of electors suggest that a matter be submitted to popular vote before it has been discussed in parliament than with referendums which take place after a project has been approved by the legislature; yet constitutions rarely allow for initiatives. Moreover, popular participation can be restricted in scope in that only some types of proposal (and often only constitutional amendments) are to be submitted to the people. There are, however, also cases when parliament (or local authorities) consult the people without being bound by the result.[30]

Much of the Western literature has been traditionally opposed to the introduction of techniques of semi-direct democracy; so have many practitioners of politics. Among the traditional arguments, two have been often put forward. First, it has been suggested that techniques of semi-direct democracy could easily be and had been abused by authoritarian leaders (from Napoleon to many contemporary rulers) and that referendums were turned into plebiscites. Second, it was claimed, on the basis of evidence primarily drawn from Australia and Switzerland, that referendums tended to be conservative and even essentially negative.[31]

Despite these criticisms, the referendum technique has been used increasingly in Western Europe since the 1950s, including in Britain, traditionally one of the strongest supporters of pure representative government. Only West Germany, the Netherlands, Finland, Luxemburg, and Iceland have never consulted the people directly on any issue between 1945 and 1990. The development is still on a somewhat modest scale, admittedly, as in most countries there has been only one referendum per decade and as, even in those which have had a few more, such as Italy or Denmark, there have been only two or three per decade. Only Switzerland uses the technique truly extensively and regularly; elsewhere, referendums which do not relate to constitutional amendments occur on a haphazard basis. There is a tendency for initiatives or referendums to take place over matters of personal status (divorce and abortion) in Italy, while they have occurred in Denmark on some aspects of social legislation; in Austria and Sweden, referendums have been called in order to solve controversies relating to nuclear energy.

Recent experience from Western Europe, Australia, and a number of states (primarily Western) of the United States suggest that referendums and initiatives do not have the effects which had been forecast. Referendums do not necessarily constitute plebiscites; some Third World leaders have used the procedure to boost their power, but they have used ordinary electoral processes to the same end and with the same effect. De Gaulle used the referendum against traditional politicians as well as against those who wished to maintain French presence in Algeria; he did win, but he later lost another referendum which aimed at modifying the constitution in ways which the people thought unjustified.[32] Overall, the influence of leaders does not appear to be necessarily larger in the context of referendums than in the context of elections.

Referendums do not seem to be always conservative either. Some of the policies adopted have indeed been conservative, as with Proposition 13 in California which introduced stringent financial rules in the state's budget; the Irish electorate also refused to repeal a constitutional clause forbidding the introduction of divorce laws in the Republic. However, other proposals of a conservative character have been rejected; the Italian people, for instance, refused to repeal a law which had made divorce legal in the country. Moreover, the conservatism of electors may lead them to reject proposals of a 'radical right' character as well as proposals of a progressive nature; the Swiss electorate thus opposed measures designed to restrict severely the situation of immigrants in the country.[33]

The real consequences of referendums and initiatives are different. They relate to the part played by parties and groups in the process, consequences which are complex and which are still somewhat difficult to assess adequately, as the number of referendums at the national levels has been small in Western Europe, let alone elsewhere, except in Switzerland. Referendums and initiatives have an effect on parties – an effect which the parties themselves tend to provoke, since referendums have frequently been called by parties which were divided internally on an issue on which they could not take a decision. This was the case with popular votes on European Community membership in Britain, Denmark and Norway (though not in Ireland); in reality, these did not solve the difficulties which the parties faced and in all three cases splits in the main Labour or social democratic party followed.[34] What does seem to be the case is that referendums tend to reduce somewhat the role of parties and can therefore be regarded as contributing to the decline of the weight of parties in the political system.

Meanwhile, groups appear to play a substantial part in provoking and, according to some, manipulating referendums, especially at the local and regional level, as is shown by many proposals made in various states of the United States; a similar influence can also be felt at the national level, as can be seen in Switzerland. Certain groups, often somewhat marginal to the political decision-making process, use the referendum technique as a means of bringing to the fore issues which parties may not want to raise. A similar tactic is also adopted by parties which are either small or outside the government and which therefore cannot make their voice heard. This suggests that referendums can lead to a manipulation of the electorate; it suggests also that the referendum and the initiative may not altogether help in linking the people directly to the political system.[35]

These conclusions are not entirely valid. Manipulation by groups and small parties can be effective only if the turnout is really low. Moreover, if groups identify problems (such as environmental problems) which traditional parties do not raise and if, in the process, the population manifests its interest in these issues, the result is a more open debate. A danger remains, namely that inconsistencies between results can occur and that it can become difficult to develop an overall policy for the nation. None the less, the clearest outcome is probably that well-established parties are shaken and lose some of their support. This may diminish the probability that comprehensive programmes will be put forward and debates may become more sectional, yet in practice this may be of relatively limited importance, since parties often do not have clearly defined programmes of the mobilising type. Nor is this the only effect of referendums, as there are instances of popular votes on large constitutional issues; these can help to reinforce the support for the political system, as occurred for instance in France in the early 1960s.

Conclusion

The relationship between people and government is, and indeed needs to be, both direct and indirect. Direct links are somewhat limited in scope, even in the West, as neither the 'mandate' of parties nor semi-direct democracy are substitutes for the action of interest groups, especially because, in particular in the West, but also elsewhere, specialised organisations play a part even in the context of these direct links. Meanwhile, however, the people shows its support for the political system in a general manner in many countries and that support itself circumscribes the actions of groups. To this extent, direct relationships play a major part, as can be seen by the fact that governments which rely on imposition attempt too to develop means of influencing directly the people even if they also create groups designed to foster ties of an indirect character.

There is therefore an interpenetration between the direct and the indirect forms of relationships linking people and government. This is why there is little basis for the fear that political systems will disintegrate merely because groups multiply in a society. The political system needs to develop direct links if it is to function effectively, but these direct links will disappear or become tenuous only if the system itself is weak, for instance because nation-building is insufficient or because the regime's goals are too distant from those of the people. In such cases, it is not so much that the groups undermine the system, but that the system does not really have enough internal strength. Authoritarian leaders instinctively know the nature of the problem; they therefore attempt to reinforce, by means of imposition, the direct lines of communication which link them to the people, though much of that effort may result in little success. Only by the maintenance of a high level of direct ties between the rulers and the ruled can political systems function effectively; only in this way, too, are groups able to represent the interests and values which they propose to promote.

Notes

1. This is the categorisation given by G.A. Almond. See Chapter 2.
2. Referendums were traditionally strongly attacked, especially in Britain, but also in other Western European countries, on a variety of grounds, the most legalistic ones being that a 'representative' system implied that parliament alone should be involved in law-making, while it was feared that referendums would lead to incoherent or irresponsible proposals. Views have been changing in this respect. See later in this Chapter.
3. This view was often presented, in particular in Britain, in terms of the suggestion that there was a 'mandate' giving the victorious party the right to carry out the proposals

which that party had put forward during the election campaign. Such a mandate would constitute a direct linkage between people and party and indeed between people and government. Although there is little evidence that it is behaviourally valid, the 'theory of the mandate' has remained broadly accepted in political circles. Theories of a similar type have been adopted in other liberal democratic countries, though less strongly or less continuously.

4. There is greater scepticism than in the 1960s and 1970s about the ability of parties to mobilise the population; but there is no doubt that parties can mobilise to an extent, at least if they are well-organised and well-staffed.

5. See Chapter 5, on legitimacy, and Chapter 19, on leadership.

6. It is generally assumed that structural differentiation goes with development; in a sense, the idea of structural differentiation stems in part from the idea of division of labour, which was associated with 'modernity' in much sociological analysis. G.A. Almond and G.B. Powell have indeed used structural differentiation as one of the characteristics of modernity: see *Comparative Politics* (1966) pp. 48–9 and 308ff.

7. Independent organisations had also markedly increased in strength throughout the 1980s in a number of Eastern European states, in particular in Yugoslavia, Hungary, and Poland.

8. The distinction was made in Chapter 7 between interest groups in the strict sense and social movements. The difference is probably much exaggerated as there can be a gradual slide from one type to the other.

9. The development of ecological groups has been rapid in a large number of countries. It may even be that, in the 1980s, the development of groups has been more rapid outside Western Europe than inside.

10. This is the pure conception of representation, which was for instance expressed by Burke in his *Letter to the Electors of Bristol*.

11. This situation is not new; it has existed in some countries for many decades, in particular in the United States. These developments did indeed lead to the strong criticisms which were expressed against the part played by interests in various legislatures (a view expressed for instance by Bryce).

12. Levels of participation are recognised as being low in all liberal democracies, at least if one excludes the types of participation which are of a ritualistic or ceremonial character. Apart from voting, political participation concerns only a minority and indeed often a small minority. See for instance S. Verba, N.H. Nie and Jae-on Kim, *Participation and Political Equality* (1978).

13. 'Green' parties developed in part out of the desire of their members to see participation increase. It is not certain that participation has markedly increased as a result, even within the 'Green' parties themselves.

14. If one takes the view that democratisation is recent and political participation needs to be slowly learned, it seems at least reasonable to expect some increase in participation in the course of the coming decades.

15. See Chapter 20.

16. Cross-cutting cleavages lead to a decrease in the intensity of beliefs. This is precisely why societies where many cleavages are cross-cutting are likely to be more stable and less violent; consequently, the mobilising capability of each of the groups (including parties) is likely to diminish, other things being equal.

17. See Chapter 12, on the development of 'independence' among American voters.

18. See Chapter 18.

19. The extent of support for the political system is large in the West, as surveys consistently show. See, for instance, G.A. Almond and S. Verba, *The Civic Culture Revisited* (1979).

20. See Chapter 5, on legitimacy.

21. See Chapter 12, on the relative weakness of anti-system parties in Western Europe since World War II.

22. On violence, see T.R. Gurr, *Why Men Rebel* (1970) and T.R. Gurr (ed.), *Handbook of Political Conflict* (1980).
23. See Chapter 6.
24. See Chapter 19, on the role of charismatic leaders.
25. See note 3 on the part played by the 'theory of the mandate' in Britain.
26. See Chapter 9.
27. See Chapter 12.
28. See A. Downs, *An Economic Theory of Democracy* (1957), *passim*. See also Chapter 12.
29. The literature on referendums is still not comprehensive. See D.E. Butler (ed.), *Referendums: A comparative study* (1978) and A. Ranney (ed.), *The Referendum Device* (1981).
30. Direct democracy in the strict sense (i.e. through the presence of the citizens on the market square) is of course very rare and can take place only in small communities (hence there are some remnants in parts of New England and in the smallest cantons of Switzerland). The most common forms of 'semi-direct' democracy are the referendum (which is a response to a proposal made by the government and/or the legislature), the initiative (which enables the people to force parliament to discuss a piece of legislation), and the recall (which enables the people to dismiss an elected official). The initiative is used fairly extensively in Switzerland, but is rarely allowed elsewhere, although there are also informal *Bürgerinitiativen* in West Germany; the recall is practised in some Western states of the United States.
31. This conservatism was said in the past to be noticeable in relation to issues of a libertarian character; it seems currently to be less pronounced or less general. The view that referendums were conservative was primarily based on the examination of earlier Australian and Swiss referendums; see W.S. Livingston, *Federalism and Constitutional Change* (1956), in particular pp. 116–28 and 183–98.
32. The referendum took place in 1969 and De Gaulle resigned as a result.
33. Substantial minorities have favoured such restrictions, however, despite the fact that the major parties were consistently against them. Thus it can be claimed with some justification that the electorate is somewhat more conservative than the parties which it elects to parliament.
34. Swiss parties are less centralised and less powerful than parties in most other Western European countries. This may be due in part to the influence of referendums and initiatives, as these clearly circumscribe the ability of parties to decide finally on many issues.
35. De Gaulle obtained support for his policies on Algeria by means of referendums in the early 1960s. In this way, the referendum helped to support the political system as a whole against those (including the military) who were attempting to 'destabilise' the regime.

24 | The future of the study of comparative government

In the course of the second half of the twentieth century, the study of comparative government has been transformed beyond all recognition. As a discipline it has existed for many centuries: originally it was concerned with the study of the behaviour of all the polities of the world, as the works of Aristotle and Montesquieu demonstrate. However, with the development of constitutionalism in the nineteenth century, analyses came to be devoted almost exclusively to liberal countries, on the assumption that all states would progressively become liberal as constitutionalism spread. This assumption turned out to be false – or at best premature. As a result, a realistic study of comparative government needed to have a broader scope: the aim had to be to understand the characteristics of all governments and to discover their dynamics.

This was the goal of those who, in the late 1950s and early 1960s, began to rethink the basis of the discipline. New conceptual frameworks had to be discovered to replace those based on constitutionalism. Not surprisingly, therefore, most of the early developments in this regard were concerned with model-making, as was particularly the case with the application of structural–functionalism and systems analysis to comparative government. Gradually, however, there came to be greater interest in the discovery of detailed findings and in the search for general relationships at the middle range, but these developments are recent and have so far produced only relatively limited results. It is worth examining the progress made and suggesting directions for future enquiries. To do so, it will be helpful first of all to return to the general framework, to the problems which it poses, and in particular to the role played by norms and institutions in structuring behaviour. The discussion will then turn to middle-range analyses in order to see where gaps need to be filled to make possible a better understanding of the life of political systems.

354

General theory: norms, structures and behaviour

Perhaps the most fundamental difficulty in studying comparative government results from the fact that behaviour is circumscribed – structured – by institutions and procedures and that these in turn are related to the norms and values prevailing in the political system. The first move must therefore be to classify polities according to these norms and, in order to do so, to refer to three dimensions relating respectively to the extent of popular participation, to the means on the basis of which political life is conducted, and to the substantive goals which the regime attempts to put forward. Two of these dimensions have long been adopted, indeed were already adopted by Aristotle; the third, the one which is concerned with policy goals, was neglected in the past, largely because constitutionalism stressed liberalism and democracy as the yardsticks according to which political systems should be classified. In the contemporary world, in which much emphasis is placed on socio-economic development, it is simply unrealistic not to regard policy goals as a major element in the categorisation of political systems. What needs to be done, therefore, is to locate political systems in the space defined by these three dimensions. All three are indeed conceptually clear; there are difficulties of operationalisation, however, and, so far at least, it has been possible to locate regimes only in a broad manner in the three-dimensional space.[1]

The second problem to be solved concerns the relationship between norms and structures. Difficulties are substantial in this respect, as they arise at both the conceptual and operational levels. All political systems have structures, whether these are defined in detail by law or constitution or have simply emerged gradually by custom. However, the way in which these structures affect the political system is unclear; each structure can perform vastly different operations or, in Almond's terms, vastly different 'functions'. These functions have been identified: there are demands which arise from a variety of points in the polity; these demands are articulated and aggregated before they become policies and are implemented. But the structures through which the demands are made and the policies elaborated vary markedly. They vary for a number of reasons, not all of which are entirely known, but at least in part because traditions differ from polity to polity and because of the role of imposition in many regimes. So far at least, there has been little systematic progress in finding means of assessing in detail the nature of the variations.[2]

A number of general points can none the less be made in this respect. First, by and large, the national government is the body primarily in charge of rule-making. It is subject to limitations, however. To an extent, these come from legislatures, though these legislatures are usually not markedly able to influence rule-making as few of them truly initiate policies. However, they may signal ideas and exercise pressure; they are also concerned with rule-application, not because they implement rules themselves, but because they attempt to scrutinise and, wherever possible, to modify the implementation of these rules. Meanwhile, bureaucracies (and the military) are involved in rule-making, despite the fact that they exist in principle to apply the policies elaborated by the government. The executive has therefore to share a substantial part of rule-making with administrative bodies.

Yet these are not the only 'functions' which bureaucracies and the military perform, while, on the other hand, the bodies which are often regarded as primarily concerned with demands, groups and parties, are sometimes concerned both with rule-making and, even more, with rule-application. Where groups and parties are created from above and constitute means by which governments attempt to strengthen their hold on the country, they do not aggregate demands, or at least do not merely aggregate demands, but instead they play a major part in implementation. In such cases, articulation and aggregation may be achieved partly in secret by bodies prohibited by the regime and partly by the bureaucracy and the military, at least within the context of the range of policies which the government broadly tolerates.

Thus the same structures can and do fulfil both an 'upward', or 'input' function and a 'downward' or 'output' function, depending on the character of the political system and in particular of its norms. This is true of parties as well as of groups, bureaucracies, armies and even courts. Indeed, it is probably the case that, everywhere, the same structures fulfil both input and output functions, but to a different extent. Bureaucracies are concerned with demands as well as with the implementation of policies; parties are involved at least with a modicum of implementation as well as with the aggregation of demands. The degree of imposition has a substantial part to play in this respect. By and large, where there is little imposition, groups and parties are mainly concerned with articulation and aggregation, while bureaucracies and armies are mainly concerned with rule-implementation, as well as, to some extent, with rule-making. Where imposition is strong, parties and at least many of the groups are likely to be deliberately set up in order to help rule-implementation, while the bureaucracy and even the military can constitute significant channels of articulation and aggregation.

The extent to which a regime is liberal or not thus has a major effect, alongside other norms, in determining both the configuration and the characteristics of institutions and procedures. This suggests that it is essential to understand the mechanics of imposition; yet it is still not known how much, or for how long, a system can be imposed. Dictatorships fall periodically, but some remain in existence for many decades. The dynamics of imposition are not well understood; it is known why governments resort to imposition, but not under what conditions or to what extent governments can increase their support, in the long run, by using authoritarian means. It is not even known how far charismatic leadership and well-organised parties can help a government to win the hearts of a disaffected population. Since 1945, much has been made of the extent to which Communist systems on the Soviet model succeeded in introducing new norms; however, the failures experienced by the Soviet Union, not only in Eastern Europe, but also in the developing world, in its attempt at exporting these norms and the structures which have been created to embody them, indeed the failures experienced in the Soviet Union itself, suggest that governments have great difficulties in setting up effective new structures. Progress in comparative government clearly requires a better understanding of the dynamics of imposition and of legitimacy-building – and legitimacy-unbuilding.[3]

Finally, this question relates to the general matter of the emergence and development of structures. New structures come into existence every day, while old structures are also modified to some extent every day. In all political systems, there are therefore large numbers of institutions at different levels of growth and maturity – some give support to others, some undermine others. There are thus, so to speak, 'baby structures', which need to be upheld and protected, and decaying structures, which are gradually disintegrating. Yet the rate at which structures grow and decay is not well-known; all that is known is that this rate is relatively slow and cannot easily be speeded up. The examination of the development of structures will lead to a better understanding of legitimacy, as the life of institutions provides a history of the support which they enjoy. A better understanding of individual structural development will in turn provide a greater insight into the life of political systems. This is the type of question with which general theory needs to be concerned in order to make progress in the study of comparative government. Only in this way will the problem of the relationship between norms and structures and the problem of the effective role of structures begin to be understood.

Middle-range theory: the dynamics of structures

In the early 1960s, emphasis tended to be placed on the need to make a theoretical breakthrough and to discover a general model of the political system. What was not sufficiently appreciated was that it was not possible to move easily from a broad descriptive framework to truly causal analyses without an understanding of the dynamics of legitimacy, institution-building, and normative change. The realisation that these problems are prerequisites to the build-up of a systematic theory led to a shift to less ambitious aims and to a greater concentration on middle-range analyses. The result has been a series of efforts designed to determine the effects of individual structures in different types of political systems.

Developments at the middle-range level have been impressive, even if much still remains to be discovered.[4] Thus the panorama of group configurations in various types of societies is better understood; this has led to contrasting those societies in which large communal groups prevail with those in which there is a predominance of 'man-made' administrative institutions, such as the bureaucracy and the military, or dependent associations, such as single parties, or of freely developing associations, such as single-issue groups. The break-up of customary bodies is slow; the move towards associationalism is patchy and somewhat uncertain, and the spread of associationalism carries with it the seeds of serious problems, since associations provide little base for aggregating demands in societies. What therefore needs to be done is to map out carefully the different ways in which polities move from dominance by customary groups to associationalism as well as the extent to which, beyond a certain point, social movements may reintroduce feelings of community and indirectly reduce what would otherwise be the excessive societal fragmentation resulting from the existence of many associations.[5]

One of the fields in which cross-national analysis is relatively old is that of political parties. Theory started in the late nineteenth and early twentieth centuries with the development of the 'iron law of oligarchy'; mass parties and the 'law' relating electoral systems to party systems have been discussed since the 1930s.[6] These theories thus form the basis for analyses in the field. Admittedly, not enough has been done as yet to extend the theory beyond competitive party systems. Not enough has been done either to understand the dynamics of party organisation, in particular in the context of parties whose mass membership is in decline, nor is it known how much 'weight' should be attributed to political parties in a polity and to what extent this weight relates to articulation, aggregation, rule-making or rule-implementation. But the point at which parties cease to need the support of a broad group, and can be said to be in 'orbit' and legitimate, is known. There is a good deal of knowledge about party systems and about their characteristics, as well as about the effect of these party systems on governmental life. The way in which parties are inserted in political systems is now becoming well-appreciated: what needs to be better understood is how and why parties seem now to be in decline or at least in difficulty in many countries.

Meanwhile, substantial analyses of bureaucracies and of the military have taken place. Indeed, the study of the military has advanced fast, now that the universal character of army intervention in politics has been recognised. The conditions maximising intervention were examined systematically; what had hitherto been a set of disjointed descriptions relating to the national character of particular nations was replaced by general propositions about the relationship between types of intervention and socio-economic development. A substantial advance has also been made with respect to bureaucracies, both in developed and in developing countries. These studies have moved from a determination of the general characteristics of administrative structures to the examination of the problems posed by administrative culture (in particular in relation to general political culture) and to the difficulties raised by the part taken by administrative bodies in rule-making.

Courts played a large part in nineteenth-century liberal institutional theory, as they were viewed as guardians of the constitution. This role has now expanded, although the expansion did not necessarily take place according to the canons of liberal judicial independence. An undue emphasis on the original model and the extension of rule-adjudication to new fields paradoxically combined to decrease for a while the interest of students of comparative government in the part played by courts. This situation changed as questions of 'control' of administration began to raise major problems for rule-makers as well as for citizens. Current studies are still limited in geographical scope, however. There is a need to introduce all types of rule-adjudicating bodies – courts, commissions, tribunals, ombudsmen's offices – into the main body of comparative government analysis, not only in the context of Western countries, but on a world-wide basis.[7]

Progress was most needed in relation to the core of the political system, as there was little real understanding in the 1950s and 1960s of the role of assemblies and of the modes of behaviour of governments and cabinets. A major effort was made in the 1970s to analyse precisely the nature of the activities of legislatures in both liberal and authoritarian systems. There was at first considerable scepticism, since it was widely noted that only rarely did these bodies truly make the rules, but it gradually became recognised that they were important in other ways and not just in terms of establishing a communication network between governments and the public. By going beyond the examination of activities on the floor of these bodies or even of activities taking place within the physical confines of the assembly building, political scientists became aware of the influence of legislatures at detailed and intermediate levels, as well as at broader policy levels. As a result, there is now a realistic awareness of what assemblies can and cannot do, even if it is still not known why some of them – such as the United States Congress – play a much larger part than others in the political life of their country.[8]

Meanwhile, the national government itself is at last becoming an object of systematic scrutiny. Analyses of the military, of the bureaucracy and of parties have led to some understanding, from different standpoints, of the limitations of the scope of governmental rule-making. Studies of individual leaders have provided a rich descriptive base, alongside the works on individual political systems. Comparative analyses have thus been in a position to begin to examine the role of governments in different institutional contexts and to assess the extent to which their members participated in decision-making. There are still many gaps, due in part to the problems of access which surround such enquiries. But progress has taken place and a comprehensive image of the most sensitive part of the machinery of political systems is starting to emerge.

All aspects of political life are thus becoming better known. What was previously thought to be too complex to study is now being investigated. Middle-range analyses can provide a basis for the development of comparative government, despite the fact that there is still no general theory of the relationship between norms, structures and behaviour, of legitimacy, and of institutional development. Perhaps it is the case that progress in comparative government on a truly cross-national basis requires a general analysis of each structure, of governments and of assemblies, of armies and of bureaucracies, of parties and of groups, before the general problems of legitimacy and of institutional development can be fully understood.

Conclusion

The study of comparative government will not provide quick pay-offs for those who expect 'recipes' for a new political order: physics and biology have taken decades to advance, even after the mathematics which they required had been developed to a point which the tools of political science have scarcely begun to reach. Other social sciences, mainly economics and psychology, have become increasingly successful, though on a rather narrow front; in some aspects of political analysis, pay-offs have also been quite large. Comparative government poses more complex problems; it needs both a concern for a detailed knowledge of countries and of their institutions and an ability to deal with general models, and it needs an interest in concrete situations together with a desire to bring these situations within a common mould. Yet, despite these difficulties, knowledge is being acquired and systematic analyses gradually replace historical accidents as the basis for most explanations. Whether comparative government has reached the 'positive' age is a matter of judgement, but there is fervour and tension in the discipline. Tension is characteristic of the take-off stage in political life: tension in comparative government may also be an indication that the discipline has now taken off.

Notes

1. See Chapter 3.
2. See Chapter 2.
3. See Chapter 5.
4. See J. Blondel, *Discipline of Politics* (1982), pp. 162–85.
5. See Chapter 7.
6. See Chapter 9.
7. Texts on comparative government still do not discuss courts to the extent that they should and do not integrate them in the general analysis to the extent that they deserve.
8. See Chapter 17.

Appendix

Party systems in the contemporary world (1950–89): stability and change

| | | Stable | | | Changing | | |
	No party (1)	One party (2)	More than one party (3)	No party ⟷ one party (4)	One party ⟷ more than one party (5)	No party ⟷ more than one party (6)	All types of change (7)
Atlantic	23	–	–	20 Australia★ Austria★ Belgium Canada★ Denmark★ Finland France★ West Germany★ Iceland Ireland★ Italy Luxemburg★ Malta★ Netherlands★ New Zealand★ Norway★ Sweden★ Switzerland★ United Kingdom★ United States★	–	2 Portugal★ Spain★	1 *Greece*★	
Eastern Europe and North Asia	15	–	6 Albania China North Korea USSR	2 *Cambodia* *Laos*	7 Bulgaria Czecho- slovakia East Germany	–	–

	Stable			Changing			
	No party (1)	One party (2)	More than one party (3)	No party ⟷ One party (4)	One party ⟷ more than one party (5)	No party ⟷ more than one party (6)	All types of change (7)
		North Vietnam Yugoslavia			Hungary Mongolia Poland Romania		
Middle East and North Africa 22	8 Bahrein Jordan Kuweit Oman Saudi Arabia United Arab Emirates North Yemen	3 *Algeria* *Tunisia* South Yemen	4 Cyprus *Israel★* Lebanon Morocco	3 *Afghanistan* *Iraq* *Libya*	2 *Egypt* *Syria*	–	2 *Iran★* *Turkey★*
South and South-East Asia (Pacific) 24	4 Bhutan Kiribati Maldives Tonga	3 Brunei Singapore Taiwan	10 *India★* *Indonesia* Japan *South Korea* Malaysia Papua New Guinea Solomon Islands Sri Lanka Vanuatu Western Samoa	–	2 *Burma* Philippines	4 *Fiji* Nepal *Pakistan* *Thailand*	1 *Bangladesh*
Africa south of Sahara 46	–	15 Angola Botswana Cape Verde Comoros Djibouti Gabon Guinea Bissau Ivory Coast *Madagascar* Malawi Mozambique Sao Tome Tanzania Zambia	3 Gambia Mauritius South Africa	7 *Ethiopia* *Guinea* Kenya *Mali* *Mauretania* *Niger* *Rwanda* Swaziland	7 Cameroon Chad Congo Senegal Seychelles Sierra Leone Zimbabwe	1 *Nigeria*	13 Benin Burkina Faso Burundi Central African Republic Equatorial Guinea Ghana Lesotho Liberia Somalia Sudan Togo Uganda Zaire
Latin America 33	–	4 Antigua Mexico Nicaragua Paraguay	12 Bahamas★ Barbados★ Belize★ *Brazil★* Colombia★ Costa Rica★ Dominica Guyana	1 *Haiti*	4 Grenada Trinidad★	11 *Chile* Cuba Dominican Republic Ecuador Guatemala Honduras Panama	1 *Argentina* *Bolivia* *El Salvador*

		Stable			Changing		
	No party (1)	One party (2)	More than one party (3)	No party ⟷ One party (4)	One party ⟷ more than one party (5)	No party ⟷ more than one party (6)	All types of change (7)
			Jamaica* St Christopher* St Lucia* St Vincent*			Peru Surinam Uruguay* Venezuela*	
Total	163	12	31	49	13	24	17	17

1. Italics denote strong or overwhelming military influence at some point during the period.
2. ★ denotes substantial opportunities for alternation of parties.

Bibliography

General works on comparative government

G.A. Almond and J.S. Coleman, *The Politics of the Developing Areas* (1960), Princeton, NJ: Princeton University Press

G.A. Almond and G.B. Powell, *Comparative Politics* (1976), Boston, Mass.: Little, Brown & Co.

D.E. Apter, *Ideology and Discontent* (1964), New York, NY: Free Press

D.E. Apter, *The Politics of Modernization* (1965), Chicago, Ill.: Chicago University Press

A. Arblaster and S. Lukes (eds), *The Good Society* (1971), London: Methuen

Aristotle, *The Politics* (1962), Harmondsworth, Mdsx: Penguin Books

J. Bill and R.L. Hardgrave, *Comparative Politics: The quest for theory* (1973), Columbus, Ohio: Merrill

J. Blondel, *An Introduction to Comparative Government* (1969), London: Weidenfeld & Nicolson

J. Blondel, *A Reader in Comparative Government* (1969), London: Macmillan

J. Blondel, *The Discipline of Politics* (1982), London: Butterworth

E. Burke, *Edmund Burke on Government, Politics and Society* (1975), Hemel Hempstead: Harvester Wheatsheaf

R. Chilcote, *Theories of Comparative Politics* (1981), Boulder, Col.: Westview Press

B. Crick, *In Defence of Politics* (1964), Harmondsworth, Mdsx: Penguin Books

R.A. Dahl, *Modern Political Analysis* (1963), Englewood Cliffs, NJ: Prentice Hall

K.W. Deutsch, *The Nerves of Government* (1963), New York, NY: Free Press

D. Easton, *A Systems Analysis of Political Life* (1965), New York, NY: Wiley

D. Easton, *The Political System* (1953), New York, NY: Knopf

P. Evans, D. Rueschemeyer and T. Skocpol (eds), *Bringing the State Back In* (1985), Cambridge: Cambridge University Press

T. Hobbes, *Leviathan* (1968 edn), Harmondsworth, Mdsx: Penguin Books

R.T. Holt and J.E. Turner, *The Methodology of Comparative Research* (1970), New York, NY: Free Press

R.J. Jackson and M.B. Stein (eds), *Issues in Comparative Politics* (1971), New York, NY: St Martin's Press

M. Landau, *Political Theory and Political Science* (1979), New Brunswick, NJ: Humanities Press

J. La Palombara, *Politics Within Nations* (1974), Englewood Cliffs, NJ: Prentice-Hall

M. Laver, *Invitation to Politics* (1983), Oxford: Blackwell

A. Leftwich (ed.), *What is Politics* (1984), Oxford: Blackwell

S. Lukes, *Power: A radical view* (1974), London: Macmillan

R.C. Macridis, *The Study of Comparative Government* (1955), New York, NY: Doubleday

J.G. March and J.P. Olsen, 'The new institutionalism', *Am. Pol. Sc. Rev.*, 78 (Sept. 1984), pp. 734–49

L.C. Mayer, *Comparative Political Inquiry* (1972), Homewood, Ill.: Dorsey Press

E.J. Meehan, *Explanation in Social Science* (1968), Homewood, Ill.: Dorsey Press

P.H. Merkl, *Modern Comparative Politics* (1970), New York, NY: Holt, Rinehart and Winston

Montesquieu, *The Spirit of Laws* (1965), New York, NY: Hafner

N.W. Polsby *et al.*, *Politics and Social Life* (1963), Boston, Mass.: Houghton Mifflin

A. Przeworski and H. Teune, *The Logic of Comparative Social Inquiry* (1970), New York, NY: Wiley

C.C. Ragin, *The Comparative Method* (1987), Berkeley, Calif.: University of California Press

J.J. Rousseau, *Social Contract* (1973 edn), London: Dent

R. Trigg, *Understanding Social Science* (1985), Oxford: Blackwell

J.H. Turner, *The Structure of Sociological Theory* (1986), Chicago, Ill.: Dorsey Press

D.V. Verney, *The Analysis of Political Systems* (1959), London: Routledge & Kegan Paul

M. Weber, *Economy and Society* (1968) (3 vols), New York, NY: Bedminister Press

P. Winch, *The Idea of a Social Science* (1958), London: Routledge & Kegan Paul

Bases of political systems; political development; legitimacy

C. Ake, *A Theory of Political Integration* (1967), Homewood, Ill.: Dorsey Press

R.A. Alford, *Party and Society* (1963), New York, NY: Rand McNally

G.A. Almond and S. Verba, *The Civic Culture* (1963), Princeton, NJ: Princeton University Press

G.A. Almond and S. Verba (eds), *The Civic Culture Revisited* (1979), Princeton, NJ: Princeton University Press

D.E. Apter, *Choice and the Politics of Allocation* (1973), New Haven, Conn.: Yale University Press

A.S. Banks and R.B. Textor, *A Cross-polity Survey* (1963), Cambridge, Mass.: MIT Press

P.L. Berger and T. Luckman, *The Social Construction of Reality* (1966), New York, NY: Praeger

V. Bogdanor and D.E. Butler, *Democracy and Elections* (1983), Cambridge: Cambridge University Press

A. Campbell, P.E. Converse, W.E. Miller, and D.E. Stokes, *Elections and the Political Order* (1966), New York, NY: Wiley

J.S. Coleman, *Education and Political Development* (1965), Princeton, NJ: Princeton University Press

W. Connolly (ed.), *Legitimacy and the State* (1984), Oxford: Blackwell

R.A. Dahl, *Polyarchy* (1971), New Haven, Conn.: Yale University Press

R. Dahrendorf, *Class and Conflict in Industrial Society* (1959), Stanford, Calif.: Stanford University Press

A. Downs, *An Economic Theory of Democracy* (1957), New York, NY: Harper

E. Durkheim, *The Division of Labour in Society* (1933), New York, NY: Free Press

M. Duverger, *De la dictature* (1961), Paris: Julliard

H. Eckstein, 'A culturalist theory of political change', *Am. Pol. Sc. Rev.*, 82–3 (1988), pp. 789–803

R. Falk *et al.* (eds), *Toward a Just World Order* (1982), Boulder, Col.: Westview Press

G. Ferrero, *Principles of Power* (New York edn, 1945), New York, NY: Putnam

J.L. Finkle and R.W. Gable, *Political Development and Social Change* (1966), New York, NY: Wiley

C.J. Friedrich, *Totalitarianism* (1954), Cambridge, Mass.: Harvard University Press

C.J. Friedrich and Z. Brzezinski, *Totalitarian Dictatorship and Autocracy* (1965), Cambridge, Mass.: Harvard University Press

H. Gerstenberger *et al.*, 'Politische Kultur', *Österreichische Zeitschrift für Politische Wissenschaft*, 13 (1984), pp. 1–121

F.I. Greenstein, *Personality and Politics* (1969), Chicago, Ill.: Markham

T.R. Gurr (ed.), *Handbook of Political Conflict* (1980), New York, NY: Fress Press

T.R. Gurr, *Why Men Rebel* (1970), Princeton, NJ: Princeton University Press

G. Hofstede, *Culture's Consequences* (1980), London and Los Angeles: Sage

S.P. Huntington, *Political Order in Changing Societies* (1968), New Haven, Conn.: Yale University Press

R. Inglehart, *The Silent Revolution* (1977), Princeton, NJ: Princeton University Press

A. Inkeles and D.J. Levinson 'National character', *Handbook of Social Psychology* 4, (1969)

W. Kornhauser, *The Politics of Mass Society* (1959), New York, NY: Free Press

G.T. Kurian, *The New Book of World Rankings* (1984), New York, NY: Facts on File

R.E. Lane, *Political Ideology* (1962), New York, NY: Free Press

J.J. Linz, *Crisis, Breakdown, and Reequilibration* (1978), Baltimore, Md.: Johns Hopkins University Press

J.J. Linz and A. Stepan (eds), *The Breakdown of Democratic Regimes* (1978), Baltimore, Md.: Johns Hopkins University Press

A. Lijphart, *Democracy in Plural Societies* (1977), New Haven, Conn.: Yale University Press

S.M. Lipset, *The First New Nation* (1963), New York, NY: Basic Books

S.M. Lipset, *Political Man* (1983), London: Heinemann

B. Moore, Jr, *The Origins of Dictatorship and Democracy* (1966), Boston, Mass.: Beacon Press

D.N. Nelson, *Elite–mass Relations in Communist Systems* (1988), London: Macmillan

D. Neubauer, 'Some conditions of democracy', *Am. Pol. Sc. Rev.*, 67 (1967), pp. 1002–9

G. O'Donnell, P. Schmitter, and L. Whitehead (eds), *Transition from Authoritarian Rule* (1986), Baltimore, Md.: Johns Hopkins University Press

N.W. Polsby, 'The institutionalisation of the House of Representatives', *Am. Pol. Sc. Rev.*, 62 (1962), pp. 144–68

L.W. Pye, *Aspects of Political Development* (1966), Boston, Mass.: Little, Brown & Co.

L.W. Pye and S. Verba (eds), *Political Culture and Political Development* (1965), Princeton, NJ.: Princeton University Press

A.A. Rabushka and K.A. Shepsle, *Politics in Plural Societies* (1971), Columbus, Ohio: Merrill

D.W. Rae and M. Taylor, *The Analysis of Political Cleavages* (1970), New Haven, Conn.: Yale University Press

W.S. Robinson, 'Ecological correlates and the behavior of individuals', *Am. Soc. Rev.*, 15 (1950), 3, pp. 351–7

R. Rogowski, *Rational Legitimacy* (1974), Princeton, NJ: Princeton University Press

S. Rokkan, *Citizens, Elections, Parties* (1970), Oslo: Universitetsforlaget

W.W. Rostow, *The Stages of Economic Growth* (1960), Cambridge: Cambridge University Press

G. Sartori (ed.), *Social Concepts* (1984), London and Los Angeles: Sage

T. Skocpol, *States and Social Revolutions* (1979), Cambridge: Cambridge University Press

C.L. Taylor and D.A Jodice, *World Handbook of Political and Social Indicators* (3rd edn, 1983) (2 vols), New Haven, Conn.: Yale University Press

S. Verba, H.H. Nie, and Jae-on Kin (eds), *Participation and Political Equality* (1978), Chicago, Ill.: Chicago University Press

T. Vanhanen, *The Emergence of Democracy* (1984), Helsinki: Finn. Sty of Sciences and Letters

T. Vanhanen, 'The level of democratisation related to socioeconomic variables in 147 states in 1980–85', *ECPR Joint Sessions*, Amsterdam (1987)

T. Vanhanen, 'The level of democratisation related to socioeconomic variables in 147 states in 1980–85', *Scand. Pol. Stud.*, 12, (1989), 2, pp. 95–127

M. Weber, *Basic Concepts in Sociology* (1962), New York, NY: Philosophical Library

M. Weber, *The Protestant Ethic and the Spirit of Capitalism* (English edn, 1976), London: Allen and Unwin

M. Weber, *The Theory of Social and Economic Organisation* (1947), Glencoe, Ill.: Free Press

M. Weiner and S.P. Huntington (eds), *Understanding Political Development* (1987), Boston, Mass.: Little, Brown & Co.

C. Young, *The Politics of Cultural Pluralism* (1976), Madison, Wisc.: University of Wisconsin Press

T. Zeldin, *The Political System of Napoleon III* (1958), London: Macmillan

Groups

S. Barnes, M. Kaase *et al.*, *Mass Participation in Five Western Democracies* (1979), London and Los Angeles: Sage

P.M. Blau, *Exchange and Power in Social Life* (1964), New York, NY: Wiley

A.F. Bentley, *The Process of Government* (1967), Cambridge, Mass.: Harvard University Press

F.G. Castles, *Pressure Groups and Political Culture* (1967), London: Routledge & Kegan Paul

H.W. Ehrman, *Interest Groups in Four Continents* (1958), Pittsburgh, Penn.: University of Pittsburgh Press

S.N. Eisenstadt, *The Political Systems of Empires* (1963), New York, NY: Free Press

S.E. Finer, *Anonymous Empire* (1966), London: Pall Mall

M. Fortes and E.E. Evans-Pritchard, *African Political Systems* (1940), Oxford: Oxford University Press

W. Galenson, *Trade Union Democracy in Western Europe* (1962), Berkeley, Calif.: University of California Press

C.B. Hagan, 'The Group in Political Science', in R. Young (ed.), *Approaches to the Study of Politics* (1958), New York, NY: New York University Press

A. Hamilton *et al.*, *The Federalist Papers* (1981 edn), Baltimore, Md.: Johns Hopkins University Press

B. Klandermans, H. Kriesi and S. Tarrow (eds), *From Structure to Action: Comparing social movement research* (1981), Greenwich, Conn.: JAI

G. Lehmbruch and P.C. Schmitter (eds), *Patterns of Corporatist Policy-making* (1982), London and Los Angeles: Sage

T. Lowi, *The Politics of Disorder* (1971), New York, NY: Basic Books

H.H. Storing (ed.), *Essays on the Scientific Study of Politics* (1962), New York, NY: Holt, Rinehart and Winston

A.J. Taylor, *Trade Unions and Politics* (1989), London: Macmillan

F. Toennies, *Community and Association* (London edn, 1955), London: Routledge & Kegan Paul

D. Truman, *The Governmental Process* (1962), New York, NY: Knopf

R. Young (ed.), *Approaches to the Study of Politics* (1958), London: Stevens

Communication

S. Ball-Rokeach *et al.* (eds), *Mass Communication* (1986), London and Los Angeles: Sage
J. Curran, M. Gurevitch and J. Woollocott (eds), *Mass Communication and Society* (1977), London: E. Arnold
M.L. De Fleur and S. Ball-Rokeach, *Theories of Mass Communication* (4th edn, 1981), New York, NY: Longman
J. Dennis (ed.), *Socialisation to Politics* (1973), New York, NY: Wiley
K.W. Deutsch, *Nationalism and Social Communication* (1953), Cambridge, Mass.: MIT Press
J.D. Halloran (ed.), *The Effects of Television* (1970), London: Panther Books
P. Lazarsfeld and E. Katz, *Personal Influence* (1955), Glencoe, Ill.: Free Press
D.D. Nimmo and K.R. Sanders (eds), *Handbook of Political Communication* (1981), London and Los Angeles: Sage
I. De Sola Pool *et al.* (eds), *Handbook of Communication* (1973), Chicago, Ill.: Rand McNally
L.W. Pye and S. Verba, *Communications and Political Development* (1963), Princeton, NJ: Princeton University Press
R. Williams, *Communications* (1962), Harmondsworth, Mdsx: Penguin Books
Lord Windlesham, *Communication and Political Power* (1966), London: Cape

Political parties; electoral systems and party systems

H.E. Alexander (ed.), *Comparative Political Finance in the 1980s* (1989), Cambridge: Cambridge University Press
H.E. Alexander, *Financing Politics* (1984), Washington, DC: Congressional Quarterly
R.J. Alexander, *Latin American Political Parties* (1973), New York, NY: Praeger
E. Allardt and Y. Littunen, *Cleavages, Ideologies and Party Systems* (1964), Helsinki: The Academic Bookstore
F.P. Belloni and D.C. Beller (eds), *Faction Politics* (1978), Oxford: ABC Clio
J. Bernard, *A Guide to Latin American Parties* (1973), Harmondsworth, Mdsx: Penguin Books
K. von Beyme (ed.), *Right-wing Extremism in Western Europe* (1988), London: Cass
J. Blondel, 'Party systems and patterns of government in Western democracies', *Can. Jour. of Pol. Sc.* (June 1968), pp. 180–203
V. Bogdanor, *What is Proportional Representation* (1984), Oxford: Robertson
V. Bogdanor and D.E. Butler (eds), *Democracy and Elections* (1983), Cambridge: Cambridge University Press
I Budge *et al.* (eds), *Party Identification and Beyond* (1976), London: Wiley
I. Budge and D.J. Farlie, *Explaining and Predicting Elections* (1983), London: Allen and Unwin
I. Budge, D. Robertson and D. Hearl, *Ideology, Strategy, and Party Change* (1987), Cambridge: Cambridge University Press
D.E. Butler, *The Electoral System in Britain since 1918* (1963), Oxford: Oxford University Press
A. Campbell *et al.*, *The American Voter* (1960), New York, NY: Wiley
F.C. Castles (ed.), *The Impact of Parties* (1982), London and Los Angeles: Sage
J.S. Coleman and C.G. Rosberg, *Political Parties and National Integration in Tropical Africa* (1964), Berkeley, Calif.: University of California Press
I. Crewe and M. Denver (eds), *Electoral Change in Western Democracies* (1985), London: Croom Helm
H. Daalder (ed.), *Party Systems in Austria, Switzerland, the Netherlands, and Belgium* (1987), London: F. Pinter

H. Daalder and P. Mair (eds), *Western European Party Systems* (1983), London and Los Angeles: Sage

R.J. Dalton *et al.* (eds), *Electoral Change in Advanced Industrial Democracies* (1984), Princeton, NJ: Princeton University Press

H.W. Degenhardt (ed.), *Political Parties in the World* (1980), London: Longman

M. Duverger, *Political Parties* (1954), New York, NY: Wiley

L.D. Epstein, *Political Parties in Western Democracies* (1967), New York, NY: Praeger

M.P. Fiorina, *Restrospective Voting in American National Elections* (1981), New Haven, Conn.: Yale University Press

J.R. Frears, *Political Parties and Elections in the French Fifth Republic* (1977), London: Hurst

G. Hand, J. Georgel and C. Sasse, *European Electoral Systems Handbook* (1979), London: Butterworths

A.J. Heidenheimer (ed.), *Comparative Political Finance* (1970), Lexington, Mass.: Lexington Books

F. Hermens, *Democracy or Anarchy* (1941), South Bend, Ind.: University of Notre Dame Press

R.L. Hess and G. Loewenberg, 'The Ethiopian no-party state', *Am. Pol. Sc. Rev.* (1964), pp. 947–50

R.E.M. Irving, *The Christian Democratic Parties of Western Europe* (1979), London: Allen and Unwin

K. Janda, *Political Parties: A cross-national survey* (1980), New York, NY: Free Press

V.O. Key, *Southern Politics* (1949), New York, NY: Knopf

E. Kolinsky (ed.), *Opposition in Western Europe* (1987), New York, NY: St Martin's Press

E. Lakeman and J.D. Lambert, *Voting in Democracies* (1955), London: Faber

A. Lijphart, *Democracies* (1984), New Haven, Conn.: Yale University Press

A. Lijphart, *Choosing an Electoral System: Issues and alternatives* (1984), New York, NY: Praeger

S.M. Lipset and S. Rokkan (eds), *Party Systems and Voter Alignments* (1967), New York, NY: Free Press

W.J.M. Mackenzie, *Free Elections* (1958), London: Allen and Unwin

H. McClosky, H.P. Hoffman and R. O'Hara, 'Issue conflict and consensus among leaders and followers', *Am. Pol. Sc. Rev.*, (1960), pp. 406–27

V.E. McHale, *Political Parties of Europe* (1983) (2 vols), London: Greenwood Press

R.T. McKenzie, *British Political Parties* (1963), London: Heinemann

P.H. Merkl (ed.), *Western European Party Systems* (1980), New York, NY: Free Press

R. Michels, *Political Parties* (1949), New York, NY: Free Press

J.S. Mill, *Three Essays on Politics* (1975 edn), Oxford: Oxford University Press

F. Muller Rommel (ed.), *New Politics in Western Europe* (1989), Boulder, Col.: Westview Press

S. Neumann, *Modern Political Parties* (1955), Chicago, Ill.: Chicago University Press

M. Ostrogorski, *Democracy and the Organization of Political Parties* (1902), New York, NY: Macmillan

S. Parkin, *Green Parties* (1989), London: Heretic Books

W. Patterson (ed.), *Social Democratic Parties of Western Europe* (1977), London: Croom Helm

D. Rae, *The Political Consequences of Electoral Laws* (1967), New Haven, Conn.: Yale University Press

V. Randall (ed.), *Political Parties in the Third World* (1988), London and Los Angeles: Sage

R. Rose, *Do Parties Make a Difference?* (1984), London: Macmillan

J.F.S. Ross, *The Irish Electoral System* (1959), London: Pall Mall

G. Sartori, *Parties and Party Systems* (1976), Cambridge: Cambridge University Press

E.E. Schattschneider, *Party Government* (1942), New York, NY: Holt, Rinehart and Winston

R.N. Tannahill, *The Communist Parties of Western Europe* (1978), London: Greenwood Press

S. Wolinetz (ed.), *Parties and Party Systems in Liberal Democracies* (1988), London: Routledge & Kegan Paul

Constitutions; federalism

C.A. Beard, *An Economic Interpretation of the Constitution of the United States* (1961), New York, NY: Macmillan
V. Bogdanor (ed.), *Constitutions in Democratic Polities* (1988), Aldershot: Gower
M. Burgess, *Federalism and Federation* (1986), London: Croom Helm
D.J. Elazar, *The Federal Polity* (1974), New Brunswick, NY: Transaction Books
T. Fleiner Gerster, *Federalism and Decentralisation* (1987), Fribourg: Editions Universitaires
T.M. Franck, *Why Federations Fail* (1968), New York, NY: New York University Press
R.T. Golembiewski, *The Costs of Federalism* (1984), New Brunswick, NY: Transaction Books
D. Jaensch (ed.), *The Politics of the New Federalism* (1977), Adelaide: Australasian Political Science Association
W.S. Livingston, *Federalism and Constitutional Change* (1956), Oxford: Oxford University Press
A.Q. MacMahon, *Federalism, Mature and Emergent* (1955), New York, NY: Columbia University Press
P.H. Merkl, 'Executive–legislative federalism in West Germany', *Am. Pol. Sc. Rev.* (1959), pp. 732–54
G. Sartori, 'Constitutionalism: a preliminary discussion', *Am. Pol. Sc. Rev.*, 56 (1962), pp. 853–64
C.G. Strong, *Modern Political Constitutions* (1963), London: Sidgwick & Jackson
M. Vile, *Constitutionalism and the Separation of Powers* (1967), Oxford: Oxford University Press
A. Vyshinsky, *The Law of the Soviet State* (1948), London: Macmillan
K.C. Wheare, *Federal Government* (1963), London: Oxford University Press
K.C. Wheare, *Modern Constitutions* (1966), London: Oxford University Press

Legislatures

W. Agor (ed.), *Latin American Legislatures* (1971), New York, NY: Praeger
S.K. Bailey, *Congress Makes a Law* (1950), New York, NY: Columbia University Press
J.D. Barber, *The Lawmakers* (1965), New Haven, Conn.: Yale University Press
A. Barker and M. Rush, *The Member of Parliament and his Information* (1970), London: Allen and Unwin
J. Blondel, *Comparative Legislatures* (1973), Englewood Cliffs, NJ: Prentice-Hall
R.F. Hopkins, 'The role of the MP in Tanzania', *Am. Pol. Sc. Rev.*, 64 (1970), pp. 754–71
Inter-Parliamentary Union, *Parliaments of the World* (1986) (2 vols), London: Gower
A. Kornberg (ed.), *Legislatures in Comparative Perspective* (1973), New York, NY: McKay
J.D. Lees and M. Shaw (eds), *Committees in Legislatures: A comparative analysis* (1979), London: Robertson
G. Loewenberg and S.C. Patterson, *Comparative Legislatures* (1979), Boston, Mass.: Little, Brown & Co.
D. Macrae, *Parliament, Parties, and Society in France* (1967), New York, NY: Macmillan
D.R. Matthews, *US Senators and their World* (1960), Chapel Hill, NC: University of North Carolina Press

D.R. Mayhew, *Party Loyalty among Congressmen* (1966), Cambridge, Mass.: Harvard University Press

M.L. Mezey, *Comparative Legislatures* (1979), Durham, NC: Duke University Press

P. Norton (ed.), *Parliament in the 1980s* (1985), Oxford: Blackwell

J. Smith and L.D. Musolf (eds), *Legislatures in Development* (1979), Durham, NC: Duke University Press

D.B. Truman, *The Congressional Party* (1959), New York, NY: Wiley

K.C. Weare, *Second Chambers* (1963), Oxford: Oxford University Press

Executives; leadership

J.D. Barber, *The Presidential Character* (1977), Englewood Cliffs, NJ: Prentice-Hall

B.M. Bass, *Stogdill's Handbook on Leadership* (1981), New York, NY: Free Press

J. Blondel, *Government Ministers in the Contemporary World* (1985), London and Los Angeles: Sage

J. Blondel, *The Organisation of Governments* (1982), London and Los Angeles: Sage

J. Blondel, *Political Leadership* (1987), London and Los Angeles: Sage

J. Blondel, *World Leaders* (1980), London and Los Angeles: Sage

J. Blondel and F. Muller-Rommel (eds), *Cabinets in Western Europe* (1988), London: Macmillan

V. Bogdanor (ed.), *Coalition Government in Western Europe* (1983), London: Heinemann

Z. Brzezinski and S.P. Huntington, *Political Power USA/USSR* (1963), London: Chatto & Windus

E.C. Browne and J. Dreijmannis (eds), *Government Coalitions in Western Democracies* (1982), London: Longman

V. Bunce, *Do New Leaders Make a Difference?* (1981), Princeton, NJ: Princeton University Press

J.McG. Burns, *Leadership* (1978), New York, NY: Harper and Row

C. Campbell, *Governments under Stress* (1983), Toronto: University of Toronto Press

H.D. Clarke and M.M. Czudnowski (eds), *Political Elites in Anglo-American Democracies* (1986), De Kalb, Ill.: Northern Illinois University Press

E.S. Corwin, *The President, Office and Powers* (1957), New York, NY: New York University Press

T.E. Cronin, *The State of the Presidency* (1975), Boston, Mass.: Little, Brown & Co.

A. De Swaan, *Coalition Theories and Cabinet Formations* (1973), Amsterdam: Elsevier

F.E. Fiedler, *A Theory of Leadership Effectiveness* (1967), New York, NY: McGraw Hill

G.M. Fink, *Prelude to the Presidency* (1980), Westport, Conn.: Greenwood Press

A.L. and J.L. George, *Woodrow Wilson and Colonel House: A personality study* (1956), New York, NY: Dover Press

F.I. Greenstein, *Personality and Politics* (1969), Chicago, Ill.: Markham

B. Headey, *British Cabinet Ministers* (1974), London: Allen and Unwin

H. Heclo, *A Government of Strangers* (1977), Washington, DC: Brookings Institution

S. Hook, *The Hero in History* (1955), Boston, Mass.: Beacon Press

R.H. Jackson and C.G. Rosberg, *Personal Rule in Africa* (1982), Berkeley, Calif.: University of California Press

B. Kellerman (ed.), *Leadership* (1984), Englewood Cliffs, NJ: Prentice-Hall

A. King (ed.), *Both Ends of the Avenue* (1983), Washington, DC: American Enterprise Institute

H.D. Lasswell and D. Lerner, *World Revolutionary Elites* (1965), Cambridge, Mass.: MIT Press

G.M. Luebbert, *Comparative Democracy* (1986), New York, NY: Columbia University Press

T.T. McKie and B.W. Hogwood (eds), *Unlocking the Cabinet* (1985), London and Los Angeles: Sage

R.D. McKinlay and A.S. Cohan, 'A comparative analysis of the political and economic performance of military and civilian regimes', *Comp. Pol.* (October 1975), pp. 1–30

J. Mackintosh, *The British Cabinet* (1962), London: Stevens

R. Neustadt, *Presidential Power* (1960), New York, NY: Wiley

R.L. Noland, 'Presidential disability and the proposed constitutional amendment', *Amer. Psychologist*, 21 (1966), pp. 232–3

G.D. Paige, *Political Leadership* (1972), New York, NY: Free Press

M. Rejai with K. Phillips, *Leaders of Revolution* (1979), London and Los Angeles: Sage

M. Rejai with K. Phillips, *World Revolutionary Leaders* (1983), London and Los Angeles: Sage

R. Rose, *Understanding Big Government* (1984), London and Los Angeles: Sage

G. Rossiter, *The American Presidency* (1960), New York, NY: Harcourt

M. Rush, *Political Succession in the USSR* (1965), New York, NY: Columbia University Press

R.C. Tucker, *Politics as Leadership* (1981), Columbia, Mo.: University of Missouri Press

A. Wildavsky, *The Nursing Father* (1984), University of Alabama Press

Bureaucracies; military; control

J.D. Aberbach, R.D. Putnam and B.A. Rockman, *Bureaucrats and Politicians in Western Democracies* (1981), Cambridge, Mass.: Harvard University Press

D.E. Butler (ed.), *Referendums: A comparative study* (1978), Washington, DC: American Enterprise Institute

G.E. Caiden (ed.), *The Ombudsman: An international handbook* (1983), Westport, Conn.: Greenwood Press

R.K. Carr, *The Supreme Court and Judicial Review* (1942), New York, NY: Holt, Rinehart and Winston

B. Chapman, *The Profession of Government* (1961), London: Allen and Unwin

M. Crozier, *The Bureaucratic Phenomenon* (1964), London: Tavistock

S. Decalo, *Coups and Army Rule in Africa* (1976), New Haven, Conn.: Yale University Press.

G. Drewry and T. Butcher, *The Civil Service To-day* (1988), Oxford: Blackwell

S.E. Finer, *The Man on Horseback* (1962), London: Pall Mall

A.G. Griffith and H. Street, *Principles of Administrative Law* (1967), London: Pitman

J.A.G. Griffith, *The Politics of the Judiciary* (1985), London: Fontana

Lord Hewart, *The New Despotism* (1929; new edn 1945), London: Benn

S.P. Huntington, *The Soldier and the State* (1957), New York, NY: Free Press

M. Janowitz, *The Military in the Development of New Nations* (1964), Chicago, Ill.: University of Chicago Press

P. Kellner and Lord Crowther-Hunt, *The Civil Servants* (1980), London: Macdonald

O. Kirchheimer, *Political Justice* (1961), Princeton, NJ: Princeton University Press

J.E. Lane, *Bureaucracy and Public Choice* (1987), London and Los Angeles: Sage

J. La Palombara (ed.), *Bureaucracies and Political Development* (1963), Princeton, NY: Princeton University Press

H. McClosky, *The American Supreme Court* (1960), Chicago, Ill.: University of Chicago Press

O. Odetola, *Military Regimes and Development* (1982), London: Allen and Unwin

O. Oyediran (ed.), *Nigerian Government and Politics under Military Rule* (1979), London: Macmillan

A. Ranney (ed.), *The Referendum Device* (1981), Washington, DC: American Enterprise Institute

J. Richardson (ed.), *Policy Styles in Western Europe* (1982), London: Allen and Unwin

F. Ridley and J. Blondel, *Public Administration in France* (1964), London: Routlege & Kegan Paul
F.W. Riggs (ed.), *Frontiers of Development Administration* (1971), Raleigh, NC: Duke University Press
E.V. Rostow, *The Sovereign Prerogative* (1962), New Haven, Conn.: Yale University Press
D.C. Rowat (ed.), *The Ombudsman* (1968), London: Allen and Unwin
G. Schubert, *Constitutional Politics* (1960), New York, NY: Holt, Rinehart and Winston
G. Schubert, *Judicial Decision-Making* (1963), New York, NY: Free Press
P. Self, *Administrative Theory and Politics* (1977), London: Allen and Unwin
H.A. Simon, *Administrative Behaviour* (1957), New York, NY: Free Press
E. Strauss, *The Ruling Servants* (1961), London: Allen and Unwin
E.N. Suleiman (ed.), *Bureaucrats and Policy-making* (1984), New York, NY: Meier

Studies of political life

General

G.A. Almond (ed.), *Comparative Politics* (1974), Boston, Mass.: Little, Brown & Co.
M. Curtis (ed.), *Comparative Government* (1990), New York, NY: Harper and Row
S.E. Finer, *Comparative Government* (1970), Harmondsworth, Mdsx: Penguin Books
R.C. Macridis and R.E. Ward, *Modern Political Systems* (1963) (Europe and Asia), Englewood Cliffs, NJ: Prentice-Hall

Western countries

W. Bagehot, *The English Constitution* (1963), London: Fontana
S.B. Beer and A.B. Ulam, *Patterns of Government: The major political systems of Europe* (1962), New York, NY: Random House
Lord Bryce, *The American Commonwealth* (1891), New York, NY: Macmillan
Lord Bryce, *Modern Democracies* (1891), New York, NY: Macmillan
R.A. Dahl, *Pluralist Democracy in the United States* (1967), New York, NY: Rand McNally
R.A. Dahl, *Political Opposition in Western Democracies* (1966), New Haven, Conn.: Yale University Press
V.O. Key, *Politics, Parties and Pressure Groups* (1958), New York, NY: Crowell
A. King (ed.), *The New American Political System* (1978), Washington, DC: American Enterprise Institute
J.E. Lane and S.O. Ersson, *Politics and Society in Western Europe* (1987), London and Los Angeles: Sage
A.L. Lowell, *Government and Parties in Continental Europe* (1896) (2 vols) Cambridge, Mass.: Harvard University Press
G. Smith, *Politics in Western Europe* (1972), London: Heinemann
A. de Tocqueville, *Democracy in America* (1947), Oxford: Oxford University Press

Communist countries

F. Barghoorn, *The USSR* (1966), Boston, Mass.: Little, Brown & Co.

L. Holmes, *Politics in the Communist World* (1986), London: Allen and Unwin

G. Ionescu, *The Politics of the European Communist States* (1967), London: Weidenfeld & Nicolson

L. Shapiro, *The Communist Party of the Soviet Union* (1960), London: Eyre & Spottiswoode

R.F. Staar, *Communist Regimes in Eastern Europe* (1982), Stanford, Calif.: Hoover Institution

S. White, J. Gardner, and G. Schöpflin, *Communist Political Systems* (1981), London: Macmillan

Developing countries

J.D. Barkan and J.J. Okumu (eds), *Politics and Public Opinion in Kenya and Tanzania* (1979), New York, NY: Praeger

P. Cammack, D. Pool, and W. Tordoff, *Third World Politics* (1988), London: Macmillan

G.M. Carter and P. O'Meara (eds), *African Independence: The first twenty five years* (1985), Bloomington, Ind.: University of Indiana Press

C. Clapham, *Third World Politics* (1985), London: Croom Helm

L. Cliffe, *One-Party Democracy: Tanzania* (1967), Nairobi: East Africa Publishing House

M. Halpern, *The Politics of Change in the Middle East and North Africa* (1963), Princeton, NJ: Princeton University Press

M.C. Hudson, *Arab Politics* (1977), New Haven, Conn.: Yale University Press

K.A. Kemal, *Turkey's Politics: The transition to a multi-party system* (1959), Princeton, NJ: Princeton University Press

J. Lambert, *Latin America* (1967), Berkeley, Calif.: University of California Press

D. Lerner, *The Passing of Traditional Society* (1958), New York, NY: Free Press

J. Peeler, *Latin American Democracies* (1982), Chapel Hill, NC: University of North Carolina Press

L.W. Pye, *Politics, Personality, and Nation-Building* (1962) (Burma), Cambridge, Mass.: MIT Press

R.E. Scott, *Mexican Government in Transition* (1964), Chicago, Ill.: University of Illinois Press

P. Smith, *Labyrinths of Power: Political recruitment in twentieth century Mexico* (1979), Princeton, NJ: Princeton University Press

W. Tordoff, *Government and Politics in Africa* (1984), London: Macmillan

R.E. Ward and D. Rustow, *Political Modernization in Japan and Turkey* (1964), Princeton, NJ: Princeton University Press

C. Young, *Ideology and Development in Africa* (1982), New Haven, Conn.: Yale University Press

Index